VICTORY AT SEA

When the United States entered World War II, her Pacific fleet of submarines was vastly outnumbered and outgunned. They learned by trial and error, paying with a terrible loss of life and material. But by war's end, the fleet had become the scourge of the enemy navy and merchant marine, sinking over 6 million tons of ships and cutting the lifeline of the Japanese empire. *Sink 'Em All* tells the whole story of the tragic setbacks and brilliant victories, and the brave commanders and crack crews whose exploits are now legend.

Under the command of Vice Admiral Charles A. Lockwood, seven skippers won the Congressional Medal of Honor, 1392 enemy ships were sunk, 504 airmen were rescued from the sea. The price was high—52 subs were lost in action, but they fought on with courage and determination until the victory was ours.

THE BANTAM WAR BOOK SERIES

This series of books is about a world on fire.

The carefully chosen volumes in the Bantam War Book Series cover the full dramatic sweep of World War II. Many are eyewitness accounts by the men who fought in a global conflict as the world's future hung in the balance. Fighter pilots, tank commanders and infantry captains, among many others, recount exploits of individual courage. They present vivid portraits of brave men, true stories of gallantry, moving sagas of survival and stark tragedies of untimely death.

In 1933 Nazi Germany marched to become an empire that was to last a thousand years. In only twelve years that empire was destroyed, and ever since, the country has been bisected by her conquerors. Italy relinquished her colonial lands, as did Japan. These were the losers. The winners also lost the empires they had so painfully seized over the centuries. And one, Russia, lost over twenty million dead.

Those wartime 1940s were a simple, even a hopeful time. Hats came in only two colors, white and black, and after an initial battering the Allied nations started on a long and laborious march toward victory. It was a time when sane men believed the world would evolve into a decent place, but, as with all futures, there was no one then who could really forecast the world that we know now.

There are many ways to think about that war. It has always been hard to understand the motivations and braveries of Axis soldiers fighting to enslave and dominate their neighbors. Yet it is impossible to know the hammer without the anvil, and to comprehend ourselves we must know the people we once fought against.

Through these books we can discover what it was like to take part in the war that was a final experience for nearly fifty million human beings. In so doing we may discover the strength to make a world as good as the one contained in those dreams and aspirations once believed by heroic men. We must understand our past as an honor to those dead who can no longer choose. They exchanged their lives in a hope for this future that we now inhabit. Though the fight took place many years ago, each of us remains as a living part of it.

SINK 'EM ALL

Submarine Warfare in the Pacific

CHARLES A. LOCKWOOD
Vice Admiral, USN Rtd.

With a foreword by
Fleet Admiral Chester W. Nimitz, USN

BANTAM BOOKS
TORONTO • NEW YORK • LONDON • SYDNEY • AUCKLAND

SINK 'EM ALL
A Bantam Book / March 1984
2nd printing . . . June 1987

*The author has rewritten, for inclusion in this volume,
portions of two articles published in The Saturday
Evening Post:* Our Pacific Sub Commander Tells
How We Gave the Japs a Licking Underseas,
(July 16, 23, 30 of 1949), and We're Betting Our
Shirts on the Atomic Submarine, *(July 22, 1950).*

Illustrations by Greg Beecham and Tom Beecham.

Map by Alan McKnight.

ISBN 0-553-26731-0

Published simultaneously in the United States and Canada

*Bantam Books are published by Bantam Books, Inc. Its
trademark, consisting of the words "Bantam Books" and
the portrayal of a rooster, is Registered in U.S. Patent and
Trademark Office and in other countries. Marca Registrada.
Bantam Books, Inc., 666 Fifth Avenue, New York, New
York 10103.*

PRINTED IN THE UNITED STATES OF AMERICA

KR   11 10 9 8 7 6 5 4 3 2

DEDICATION

*To my comrades
of the Silent Service,
and in memory
of those
who did not return.*

FOREWORD

By Fleet Admiral Chester W. Nimitz, U.S. Navy

For this factually accurate and technically correct account of operations of United States submarines in the Pacific in World War II no more appropriate title could have been chosen than *Sink 'Em All*, a statement easily confirmed by the record. As British airmen are credited with saving Britain in those critical days after Dunkirk, so our gallant submarine personnel filled the breach after Pearl Harbor, and can claim credit, not only for holding the line, but also for carrying the war to the enemy while our shattered forces repaired damages following the treacherous initial attack of the Japanese, and gathered strength for the long march to Tokyo. Because of the complete absence of publicity regarding our submarine operations during the war, and due to an understandable letdown in public interest in war news following the surrender of the Japanese in Tokyo Bay, the American public is largely unaware of their great debt to that relatively small but closely knit force which had, at its peak, not more than 4,000 officers and 46,000 men, of which number some 16,000 actually manned the submarines.

It is to be hoped that this interesting narrative will be widely read, and that the exploits of our "Silent Service" will take their proper place in the minds of our citizens. Certainly no one is better qualified to tell this story than the author, Vice Admiral Charles A. Lockwood, U.S. Navy, retired, who commanded our submarines in the Pacific during the greater part of the war. He writes with complete authority and authenticity, and has skillfully added to an official account that friendly human touch that makes its perusal an exciting pleasure.

Of particular interest to coming generations of submariners is his account of the troubles and frustrations due to faulty design of the exploders in the submarine's principal weapon—the torpedo. In the correction of these defects the author played a leading and very personal part—as indeed he did in all aspects of the submarine war against the enemy, culminating in the penetration of the mine barriers blocking the entrances into the Sea of Japan in the last year of the war. The author was prevented from leading his submarines through the dangerous minefields by the firm refusal of his "Boss," the writer of this Foreword, who could not afford to risk his Commander Submarines Pacific in such a hazardous venture. We had many fine submarine captains but only one Lockwood.

There are few families in this country who were not touched by the war through the service of sons, daughters or near relatives, and there are still fewer servicemen and women who are not indebted to our submariners in some way or other. I have in mind particularly the 504 airmen of all the services who were rescued from almost certain death of drowning, or worse, by the timely presence of lifeguard submarines. And this is only one of the numerous phases of submarine activity during the war. From lone wolf tactics to large scale coordinated actions with the surface fleets the submarines played their part with uniform success.

Reconnaissance missions and clandestine visits to enemy-held islands for supply and personnel rescue were commonplace. But let the author tell these tales of valor and daring.

What part can we expect our submarines to play in future wars? It is a sad commentary that weapons of war are seldom (if ever) outlawed or eliminated for reasons of humanity. It is only when such weapons become inefficient or ineffective against their counter measures that nations no longer include them in their arsenals. By this standard submarines will continue to be an important part of navies for the predictable future. And for this reason this narrative—"Sink 'Em All"—will be an important addition to the reading list of all who like to be well informed. It will undoubtedly be interesting reading to former Japanese shipowners and naval men, and to (disturbing thought) possible aggressors whose plans run counter to the interests and security of our country.

Because of the high standard of daring of the many submarine captains involved in this account, there will appear to the readers to be a certain similarity in the story of each individual submarine's operations. However, in fairness to each individual crew of officers and men it would be wrong to compress the story into smaller space because to do so would necessitate omitting important successes. The very repetition of the many exploits of high standard are a tribute to the efficiency of the submarine as a whole and to the officers and men who trained them for battle.

AUTHOR'S PREFACE

Just after his appointment as Secretary of the Navy, I received a most gratifying letter from the Honorable James V. Forrestal. It ran:

My dear Admiral:

I have been getting quite a number of congratulations lately and I feel this morning like congratulating somebody else, so this is to tell you that I think the work of your submarines recently has been splendid. That is an understatement, but some day I hope the full story can be told.

James Forrestal

This gracious and sincere tribute from a very great Secretary I passed to all submarines in our nightly news letter.

In *Sink 'Em All*, I have attempted to tell the full story in so far as I know it. Due to space limitations of this book, many fine stories of daring exploits have been omitted much to my regret. To present the complete picture of the soul stirring exploits of the "Silent Service" would require a volume several times the size of this one. Many of the tales it contains were related to me by commanding officers, just in from a patrol, over a cup of coffee in the wardrooms of their own submarines with the soft whirr of ventilation fans and the acrid smell of diesel oil lending realism to their words. Others have been drawn from patrol reports, from the booklet *U.S. Submarine Losses, World War II*, and from the original *Submarine Operational History, World War II*, compiled by my Staff and that of my successor, Rear Admiral Allen R. McCann, during or just after the war. My diary and personal files have been used to verify names, dates and incidents.

So many shipmates and friends have assisted me that it is impossible to name them all. High on the list of these are Captain Jasper Holmes and Commanders Barney Sieglaff and Chick Clarey.

Percy Finch assisted in cutting and "tightening up" the original manuscript to get it down to size.

Last but not least of those to whom I am grateful is my wife, Phyllis Irwin Lockwood, without whose enthusiasm, keen advice and tireless fingers, the work could never have been completed.

CHARLES A. LOCKWOOD
Vice Admiral, U.S.N., Rtd.

Twin Dolphins, Los Gatos, California
November 7, 1950

SINK 'EM ALL

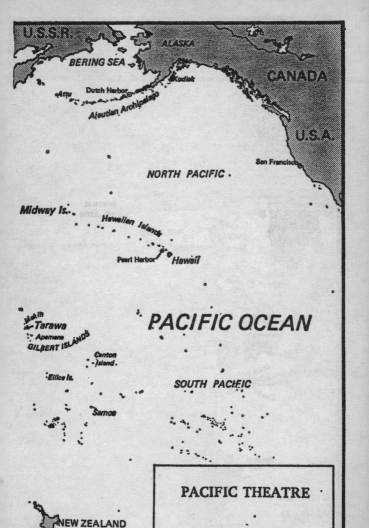

CHAPTER 1

Dusk of a rain-swept day in early May, 1942, was settling over the little frontier town of Albany, Western Australia, sprawled among the hills surrounding spacious Princess Royal Harbor. The cold winter rains of the land "down under" began early that year.

The Japanese hordes that had overrun Malaya, the Philippines and the Netherlands East Indies were now massing at bases in the Malay Barrier for a thrust into Australia. The battered remnants of our once powerful Asiatic Fleet and Allied naval forces had retreated to Fremantle, on the west coast of Australia, to repair battle damage and replace casualties.

Part of the Submarine Force, U.S. Asiatic Fleet, had been dispersed to this most southwestern port. Normally a prosperous wheat, wool and cattle shipping town, the harbor now was empty of merchantmen and only the submarine tender *Holland,* with a half dozen of her brood, represented the naval power of the United States. The shore defense consisted of perhaps 100 home guards and two ancient 6-inch guns.

The west coast of Australia was as wide open as a dead clamshell to enemy invasion and, if Australia fell to the Japanese, it looked as if our next base might be Marie Byrd Land in Antarctica.

This was the bleak outlook when I took over my new, and, so far, my highest, command—Commander Submarines Southwest Pacific—after 18 years of service with submarines.

Lights were beginning to show in the buildings bordering streets that could have been those of a typical Kansas boom town as my jeep slithered and bounced along toward the Freemasons Hotel where Captain Jimmie Fife, my Chief of Staff, and I had planned to have dinner.

As we entered the lobby, a burst of song greeted us from the direction of the lounge—a song that I hadn't heard before but one which sounded like it had stuff in it. A dozen young submarine officers, with a few girls, were gathered about the hotel piano and singing at the top of their lungs:

1

Sink 'em all, sink 'em all,
Tojo and Hitler and all:
Sink all their cruisers and carriers too,
Sink all their tin cans and their stinking crews, . . .

At first I thought that Australian beer, well known for its potency, was responsible for this sudden burst of optimism but there were very few glasses in hand—none among the girls. This was sheer exuberance of youthful spirit shouting defiance to the swarms of Japanese to northward who had already taken grim toll of our submarines and now threatened to overrun our temporary refuge. Sung to the tune of the Australian song "Bless 'Em All," these fighting words were destined to keynote our entire submarine campaign in the Pacific and their defiant ring bolstered many a man's courage in the dark days that were to come.

The heroic last-ditch defense of our Army and Marines on Bataan and Corregidor had been a tremendously inspiring example to all of us, Americans and Australians alike. Many of our submarines had run the Japanese blockade into Corregidor carrying cargoes of food, medicines and ammunition and bringing out evacuees, records, etc. The *Trout*, a Pearl Harbor–based submarine, early in the war had brought out 20 tons of gold, silver and securities—the Philippine currency reserve.

The stories of heroism and hardship which these evacuees from the Philippines brought, steeled our hearts with the resolve that we, too, would go down fighting. For my own inspiration, I needed to look no farther than my own submarine officers and men, lads to whom nothing appeared too difficult or dangerous to undertake. All they wanted between patrols were a few necessary repairs, stores, diesel fuel, torpedoes and the assignment of a good area for their next patrol—an area where plenty of Jap targets might be found. They were even making bets that we would have all Japan's shipping sunk by July, 1943!

Beyond a doubt, their stouthearted front and resolute faces concealed many secret, questioning thoughts as to their chances of returning from these 50-day patrols into badly charted waters, infested with Jap planes and antisubmarine craft but, thank God, they gave no sign of faltering for I myself was never free from a haunting fear that I was sending them to their deaths. They were all youngsters I had watched grow up in the submarine service and I felt a deep personal responsibility for them. Not once throughout the war, was I able to watch a submarine shove off for patrol without a twinge of sorrow and a period of soul searching as to whether or not I and my Staff had done everything humanly possible to insure the accomplishment of its mission and its safe return. The courage and determination of our submarines were always a sturdy buttress to my sometimes wavering resolution.

H.M.S. Prince of Wales

I had come a long way to find the spirit that I found there in our submarines down at the ends of the earth. In March, 1942, I had left my post as Naval Attaché in London in an atmosphere thicker with gloom than one of that city's famous fogs. The *Prince of Wales* and the *Repulse* had been sunk off Malaya by Jap planes; the fortress of Hong Kong, often stated to be another Gibraltar, had been overrun; and the disastrous Singapore campaign had drawn to a humiliating close.

In Washington I had found the usual rat race in progress. Indecision existed as to the line of advance to be followed back across the Pacific in regaining our lost territory. Our strategy in both the Atlantic and the Pacific was a matter of debate. I was speeded on my way to the Antipodes with the uninspiring information that we were destined to

fight a holding, delaying war in the Pacific until our armies
could clean up Europe. That operation, from the state of affairs I had seen in England, would require some years.

At Pearl Harbor I paused only long enough to pay my
respects to the new Commander in Chief U.S. Pacific Fleet,
Vice Admiral Chester W. Nimitz, check on the submarine
set-up there and obtain transportation to Brisbane, Australia.
I got passage on an Army bomber which was being flown
down for delivery to General MacArthur's meager forces and
soon I was out among the lads whose language I spoke and
who were really doing the fighting!

After reporting in to Vice Admiral H. F. Leary, Commander Southwest Pacific Area, at Melbourne, I flew across
the dreary stretches of the great Australian desert to Perth on
the west coast and reported to Rear Admiral W. R. "Speck"
Purnell for duty as understudy to Captain John Wilkes, Commander Submarine Asiatic Fleet, who was due for return to
the United States.

It was a grim-faced crowd that I met that first night at
the Perth U.S. Navy Headquarters. All of them had taken
part in the retreat from Manila to Soerabaja and had been
targets for Jap bombings almost daily. Finally, after Java and
the Malay Barrier had been invaded, they had made their
way, minus most of their personal effects, first to Darwin and
then to Fremantle, the seaport of Perth, with their decimated
naval forces and the ghost of Patrol Wing 10. This remnant
of the Asiatic Fleet had lost most of its planes and surface
ships. The surviving forces were in desperate need of torpedoes, ammunition and spare parts. In the bombing of Cavite, the submarines had lost some 233 torpedoes. When
Bataan fell, it was necessary to sink the gallant old *Canopus,*
a submarine tender which, on account of bomb damage, we
were forced to leave behind. Our two remaining tenders, *Holland* and *Otus,* had 20 submarines to care for, which meant
that most of the work fell to the lot of the former, since the
Otus was merely a C-3 cargo ship in process of being
converted to a tender at the outbreak of war.

The tenders were crowded with survivors from other
units, hence there was no spare space aboard to accommodate the crews of submarines while refitting. These unfor-
tunates had to live and try to sleep aboard their own boats
even when repair gangs were working in them night and
day. Nobody got the rest he so badly needed during refit peri-

ods and all hands went back on patrol almost as weary as when they came in.

Something had to be done about this—and soon. Those submariners needed complete rest, as much as we could give them, between patrols. They must go back fit, mentally and physically, to stand the strain of 50-day patrols in enemy-controlled waters where every man's hand was against them, to sink the maximum number of Jap ships and to bring their own boats safely back to base to prepare for another patrol. There were plenty of material problems confronting us at Perth Headquarters, such as lack of spare parts and torpedoes, and correction of torpedo defects, but paramount to me was the problem of physical reconditioning. If your submarine crews are exhausted and thereby drained of their morale, it won't matter much whether your torpedoes function or not.

The thin faces of the officers and men, their unnaturally bright eyes, told of the tension on their nerves and the drain on their vitality produced by those long weeks submerged in tropical waters—weeks of peering into the sun glare or into the darkness for enemy targets, of sweating out depth charge attacks by Jap planes and antisubmarine vessels. One of our leaders in the Jap-sinking game, Lieutenant Commander W. L. Wright, of Corpus Christi, better known as "Bull," was just back from a very productive patrol during which he had lost 27 pounds from his already spare Texas frame. Even half of that amount was far too much for anyone to lose in one patrol. The need for proper recuperation facilities was obvious and most urgent.

Admiral Nimitz, at Pearl Harbor, had directed the leasing of the Royal Hawaiian Hotel as a rest camp for submariners and aviators back from war operations. Quotas of personnel from other forces were also rehabilitated there to the extent of the capacity of the hotel. The officers and men, removed from their ships immediately upon return from patrol, were given two weeks in which to relax completely, to lie in the sun, swim and indulge in athletics. Meanwhile their ships were repaired by expert refitting crews and when their rest period was completed, the submariners returned to their boats rested and keen to get back into the war.

Something of this sort, but on a smaller scale, was what I wanted to initiate in Fremantle and Albany—the latter a port 250 miles south of Perth. The idea was looked upon askance in some quarters as being too much in the line of pampering our personnel but the rehabilitation of our crews throughout the war paid large dividends in the form of better performance on patrol, better physical and mental health. As a natural consequence, I am convinced, we lost fewer submarines. The idea of rehabilitation was not new. The Germans initiated it in World War I, and no one ever accused them of pampering their men.

Investigation was immediately started as to availability of rest-camp facilities in the vicinity of our bases. In a short while we leased, through the Australian Army on Reverse Lend-Lease, four small hotels—two on the beaches—into which our men moved immediately with their own cooks and rations, to the great improvement of overall conditions.

The then unused Quarantine Station at Albany was very generously loaned to us by the Australian Immigration authorities to take care of about 250 raw recruits who came to us after only six weeks' training. These lads, I may add, though green as grass, after about six months on patrol in submarines, developed into excellent men, many of them ready for advancement in rating—which shows the speed-up in training which can be effected when stern necessity is breathing down the back of one's neck.

During May, 1942, I relieved Captain Wilkes and became Commander Submarines Southwest Pacific; also I relieved Rear Admiral Purnell, who had been ordered home, and became Commander Allied Naval Forces based in Western Australia, with the rank of rear admiral.

The Allied naval forces under my command consisted of two Dutch, one Australian and one U.S. cruiser; two Dutch and two Australian destroyers; three U.S. seaplane tenders (ex-old destroyers), a squadron of PBY's, the *Isabel* (a converted yacht of World War I vintage), plus my submarine force of two tenders, two rescue vessels, and 20 Fleet-type submarines. The S-class submarines originally with us, had been ordered to Brisbane where they, plus six more S-boats, operated under command of Captain R. W. Christie, on patrols in the New Guinea-Bismark-Solomons area.

Four submarines had already been lost. *Sealion*, Lieutenant Commander R. G. Voge of Chicago, Illinois, was bombed while undergoing overhaul alongside the Submarine Base at Cavite, Philippine Islands. We destroyed her on Christmas Day, 1941, to prevent her falling into enemy hands. S-36, Lieutenant J. R. McKnight, Jr., of Oklahoma City, Oklahoma, grounded on Taka Bakang Reef in Makassar Straight on January 20, 1942, and was destroyed. *Shark,* commanded by Lieutenant Louis Shane, Jr., which had evacuated Admiral Thomas C. Hart and his Staff from Manila to Surabaya, Java, was lost, probably near Menado, Celebes Islands. *Perch,* Lieutenant Commander D. A. "Dave" Hurt, was mortally damaged by depth charges and scuttled in the Java Sea. After the war, when Commander Hurt and 52 of the ship's complement were returned from Japanese prison camps, nine had died while POW's.

My second in command in the Allied force was Commodore John A. Collins, Royal Australian Navy, who as captain of the Australian cruiser *Sydney* had sunk the Italian cruiser *Collini* at the battle of Cape Matapan. He was a tower of strength and possessed a fine sense of humor which endeared him to all of us "Yanks," as we were universally called throughout Aussieland.

Our position in Australia was a curious one for while we were received with the most openhanded hospitality and welcomed as very valuable additions to their meager armed forces, there were many of our new-found friends who did not always appreciate our breezy ways, our jokes—often told at their expense—nor our complete confidence that everything American was better than anything to be found in any other land. An American bluejacket in a pub, having a few drinks with some Aussies, was trying to reassure them as to the state of their defenses. He slapped one of them on the back and said, "Cheer up, Buddy. Everything is going to be all right now—the U.S. Navy is here to defend you."

"Oh," said the Aussie, "is that why you're 'ere? I thought per'aps you were bloody refugees from Pearl 'Arbor!"

In the same vein was a wheeze which I heard in London after the Pearl Harbor disaster. Admiral Lord Fraser, now First Sea Lord, then the "Controller" in the British Admiralty and later the British Commander in Chief in the Pacific, loved a good joke, even if it were on himself. One morning when I visited him in his office, the Admiral greeted me with:

"I say, Lockwood, had you heard that the American Navy has requisitioned 30,000 kilts from us on Reverse Lend-Lease?"

Nothing would have surprised me at that stage of the

war, otherwise I might have smelled a rat, but I swallowed
the bait, hook, line and sinker.

"No, Admiral," I said, "what are they for?"

"So you Americans won't get caught with your pants
down again!" gently explained the Admiral.

Remembering the blasting of the *Prince of Wales* and
Repulse, the overrunning of Hong Kong, and the evident fact
that Singapore was tottering to its fall, that one I could also
take with a laugh. In fact, I felt that the Controller was, in
reality, saying, "We're all in the same boat, now."

The entire west coast of Australia was under the military
command of Lieutenant General H. Gordon Bennett, with
headquarters in Perth, and to him I reported for coordination
of our defense. General Gordon Bennett had escaped from
Singapore after the capitulation of that base.

My own Staff was top notch, while the submarine
squadron and division commanders and the VP squadron
commander were likewise officers of high caliber. Many of
them were submariners with whom I had served for years
and four had been skippers in Submarine Division 13 when I
commanded it back in '35–'37. Among the key men in my
Western Australia submarine, surface ship and air organization were such stalwarts as Captains Jimmie Fife, S. S. "Sunshine" Murray, Homer L. "Pop" Grosskopf, H. H. "Tex"
McLean, Perley L. Pendleton, W. G. "Bill" Lalor; Commanders E. H. "Swede" Bryant, J. A. "Joe" Connolly, W. B.
"Pinky" Thorp, J. M. "Dutch" Will, J. V. "Pete" Peterson,
John P. Dix, and F. C. "Kraut" Dettmann.

No outfit boasting such an array of talent, given half a
chance, could fail to produce. There was not a "Yes" man
among them. Each had very definite ideas as to how his particular ships should be employed and how the war was to be
won. They were agreed on but one thing, that the war *was to
be won—and soon.* This set-up suited me perfectly, for it insured that in any critical situation, the different angles from
which it was certain to be attacked by my top advisors would
result in a correct, perhaps brilliant, solution.

Before our submarine offensive, which sank nearly 6
million tons of Japanese shipping, became effective, one serious problem had to be solved—our torpedoes.

Ever since the outbreak of war, our submarines had experienced discouraging results from their torpedo fire. Apparently they were running too deep, i.e., deeper than the

desired depth which had been set on the regulator dial. Skipper after skipper reported seeing the air bubble trail from their torpedoes pass under the stern or slightly astern of their targets. Allowing for the time required for the bubbles to rise to the surface and for the advance of the target during that short interval, a bubble trail seen in such a location would indicate that the torpedo itself had actually passed under the target. The S-class submarines used a torpedo equipped with a mechanical contact exploder, hence that type had to strike the target to explode. However, the Fleet-type submarines used a magnetic exploder designed to explode on activation by the magnetic flux of the steel hull just as the torpedo passed *under* the target ship. If torpedoes were running deeper than the set depth, it meant that those used by the S-class would not strike the target and that those used by the Fleet-type subs would pass so far under the target's hull as to be below the influence of its magnetic field.

In some quarters, including the Bureau of Ordnance, it was evidently believed that these stories from our submarine captains were merely alibis for misses. However, so much evidence was piling up and our submariners were becoming so discouraged by repeated misses which should have been hits, we decided to do a little torpedo testing on our own. Thereupon, at the suggestion of Captain Jimmie Fife, we bought 500 feet of net from a fisherman in Albany, moored it just outside the harbor in King George Sound and fired a series of torpedoes through it from a distance of 1,000 yards, which was about the normal attack range. When the net was examined by divers it was found that our skippers were probably correct in their observations. Measurements showed that torpedoes used by Fleet-type submarines (we had no S-class in Western Australia at that time) were running an average of 11 feet deeper than set. This could make a whale of a difference in the performance of our magnetic exploder and we immediately made the necessary changes in our depth settings.

The Bureau of Ordnance questioned our procedure in making these tests—also the accuracy of our data. However, it did admit, some time later, that Torpedo Station tests showed a 10-foot error instead of the 11 which we had found.

The result of our tests brought a wave of confidence because we believed the trouble had been located and we had the satisfaction of having found it all on our own. Hope sprang up anew in the hearts of frustrated submarine commanders but, alas, this was not the end of our torpedo sorrows. Bringing our torpedo runs closer to the surface seemed to multiply the number of premature explosions of war heads as well as the number of times in which torpedoes could be heard to thud against the side of a target without exploding. Premature explosions sometimes occurred as soon as the torpedo had "armed" itself after leaving the tube and sometimes so close to the target that they were mistaken for good hits.

These increased troubles, unfortunately, were destined to be with us for about a year more, during which time our torpedo shops in bases and tenders were working feverishly on the delicate insides of our temperamental magnetic exploder. Bureau of Ordnance sent expert trouble shooters into the Pacific in an effort to help us to eliminate its defects—all to no avail. The whole design was sour. It must have been known in the Department that both the British and the Germans had abandoned this type of unreliable exploder early in the war, yet our experts clung to it "like grim death to a dead cat" for many months more.

In spite of our difficulties in getting hits, occasionally our exploders did function as designed, thereby lifting our morale at the same time they confused the problem. As one submarine captain said, "There's no better morale booster than the sound of your own torpedoes exploding against an enemy ship."

While we were getting the bugs out of our torpedoes, the successful accomplishment of several secondary missions also cheered us. Our boats showed themselves capable of doing many things not contemplated in peacetime thinking. The *Searaven*, Commander Hiram Cassedy of Brookhaven, Mississipi, went in to the south coast of Jap-held Timor one black night to pick up 33 Aussie flyers who were hiding there. The submarine's tiny dory was rowed in to the beach and anchored outside the surf. Ensign G. C. Cook, the boat officer, swam in through the breakers and, with a line, succeeded in getting 16 of those in the best physical condition out to the boat. However, he had twice to go to the rescue of men who got adrift. Next night 17, some in pitiable condition, were got out in spite of a catastrophe when the anchor line parted. The boat was thrown ashore and it required superhuman efforts on the part of Ensign Cook and his boat's crew to launch her through the surf. Six Australians, too weak to be hauled out by a line, were placed in the boat before this truly Herculean feat was attempted.

On the *Searaven*'s way back to Fremantle, this expedition nearly ended in disaster when a fire in her electric control panel put all engines and motors out of commission. She rolled around for two or three days, a perfect sitting duck, in waters where Jap submarines had been sighted frequently, until a sistership could be sent out to tow her in.

The people of Perth were delighted with this rescue. A service men's organization gave Cassedy and his crew a fine party as a testimonial. Ensign Cook was rewarded for his daring by the award of a Navy Cross, which, I believe, was the first one given a reserve officer in the submarine forces.

Lieutenant Commander J. C. "Jimmy" Dempsey of Philadelphia, Pennsylvania, brought the *Spearfish* into Fremantle one blustery May morning with a passenger list of about 27 evacuees from Corregidor who were especially happy to be with us. They had embarked in the submarine during the night about 48 hours before "The Rock" surrendered. Captain Sackett, the Commanding Officer of our tender, *Canopus*, was one of them. His ship had acted as a work-shop for all sorts of Army and Marine jobs after being damaged by a bomb in Manila Bay, and had been scuttled when Bataan fell. We mourned the loss of her fine crew, many of whom were never to come back from Japanese prison camps. We likewise mourned the loss of machine shop equipment and spare parts which she carried to the bottom of Mariveles Bay.

Among the *Spearfish*'s other passengers were one Navy and 12 Army nurses. They had made the 15-day trip in the Chief Petty Officers' tiny four-bunk quarters where they slept in watches and occupied their waking hours helping the mess cooks and making pies and cakes in the ship's galley, to the great pleasure of all hands. All were apparently in good health and spirits. One pint-sized girl in a makeshift costume of mixed slacks and uniform, came up the submarine's hatch and onto the dock where she quietly walked from one end of the submarine to the other, looking over it carefully. Noticing that I was regarding her quizzically, she came up and said, "I just wanted to see what the darned thing looks like. I've been inside it, like Jonah in the whale, for 15 days, but have never seen the outside."

During the first part of this trip, while en route from Fremantle with a cargo of antiaircraft ammunition for Corregidor, Captain Dempsey had added to our tonnage score by sinking two Jap cargo carriers totaling 11,000 tons.

On one trip *Permit* brought down a stowaway. He said he was "just a spare pumphandle" and could see no use in remaining to be a POW. A general court-martial was indicated in this case but we needed men and I could ill afford to spare officers to form such a court, so we put him to work.

Other additions to our bag kept coming in as submarines returned from their 50- or 60-day forays into enemy-controlled waters—which control we were vigorously contesting.

The *Skipjack*, Lieutenant Commander J. W. "Jim" Coe

of Richmond, Indiana, later lost in the *Cisco*, sank three freighters off Indo-China for a total of about 12,000 tons. Coe, who had a keen sense of humor, also brought in a diverting yarn about his last overhaul at Mare Island. His ship had submitted a number of requisitions for supplies, among them one for a case of toilet paper, which was returned, stamped "Item cannot be identified"! Whether this happened by mistake or some joker was trying to pull his leg, Jim didn't know, but the two-page letter which he wrote to the Supply Officer more clearly identifying the item, is a classic which will live long in submarine annals.

U.S.S. Tautog

The *Tautog*, Lieutenant Commander J. H. "Joe" Willingham of Pell City, Alabama, came in from a patrol which began in Pearl Harbor and ended at Fremantle, with a thrilling tale of having sunk three enemy submarines. She was one of the first of the new submarines which were being sent down to us by Rear Admiral R. H. "Bob" English, Commander Submarines Pacific Fleet, to make good our losses and replace older boats which were due for navy yard overhauls. Such exchange submarines were routed through the Marshalls and other Mandated Islands with instructions to pay particular attention to Kwajalein, Truk and the Palau group. The *Tautog* had patrolled those hot spots on her way down. She got no shots at surface ships, but had fired at three enemy submarines, all of which Willingham claimed as dead ducks.

The first encounter took place northeast of Johnston Island when *Tautog*'s Officer of the Deck sighted a periscope. It could belong only to an enemy since no other American sub was in that area. The Jap was in good position and probably just about to fire. The OOD, Lieutenant Barnard, handled the situation perfectly by ringing up full speed and swinging away from the enemy with hard over rudder, meanwhile burning up the intercommunication system with frantic orders to the after torpedo room to get the tubes ready to fire. The torpedo crew broke all existing speed records for that maneuver and, when the *Tautog*'s stern swung onto the target, the OOD fired one torpedo which exploded in about the proper place. There was always the chance this might have been a premature explosion but postwar investigation shows that the career of the RO-30, 960 tons, ended there.

Three weeks later, while patrolling submerged one bright morning off the South Pass of Truk, *Tautog* sighted at about one-hour intervals, two enemy submarines heading for port. He failed to get a shot at the first but did fire at the second and heard an explosion. However that must have been from a premature for the Japanese do not admit the loss of a boat at that time. Later in the forenoon watch a third submarine, also on surface, came down the same course. Her rising-sun flag was proudly flying and numerous personnel were on the bridge. She was probably returning from patrol down Solomons way and anticipating a warm welcome from her division mates—and perhaps some dusky belles—at Truk. Willingham said the Jap was so close that he felt sure he would recognize the Officer of the Deck if he ever saw him again. Joe fired two torpedoes and got one hit which disabled the Jap but did not sink her. Willingham then fired again and we know now that, in the shower of debris and bodies that resulted from the ensuing explosion, all earthly plans ended for the 1-28, 2,212 tons.

Another new submarine, the *Grampus*, Lieutenant Commander E. S. Hutchinson of Germantown, Pennsylvania, came in shortly after the *Tautog* had stirred up the Japs at Truk, with a story of near disaster which showed that the enemy was tightening up their antisubmarine patrols. I went down to meet *Grampus* on her arrival at Fremantle and found her with a very neat shell hole about three feet in diameter through the starboard side of the cigarette deck spray shield. It looked as though some large, seagoing rodent had been at work. The shell had evidently exploded on contact, for the port side of the fairwater was torn to shreds. Off Truk one night, Hutchinson had encountered a patrol vessel which immediately made a dash for him. "Hutch" crash-dived with all speed but before the conning tower got under, the Jap registered a hit. Thank God his sights were a little high, for had his hit been three feet lower, *Grampus* would have been on her way to Davy Jones's locker instead of Fremantle.

About this same time, good news arrived by dispatch one night from the *Salmon*, Lieutenant Commander E. B. "Gene" McKinney of Eugene, Oregon, who reported sinking a cargo-passenger ship plus the cruiser *Yubari* off the Indo-China coast. The ship he had identified as *Yubari* was actually the naval repair ship *Asahi*—named, no doubt, after that excellent brand of Jap beer—but 11,441 tons, with her invaluable machine shops, made a very handsome item on our list of sinkings. Gene got in a perfect attack on her and had the unusual pleasure of seeing all four of his shots hit—and explode—right where he had aimed them. The *Yubari*, incidentally, was destined to bear a charmed life until April, 1944, when *Bluegill* got her south of the Palau group.

Looking back on the first five months of World War II, we, as a nation, had little with which to lessen the sting of our defeats but the courage and determination of our Armed Services. Attacked with blackest treachery, outnumbered at every point, and handicapped by inferior armament, they, nonetheless, fought to the last ditch and died confident that others would seize the weapons from their failing hands to avenge their deaths and to wipe barbarism and imperialism from the face of the earth.

Numerically one of the smallest branches of the Armed Forces, one whose handicaps at the beginning were very great, yet one whose contribution to final victory was out of all proportion to its size, was the Submarine Force.

Starting, initially, with 51 submarines in the Pacific— some long overage for modern combat—the Submarine Forces based in the Central Pacific and in the Southwest Pacific reached their nadir in those first bloody months. Torpedoes were unreliable, spare parts and radar were nonexistent, personnel replacements were nill—even torpedoes had to be rationed.

Meager as was their force at the outset, and great as were their handicaps, singlehanded they fought for almost two years, in enemy-controlled waters, thousands of miles from their bases, to destroy Japanese sea-borne communications and supply lines, and swept on to make themselves the scourge of the ocean to the enemy navy and merchant marine.

Never in the course of the war did the Submarine Forces exceed 4,000 officers and 46,000 enlisted men—about the equal of two Army or Marine divisions. Our peak in submarine strength was 169 Fleet-type and 13 S-type.

Yes, we reached our lowest ebb in those first heartbreaking months but in Australia, as in Pearl Harbor, the tide was making, a mounting flood, which, before V-J Day, was to sweep from the seas 1,178 Japanese merchantmen and 214 ships of the once arrogant Imperial Japanese Navy— 6,000,000 tons of shipping on which the very life of the Empire depended.

CHAPTER 2

The Battle of Midway was the turning point in the naval war against Japan. It also helped turn the tide in the submarine onslaught on the enemy. Possession of the Midway Islands was of great strategic importance in the entire Pacific picture and of operational importance to submarines based on Pearl Harbor. Situated 1,200 miles west by north of Oahu, their replenishing facilities added 2,400 miles to the cruising radius of the boats commanded by Rear Admiral Robert English, Commander Submarines Pacific.

Ever since I took command at Perth, I, too, had been seeking a way to increase the cruising radius of my own submarines. The distance to the Indo-China coast, then our best hunting ground, was about 3,300 miles, a 6,600-mile round trip. Since the cruising radius of our subs was in the neighborhood of 10-12,000 miles, at economic speeds, this long trip seriously cut into the fuel available for high-speed operations in the combat areas. If I could arrange, nearer to our targets, a refueling base such as the Central Pacific subs had at Midway, the time necessary for our boats to reach their assigned stations would be cut. They could proceed at higher speeds, their on-station period would be lengthened and more enemy ships would be sunk.

The ports of northwest Australia offered little promise. They had practically no fuel storage facilities and I couldn't spare a tender to anchor in one of them for use as a tanker. Tankers were as scarce as hen's teeth and the only one we had in Fremantle, a Norwegian, had been so badly mauled by Japanese bombs that she would be out of commission for a long time.

Darwin, on the north coast, and Broome, halfway up the coast to Darwin, appeared to be the best available spots for submarine advance bases and therefore I took off by air to inspect them at firsthand. Darwin proved impracticable. Its defenses were meager. There was nothing to stop the Japanese, sitting on Timor, from coming over any time they liked and the city, deserted by its civilian population, was in ruins from Japanese air raids, which still continued. Broome, once the wealthest pearling town in Australia, was another ill-defended ghost town. It would have been foolhardy for me to risk a tender in either of these two ports.

On one of my trips east I took up the question of an advance submarine base with General MacArthur at Brisbane. He was never too busy to listen to the problems of Allied Naval Forces based in Western Australia and was particularly interested in the lastest news of submarine operations.

He discussed current operations and future plans with the greatest frankness. I pointed out to him the urgency of our need for another base but said I couldn't afford to risk one of my few submarine tenders at Darwin so close to

Japanese air bases at Koepang and Dilli, on the island of Timor. MacArthur immediately replied that he intended capturing Timor before the end of the year—1942. Unfortunately, for our plans, this optimistic assumption was never realized. The Japanese push, late in 1942, over the towering Owen-Stanley mountains of New Guinea toward Port Moresby fully engaged his attention and Timor remained in Japanese hands until the end of the war.

Exmouth Gulf, on the northwest corner of Australia, 700 miles north of Perth, was the answer to my problem, although it did not completely meet requirements. For some time Exmouth Gulf had served as a patrol base for four or five of our Catalina flying boats and there eventually we based a tender, giving the new refueling depot the name "Potshot."

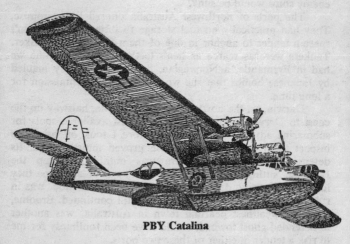

PBY Catalina

Exmouth Gulf is a large body of water with depths suitable for netting against midget subs and torpedoes and, in general, too shallow for submerged attacks by regular-sized submarines. However, our seaplane tenders were wide open to night surface attack and we actually wondered why some Japanese submarine skipper did not make the attempt. The Gulf is almost landlocked but the flat terrain of that section of Australia afforded little protection against willy-willies, the dreaded windstorms of the region, which frequently flattened the frame-built, pearl-fishing villages along that desolate coast. Planes had been damaged at their anchorages but those were hazards we had to accept in return for the partial security afforded by the patrol. For my submarine plans, this location had suitable characteristics but was not nearly as far from Fremantle as was desirable.

Although it added only two days each way to the cruising radius of our submarines, I decided to obtain, if possible, a "dumb" lighter (one with no motive power) of 500-ton capacity and anchor it in the Gulf, under the guns of the seaplane tender, so our submarines could top off their fuel supply there on their outward journey and use it for an emergency fueling stop on the return trip. With this as a beginning, we could then make further plans for putting a tender there for refitting submarines—and possibly a recuperation camp.

On my return to Perth, I proposed this plan to Vice Admiral Leary, Commander Southwest Pacific. He concurred and in less than two months the Australian Commonwealth Naval Board ordered a dumb lighter towed from Sydney, via Torres Straight, and had it anchored, full of diesel fuel, in Exmouth Gulf.

This was the initial move toward what later grew into the advance base, need for which was so clearly recognized. As things turned out, its existence was destined to be short lived. The outlay of funds and materials was not great, whereas the experience my Staff and I gained in planning and establishing such bases, was invaluable to us later at Midway, Majoro, Saipan and Guam.

At Perth we still had to struggle with engineering difficulties. The west coast of Australia boasted of nothing in the line of a dry dock. Melbourne or Sydney had to take the more serious docking jobs. At Fremantle, the port of Perth, we had only a small slipway too small to haul out a 312-foot Fleet-type submarine. Until this slipway could be lengthened and strengthened we had to rely on divers or jury-rigged caissons for shifting propellers or making small underwater repairs. The supply question was also difficult. Owing to the many gauge changes on the Australian railways, the freight service across the country was so slow that we found it quicker to ship our torpedoes by boat from Melbourne to Western Australia.

The Australian authorities authorized the necessary alterations to the slipway and Lieutenant Commander W. T. "Bill" Jones, our naval constructor, worked tirelessly with its manager to expedite the work. Divers from our submarine tender at Fremantle were in constant demand for extending the rails into deeper water and one of the main motors of the old Dutch submarine K-8 was pressed into service to augment its power for hauling out larger ships. Progress was slow, partly because there were few Australian workmen assigned to the job and secondly because they were not very energetic workmen. Finally, in early August, I arranged a conference with the authorities which resulted in obtaining augmented civilian working forces which we supplemented by special details from our tender crews. Some of our submarines had not been docked in 19 months, with the result that fouling of their underwater hulls had seriously reduced their speed and had increased fuel consumption. I wanted, at all costs, to avoid the 2,100-mile trip to Melbourne or the 2,500-mile trip to Sydney for docking and bottom cleaning. Nevertheless, with all the pushing that Bill Jones and I could do, it was not until September 30 that our first submarine was hauled out for cleaning and underwater repairs.

As if the sum total of all these difficulties was not sufficient to sear the soul of anybody but the resourceful submariner, we ran into trouble from another source—a new broom. In the first part of July we received from the Atlantic a new Commander Allied Naval Forces based in Western Australia, who relieved me of that responsibility and left me in the billet of Commander Submarines Southwest Pacific.

I had desired from the beginning of my duty in Australia to be assigned only to submarine duties and, when Vice Admiral Leary informed me this officer was designated to relieve me of top command in Perth, I was greatly pleased. That change, I believed, would permit me to devote full time to prosecution of the submarine war.

The new boss desired to change practically everything in our set-up and operations. First, the organization had to be radically altered. The tenders, the heart and soul of all submarine squadrons, had to be put in a separate task group. Everything had to be patterned on the Atlantic Fleet. I heard how things were done in that Fleet so often that I felt ready to shoot on sight the next Atlantic sailor I met.

Second, the rest camps should have been set up out in the country away from all distractions—not in beach hotels.

—Certainly the discontent of our crews at being exiled to such recreation camps would have nullified any gain that might have been achieved by keeping them away from wine, women and song. Admiral Nimitz had established a rest camp at the Royal Hawaiian Hotel in the heart of Honolulu without, I feel sure, any idea of monastic seclusion.

Third, our submarines should use pure English in dispatches. The use of slang such as "fish" or "pickle" instead of "torpedo" was all wrong. Our simple "slipstick" codes, we felt sure, were not proof against decryption by the enemy and our communication officers urged that we use the widest possible range of words in radio messages—naturally, slang words and phrases crept in. While my skippers did not go in for the less reputable of the Anglo-Saxon words, they may have obtained a few ideas from a message which Admiral Bill Halsey sent to a submarine operating with his forces in the Solomons. It read: "I like your guts. You can play on my team any time."

Lastly, our submarines were not sufficiently aggressive. This I could not take lying down. My skippers were prying into every nook and cranny of Far Eastern waters from Christmas Island, where *Searaven* sank a Jap ship at the dock, to the South China coast and the roadstead at Kema, Celebes, where *Swordfish* had sunk one ship and damaged another.

In all Australia we had, at that time, only 31 submarines and even with defective exploders, 260,000 tons of merchant shipping and 10 men-of-war had been sunk or damaged. True, we were not making the records the Germans were piling up in the Atlantic but they, after all, had an excellent torpedo, a reliable exploder and many times the number of targets.

I knew most of my officers too well ever to doubt their courage, determination and skill, and, when our torpedo and exploder troubles were solved, they proved my confidence was not misplaced.

In spite of the additional tension which this temporary change created in the command, operations against the enemy proceeded apace. *Sculpin*, Lieutenant Commander Lucius H. Chappell of Columbus, Georgia, came in on July 17 with a count of four ships all of which he believed had sunk. In each case, however, he had been kept down so long by depth charging that he had not actually seen them sink. Postwar records credit no sinkings at that time but undoubtedly some of his targets were damaged. Probably some of his supposed hits were actually premature explosions.

It was customary for the Staff to meet each returning submarine at the dock and then I would run through the Commanding Officer's report over a cup of coffee in the submarine's wardroom. This gave me a chance to look over the ship and crew to observe how both had stood up under the punishment they had received. In this case I noted that Chappell looked a little drawn but the rest of the crew looked fine. Three officers, hardly old enough to shave, had grown beautiful apostolic beards.

The *Sculpin* was scheduled for refit at Albany and I made plans to take passage in her in order to keep in touch with current diving technique, to acquaint myself with the spirit of the command, and to meet our new tender, the *Pelias*, which was due to arrive there on July 22. She was coming out from the U.S. and I hoped to find her loaded to the Plimsoll mark with spare officers, men and torpedoes to fill our empty magazines.

On the trip south in *Sculpin* we took another passenger, Lieutenant Colonel Duffy of the Australian Imperial Forces, a member of General Gordon Bennett's Staff, who had flown with me in June to look over the Darwin situation. The Royal Netherlands Navy cruiser *Von Tromp*—Captain J. B. de Meester—accompanied us to act as escort.

On the morning of July 22 we arrived at Albany but found no *Pelias* there. As the day advanced, no *Pelias* showed up and we grew somewhat anxious as an enemy submarine had been reported in the Great Australian Bight. Late in the afternoon I sent out one of the scouting planes stationed at Albany to look for her and it returned without sighting anything. However, the weather was bad to eastward and we believed this accounted for her delay. It seemed unlikely she could have been sunk without getting off an SOS.

Next morning the weather had improved and, at 10 A.M. *Pelias*—Commander Wm. Wakefield of Humboldt, Kansas— was reported standing in. As soon as she had secured, transfer of details between her and *Holland* began and at 4 P.M. the latter, with her escorts, sailed for Fremantle.

To my sorrow I found that *Pelias* had brought almost no reinforcements in officers or men and only her regular allowance of torpedoes. These last mentioned were still in short supply back in the U.S. and our reserve stock was so low that submarines going on patrol were issued only 20 of the 24 torpedoes which they should carry.

However, *Pelias*, tender for Subron 6, did bring Commander Allen R. McCann, Commander Submarine Squadron 6; Lieutenant Commander H. H. "Tex" McLean, a division commander; and Lieutenant Commander "Joe" Thew, the squadron engineer officer. All three of these officers were submariners of many years' experience and most welcome additions to our struggling organization. Several submarines had arrived ahead of the squadron commander and were already on patrol in or about the South China Sea.

With the replacement of *Otus* at Fremantle by *Holland,* our capacity for effecting repairs to our submarines was greatly improved. In addition to the facilities of our tender's shops we had, through the efforts of Commander "Dutch" Will, our very efficient Force Engineer Officer, obtained the assistance of the State Engineering Works—Mr. G. C. Kekwick—of North Fremantle to absorb some of the *Holland*'s overload. It was my desire to set up a repair unit and storage battery overhaul shop ashore in Fremantle, of capacity equal to that of a submarine tender so we would have a tender free to be moved to "Potshot." In pursuance of this plan, we leased from the Fremantle Harbor Trust one of the enormous wheat sheds where, in normal times, grain was stored awaiting shipment to England. The manager of the Harbor Trust, Mr. G. V. McCartney, was most cooperative in every way.

Before each submarine left on patrol she had to be degaussed, an operation intended to neutralize the permanent magnetism of her steel hull and equipment so that she would not detonate enemy magnetic mines. Our tenders had no equipment for this purpose so we made use of the RAN auxiliary vessel, the *Springdale,* anchored in the Swan River at Fremantle. Degaussing was of value in giving a sense of added security to our submariners but we found toward the end of the war that the Japs had no magnetic mines. Hence all this work had been unnecessary except that it possibly might have protected a submarine from a circling run of one of its own torpedoes armed with a magnetic exploder.

In order to keep in closer touch with submarines and to be on hand for the numerous night alarms—usually false—I took up quarters aboard the *Holland.* She, our oldest tender, was a beehive of activity and usually sounded like a boiler factory most of the night—so much so that Commander Pendleton, her Commanding Officer, had moved most of his men, who normally slept near the shops, onto cots in our newly acquired grain shed.

Our spirits were cheered by performances of *Sturgeon*, under the redoubtable Bull Wright, and *Seadragon*, Lieutenant Commander W. E. Ferrall of Pittsburgh, Pennsylvania. The former, on the first day of July off the west coast of Luzon, sank the 7,267-ton transport *Montivedeo Maru* while the latter, on July 12, 13 and 16 off the Indo-China coast, sank *Hiyama Maru*, *Shinyo Maru* and *Hakodate Maru* for a total of 15,636 tons.

The *Seadragon* had an old score to settle with the enemy. She was lying alongside *Sealion* at Cavite docks on December 10, 1941, when the Jap bombers attacked. Two bombs struck the *Sealion* and sank her. Fragments from the first of these two bombs pierced the side of *Seadragon*'s conning tower, killing Ensign Sam Hunter. He was the first casualty of the Submarine Force in World War II. *Seadragon*'s superstructure still bore the scars of that bombing and her CO (Commanding Officer) wanted them to remain there as a reminder to all hands of the debts she would always owe a treacherous enemy.

Contacts with enemy ships dropped off somewhat during July, 1942, probably due to wide changes in the routing of enemy ships. They evidently were learning just as our own convoys were learning in the Atlantic, that proceeding via the longest way around frequently made the difference between arriving at their destination or in Davy Jones's locker. The submarines available to us in Western Australia were too few in number and had to cover too many important points to permit the use of coordinated attack groups—or "wolf packs" as the Germans called them.

The approaches to Manila, Davao, Soerabaya, Singapore, Saigon, Camranh Bay, the oil ports of Miri and Tarakan in Borneo, all had to be watched continuously, if possible. An attack group guarding each of these undoubtedly would have paid handsome dividends. Other wolf packs in Makassar Straight and off the Indo-China coast were urgently needed. There just were not enough Fleet-type submarines in the Navy to supply me and Commander Submarines Pacific— whose work was equally important—with a sufficient number to cover our areas properly. This was indeed a misfortune.

At the beginning of the war, enemy antisubmarine forces were few and inexperienced, submarine attack methods were not generally known and many merchantmen were poorly armed or not armed at all. Furthermore, the enemy was storing stockpiles with strategic materials from captured territories and laying in reserves of oil and gasoline which were to cost us dear.

A strong force of Fleet-type submarines in this opening period—say, 100 instead of the 39 we actually had—would have reaped a rich harvest. That undoubtedly would have shortened the war,—perhaps by six months, thus saving billions of dollars and thousands of American lives.

The other half of my administrative command, Submarine Squadron 5—Captain R. W. Christie—based at Brisbane on the new tender *Griffin* and operated 11 S-boats in the torrid waters of the Solomons, Bougainville, New Ireland, New Britain and New Guinea. Conditions in that area were particularly difficult because of the lack of air conditioning in these older submarines. This resulted in almost intolerable heat in the boats when submerged. The temperature of the main storage batteries frequently ran up to 125–135 degrees Fahrenheit so that the crews lived in a continual sweat bath from which they emerged at the end of a 30-day patrol looking like something you find under a rock.

When I saw them they were none too cheerful. They had a continual struggle to keep their aged ships in operating condition. The inevitable corrosion and pitting of the strength of the hulls had so weakened them that their successful resistance to a close depth charging was in grave doubt. Before the war, it had been the plan to allow the S-boats then in the Asiatic Fleet to live out their few remaining years of usefulness and then scrap them at Cavite.

However, they could still do a wartime job of training new crews and acting as electric rabbits for antisubmarine vessels, so eventually the Department decided to relieve the S-boat divisions at Brisbane with Fleet-type boats from Pearl Harbor and Western Australia and send them back to the U.S. This change was carried out in the early fall of 1942 and these weary, battle-scarred veterans departed homeward, leaving behind them a very creditable record of patrols made, enemy ships sunk and coast watchers landed in enemy-held territory.

Midget submarines were another subject continually entering the Australian picture. Hauled out on Clark's Island in Sydney Harbor were two of the Japanese midget submarines, which made an attack on shipping there on the night of May 31. It was believed that four midgets had taken part in this attack launched from I-class submarines outside the harbor. Three had been accounted for and the fourth may have been lost or may have got back to her mother ship. In any case, only two torpedoes had been fired, both of which missed our heavy cruiser *Chicago*. One torpedo ran up onto the beach without exploding, while the other struck an ex-ferryboat in use as a naval receiving barracks, killing several men and breaking numerous storage battery jars in the Dutch submarine K-9 which was moored close by.

One midget had apparently tried in vain to open the caps which covered the outboard ends of her torpedo tubes. Failing in this she had settled to bottom in a quiet cove and the captain and his mechanic shot themselves. Another had become entangled in an antisubmarine net and, evidently becoming discouraged, the skipper had blown the boat up with his demolition charge. A third was reported destroyed by depth charging.

The midgets themselves were beautifully built little vessels, practically just oversized torpedoes, designed to be carried securely strapped onto the decks of larger submarines. They carried two "fish" and had a bottom hatch through which they could be entered from the mother submarine. Thus they could be carried submerged, right up to the target area and then released. The crew of each consisted of one officer and one enlisted man, who undoubtedly never expected to see home again. Few, if any, ever did.

For the amount of damage these four accomplished at Sydney, their construction seemed wasted effort. We learned after the war that Japan expended thousands of tons of steel and countless man-hours in building hundreds of these craft, intended for special missions of this sort and for the last-ditch defense of the homeland against invasion. Naturally, the diversion of material and labor into this sideshow reduced the resources which could be put into building seagoing types and thus operated to our advantage.

Several times during the course of the war, recommendations were made to the Navy Department that we also engage in a midget building program. These proposals I always opposed for I felt they proceeded from misguided thinking and lack of information as to the real situation in the Pacific. The principal harbors in Japan and the Inland Sea are so shallow as to permit adequate protection by mines and nets and offer no possibility of evading depth charging counterattacks by deep running. Entry into such enemy refuges, therefore, amounted to suicide for submarine and crew, a desperate type of mission which I felt would never be required and which I, myself, never would have advocated. I felt that when our submarines had swept the seas clean of all enemy shipping, the Army and Navy Air Forces would be able to take care of remnants in Japanese-held ports.

I was glad indeed that none of these ill-considered brain children ever progressed beyond the drawing-board stage and that we continued to build all through the war, with practically no changes, the excellent all-purpose submarine which had been designed for just the type of warfare that we were waging in the Pacific. Specifications for this submarine were written with great care and after much study, in 1938, by the Submarine Officers' Conference in the Navy Department, aided by such outstanding naval constructors and engineering talents as Captain A. I. "Andy" McKee, Captain Armand "the Silent" Morgan, Captain E. H. "Swede" Bryant and Captain W. D. "Legs" Leggett, Jr.

CHAPTER 3

The Japanese, stung by their heavy shipping losses, evidently decided to strike back at Australia. They obviously did not know of our base at Exmouth Gulf for, on the night of July 29, Port Hedland, a pearl-fishing town and Australian Air Force base on the northwest coast, 150 miles away, was raided by nine Japanese bombers from Timor or Ambon.

Damage was minor but the raid drew our attention sharply to the danger which our Exmouth project faced. The recapture of Timor seemed the obvious answer but in view of the microscopic forces available on the west coast of Australia and the preoccupation of Allied forces on the east coast, the chances of such an event looked slim. Nevertheless, spirited discussions of the operation took place at General Gordon Bennett's weekly conferences.

Disturbing rumors kept coming in of increased enemy activity to the north and the northeastward. The Japanese were preparing to move: in fact, Tokyo Rose boasted that the Imperial Japanese Army would take Perth before the first of the year. The first Battle of Savo Island, in which we suffered disastrously, added to this uncertainty that might upset all our submarine plans. The complete losses and the fact the Japanese fleet got away scot-free were kept secret in Western Australia, although we did know that the S-44 had sunk the *Kako*, an enemy heavy cruiser, off Kaviang.

U.S.S. Nautilus

Our radio broke the wonderful news later that our Marine First Division had landed on Guadalcanal. Our offensive had started at last! The reaction of the Australians, as well as ourselves, was tremendous. We felt that nothing could stop us now and our admiration for the Marines knew no bounds. Coupled with this news came dispatches telling of our bombardment of Kiska in the Aleutians. A few days later, the announcement was made that Marines from *Argonaut* and *Nautilus* had raided Makin Island in the Gilberts.

All this activity made for unrest among my Staff and officers of the tenders. Several were of sufficient rank for command of cruisers or transports and they wanted to get out where things were popping. As a sedative, and also for the purpose of giving these lads some firsthand submarine combat experience, I promised two or three they would be allowed to make a war patrol. Commander Tex McLean was the first to go.

Even my Filipino mess boy came to me, practically in tears, to ask for combat duty. He said, "My family gone, my money gone, my country gone. Me, I want go out fight and forget my troubles."

Perth was full of refugees from Hong Kong, Malaya, Java—women and children practically destitute, whose homes and possessions were then being enjoyed by the enemy. What had become of their menfolk, few, if any, knew. The courage of these refugees under hearbreaking conditions and their determination to help in some sort of war work was inspiring.

Few of the officers or men of the Dutch naval forces in Fremantle had any idea what had become of their families. Their enforced inaction was most irksome to them and they welcomed any exercises, escort duties or projects which would occupy their time and thoughts.

Thresher, Lieutenant Commander W. J. Millican of Valley Stream, Long Island, came in on August 15. She was one of the new submarines sent down from Pearl Harbor and had patrolled en route the hottest spots in the Mandates. Millican claimed two ships as sunk but postwar reports credit him with only one, a motor torpedo-boat tender which he sank in the Marshall Islands. He also reported a unique experience while patrolling off the north entrance to Truk lagoon.

One black night *Thresher* and a Japanese patrol boat discovered each other close aboard and on collision courses. The submarine captain naturally maneuvered to avoid a collision, cleared his bridge and sounded the diving alarm, praying that he could get under before the enemy rammed him. The Jap, however, probably mistaking *Thresher* for another patrol boat, maneuvered deftly to avoid collision with the result that the two vessels came to a stop on parallel courses almost rubbing sides. The Jap was just far enough forward of her quarry so her forward gun—the only one manned—could not be brought to bear on the submarine. Millican said that as he slid down the conning tower hatch, the Jap skipper was screaming at his gun's crew—probably not in printable language—and they were desperately trying to get the cover off the after gun. It was a close call, but the depth charges, when the patrol boat captain finally thought of dropping them, merely knocked a few wrenches off the air manifolds.

When the excitement died down *Thresher* had time to enjoy a hearty laugh at the Jap's expense. Just how was he to explain to his division commander that, by skillful maneuvering, he had managed to avoid ramming an American submarine? Did they chop his head off or was he allowed to commit hari-kari?

One or two other small bags were reported about this time, and then came bad news from Brisbane. S-39, Lieutenant F. E. Brown of Reno, Nevada, had run on a reef off Rossel Island and was a total loss. Lieutenant C. N. G. Hendrix and Chief Commissary Steward W. L. Schoenrock courageously carried a line ashore and all hands were got through the surf without loss of life.

We proceeded with our Exmouth Gulf plans. An expedition led by Commander "Pinky" Thorp and accompanied by several other officers, including our very able and resourceful civil engineer officer, Lieutenant R. E. Hollister, USNR, made a trip by car to Exmouth Gulf to look into the proposition of establishing a camp site as near as feasible to the anchorage of our fuel barge. When we moved a tender to this anchorage for refitting submarines between patrols, it would be necessary to have a quonset-hut camp on shore to house our repair unit personnel and to recuperate our resting submarine crews. True, the recreation afforded by such a camp would have to consist chiefly of swimming, hunting, fishing and movies. The charm of feminine society would be completely absent. However, I planned to use the fairly speedy, ex-yacht, ex-Yangtze gunboat *Isabel* as a ferry to Fremantle to allow a few days' liberty in Perth for each crew.

Pinky's expedition returned with such tales of the hazards of Australian roads in the "bush"—"bush tracks" the Aussies called them—that it was apparent ferries would have to be the chief source of supply to any advanced base.

A letter arrived from "Bob" English asking me to give him Dick Voge, CO of *Sailfish*, for duty as his Operations Officer at Pearl Harbor. I agreed reluctantly, for experienced submarine skippers were at a premium. Little did I guess how important a change this would be, or what an extraordinary Operations Officer Dick would become. I wanted to talk the matter over with Voge, whose ship was in Albany, so I went down there via *Gar*. When I went aboard the *Sailfish*, I found Dick in a characteristic attitude—bowed over his tiny stateroom desk, working on an ingenious diagram for setting up different types of torpedo spreads. Dick's inventive brain was always engaged in some new and clever project, a habit that was to work wonders for the Submarine Force Pacific Fleet when he became its Operations Officer.

I drove back to Perth the next day but before leaving the *Pelias*, I called all officers into the wardroom for a conference. A former Submarine Force Commander, Rear Admiral W. L. "Big Eph" Friedell, whose Chief of Staff I had been in '39 and '40, had a great habit of what he called "haranguing the troops." Before a special operation—or just whenever the thought occurred to him, he would call all his officers together and talk to them. Sometimes he'd cuss them out, sometimes he'd give them a pat on the back, but during the process he would have a free discussion and collect a number of useful ideas.

It worked fine and I adopted it wholeheartedly. Nothing is so black that it can't be lightened by picking it apart and finding out just how bad it is. Big Eph was not too proud to take advice from anyone, no matter what his rank or rate, and when he gave a man a job, he let him do it without breathing down his neck all the while. These were virtues I wanted to emulate. Certainly I found throughout the war that "haranguing the troops" every now and then, especially when visiting a new station, paid good dividends in contacts established and ideas produced.

We discussed several special situations on this particular occasion, including marriage and publicity. One of my additional duties was to operate a marriage bureau. Commander Southwest Pacific had issued orders based on a directive from high in the Government—so it was rumored—that naval personnel could not marry foreign girls without first obtaining permission from the Force Commander. The order required that the prospective bridegroom declare his intentions in an official letter and that a period of six months must elapse before the wedding could take place. The Force Commander was charged with the delicate duty of ascertaining that the lady in the case was thoroughly reputable. Just how legal the order was, I do not know. Fortunately we never had a test case. I tried in vain to have the "cooling off" period abolished or at least reduced to three months. The standing of the prospective bride was usually easily obtainable by a letter to the pastor of her church. The girls of Western Australia were exceptionally fine-looking, usually of the athletic type, so it was not surprising that our lads were attracted to them.

Publicity was another one of our headaches. In an effort probably intended to bolster public morale at home, great pressure was being put on the Navy Department to publish play-by-play accounts of the war. We of the submarines wanted no part of this. We would have preferred to publish nothing at all, not even the score of enemy ships sunk by each returning submarine. To keep the enemy guessing about what became of his ships which never reached port would, I felt, not only wear down his nerves but would deny him information on which to base changes in his routings or improve his antisubmarine measures. We wanted him to think that his existing methods were highly effective and that every time he dropped a depth charge, another American submarine went to Davy Jones's locker. I even recommended making a press release to the effect that the Navy Department was deeply concerned about its submarine losses. Admiral Doenitz, the German Submarine chief, had made a speech a short time before in which he intimated that his losses were heavy. This was undoubtedly intended to make the Allies believe that their antisubmarine warfare was successful, which definitely was not the case.

A rumor reached us that a public official had boasted in a press release that American submarines did not fear Japanese destroyers because their depth charges were neither heavy enough to damage them nor set deep enough to reach them. The value of this information to the enemy can be readily appreciated. Whether or not this rumor was founded on fact, it is true that in the autumn of 1942 the Japanese radically increased the setting of their depth charges. We lost only three submarines in 1942, presumably due to depth charging, but the first months of 1943 saw six boats reported "overdue, presumed lost."

Submariners, I feel sure, were fully convinced that they must become "the Silent Service," but we were never successful in stopping all leaks.

Gudgeon, which, early in the war under Commander Joe Grenfell, sank the I-173, the first man-of-war victim of an American submarine, came in on September 2, after a patrol which started at Pearl Harbor and touched the principal centers of enemy activity in the Mandates. Her present skipper, Commander W. S. Stovall of Picayune, Mississippi, claimed four rising suns "sunk or probably sunk." However, three must have managed to make port, for postwar reports credit her with only the 4,858-ton *Naniwa Maru,* sunk southwest of Truk. *Gudgeon's* executive officer was Lieutenant Commander R. E. "Dusty" Dornin of football, baseball and basketball fame at the Naval Academy, whose illustrious career as a destroyer of Jap shipping was just beginning.

Before each submarine went on patrol she was carefully tested to see whether any item of her machinery was making too much noise. The listening gear of the Jap destroyers was excellent and the ability of our submarines to "run silent" was most important. I went out on *Spearfish* one early morning to observe her final tests. We selected a beautiful little cove in Cockburn Sound outside the entrance to Fremantle and there spent the morning with a portable decibel meter, checking the sound level of each separate piece of machinery. If any item was too noisy the cause was ferreted out and corrections made until the ship was satisfactorily silent. Most submarines had no trouble in passing the test but as their main reduction gears grew older, sometimes the allowable noise limit would be exceeded. In that case there was nothing to be done except assign the submarine to a patrol area where the enemy antisubmarine craft were not "on the first team." As soon as hard-pressed Mare Island or Hunters Point could take on the job, we would send the boat back for gear regrinding.

Three or four submarines returned to Fremantle from patrol about this time with small bags, notwithstanding the fact that they covered their areas thoroughly. *Tautog* got the biggest prize, the 5,872-ton passenger-cargo ship *Obio Maru,* which she sank off the bulge of Indo-China. Lack of targets in the China Sea–Philippines area probably was due to the intense enemy activity along the northeast New Guinea coast, in New Britain, New Ireland and Bougainville. The Japanese were evidently using most of their tonnage for troops and supplies to strengthen their South Pacific outposts against our advancing Marines and Army in the Solomons.

The Brisbane-based submarines got several sizable enemy ships, including the 12,752-ton transport *Brazil Maru*, sunk by *Greenling*, and the 5,628-ton transport *Meiyo Maru*, sunk by S-38, which brought the August merchant-ship score for Submarines Southwest Pacific up to a neat 38,057 tons. The number of transports included in these sinkings was especially pleasing. Torpedoing of the heavy cruiser *Kako* by S-44, brought our grand total up to 46,857 tons.

Meanwhile our plans were going forward for establishing a quonset-hut camp at Potshot. On September 11 Commander Joe Thew and I took Brigadier B. E. Klein, AIF, and Colonel J. S. Young, AMF, both of General Gordon Bennett's Staff, to Exmouth Gulf via Navy seaplane to make initial plans for the Australian part of the project. We took up quarters on the seaplane tender *Wm. B. Preston*, Lieutenant Commander Grant, and set out in one of her dories to explore the site tentatively chosen by Commander Thorp. One of our submarines, the *Spearfish*, was topping off with fuel at our recently acquired oil barge, so I took advantage of the opportunity to go alongside and inspect this new facility.

On arrival ashore we found that our exploring party had picked an excellent site with a shelving beach, where a makeshift pier for small craft could be built. Backing up the shore line were 40-foot dunes behind which the quonsets would be somewhat protected from the wind. About a mile away was plenty of flat land, where a fighter strip could be constructed without much labor. We planned to keep a few fighters there ready to counter any bombing raid such as Port Hedland had suffered in July. The fighter squadron base, according to tentative plans made with the RAAF, was to be about 20 miles east at Yanrey and would be manned by Aussies, flying Spitfires.

It was the unanimous opinion of our group that the establishment of a submarine advance base at Potshot was entirely feasible and would result in a sufficiently important gain in cruising radius to justify the expenditure of the funds and material which would be involved. We also considered the psychological effect of even this small advance toward the enemy as important.

On my return to Perth, conference with the officer in command of our Naval Supply Depot at Fremantle, Commander J. J. Levasseur, revealed an excellent supply of advanced base equipment with materials sufficient to build several such camps. A self-propelled pontoon barge, suitable for moving heavy equipment and AA guns from ship to shore, was ready to be assembled, while caterpillar cranes (cherry pickers) and bulldozers were also on hand. Not the least valuable of Levasseur's gear were the perforated pressed metal sheets and wire mesh intended for landing strips, which we could also use for roads in deep sand areas.

After receiving assurance from General Gordon Bennett that the AMF stood ready to support us by drilling wells and furnishing an AA battery of eight 3.7-inch guns, I sent a dispatch to the Commander Southwest Pacific Force (new name for Southwest Pacific Area) requesting permission to initiate the move.

However, various delays occurred while higher commands decided whether or not the major portion of my submarine force would be maintained at Fremantle or Brisbane. My hope was to have, eventually, 48 submarines in Submarine Force Southwest Pacific, based at Fremantle, Brisbane, Potshot and Darwin. With half based on Brisbane, we could patrol all the Mandated Islands south of the latitude of Guam, thus relieving Pearl Harbor submarines. With the remainder patrolling the South China Sea, I felt we could absolutely deny the Philippines, Malaya and Indonesia to Japanese seaborne traffic.

Unfortunately, there were not yet enough submarines in commission to give me such a force. A distribution of those available, and of submarine tenders, was in a state of flux, hence it was not until November 2 that the mine sweeper *Heron* left Fremantle with a working party and the initial supply of gear necessary to establish Potshot.

At this point I made a hurried trip via amphibian to Brisbane to confer with Commander Southwest Pacific Force, Vice Admiral Carpender, and Commander Task Force 42, Captain Christie, regarding Potshot and the supply of torpedoes. Although, due to scarcity of targets, we had fired only 76 torpedoes in the month of August and 77 in September, our supply was dwindling toward zero and the best promise that I had been able to obtain from the Bureau of Ordnance was for delivery of 48 per month. That promise had not been kept and during August and September we had received only 36 in all.

My Staff already had selected six advantageous locations for laying mine-fields and, of necessity, we were planning to employ *Thresher, Tambor, Gar, Tautog* and *Grenadier*. It was desirable to lay all fields at the same time, so that the enemy would not have a chance to learn progressively our mine tactics and the characteristics of the mine. This latter part of the plan we were not able to carry out. The type selected was the MK XII magnetic, the same type with which the Germans had such great initial success in European waters.

No relief for the torpedo situation was in sight at headquarters in Brisbane, consequently the mining plan was put into operation and during October and the first part of November, five fields were laid between the northernmost part of the Gulf of Siam and the Hainan Strait. Each submarine carried eight torpedoes in addition to her mines. We had no information as to whether the Chinese had done any mining of their own waters. That was a risk we had to accept.

Arriving at Perth, I found that one of our patrol planes had bombed and, fortunately, missed the Dutch K-12, regarding whose reception at Fremantle we had just made arrangements. Failure to give the correct recognition signal was stated as the reason. Two days later the *Snapper* was similarly bombed without damage. This led to an order that later in the war was to apply over most of the Pacific Ocean Area. I forbade planes to bomb any submarine in West Australian waters not positively identified as enemy. We had far too few submarines to be able to take chances on the bad aim of some trigger-happy aviator.

Late in October dispatch orders came detaching Captain Jimmie Fife and ordering him to special duty with Vice Admiral Carpender. This was a blow, but when we learned that he was to be liaison officer for the Navy on General MacArthur's Staff, I felt better about it, for I was anxious to get a friend at court, who could perhaps convince the Army Air Force that they shouldn't bomb our submarines. Fortunately thus far only one submarine had been damaged—*Sargo* had both periscopes wrecked by an RAAF bomb—but there was no telling when carelessness about observing the sanctity of safety lanes for submarines might result fatally. I would have preferred that the fly-fly boys pass up a hundred chances to attack what, perhaps, might be enemy submarines, rather than dash in precipitately and sink one of our own.

On top of these discouraging happenings came news that the RAN destroyer *Voyager* had dragged onto a reef off the coast of Japanese-held Timor and was a total loss. She had been sent to evacuate some 600 refugees, Australian and Dutch, who still were holding out against the Japs in an inaccessible spot in the south of Timor. She anchored as close in as possible and heavy currents swept her onto the reef. Jap bombers then came in and finished the job. Thus about 100 men who got ashore from *Voyager* were added to the refugees.

There was nothing that could be done about this matter instantly, for the Dutch destroyers *Van Galen* and *Tjerk Hiddes,* the only remaining destroyers in my task force, were out with a convoy. Submarines would require many trips to evacuate so large a number. Eventually I was directed to send the *Tjerk Hiddes* to Darwin to undertake ferry trips for the refugees. By timing her runs so as to arrive off the coast of Timor at night, and using high speed, the *Hiddes* did a beautiful job and, in two trips, brought off all hands. In the below deck spaces people were packed like sardines and on deck there was standing room only. She returned to Fremantle with no casualties except a damaged rudder. I had the pleasure of recommending her commanding officer for a Legion of Merit.

I spent a good part of September 30 making trips to the marine railway at Fremantle to see *Salmon* hauled out—our first submarine to use this new facility. The job of getting her up took all day and my diary contains the following entry: "Aussie labor awful, awful slow. Will call on the Premier (of Western Australia) soon, I think, and ask to lease the whole shebang if work doesn't go faster." In this resolve my hand was forced for, on the following night, the manager discharged a bottom cleaner for flagrant loafing and the whole crew of laborers walked out. Lieutenant Commander Bill Jones was present at the time and took the play from there. He went immediately to the *Holland,* asked for and received a working party of 50 men, and completed the job of cleaning and painting bottom in record time. My call on the Premier of the state of Western Australia next morning, therefore, took on a different aspect. I expected that Jones's action, which I fully approved, would result in a strike of the entire dockyard and I came prepared.

I informed the Premier of the situation and explained that the exigencies of war did not permit us to take time out for labor troubles. The Premier was very courteous and apparently in agreement. We continued to employ our own working parties on the slipway as long as I remained in Perth and no further trouble developed. As can be imagined, that marine railway was worked to death in the first few months of its availability. Most of the submarines had been out of dock for so long that their bottoms looked like marine gardens and only those newly arrived from Pearl Harbor could make more than 16 knots.

Our estimates regarding enemy ships attacked by Submarines Southwest Pacific in September were that eight had been downed while five had been damaged. Postwar reports cut the sinkings in half, hence the score should read four sunk, for a total of 17,041 tons, and nine damaged. The biggest of these targets was the 8,606-ton aircraft ferry *Kanto Maru* sunk in Makassar Strait by *Saury*, Lieutenant Commander L. S. "Tex" Mewhinney of Buckholt, Texas.

Rear Admiral F. W. Coster of the Royal Netherlands Navy, the senior Dutch naval officer in Australia, flew over from his headquarters in Melbourne to inspect the RNN

ships and personnel under my command in Western Australia. Admiral Coster was an enthusiastic submariner, having served in Dutch submarines in his youth. He was among those responsible for installing air conditioning in their undersea boats. The first such installation that we U.S. submariners saw was in the Dutch K-13, which passed through Panama about 1929. We were enthusiastic about the idea but it was not until 1934 that an installation was made in U.S. submarines. This new equipment was strongly objected to by many as being "hotel accommodations" but it certainly pulled its weight in the boat in terms of health and endurance of submarine crews operating in torrid waters.

The Dutch have always had smart submarines. It was they who invented the device which we call a "poppet valve" for eliminating the telltale air bubble which normally boils to surface when a submarine torpedo tube is fired.

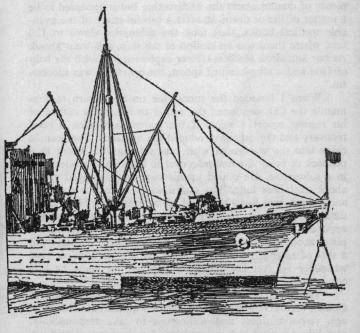

U.S.S. Holland

At just about this point *Seadragon* returned from patrol with a bag of one down and two damaged. Her skipper also made an amazing report of an appendectomy performed on board. She was the first of three submarines to perform this feat before the "medicos" issued instructions to all pharmacist's mates forbidding resort to surgery in appendicitis cases occurring on patrol.

While off the coast of Indo-China, 3,000 miles from base, D. D. Rector, S1/c, USNR, came down with an acute appendix. Of course the submarine carried no doctor, but the pharmacist's mate first class, W. B. Lipes, in charge of the medical department aboard, correctly diagnosed the case. This was before we had learned how to keep such attacks under control with sulpha drugs. The usual ice packs seemed to bring no relief and the patient was in such pain that he begged the "Doc" to operate. No doubt all concerned, including the captain, Lieutenant Commander W. E. Ferrall, had plenty of qualms about the undertaking but it appeared to be a matter of life or death, so after a careful study of the available medical books, they took the submarine down to 120 feet, where there was no motion of the ship, and went ahead. As our Squadron Medical Officer expressed it, "With the help of God and a long-handled spoon, the operation was successful."

When I boarded the submarine on her return to Fremantle the CO mentioned the matter to me in the course of his regular report. I asked if the patient had made a good recovery and the captain produced the evidence. The seaman came into the wardroom with eyes shining and proud as a peacock of being the first man ever to have an appendectomy in a submarine. He pulled up his shirt and displayed a scar about six inches long. The pharmacist's mate was called in and he, too, was justly proud of his achievement. He said the difficulty was not in opening the abdomen but in finding the appendix. I asked how long the operation took and he replied, about two-and-a-half hours! "Good Lord," I said, "will a shot of ether last that long?" "Oh, no, sir," he replied, "but whenever I'd feel his muscles stiffen up, I'd know he was coming out of it and I'd give him another shot!"

The CO recommended his corpsman for promotion to Chief Pharmacist's Mate and I heartily concurred. His courage, resourcefulness and willingness to take responsibility, certainly deserved high recognition. I was surprised and disappointed, however, to find that the Squadron Medical Officer "took a poor view" of the matter. According to him, the patient had a much better chance of survival if kept packed in ice and put on a starvation liquid diet than in undergoing an ordeal such as this operation. Perhaps that was true, but we got the "Doc" promoted, anyhow.

The worst blow of the month of October came when I received orders to send *Holland* and eight submarines to base at Brisbane. That left me with one tender, the *Pelias*, and 12 submarines. Of course, this removed any further need for Albany, so I drove down there and organized a sortie of all our ships. The announced purpose of this maneuver was to hold target practice for the tender and minesweepers and return to Albany that night. The RAN cruiser *Adelaide* came down from Fremantle, ostensibly to join in the practice. We steamed out on the morning of October 23 and that was the last any of us ever saw of Albany—a fine town, with a lot of helpful, warmhearted people, and a splendid harbor. One of the treasured possessions of the Albany Club was a picture of the U.S. Fleet which girdled the globe in 1908–09, steaming into their anchorage.

The reduction of our force was a severe handicap to our operations, but we tightened our belts and dug our toes in. Commander Tex McLean returned to my Operations office after a two months patrol in *Sargo* off the Indo-China coast. He looked a little pale from lack of sunlight and a little drawn, as did most submarine officers at the end of a patrol. However, as a passenger he had had many hours to mull over our problems and came home full of ideas as to possible improvements in operating methods.

There could be no doubt that the technique of our submarine captains was improving rapidly. At the beginning of the war we believed that enemy antisubmarine ships and planes would force all submarines to remain submerged by day, surfacing only at night. This obviously limited coverage, even though lookouts and sound operators became very expert. Now, in actual war, our submarine skippers were discovering that enemy antisubmarine measures did not cover the entire ocean and that daylight surface running was quite feasible.

Also at the beginning of the war we lacked actual experience in night attacks. Target practices, of course, were held, simulating night attacks under war conditions. However, so many safeguards had to be thrown in to minimize risk of collision and loss of torpedoes that much of the necessary realism was missing. Now night attacks were becoming more and more frequent, and once a target was located, it actually was found easier to attack in the dark than in daylight. For one thing, the enemy usually did not zigzag at night. On bright nights, however, the attacking submarine was forced to submerge to avoid detection. We suddenly realized that our periscopes gave pretty fine vision even at night. Periscope lenses were now being "light treated" by a newly discovered process which greatly improved light transmission and thus increased the effectiveness of the periscope for nightwork.

Our skippers discovered also that taking a "single ping" range with the echo-ranging gear, in the last stages of an attack, was feasible and unlikely to be overheard by the enemy. One of the most important things that remained to be done, was improvement of our instruments used for taking target bearing from the bridge at night. Another thing that remained to be improved was our camouflage. Gray paint was found to be much less visible at night than the black with which we began the war.

With improved technique, naturally, sinkings and damagings of enemy ships increased. Moreover, the number of targets was increasing. Evidently the Japs were beginning to get production from the oil wells, refineries, sugar mills, etc., of Malaya, Indonesia and the Philippines. After these resources of supply had been wrecked by the defending forces, it required several months before the conquerors could repair damage, reassemble workers and get plants running again. This initial nonproductive period undoubtedly was another contributing factor to the lack of targets in that area during the spring and summer months of 1942.

By our best estimates, during October, 14 enemy ships were sunk and five damaged by submarines of the Southwest Pacific, but postwar reports cut this down to nine sunk for a total of 39,789 tons. The most important target of the month was the aircraft ferry *Katsuragi Maru*, 8,033 tons, sunk in the Bismarks by the veteran *Sturgeon* under her new CO, Lieutenant Commander H. A. "Pie" Pieczentkowski of Middletown, Rhode Island. Stovall, in *Gudgeon*, scored again with the 6,783-ton cargo-passenger ship *Choko Maru* and smiling Jim Coe, in *Skipjack*, contributed the 6,781-ton freighter *Shunko Maru*. Two ships observed to sink are listed as "Unknown Marus" in the Joint Army-Navy Assessment Committee report, compiled after the war, which reveals the sad state of Japanese records.

CHAPTER 4

I took off in a Catalina for Exmouth Gulf on November 6, with Australian staff officers from Melbourne Headquarters, who desired to learn at first hand all the plans for Potshot before giving final approval of the Australian commitments involved. General Whitelaw and Commander Buchanan represented the AMF and RAN, respectively. Brigadier Klein represented General Gordon Bennett.

About one hour after we took off, the pilot sent back word to me that the port engine was leaking oil badly, so it would be necessary to sit down at Geraldtown (200 miles north of Perth) for repairs. Minutes later the port engine stopped and the plane lurched sharply downward before the pilot could regain control. The messenger again came aft and reported, "The pilot says the port engine has stopped. He is heading back for Perth and will keep her in the air as long as possible." Looking down at the desolate coast line below us, my fervent hope was that nothing would prevent him from "keeping her in the air." We reached the Swan River at Perth with about 50 feet of altitude left, landed, shifted to another plane and reached Exmouth Gulf without further incident.

The Australian staff was convinced that the move to Potshot, and the arrangements therefor, were entirely practical. A few days later I got the green light from Commander Southwest Pacific to start building the camp. Shifting a tender there was to be held in abeyance until sufficient facilities had been set up in our leased grain sheds in Fremantle to handle the maintenance of submarines at that port.

On November 9 (East Longitude date), the world again was electrified by a surprise move which had been kept so secret that we in the Antipodes didn't even know it was in immediate prospect. Our troops had landed in North Africa and all landings appeared to have been successful. Submarines acted as beacon ships for several of these amphibious at-

tacks. Rapidly following this news came dispatches telling of
our decisive naval victories on November 12–14 off Guadalcanal. We had sustained heavy losses in ships and men but
the backbone of the Japanese offensive in the Solomons was
broken.

Now the preliminary construction for the Potshot move
could progress speedily and safely. The officer in charge of
the advance party—and later assigned as Commanding Officer of the base—was Lieutenant W. J. R. "Bill" Hayes who
worked day and night with his men landing materials and
getting the huts set up. Lieutenant Robert E. Hollister, CEC,
USNR, in charge of construction details, had developed a
rectangular, portable, galvanized-iron hut which he called the
Perth hut. We used these for mess halls, storehouses, etc., and
saved the insulated quonsets for living quarters, sick bay, and
other spaces that needed protection from the blazing heat of
the tropical sun.

Tautog returned from patrol with a bag of one 4,000-ton
passenger-cargo ship definitely sunk, and two others hit but
not known to have gone down. In addition she brought in
four Filipino youths who hailed from Zamboanga. *Tautog*
had encountered the 75-ton fishing schooner, *Sea Food II*, in
the Sulu Sea. The fisherman hove to in response to a shot
across her bow and hoisted Japanese colors. When brought
alongside she was found to be manned by 12 Japs and four

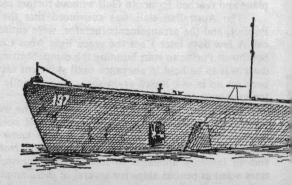

Filipinos. The latter were taken aboard the submarine. The Japs abandoned ship in one of the schooner's boats and were given food, water and directions to the nearest land. The schooner was then sunk by gunfire. The Filipinos said they had been impressed by the Japanese, given no pay and kept as prisoners aboard the fishing schooner. They brought the important news that many American and Filipino guerrillas were still fighting in Mindanao.

Thresher returned from a patrol which included laying 32 magnetic mines in the northernmost part of the Gulf of Siam. She reported that two mines exploded as soon as they became armed. The safety period between planting and arming is sufficient to permit the mining vessel to get clear of the field. *Thresher* had only eight torpedoes on this patrol. She made several attacks and expended all of them.

While on her way home, passing along the west coast of Celebes Island, *Thresher* sighted a ship close in to the beach, apparently aground. Captain Millican dived and approached cautiously, trying to figure out some way of destroying this target without putting his submarine in too much danger from enemy air, for he knew the Japs had airfields at Makassar City about 25 miles distant. He decided to wait for nightfall and then sink her with his 3-inch gun. The Jap, however, was making energetic efforts to get his ship off the reef. He could be seen pumping his ballast water overboard and the

U.S.S. Seawolf

crew struggled manfully to lay out an anchor astern. Finally
with about two hours of daylight still remaining, he hove his
ship off the reef and started picking up his anchor. This was
too much for Millican. He just couldn't let that ship get
away. So, air cover or no air cover, he "battle surfaced" and
sunk her with gunfire. Postwar reports do not credit *Thresher*
with any sinkings by torpedoes on that patrol but this last
ship is credited as "Unknown Maru—probably sunk."

Millican had demonstrated that he knew how to handle
a minor-caliber gun so I gave him a better one, a five inch
that had just been shipped out to us, one which had graced
the deck of the old V-3 when I commanded her in '26-'28. I
went out with him to watch gun and torpedo practice after
the gun was installed. It was reassuring to note the realism
which had been introduced into our training exercises. If the
submarine skipper used his periscope too much and it was
spotted by the target ship, she immediately charged down at
the sub's periscope. This forced the submarine into a hasty
shot at a much reduced target and rapid deep submergence to
avoid the "ash cans" which could be expected from an enemy. At the end of the exercise the target vessel dropped a
string of live depth charges 300 yards from our periscope to
accustom new crew members to the spine-chilling sound of
their explosion.

During October and November 1942 the Brisbane submarines, Task Force 42, were reinforced by submarines from
Squadron 8, Captain W. M. Downes, and Squadron 10, Captain C. W. Styer, from Pearl Harbor. The new tenders, *Fulton* and *Sperry*, which were the flagships of those squadrons,
arrived at Brisbane during November. With increased numbers of modern submarines, cooperation with Admiral
Halsey's South Pacific Force in the battle of Guadalcanal improved greatly.

The primary mission for which Task Force 42 had been
established on the east coast of Australia was to help disrupt
enemy surface operations and supply lines into the Solomons.
For a time the whole of Task Force 42 was placed under the
operational control of Commander South Pacific Force to effect closer cooperation with the fleet. Admiral Halsey, however, did not want to take on the job of maintaining them
and assigning them to stations. He therefore directed that
Commander Task Force 42 at "Adobe" (code name for Brisbane) perform those duties. He outlined his desires for their

employment in a dispatch typical of his bold, direct character. After specifying the areas he particularly wanted patrolled, Admiral Halsey concluded: "Maintain maximum coverage in areas. Priority of targets: men-of-war, tankers, loaded transports, supply vessels. Your task is to destroy enemy vessels."

In addition to purely combatant duties, these submarines performed numerous services in landing coast watchers and scouts. At a time when the aviation gas supply had dropped to a dangerous low on Guadalcanal, *Amberjack,* Lieutenant Commander J. A. Bole, Jr., of Wallhill, New York, delivered 9,000 gallons, plus two hundred 100-pound bombs and 15 Army fighter pilots, to Tulagi.

The sinkings in November, according to postwar reports, were not as high as in the preceding month, although our best estimates at the time showed them to be higher. Enemy antisubmarine operations in the New Guinea, New Britain and Solomons areas were getting really tough and CO's seldom had a chance to see whether or not their targets actually sank.

The best bag was brought in by a west coast boat, the *Seawolf,* who did her customary excellent job by sinking three ships for a total of 13,000 tons, in and about the Gulf of Davao in Mindanao. Her skipper, Freddy Warder, came in with his usual quiet, confident air—and ready to take a poke at the nose of anyone calling him by the nickname, "Fearless Freddy," which he had so thoroughly earned.

Warder's most exciting adventure occurred during the morning of November 3 in Taloma Bay, 50 miles up the Gulf of Davao. The day before *Seawolf* sank a 3,000-ton cargo boat at the entrance of the gulf. He watched it sink, hoping a destroyer might come out to pick up survivors but none showed up. Freddy then stood in toward the city of Davao to have a look-see.

Next morning he found two small freighters in Davao Harbor but the prize objective was a big passenger-cargo ship at anchor at Taloma Bay. There were no evidences of minefields, in fact, the water is so deep right up to the anchorage that he felt confident no mines had been laid. He approached deliberately, checking his ranges with single pings. This was really a sitting duck. At 1050 the range was down to 1,100 yards and Warder fired a single torpedo, set for 18 feet. It ran under the ship and exploded on the beach. Freddy set his next one for eight feet, which hit exactly where he had aimed. The ship listed badly, then righted herself and did not appear to be settling much. *Seawolf* then fired two more deliberate shots, both of which apparently passed under the ship but did not explode. The magnetic exploder evidently was not feeling well that day. By this time two guns were shooting at *Seawolf*'s periscope but got no hits.

Warder hauled out, reloaded and stood in again. Both guns were still shooting but hit nowhere near the periscope. The next torpedo shot hit aft and cleared the deck of the spectators who had been lining the rail. Small boats began ferrying people ashore. *Seawolf* then swung around and fired one last torpedo from a stern tube. This finished the battle for with its explosion, fires broke out and the 7,189-ton *Sagami Maru* sank by the bow. A few minutes later, as *Seawolf* was standing out, three planes arrived, zoomed her periscope and dropped "ash cans." Warder headed for the open sea where on November 8 he sank a converted gunboat.

A dispatch was received from Commander Southwest Pacific Force to the effect that the Dutch were anxious to land a small party of agents—all soldiers—in Java. I replied that *Searaven* was preparing to sail and please to rush the party. For some reason they were sent by rail, with quite a lot of equipment. The resulting difficulties gave an excellent example of the confusion which could be produced by the many changes of trains required during the long transcontinental trip. Their arrival seemed interminably delayed and I was getting more and more irate when they finally showed up, but without any of their baggage and equipment. Even the Commanding Officer's pistol had been lost on the trip across! Another day's delay was required to retrieve their gear and at long last we got them aboard the *Searaven* which sailed under secret orders.

This, however, was not to be the last untoward incident in launching the expedition. *Searaven* sailed in the afternoon and about midnight that same night one of my Staff reported he had heard a conversation between two civilians at the Esplanade Hotel which revealed they knew full details of the expedition. The leak had evidently come from a boastful member of the Dutch party. Under the circumstances, there was nothing to do but cancel that part of the orders to the *Searaven*. She dropped her passengers at our advanced base at Exmouth Gulf, whence they were flown back to Perth for indoctrination in security and to await a more favorable opportunity.

I flew up to Potshot to spend Christmas and had a holiday that boosted my morale in spite of the boiling heat of that desert land. The flies were terrific. Those of you who haven't met Australian flies just don't know what flies are. They swarm out of the desert in uncounted millions. People walking along the streets are constantly giving what we called "the Aussie salute"—brushing at flies. Some seem to get used to them, for I've seen an Australian sentry standing at his post calm as a Yogi, with flies literally covering his face, hands and bare legs.

The construction crew at Potshot, four officers and 65 men, were in fine fettle. Most of them were hardly more than kids and this was adventure to them. They were allowed to grow beards and to wear a minimum of clothing. Except for a few practice alerts and instruction in machine guns, rifles and pistols, there were no drills and, when off watch, they slept, swam, hunted or made collections of sea shells. They certainly proved to me that the love of outdoor life and adventure is not dead in the American youth, particularly when they land in out-of-the-way spots like the Australian bush. Life was not easy. I had a group of men training at a radar camp at Kalamunda and dropped in to see how they were getting on. Housed in tents, they were in the best of health and spirits. Before I left I asked them if there were anything special they wanted in the line of a Christmas treat. The petty officer in charge hesitated, and then said: "Well, sir, we would certainly appreciate a side of beef. We get this damned goat (meaning mutton, a staple Australian dish) three times a day."

Exactly opposite was the request made at Potshot, where our supply officer, Lieutenant Commander "Chuck" Osborne, furnished rations to the Australian gunners manning the antiaircraft guns. They couldn't take our constant diet of beef and implored us to buy sheep from a nearby station.

On Christmas Day Commander Joe Thew and I took a 10-wheeled truck and some wire mesh and started out to see the lighthouse at North West Cape. Our planning section wanted to put a type-271 radar there and another near Onslow, 60 or 70 miles up the coast to northeastward. I wanted to see if the 30-mile stretch of bush track which led to the light was passable for cars and to select a suitable location

for the equipment. The road was terrible, but at the expense
of two blowouts and with the aid of the wire mesh to get us
over the worst sand stretches, we made it. I considered that
setting up a radar was entirely feasible and planned to search
for a supplementary site near Onslow. My observations were
confirmed by a radar and communication expert, Flight Lieutenant Grout-Smith of the RAAF, who flew to Exmouth
Gulf.

The December score for Submarines Souwestpac was an
improvement over previous months. It included eight merchantmen, the big submarine I-4, sunk by *Seadragon*, Lieutenant Commander Ferrall; the light cruiser *Tenryu*, sunk by
Albacore, Lieutenant Commander R. C. Lake of Goshen, Indiana, and Patrol Boat No. 35—an old destroyer which succumbed to the torpedoes of the *Greenling*, Lieutenant
Commander H. C. Bruton of Little Rock, Arkansas. Two of
the eight merchant ships mentioned above were likewise
contributed by Bruton.

Thresher scored again, this time with the 5-inch gun
which we had just given her. Encountering the *Hachian Maru*
in the Java Sea north of Soerabaya, on the night of December 29, Millican stood cautiously in and fired two torpedoes
which missed—but without alarming the intended victim.
Again *Thresher* approached and again no cheering explosions. Infuriated by this performance, the Captain called
for his 5-inch gun crew. Unfortunately, my old gun had arrived minus its telescopic sights, so we had installed an open
ring sight, but the pointer found that, in the dark, he couldn't
see the target through the sights. Millican came to the rescue
with his binoculars. He lashed them tightly to the sight yoke
and, by adjusting the range and deflection dials while peering
at the target through the bore of the gun, he finally decided
the bore-sighting was sufficiently correct.

During this preparation the target had taken no alarm.
At the first shot, however, she opened fire with a gun in the
bow and turned to ram. Millican's gun was mounted abaft
the conning tower and, as he swung away to avoid being
rammed, his gun's crew was able to pour a steady stream of
shells into the enemy's forward section. The merchantman's
gun was silenced in the first few shots and evidently he received damage in the engine room, for the ship swung off and
stopped. Millican concentrated then on the mid-section and,
as he expressed it, "Before she sank there was a hole below

her stack big enough to drive a truck through!" He reported
that our new 5-inch ammunition exploded nicely on contact
and that there were no duds.

The new year opened full of encouragement for our
boats. Dispatches indicated that January was to be another
fighting month. *Grayback,* Lieutenant Commander E. C. Ste-
phan of Washington, D.C., started the ball rolling on the 2nd
by sinking the 2,180-ton Japanese submarine I-18 in the Solomons.

Suddenly on January 11, tragedy stalked into our reports. An Army plane, with all bombs expended, witnessed a
battle between an enemy convoy and a submarine which must
have been the *Argonaut,* largest in the Navy. The plane reported it had seen one destroyer hit by a torpedo and two
other destroyers blown up. After a severe depth charging, the
submarine partially surfaced and the destroyers fired into her
bow, which was sticking up at a sharp angle. Commander J.
R. Pierce and his crew of 106 officers and men were never
heard from after this report.

Postwar investigation makes it quite certain that *Argo-*
naut, on January 10, attacked a convoy bound from Lae to
Rabaul and was sunk by the escorts. *Argonaut* (originally the
V-4) was designed as a mine layer and had a huge mine
room aft which she had used to quarter troops when she assisted *Nautilus* during August, 1942, in transporting 211 officers and men of the Second Marine Raider Battalion to
Makin Island.

Reports of enemy sinkings continued to pour in as the
month advanced and our spirits rose correspondingly. *Guard-*
fish, Lieutenant Command T. B. "Burt" Klakring of Annapolis, Maryland, on a patrol which was to win her a
Presidential Citation, sank, among other ships, Patrol Boat
No. 1 and the destroyer *Hakaze.*

The location of our radar set in the vicinity of Onslow
came up for decision, so I borrowed an amphibian from Patrol Wing 10, picked up Flight Lieutenant Grout-Smith and
headed for Exmouth Gulf. We stayed overnight at Potshot,
then flew on to Onslow. We landed at the airport, met Group
Captain Sampson, RAAF, who was in command, and borrowed a "blitz wagon."

Grout-Smith and I hiked over a lot of terrain in locating
an advantageous spot for our radar and, foolishly being in
shorts, had our legs so punctured by the sharp, pointed

spinifex grass that we looked like a pair of chicken-pox patients. However, we found an excellent situation where the screen could have nearly a 360-degree sweep without interference from hills or buildings.

I arrived back at Perth, on January 30, to find that we really had harvested a bumper crop. All reports, of course, had not come in, but postwar assessment credits Submarines Southwest Pacific with three men-of-war, two transports, two passenger-cargo and nine cargo ships.

Lieutenant Commander Barney Sieglaff, of Albert Lea, Minnesota, brought the *Tautog* in from a patrol in the South China Sea. He had sunk two freighters in the Flores Sea and had hit two other targets—one of them a light cruiser. *Tautog* was badly shaken up by depth charges but had received no serious damage.

The *Guardfish*, in addition to sinking three ships, had added to her reputation for daring by penetrating Rabaul Harbor, a stunt which many a submarine skipper had planned but which none had accomplished. As Klakring came into Blanche Bay during the forenoon of January 28, he could see several ships anchored in the lower reaches of Simpson Harbor. They made an overlapping target and Burt decided to fire all six bow tubes with torpedoes set for low speed, as soon as the range shortened to 8,000 yards. Unfortunately, with only one minute left to go, his periscope was zoomed by a plane and shore batteries opened fire. The forward torpedo room reported that the hull had been struck above the wardroom. Possibly the plane had dropped a depth charge which was a dud. Possibly the object was a spent projectile. In any case, with two patrol vessels standing in his way, discretion appeared the better part of valor and *Guardfish* hauled out as rapidly as conditions permitted.

The *Wahoo*, Lieutenant Commander Dudley W. "Mush" Morton of Miami, Florida, got the best tonnage for the month and set a couple of marks which were to stand for a long time. En route to patrol station, Morton had been ordered to reconnoiter Wewak Harbor, on the northeast coast of New Guinea. He determined to penetrate into the harbor but found he lacked charts. However, one of his engine room crew, D. C. Keeter, MM1/c, had purchased an Australian school atlas and, with its aid, Mush dove at daylight and stood into the harbor. He avoided two Chidori-type destroyers on the way in.

Just after noon he sighted a Fubuki-class destroyer at anchor off the town of Wewak, with several RO-class submarines alongside. Here was a target worth while, so Morton commenced an approach, planning to fire at 3,000-yards range in order to keep his ship in fairly deep water, thus facilitating his exit.

On his next periscope observation, the destroyer was seen to be underway, heading out for sea. It appeared that she would pass astern of the *Wahoo*. Torpedoes were got ready aft but a zig of the target made her cross the submarine's bow. Three torpedoes were fired at 1,800-yards range, with a hurried set-up allowing for 15-knot speed of the destroyer. Mush saw that the torpedoes were going to miss astern and fired a fourth shot set for 20 knots. This one the destroyer avoided by turning away, then circled to the right and charged for the *Wahoo*'s periscope.

Morton kept his periscope up, not only to get his own data, but also to keep the destroyer on a steady course headed for *Wahoo*. At 1,200 yards he fired a fifth torpedo, which either missed or did not explode, then with the range down to 800 yards and closing at a terrific rate, Mush fired the last torpedo of his forward tube nest. At 25 seconds on the stop watch, the torpedo exploded with a terrific detonation and broke the destroyer's back. Evidently she managed to beach herself. Nevertheless, she was out of this action and *Wahoo* began her nine-mile return trip to open water, to the accompaniment of shellfire and a couple of aircraft bombs.

For once our often-cursed Mark VI magnetic exploder had functioned as designed and thereby probably saved *Wahoo* and all on board. With an angle on the bow of zero, the chances of hitting with a straight contact exploder are extremely small and in striking a glancing blow on the fine lines of a destroyer, the jar might not be sufficient to actuate the exploder mechanism. However, the Mark VI had caused us too many lost targets, too many prematures and too many punishing depth charge attacks to let us feel that we could wash the slate clean and put its picture back on the piano. I still wanted its temperamental characteristics corrected or the whole magnetic feature removed.

Next morning, *Wahoo* set a base course for Palau and made wide zigzags across the expected enemy traffic lanes. Just before dawn of January 26 two merchant ships were sighted on the horizon. *Wahoo* raced ahead, keeping just over

the horizon from them, reached a favorable position and
dived to attack.

Morton had planned to attack with his six bow tubes but
found himself too close to the track of his intended victims,
so he reversed his course and used his four stern tubes. From
these four shots Mush obtained two hits in the first target and
one in the second. Both were frieghters. *Wahoo* swung
around to bring her bow tubes to bear in case additional
shots were needed. As she did so a third ship was sighted, a
big transport which had been hidden by the second target.
Here was luck indeed! Whether the transport captain was too
surprised and confused to act, or whether he held his course
to pick up survivors, we probably will never know, but the
net result was two torpedo hits which stopped his engines.
Morton then turned his attention to the damaged second
freighter which, when last observed, had been turning toward
Wahoo's periscope. The freighter was still coming at slow
speed, evidently trying to ram. Morton fired two "down the
throat" shots and got one hit, but even that didn't stop the
Jap and *Wahoo* had to go to full speed, duck and change
course to avoid him.

A periscope look eight minutes later showed the first
freighter had sunk but the transport was still afloat. The second frieghter, which had tried to ram, was now attempting to
escape but evidently was having steering troubles. Morton decided to finish off the transport and fired a torpedo from perfect position at 1,000 yards, which passed under the target
but failed to explode. Another mark against our magnetic exploder! However, a second shot blew the amidships section
"higher than a kite," as Mush reported.

Wahoo swung close to the still floating frieghter but her
electric storage battery was running low and a report of
"cruiser tops" on the horizon decided Morton to hold fire.
Perhaps more important game could be lured his way!
Shortly afterward the newcomer changed course and showed
a typical tanker silhouette. It had been a busy morning with
all hands manning battle stations, at high tension since daylight, so Mush passed the word "prepare to surface." He
planned to take two or three hours to get his battery charge
well started, then make an "end round" run on the escaping
tanker and damaged freighter and attack submerged from
ahead of his targets.

When *Wahoo* surfaced she found about 20 of the

transport's boats, landing craft of various types, in the water.
She approached them to pick up a few prisoners for intelligence purpose and was received with rifle and machine-gun
fire. There was nothing to do then but sink them all, which
Wahoo promptly did. This was an attitude on the part of our
enemy which our submarines were to encounter often in the
months and years to come. They fought so long as they had a
weapon and, even when found helpless in the water, refused
to be rescued.

At 1530 *Wahoo* began to chase the two fleeing ships. At
1830, when darkness was fast closing in, three bow shots at
the tanker were delivered and one torpedo hit. Both ships
kept going and turned away. *Wahoo* surfaced on a dark
night. She had only four torpedoes left, and those all aft. After an hour and a half filled with futile attempts to gain position for a good stern shot, *Wahoo* paralleled the tanker at
less than 2,000 yards range, then twisted with full power.
Two torpedoes broke the tanker's back and she went down
rapidly.

Then followed a similar period of jockeying for position
on the freighter, during which wild, radical zigs and much
gunfire from the freighter made the problem extremely difficult. At 2100 a large searchlight commenced sweeping from
over the horizon. An escort was hurrying to the scene, and
Wahoo's coup de grace had to be delivered in a hurry.

As the target headed straight for the destroyer and protection, *Wahoo* gained position for a straight stern shot at
2,900 yards, and fired her last two torpedoes to hit. Both did.
As the belated escort was now coming over the horizon, sil-
houetting the freighter in her searchlight, *Wahoo* set a course
for Pearl Harbor. Fifteen minutes after being hit the freighter
sank, leaving the destroyer's searchlight sweeping an empty
ocean.

Thus ended the daylong battle of our first "one man
wolf pack." *Wahoo*, under command of Dudley Morton, was
first to sink an entire convoy. It was the fighting start of a
fighting skipper and a fighting ship. Morton's dispatch, reporting this event, was typical of the man, terse and to the point:
"In 10-hour running gun and torpedo battle destroyed entire
convoy of two freighters, one transport, one tanker. All torpedoes expended. Returning home."

Next morning *Wahoo* encountered a five-ship convoy of
freighters and tankers. Morton had no torpedoes but trailed

the convoy on surface, hoping for a breakdown or a laggard whom he might sink with his gun. Luck was not with him that day for about midmorning a Japanese destroyer came boiling out from the midst of the convoy and gave chase. *Wahoo* continued on surface at best speed, showing her stern to the enemy, but at 7,000 yards salvoes began falling too close for comfort and Morton dived. The destroyer delivered a pattern of six depth charges but inflicted no damage.

Morton's report of this affair was also typical: "Another running gunfight. Destroyer running. *Wahoo* running." For this outstandingly aggressive patrol, *Wahoo* was awarded the Presidential Citation.

Although I did not know it, my tour of duty in the Southwest Pacific was drawing to a close. On January 27, press dispatches announced that a Pan-American plane flying from Pearl Harbor to San Francisco, carrying Rear Admiral Bob English and nine other officers, was long overdue. This was terribly bad news, for Bob English was the heart and soul of the Pacific submarine set-up—a man we could not afford to lose.

In a personal letter to my former submarine boss, Vice Admiral R. S. Edwards, then Chief of Staff for the Commander in Chief U.S. Fleet, I said, "If it is true (that the plane is lost) I hope no one thinks of sending me to Pearl Harbor. By all means let someone else have Pearl Harbor."

When I was called in the early morning of February 5, a dispatch was handed me which detached me from duty as Commander Submarines Southwest Pacific and ordered me to report to Cincpac for duty as Commander Submarines Pacific Fleet. Bob's plane had crashed. My letter to Admiral Edwards had not reached him and he told me afterward that it probably would have made no difference.

With Bob English, a gallant and brilliant submarine officer, a veteran skipper of submarines in World War I, died, among others, Captain Bob Smith, Commander Riley Coll and Lieutenant Commander John J. Crane, all members of his Staff and submariners of long experience.

My sorrow at the tragic news was intensified by the thought of leaving Australia. We were closer to the fighting front in Perth than I would be in Pearl Harbor. The areas vital to the Japanese and from which they must be cut off— Malaya, the Netherlands East Indies, the Philippines—were closer to Fremantle and Brisbane than to Pearl Harbor. It seemed that I was taking a step backward. My Staff threatened to send me a white feather for desertion in the face of the enemy, but instead they presented me with a beautiful little wrist watch, the first I had ever owned and which I wear today with great pride.

Then, too, the organization and plans which we had built up in Australia had taken a lot of blood and tears and I wanted to follow through. Rear Admiral Ralph W. Christie was ordered as my relief.

With regret, I paid my departing respects to the Lieutenant Governor, the Commanding General, the Lord Mayor and to my Australian and Dutch comrades in arms. My short stay among the people of Perth, Fremantle and Albany had been so filled with examples of consideration, cooperation and hospitality that saying good-bye to them was like parting from lifelong friends.

CHAPTER 5

Passing through Brisbane in February, en route to my new station at Pearl Harbor, I reported to Comsowestpac for a final conference. After our affairs were settled, Vice Admiral Carpender directed me to report my departure to General MacArthur, whose office was two decks up in the same building.

The General said that he had a message which he wanted delivered personally to Admiral Nimitz. "I want to present most urgently to Cincpac," he said, "the need for a stronger naval force in the Southwest Pacific. I am not interested in who commands these ships. It makes no difference to me whether they come under my jurisdiction, under Admiral Halsey or under Admiral Nimitz. Coordination can be arranged. Frankly, I am worried about the evidence piling up of Japanese reserves in the Malay Barrier. I estimate that the enemy has 200,000 troops in that area. If they overrun Australia, the results to the Allies will be disastrous and set back final victory for years."

I jotted down cryptic notes, which would mean nothing if they fell into hostile hands, made my respectful adieus and departed.

I then paid a farewell visit to Fulton at New Farms Wharf, where Captain Jimmie Fife, the new Commander, Task Force 42, flew his broad command pennant. I found them mourning the loss of Commander Howard W. Gilmore, Ensign W. W. William and W. F. Kelley, FN3/c, killed by enemy machine-gun bullets during a collision between Gilmore's submarine, the *Growler,* and a Jap patrol boat. Alongside the tender lay the *Growler,* her bow looking like the twisted snout of an elephant seal. Her bridge and conning tower fairwater had been riddled by machine-gun fire.

Gilmore, who in previous patrols had earned the reputation of being an outstanding submarine captain, had met death with gallantry and utter devotion to duty. He gave to the Submarine Service the deathless slogan for which his name will always be remembered, "Take her down."

Growler had left Brisbane on January 1, 1943, for a patrol in the western Solomons, athwart the traffic lanes from Rabaul to Jap strongholds to the east and south. On the 16th, *Growler* sank the freighter *Chifuku Maru,* after a brilliant approach had placed the submarine inside the screening escorts. He made three more attacks and then ran into trouble. On February 5, while making a radar night surface attack on two merchant ships, with two escorts, *Growler* was fired on and then depth charged. Number one ballast tank manhold was damaged and the forward torpedo room began flooding at an alarming rate, but temporary repairs were successfully made.

At 0110, on February 7, *Growler* sighted a ship on the starboard bow, on an opposite course, range 2,000 yards. Gilmore turned away, made all tubes ready and swung around to close for an attack. When *Growler* was in position 2,000 yards on the enemy's starboard quarter, the target sighted her and reversed course to attack. The Commanding Officer, Officer of the Deck, Assistant Officer of the Deck, the quartermaster and three lookouts were on the bridge. Although radar immediately caught the enemy course change, it apparently was not seen by bridge personnel.

At 0134 radar indicated that range was too short to allow torpedoes to arm. At that instant the order came down the hatch, "Left full rudder"; and the collision alarm sounded. A moment later *Growler* plowed into the enemy ship at 17 knots, with a terrific impact, knocking everyone off his feet. *Growler* heeled over about 50 degrees, then righted. The enemy opened fire with several machine guns at point-blank range. With a hail of bullets pouring into the submarine, the Commanding Officer gave the order, "Clear the bridge." The OOD and quartermaster descended, followed by two wounded lookouts who were pulled through the hatch. Then came the immortal words—"Take her down." Everyone hesitated. Seconds ticked by, and no one appeared at the hatch. Then *Growler* submerged, with the enemy still spraying the ship with machine-gun fire. The Commanding Officer, Assistant OOD and one lookout, left on the bridge, presumably were killed by enemy fire.

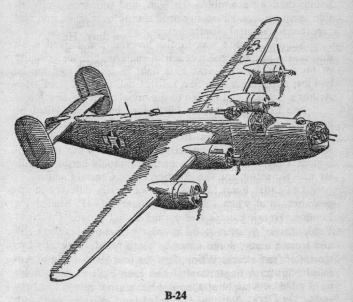

B-24

For personal heroism in ordering his ship submerged as he lay wounded on deck, knowing he would be lost, Commander Howard W. Gilmore became the first member of the Submarine Force to be awarded the Congressional Medal of Honor. Through his inspiring spirit of self-sacrifice, his ship, though seriously wounded, lived to fight again, and to add to her already high score of enemy shipping destroyed.

The flight to Pearl Harbor via New Caledonia, Fiji and Canton Island was made in an Army B-24 packed to the limit. Among the passengers was Colonel Clifton B. Gates. USMC, whose First Marine Regiment had just come out of Guadalcanal. We arrived at Hickam Field, Pear Harbor, on Sunday, February 14, in clear, beautiful Hawaiian weather. Captain John H. Brown, "Babe" Brown to thousands of Navy football fans who had watched him lead the team in trouncing Army back before World War I, had fallen heir to command of Task Force 7, Submarines Pacific Fleet—on the death of Bob English. John, his Chief of Staff, Captain John Griggs, and I went into a huddle, which lasted practically 24 hours; then we assembled the Staff, and squadron and division commanders. I read my orders, took over command and reported to Admiral Nimitz.

Admiral Nimitz was in the hospital and looked a bit drawn. He had suffered a touch of malaria, but the geniality of his smile and the clear blue light in his eye told me he had lost none of his dauntless spirit. I delivered General MacArthur's message and retired to dig myself into the new job.

Bob English's schedule lay before me. When killed he had been on his way to a conference at Mare Island, to be followed by an inspection trip to our submarine facilities at Kodiak, Dutch Harbor, and San Diego, plus a trip to Washington. They would have to wait until I should become familiar with the set-up and the situation in the Central Pacific.

The entire Pearl Harbor area was vastly different in appearance from when I left it in January, 1941, headed for London. Housing areas had sprung up all around the Navy Yard, officers' quarters stood in orderly rows of Makalapa Hill and from a mud-colored concrete bomb proof, topped by two stories of frame construction, flew the four-starred flag of Admiral Nimitz. A huge hospital had been built in Aiea; fields were piled with supplies. Quonset-hut marine camps lined the roads into Honolulu, and Ford Island was packed with planes.

An equally great change had taken place in the atmosphere since I passed through in April, 1942. Then, gloom had hung like a pall over Pearl Harbor; now, the spirit of confidence, determination and self-sacrifice was paramount. What an amazing difference the capture of a little territory at Guadalcanal and the sinking of a few men-of-war and merchant ships had made in our inner selves.

The sinking score during February for Submarines

Pacific was not high but the bag turned in by *Tarpon*, Lieutenant Commander T. L. "Tommy" Wogan of Philadelphia, Pennsylvania, was outstanding. Tommy had succeeded in downing the 10,935-ton passenger-cargo ship, *Fushimi Maru*, and the 16,975-ton transport, *Tatsuta Maru*, south of Honshu. The average enemy merchant ship was not large—say 5–7,000 tons—so these ships which *Tarpon* sank were really worth while.

The old *Tarpon* had been a hardluck ship. Misfortune dogged her for the first year of the war. Her escapes from disaster were numerous and close. She almost foundered; she was stranded in the Java Sea, and virtually abandoned, only to be refloated and saved. She did not fire a torpedo in anger until November, 1942.

Tarpon's luck did not change until the evening of February 1, 1943, when she sank the *Fushimi Maru* and then went on to get the *Tatsuta Maru*, the third largest Japanese merchantman sunk during the war.

The *Tatsuta* was sunk on the Truk route, about 80 miles south of Tokyo Bay. Contact was made at night by radar, at a range of 10,000 yards. Very shortly, Wogan knew he had a large, high-speed, heavily escorted target. There would be no second shot at this fellow. The approach followed a familiar pattern: full surface speed on collision course, followed by the submerged periscope-radar attack. During the approach the target was recognized as a larger passenger liner, a two-stacker.

A half hour after contact *Tarpon* commenced firing—a spread of torpedoes from her four bow tubes. It was a perfect shot from a range of 1,500 yards. There was no time to tarry; Wogan began a strategic retirement the moment his torpedoes left the tubes. Within a minute torpedoes began thudding home—not one, not two, but all four. The explosions were terrific. *Tarpon* had the most satisfying experience that a submarine can enjoy—four shots, four hits, target sunk.

Prolonged and severe depth charging followed. The escorts gave the submarine a rough time, but their best efforts served only to punctuate her success. The depth charging continued until well after midnight, but Wogan, evading at deep submergence, finally shook off the pursuers without suffering any damage except to nerves.

While in Australia a story found its way down to us

about a submarine which had entered Tokyo Bay and
watched the horse races, at some track close to the shore line.
It sounded very unlikely to me, since Tokyo Bay is far too
shallow for a big submarine to penetrate submerged. After
arrival at Pearl, I heard the true story of how this remarkable
yarn originated and, because so many people have asked me
about it, I am retelling it here for the benefit of those who
have not yet heard the straight of it.

One bright August day in 1942, *Guardfish,* Commander
Burt Klakring, ran so close to Yagi, a port north of the
smog-ridden iron and steel city of Kamaishi, northern Honshu, that through his periscope the skipper spotted the town's
race track. There was no activity on the track—and nothing
smacking of aviation, a matter of much interest to *Guardfish.*

Officers and men peeked through the periscope. A lot of
kidding went on around the control room about bets and
daily doubles. Burt Klakring jokingly promised he would
bring the boat back for the next races.

What really intrigued Burt was a railroad trestle crossing
an inlet near the track, which reminded him of the old Short
Line bridge across College Creek in Annapolis. A torpedo
well placed at the moment a train was crossing, would make
the *Guardfish*—so the torpedo officer promised—"the first
damned submarine in the U.S. Navy to torpedo a train."

The skipper toyed with the idea for the best part of the
day, but, as no train appeared, he went about his patrol,
which netted him 70,000 tons of enemy shipping and a
Presidential Citation. The New York State Racing Commission sent Burt an honorary membership, after a much embel-
lished account hit the press reports. A crew member, back in
Pearl Harbor, romanced outrageously that they actually saw
the races—a submarine wartime myth Klakring has been trying to kill ever since.

Another yarn current at that time concerned a submarine
which watched an aircraft carrier building at a coastal
dockyard, waited for her completion, and sank her just after
she slid down the launching ways. It made a good newspaper
story but was pure fiction.

From Brisbane came a report that *Albacore* had added
to her warship score by sinking a mine layer and a destroyer.
On February 20 she encountered two destroyers, escorting a
mine layer. Some might have considered this a dangerous
outfit to attack, but not Lieutenant Commander R. C. Lake.

He bored in and sank the mine layer and one of her escorts. The other got away. Captain Lake had begun his warship blitz the previous month by sinking the light cruiser *Tenryu*.

The *Tunny*, Lieutenant Commander John A. Scott of Grand Rapids, Michigan, turned in a score of only one ship sunk, a 5,000-ton cargo carrier, but the story of that sinking was a tremendous morale booster. *Tunny*, on her first patrol, was stationed in the south end of Formosa Strait. On February 8 she was forced down by a plane and, on surfacing just after sunset, she found a large freighter about 10,000 yards distant. She immediately crash-dived and checked the course of the enemy ship as it passed out of sight. Then *Tunny* surfaced, located the target by means of radar, and raced to get ahead of her quarry. After obtaining desired position, Scott submerged to 40 feet in order to reduce her silhouette, closed the range to 830 yards and fired two torpedoes. The sound operators never heard one of them (probably it sank) but the other one made an erratic run and missed the target. *Tunny* then surfaced, checked the bearing of the enemy ship by radar, and circled for another shot. However, the target sighted her and opened fire with two guns. Captain Scott was thoroughly exasperated and determined not to let that ship get away. Poor torpedo performance had made his entire patrol a nightmare. John stuck his chin out and gave the order to head for the target, disregarded the enemy's fire, and stood in to a range of 980 yards, where two more torpedoes were launched. One was a straight run but missed. The other circled.

By this time the entire fire control party was furious and swore to get that ship. *Tunny* hauled out, reloaded, and came in again to the accompaniment of enemy shellfire and, at a range of 1,020 yards, fired three torpedoes. The first one hit, the second missed ahead and the third, after zigzagging down the course, hit its target. *Tunny*'s luck was certainly with her that night, for she came out untouched. Her victim sank in 20 minutes.

Prematures and duds were occurring with the same discouraging frequency in Pearl Harbor boats as in Southwest Pacific, and torpedo experts had no better answers than we had in Australia. The Bureau of Ordnance contended that the percentage of prematures was not high and that, after all, we *were* sinking ships. This might be true, but nearly every premature allowed the target to escape, because it gave her sufficient warning to evade the other torpedoes. Too, it gave the enemy escorts a perfect mark from which to start their search curves, thus increasing the punishment from depth charges which our submarines had to endure. The submarine skippers were resentful and discouraged. As one of them said, "It's a helluva thing to go all the way to the China Coast to find out your damned torpedoes won't work."

When a 3,000-pound torpedo, with its 700-pound TNT war head, is fired from one of the 10 tubes of a submarine, it is perfectly harmless. This precaution is necessary to protect the submarine from accidental explosions at dangerously close ranges. When it has run about 300 yards, a mechanism in the exploder operates to free the firing pin. After thus arming a magnetic exploder, the firing pin is ready to strike the caps, which detonate the explosive charge when the torpedo passes under a steel target. In the case of a contact exploder, the torpedo must strike the hull of its victim, thus jarring the firing pin into activity.

Our Mark VI exploder was built to operate in either of

H.M.S. Victorious

these two ways but, unfortunately, in many cases it operated in neither. The question came from all sides, "Shouldn't we inactivate the magnetic feature of the exploder until a simpler and more foolproof exploder is invented?"

I was loath to inactivite, because the effect of the torpedo's explosion under the target's keel was devastating, and also because the magnetic feature was almost a "must" in making a down-the-throat shot. However, my belief in our ability to correct its defects was weakening—as was reflected in my letters to the Chief of Bureau of Ordnance.

The Torpedo Officer of HMS carrier *Victorious* gave me some valuable data on British experience with magnetic exploders, which they had abandoned early in the war, and on the new design, which they felt might be successful. This latest attempt employed dry batteries as a source of power instead of our pocket-sized generator, the source of so much trouble. Their exploder was about half the size of ours, hence it required a smaller opening in the shell of the torpedo, which thereby was made less liable to leakage—a frequent cause of prematures. All this data I passed on to the Bureau of Ordnance, with the suggestion that the Naval Attaché in

London would undoubtedly be glad to get them a sample of this new gadget.

The repair facilities at Pearl were also matters of great interest to me after the struggles we had gone through in the Southwest Pacific. I found that the 2,500-ton floating dry dock ARD-1 had been turned over for the exclusive use of the Submarine Base, and that its sides fairly smoked from the friction of its frequent submergences and emergences, made in keeping up with underwater repairs and bottom cleaning. The 3,500-mile trip out to the hunting grounds off Japan made it imperative that fuel be conserved, hence bottoms were cleaned and painted every time a submarine refitted at Pearl. As yet we had no docking facilities at Midway Islands. The Submarine Base repair division, under the leadership of Lieutenant Commander D. T. "Tom" Eddy, was doing an excellent job of refitting. Shops operated on a 24-hour basis and refit crews relieved the submarine's crew of all responsibility during their recuperation period. Boats requiring a full overhaul—ordinarily this came every 18 months—were sent to the Navy Yards at Pearl Harbor, Mare Island, or Hunters Point.

Having acquainted myself with the situation and facilities at Pearl Harbor, my next interest lay in Midway. I had seen the beginning of development of Sand Island as an air and submarine base in July, 1940, and believed that it had great possibilities. I included in our war plans of January, 1941, a scheme to station a tanker at Midway for topping off fuel tanks of submarines outward bound.

For the future, however, I had larger plans for Midway. I hoped to move my entire headquarters there and to refit about half of our submarines at that base. By so doing, we would save 2,400 miles of wear and tear, plus fuel, on every patrol, except those starting from Pearl Harbor.

Hence in late afternoon of March 1, I took passage in the *Scamp*, Lieutenant Commander W. G. "Wally" Ebert, a brand-new boat built at Portsmouth, New Hampshire, and in beautiful condition. She had many war-born improvements and reflected great credit upon her builders. A subchaser escorted us until dark, to insure identification by our own patrol planes, blinked "Good-bye and good hunting," and then we were on our own.

When Eastern Island and Sand Island, which constitute the Midway group, hove into view on the morning of March

5, they presented a far different picture than when I last saw them in 1940. At that time, civilian contractors were just getting started on the submarine and air base development and the only completed installations were those on Sand Island, where the cable station and Pan-American Airways had established themselves. Now, both islands bristled with radio and radar towers, operation towers, water tank towers and AA-gun emplacements.

The reef which enclosed the wide lagoon had been pierced and a 400-foot channel dredged. A wood and steel dock had grown out into the lagoon from Sand Island, an oil tank field had appeared, and all space not reserved for airstrips was crowded with shops, office buildings, warehouses, quarters and barracks. Eastern Island was all aviation, while Sand Island was shared by submarine and aviation installations. This was chiefly the work of Rear Admiral Ben Moreel, Chief of Bureau of Yards and Docks, and his "Seabees."

Midway, a part of the Fourteenth Naval District, was under command of Commodore H. M. "Beauty" Martin, an aviator who had been in command of our air base at Kaneohe on that fatal December 7. Our Submarine Base commander was Commander W. V. "Micky" O'Regan. The Marine Defense Battalion of 1,500 men was commanded by Lieutenant Colonel Hahn, USMC.

A tremendous amount of work had been put into developing Midway, but much remained to be done. The Submarine Base, which was intended to have facilities equivalent to those of one submarine tender, i.e., to be able to refit three or four submarines simultaneously, was coming along nicely. Recreational facilities for submariners recuperating there were not good but buildings and playing fields were being constructed. Our schedule was so arranged that each submarine refitted once at Midway and twice at Pearl.

Refitting facilities also required improvements. The "tanker" dock, at which our submarines moored inside the three-mile wide lagoon, was fully exposed to the normal trade winds. At times the seas kicked up were so heavy that the submarines had to anchor out in the lagoon, necessitating boating and loss of time for repair crews. During winter gales, sometimes reaching 75 m.p.h., all boating ceased.

What we urgently needed was a sheet-steel, cellular breakwater to complete the shallow harbor built for Pan-American seaplanes, and dredging to make it usable for tenders and submarines. With such a refit basin, we eventually could move three or four tenders to Midway and repair 12 to 20 submarines continuously in all weather. To complete this ideal set-up, another 2500-ton floating dry dock was required. On the accomplishment of this new task, I now set my sights.

On returning to Pearl, I wrote a letter to Rear Admiral Moreel, congratulating him on the spirit, appearance and effectiveness of his Seabees. I explained what we needed at Midway regarding dredging and a breakwater to make an all-weather refit basin. I had already discussed the matter with the Fourteenth Naval District Civil Engineer, Commander T. A. Hartung, who considered the plan feasible. I asked Ben to look the proposition over and be ready to give it a fair breeze as soon as I got permission from Cincpac to proceed. There, however, I struck a snag. Cincpac wanted Midway lagoon to be dredged sufficiently to provide anchorage for a cruiser task force, and would not agree to diverting dredges from that work to undertake the necessary deepening of my proposed refit basin. Another dredge for Midway was in prospect, so I did not take this answer as final. However, it was months before I got the "go ahead" sign.

We had plenty of worries during the month of March. Our stocks of Mark XIV torpedoes, whose magnetic exploders were such a headache, were running so low that we had to plan mining operations for the next three boats scheduled for patrol, in order to relieve the pressure on our dwindling supply of "fish." The Mark XVIII electric torpedo, which left no wake and therefore was eagerly awaited, had not made its appearance in our areas and word came from submariners in Newport that not much attention was being given it. I found, years later, that this apparent neglect was investigated by the Naval Inspector General. Additionally, a recommendation had been made to Cominch that a "Directior of Submarines" be set up in Washington, from whom would emanate all administrative orders to commanders of Submarine Forces. I viewed this proposal with concern, for it meant introducing an extra gear between submarines at sea and Cominch, who would always have the final word. I protested vigorously against the idea.

Word came from Subsowestpac that *Amberjack*, Lieutenant Commander J. R. Bole, Jr., and *Grampus*, Lieutenant Commander J. R. Craig, were "overdue and presumed lost." Postwar reports indicate the *Amberjack* fell a victim to patrol craft depth charges southeast of New Britain on February 16. The *Grampus* was presumably sunk by seaplane attack in about the same area on February 19.

The final worry of the month came when Cincpac received a dispatch from Cominch, asking what we knew about the sinking of the Russian freighter *Ilmen*. The position given was southeast of Kyushu, the southernmost island of Japan, 50 miles from the spot where *Sawfish* sank a ship just before daylight about that same time. Checking back and forth brought out details indicating that *Ilmen* had, indeed, been the unfortunate victim of torpedoes from the *Sawfish*. To make matters worse, the *Sawfish* had sunk, during the following night, a ship which might have been the Russian freighter *Kola*, which also was reported to have been torpedoed.

These ships had been routed south of Japan, through Van Dieman Strait, at a time when our information was to the effect that Russian ships bound for the United States were using La Perouse Strait. Actually, La Perouse had become icebound on January 15, forcing the use of the Tsushima–Van Dieman route, but we had received no word of this change. Both ships admittedly were showing navigational lights "at half strength." *Sawfish*, because of approaching daylight, in the case of *Ilmen*, and brilliant moonlight, in the case of the supposed *Kola*, had made submerged attacks, using the periscope, and had not seen these dim lights.

After these incidents the Russians began to inform us, through our Consul General at Vladivostok, of individual ship movements and general traffic routings. Eventually they also began the use of special identification markings.

On the credit side of the ledger were 16 enemy merchant ships, officially credited to Subpac as having been sunk. Our records credited us with damaging 16, which figure was probably higher, since some of our claims for ships sunk were disallowed, and these also undoubtedly limped home to overcrowded enemy repair yards.

Wahoo had asked for and received a patrol assignment in the Yellow Sea, an area practically untouched. There she performed the so far unparalleled feat of sinking, singlehanded, eight cargo ships and a transport in 10 days. Captain Mush Morton, not satisfied with his January record, had proceeded to hang up a new one.

Plans for carrying out the inspection trip, on which Rear Admiral English had been killed, finally matured in March.

My first request was to go by submarine to Dutch Harbor
and then work back along the Aleutian chain by air. Flying
weather in Alaska at that time of year is unpredictable and I
wanted to be sure of getting to our submarine base at Dutch
without wasting too much time.

However, Cincpac did not approve diverting a submarine from the "production line" for even a few days, and
therefore I left Pearl by clipper plane on the afternoon of
March 21, arriving in San Francisco the next forenoon. I flew
to Kodiak. There, I found that Rear Admiral J. W. "Jack"
Reeves, Commander Alaskan Sector, had shifted his HQ to
Dutch Harbor. The Submarine Base, administered by Lieutenant Commander G. W. "Smoky" Snyder, though overhauling no submarines, was doing a useful job in caring for the
many small craft and surface ships which filled Womens Bay.
A wooden, floating dry dock had been assigned and, with no
previous docking experience, the Submarine Base carpenter
had docked some 50 ships.

At Dutch Harbor I found Admiral Reeve's office in the
"explosion chamber" of a concrete bomb proof. Space was at
too much of a premium to waste this upper story, in which
aerial bombs were supposed to explode. The Submarine Base,
commanded by Commander C. W. "Duke" Gray, was still in
the building stage. Its shops were pretty much of a "jury rig,"
but a full-scale combination machine shop, which could
handle anything from periscopes to storage batteries, was
nearing completion.

Despite the grimness of the setting, and the continual
battle which the ancient S-class submarines stationed at
Dutch had to wage with Arctic gales and seas, there was
plenty of fight left in our lads.

Just how rugged were these battles this story tells: S-35,
Lieutenant H. S. "Hank" Monroe of Ellsworth, Maine, had a
terrifying experience with Arctic weather. She had been on
patrol about 10 days and December 21 found her off Amchit-
ka, struggling along on surface in the midst of a typical Aleutian storm. Heavy seas breaking over the bridge had flooded
considerable water into the control room and the bilges were
being pumped constantly. In the pitch blackness of early
night, a huge comber swept the bridge and smashed the skipper into the hatch, badly spraining one arm and one leg. He
was helped below and was just turning into his bunk when the
cry of, "Fire in the control room" was heard. Bright electric

arcs and blue flames from the main power cables illuminated
the after starboard corner of the compartment. Salt water apparently had saturated the insulation, causing a short. No
sooner had this fire been brought under control than a similar
one broke out in the forward starboard corner of the control
room. Again and again, electrical fires broke out, until finally
it was necessary to stop the engines, abandon and seal the
control room.

Then followed a three-day nightmare, in which the in-
terior of the submarine frequently had to be abandoned for
hours at a time because of fires and suffocating smoke. During these crises, all hands took refuge on the ship's tiny
bridge, or lashed themselves on the conning tower fairwater
to prevent being swept away by icy seas. None were lost
overboard or died of exposure!

The day before Christmas, S-35 limped into Adak,
where first aid and emergency repairs were rendered by the
destroyer *Gillis*.

During the period preceding the invasion of Attu and
Kiska by U.S. amphibious forces, the mission of these aged
S-boats was to cut off all supplies to those islands. Postwar
reports show that, in spite of terrific hardships, these gallant
little ships performed that duty to the extent of sinking a
converted gunboat and four freighters for a total of 15,026
tons. Several other enemy ships were damaged. These severe
losses undoubtedly weakened the final desperate defense of
Attu and probably strongly influenced the Japanese decision
to abandon Kiska.

I had no business at Adak, but my orders from Admiral
Nimitz were sufficiently elastic to permit the trip. There I
found Rear Admiral Kinkaid, Commander Task Force 16,
living in a quonset, with his Chief of Staff, Captain O. S.
"Ozzie" Colclough, an old submarine hand. His mess
consisted of Major General Simon Bolivar Buckner, Alaskan
Department Commander (absent at the time); Major General Corlett, Island Commander; Major General Butler, Commander Eleventh Air Force, and their Staffs. An excellent
spirit of friendliness and cooperation prevailed—a condition
which, to my fairly wide observation over the Pacific, seemed
to exist all along the line. It was not until the war was practically over that we began hearing from the waffle tails and po-
liticos, who had sat out the war in Washington, how badly

the armed services got along together and how much we needed "unification."

The 3,400-mile haul back to San Francisco, which I began on April 2, was made in almost perfect flying weather—a great rarity at that time of year. After a two-day stop in the Bay Area to inspect submarine repair facilities at Mare Island, Hunters Point and Bethlehem Steel, I hurried on to San Diego to look over similar facilities there. Likewise, I wanted a look at my family in Coronado, which I had seen only *en passant* since 1939.

The submarine situation at the Destroyer Base in San Diego was not good. S-boats down from the Dutch Harbor base were requiring four or five months for overhaul, as compared to 40 or 50 days in which Mare Island, Hunters Point and Bethlehem Steel were overhauling the much larger Fleet submarines. The blackout regulations were so stringent as to discourage nightwork on the docks or on the outsides of any ships. Blackout was much more strictly enforced there than in Australia or Pearl Harbor—while only half a mile from the Destroyer Base an aircraft factory blazed with lights all night. With the Japs some thousands of miles away, I thought these

U.S.S. Narwhal

precautions a bit overdone. My proposed report to Cincpac on these matters was discussed on the spot with the Commanding Officer and with the Commandant of the Eleventh Naval District.

At the Destroyer Base, I found *Narwhal* being prepared to transport half of a Scout company of Army troops. She and *Nautilus* were scheduled to land commandos on Attu, during the forthcoming invasion of that island. All torpedoes and torpedo racks were removed from her forward torpedo room and tiers of bunks installed. The soldiers were certainly packed in like sardines and, by putting four bunks in a tier, about 108 men were accommodated in each of the two submarines.

Early one morning I went to the San Diego Naval Laboratory of the University of California Division of War Research (UCDWR) at the invitation of Dr. G. P. Harnwell. He said they were developing gadgets for both submarine and antisubmarine warfare and that perhaps I might be interested in them. Thus, by a casual visit, was begun one of the most valuable contacts which submarines had with the scientific world. They did indeed have gadgets in which I was interested: noisemakers to jam enemy listening gear; decoys to throw antisubmarine craft off the track of hard-pressed submarines and an FM Sonar (Frequency Modulated Sonar), which could be used for locating submerged objects.

We went out into the bay in a small surface craft and Dr. Harnwell demonstrated how the instrument could locate shoals, on either side of the channel, and nets at the entrance. Passing small craft could also be seen on the PPI (Position Plan Indicator) scope. The doctor felt it would be valuable to submarines running totally submerged while entering an enemy harbor or locating entrances through nets. Undoubtedly, it could be used in that way, but it appealed to me as an instrument with which a submerged submarine, under attack by surface vessels, could locate and torpedo his pursuers. The steel hull of a ship or buoy gave back a clear, ringing echo in addition to appearing as a blob on the scope, from which the range and bearing of the object could be obtained. It was not until later that the suitability of this gadget as a mine detector occurred to me. I immediately started planning to get a trial installation made on a submarine.

Every time I came to the U.S. during the war I made a special visit to UCDWR, San Diego, and between visits kept in close touch through the submarine squadron commander stationed in that port. The prosubmarine gear, which this group produced, was of utmost importance and undoubtedly saved many a submarine from destruction. Dr. Harnwell, Dr. F. N. D. Kurie, Professor Malcolm Henderson and Dr. R. O. Burns were the members of the organization with whom we had most dealings and their cooperation and visits to the Pacific areas for technical assistance were tremendously helpful. On our part, we provided submarine services whenever possible to further their work. It was due to this same FM Sonar that we were able to penetrate the Japanese minefields and raid the Sea of Japan.

Unexpected orders came for me while at San Diego to proceed to Washington, for various conferences at the Navy Department, so I departed by air on April 13 and arrived at the Department the next morning. Captain Merrill Comstock, Submarine Material and Operations Officer for Chief of Naval Operations, was on hand to meet me and guided me through a whirlwind two days of conferences. We needed so many things out in the Pacific submarines and this was my chance to get our name into the pot.

I reported first to Cominch, Admiral King. Rear Admiral Freeland Daubin, Comsublant (Commander Submarines Atlantic Fleet), was in Washington and together we called on the Big Boss. Between the two of us, Freeland and I commanded most of the submarines in the Navy. Strangely enough we had grown up together in the little town of Lamar, Missouri—a long way from salt water.

Admiral King was fully aware of the situation regarding submarines in both oceans and his comments on training, distribution and most profitable areas to be patrolled were right to the point. The only subject on which I could not agree with him was that of providing better AA armament for submarines. I did not want my submarines to attempt to shoot it out with planes. After a few successes against our aircraft, the German submarines in the Atlantic were losing a lot of boats in such unequal battles. A submarine's best defense against planes is a crash dive and that was the tactic I wanted my boats to use.

Merrill Comstock asked me to address a meeting of submarine officers from all Bureaus. Perhaps it was not such a good idea for, stirred up as I was about the poor performance of our torpedoes and the lack of guns big enough to use in sinking enemy ships, I voiced some criticism that trampled on highly placed toes.

"If the Bureau of Ordnance," I said, "can't provide us with torpedoes that will hit and explode, or with a gun larger than a peashooter, then, for God's sake, get Bureau of Ships to design a boat hook with which we can rip the plates off the target's sides!"

I also extolled the virtues of the so-called "hotel accommodations" (improved toilets and air conditioning) which the General Board had given us back in '38—much against their better judgment. Members of that General Board were present, but I feel sure they were good enough sports to see the strategic value of these innovations and admit that sometimes "young squirts" have better specialized information than "old fuds."

That afternoon, I went to see my old friend Rear Admiral W. H. P. "Spike" Blandy, Chief of Bureau of Ordnance. I had known and admired Spike for many years. He stood one in his class at Annapolis and had devoted his career to Ordnance, in which he was acknowledged the Navy's top expert. However, he was no torpedo man, and I felt he was getting some bad advice.

When I arrived in his office, Spike was boiling. He had been told of my criticism of the morning.

"I don't know whether it's any part of your mission," he said, "to discredit the Bureau of Ordnance, but you seem to be doing a pretty good job of it."

"Well, Spike," said I, also heatedly, "if anything I have said will get the Bureau off its duff and get some action, I will feel that my trip has not been wasted."

From there we went on to get down to cases and, in the course of an hour, got some constructive things done. The Bureau demanded submarine torpedo experts. Ill as I could afford to lose them, I gave two instantly and three more later on. We didn't solve the problem of the defective exploder at that time, but perhaps some seeds were sown, which brought about an acceptable solution four months later.

Before heading back to Pearl Harbor, I went in to pay my respects to the Secretary of the Navy, James V. Forrestal. I first me Mr. Forrestal aboard the British battleship *Rodney* when, as Under Secretary of the Navy, he came to England in 1941. I found him unchanged from London days except, perhaps, with a firmer set of the jaw—if that were possible.

One look at James Forrestal would convince anyone that the
naval end of our war would be carried through on schedule
and that men on the fighting fronts would be supported with
every power at his command.

"I am proud of the performance of our submarines," he
was kind enough to say, "and, with increased production, we
soon will have enough to sweep the Pacific clean of enemy
shipping."

CHAPTER 6

Early morning of April 19 found me back at Pearl Harbor. My aerial jaunts added up to 16,578 miles and 28 days'
absence from my office, but the firsthand information and the
contacts made more than compensated for the separation
from the main job. Commander Submarine Squadron 4, Captain John Brown, and my Chief of Staff, Captain John
Griggs, had kept the ball moving forward while I was away.

During my absence, Cincpac had directed more mining
of enemy coasts. I am no advocate of mines to replace torpedoes, but our supply of torpedoes was dangerously low.
Cincpac not only wanted to take the pressure off our dwindling torpedo reserves, but also to lay mines for nuisance
value. Mining would force the enemy into extensive sweeping
operations which, according to the experts, would necessitate
large expenditures of copper wire and rubber—both strategic
materials that the Japanese had to import. There was a critical shortage of copper in Japan. Dr. C. W. Michels was the
senior Mine Warfare technician on Cincpac's staff and with
his close cooperation, five submarines had been dispatched to
lay mines in the approaches to Hong Kong, Shanghai, Wenchow Bay (China), off the steel manufacturing port of Muroran on the northern island of the Japanese Archipelago, and
at Kashima Nada, on the east coast of Honshu.

Cominch, about this time, issued a directive that "wolf
pack" tactics be developed. I had long entertained a hope
that we might soon have a sufficient number of operating
boats to permit such tactics. The idea was not new, having
been explored in the middle 1920's under the designation of
section attacks. Extensive literature was written on the subject

at that time, but it was abandoned because of its restrictions
on the freedom of action of the individual submarine and the
attendant risk of submerged collision. The hazards for peacetime training were greater than any advantage gained.

Just before the war, experimental night practices were
held, which attempted simultaneous attacks by several submarines, but communications were not good enough to insure
the degree of safety necessary in peacetime operations. Now
conditions were different; radar had been perfected; high-fre-
quency radio phones had been installed, no longer did the
old, slow, toilsome methods of coding and decoding prevail.
In communications lay the key to the solution of the problem
and we now had excellent communications. In short, we had
everything except sufficient submarines.

Nevertheless, Captain John Brown, with his lads in the
Training Section of Submarine Squadron 4, turned to the
preparation of coordinated attack doctrine and initiated what
they called the "Convoy College." The dance floor of the
Submarine Officers' Mess at Pearl Harbor was a checker-
board of one-foot-square black and white tiles. This made an
excellent game board and, using submarine captains and their
fire control crews, they started working with three-boat coordinated attack groups.

Every day during their refresher training periods, when
not shooting torpedoes at sea, these lads would gather at the
dance floor and, behind screens in best War College style, depending entirely on communications and infrequent "periscope looks," after the targets had "come over the horizon,"
would proceed to wipe out an enemy convoy.

Later, by permission of Cincpac, we would warn Pearl
Harbor-bound convoys from San Francisco that they would
be "attacked" by our submarines one night and day before
they reached their destination. Rear Admiral John Dale
Price's planes from Kaneohe would locate the convoy when
four or five hundred miles from Diamond Head, and then the
wolf pack would go to work. Frequent narrow escapes from
collision took place, but the submarine captains learned fast
and radar made the darkened target convoy as visible to
them on their PPI scopes (Position Plan Indicators) as they
would have been in daylight. This training produced rich har-
vests for us.

Poor torpedo performance was plaguing us more than
ever. The percentage of prematures had risen from 5 to 9 per

cent. Submarine captains returned from patrol ready to turn
in their suits. The best experts of the Bureau of Ordnance
could send us made no improvement. As an experiment, we
ordered eight submarines to inactivate the magnetic feature of
their exploders, with the intention of reactivating them for
their subsequent patrol, in order to obtain comparative data.

In spite of our torpedo troubles, the submarines were
still stinking ships. Postwar reports for April, 1943, credit
Subpac and Subsowestpac with sinking 18 ships. Probably
twice as many were hit, but managed to make port.

The prize for that month went to *Gudgeon,* Lieutenant
Commander W. S. "Bill" Post of Los Angeles, California. On
a patrol starting at Fremantle and ending at Pearl, she encountered, on April 28, in the Sulu Sea, the 17,526-ton
transport *Kamakura Maru.* The attack was made at night,
and since *Gudgeon's* speed was barely sufficient to overtake
the big ex-liner, Post was lucky to get his shots off from
about 170-degree track, i.e., 10 degrees from dead astern of
her. He got two hits in the *Kamakura's* stern and instantly
she was seen to be in serious trouble. Almost before Bill had
finished counting his hits, she sank by the stern, leaving the
water littered with lifeboats, rafts and screaming Japanese.
Evidently the captain had not been careful about his watertight bulkhead doors, for two hits astern should not have
sunk a big ship like the *Kamakura.* Later the *Gudgeon* sank
a 5,800-ton freighter and an enemy patrol boat. She salvaged
three Filipinos from the latter.

If we had had a prize for "picture of the month" that
award should have gone to Lieutenant Commander R. L.
Gross of the *Seawolf,* for his series of eight excellent periscope pictures portraying the sinking of Patrol Boat No. 39,
an autographed copy of which now hangs over my desk.
Gross came in from patrol which had taken him through the
Marianas into the Strait of Luzon. He sank a 4,575-ton
cargo ship northeast of the Marianas and a destroyer
southeast of Formosa.

Postwar reports classify his "destroyer" as an old
destroyer designated as a patrol boat of 820 tons. Gross was
rather apologetic about this latter victim, for in those days of
a scanty torpedo supply we did not deliberately attack
destroyers. They were not considered to be worth a torpedo.
This one, however, had got in his way and frustrated his attack on a good target and, in anger, Gross "let her have it."

The result was spectacular. The patrol boat, hit below the forward stack, gracefully settled forward, brought her rudder and propellers out of the water, assumed a perfect vertical position and finally plunged for bottom, leaving only a smudge of black smoke to mark the spot where she had disappeared. She was one of the approximately five score smaller Japanese escort vessels which our submarines erased from the register of the Imperial Japanese Navy.

The *Kingfish*, Lieutenant Commander V. L. "Rebel" Lowrance of Catawba, North Carolina, returned ahead of time from an area off Formosa. He reported that he had been worked over by the Dean Emeritus of the Tokyo Sound School and had sustained considerable battle damage. He claimed a fully loaded transport, a trawler and, possibly, a freighter. JANAC allows him the *Takachiho Maru*, transport, of 8,154 tons. His damage was sustained during a counterattack by escort vessels, one of whom planted a close pattern onto him, which slammed him down to bottom at 350 feet. Rebel thought that was a good place to remain, so he stopped every moving bit of machinery and sat there.

During the escort vessel's next firing run, one of the electricians was down in the motor room, checking on possible damage. Just then a batch of depth charges arrived and exploded terribly close. The electrician came streaking it up the hatch into the maneuvering room, swearing that flames had come in through the packing glands around the propeller shafts. His shipmates pooh-poohed that possibility, but on the next run the engineer officer and two more electricians each swore they also saw flames. A scientist explained this to me by saying that undoubtedly what they saw were sound waves of frequency high enough to approach the speed of light waves. Nevertheless, *Kingfish* personnel, who witnessed this phenomena, still swear they saw flames.

That *Kingfish* came back at all is miraculous and a high tribute to her designers and builders. Her hull was so badly dimpled and strained that her ribs were showing like those of a well-conditioned race horse. We sent her back to Mare Island to be fattened up.

The *Haddock*, Lieutenant Commander R. M. Davenport of Kansas City, Kansas, also got a bad working over in the Palau Island area. She brought back two scalps, one the *Arima Maru*, a passenger-cargo ship of 7,389 tons. She also brought back two dimples in her conning tower plating. The first was definitely the result of a very close depth charge, received at 300 feet, but the second was noted when the ship was at 415 feet, and undoubtedly was due to the 183-pound per square inch pressure of the water at that depth.

We also sent her back to Mare Island for repairs. I was informed later by the Chief of Bureau of Ships that these dimples were the result of an error in a design detail in the conning tower framing. If that were correct, it is one of the few errors committed in submarine designing by the excellent Bureau of Ships and its Chief, Vice Admiral Ned Cochrane.

Thus far, our ships had stood up well under the punishment of enemy depth charge attacks, but the Japs were definitely getting better with their depth charges. Perhaps the information they received earlier in the war by indiscreet news releases was beginning to pay off—for them. However that may be, they were setting them deeper and there was a rumor that they had increased the explosive charge to 1,000 pounds.

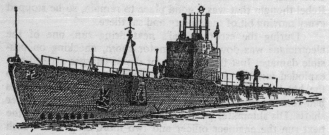

U.S.S. Pike

Pike, Lieutenant Commander W. A. New, came in from a brief patrol in the Marshalls. She had received an accurate depth charging, which shattered the insulation around her main control cubicle bus bars, which were hung from the hull overhead. The resultant arcing of heavy amperage currents forced her return to base. The only cheering thing in this encounter was that the welded hull plates, above her motor room spaces, had held perfectly. There had been many arguments among designers and builders as to whether welded seams would stand up against depth charging as well as rivetted seams. The *Pike*'s experience seemed to answer the argument in so far as welded seams were concerned—they definitely stood up all right. With shock-proofing to the mounting of her control cubicle, and a more resilient type of insulation, *Pike* was ready for sea again.

However, our feeling of assurance as to the ruggedness of our hulls was disturbed and all hands saddened by the news that *Pickerel*, Lieutenant Commander A. H. Alston, Jr., was overdue from a patrol in northeastern Empire waters and that *Triton*, Lieutenant Commander G. K. MacKenzie, was long overdue from a patrol north of New Guinea. Postwar reports indicate that both were lost due to depth charging. JANAC (Joint Army-Navy Assessment Committee) tells us that *Pickerel* sank a submarine chaser and a freighter on her last patrol. According to the same authority, *Triton* took one freighter with her to the bottom.

The submarine bringing in the most numerous bag for April was *Flying Fish* which sank three ships in the area between Honshu and Hokkaido—the approaches to Hakodate in the north of Japan. These northern areas were the toughest in enemy waters and we finally shut them down for a few months because of our losses. *Flying Fish*'s skipper, Lieutenant Commander G. R. "Donk" Donaho of Normangee, Texas, was a lad who seemed to have no nerves in his body and apparently had no muscles in his face—except every now and then a slow, rather nice smile. Sinking ships was just a matter of applied sciences with Donk.

We sent Donk and "Mike" Fenno, the man who brought the Philippine currency reserve out of Corregidor, back to the States on a recruiting drive.

Scorpion returned from patrol in the Empire area on May 8, reporting the loss of her Executive Officer and the sinking of the two ships, one of them the passenger-cargo ship *Yuzan Maru* of 6,380 tons. On her homeward run *Scorpion* had encountered one of the dozens of small radio-equipped patrol boats, converted trawlers, which the Japs maintained about 600 miles off the home islands. The submarine stopped the Jap, with a shell hit in the engine room, but the small 3-inch gun, which our boats carried, seemed unequal to the task of sinking her. *Scorpion*, still on surface, eased in to about 1,000 yards and fired a torpedo. At that instant a final burst of machine-gun fire from the doomed enemy killed Lieutenant Commander Reg Raymond, a brilliant young officer who had been with me in London before Pearl Harbor and had patrolled as an observer in British submarines. I deeply regretted his loss.

Casualties from enemy machine-gun fire, such as we had suffered in *Growler* and *Scorpion*, raised the question of better protection for personnel on submarine bridges. I certainly did not want to encourage my skippers to fight "yardarm to yardarm" battles—a submarine is too vulnerable to be able to afford taking chances by standing up to enemy gunfire. However, surprise night encounters were always a possibility. When the matter was put up to the Bureau of Ships, Vice Admiral Ned Cochrane immediately replied that special treatment steel (STS) was being used in all new construction and was to be installed in all other submarines at the first opportunity.

Ned had as assistants a fine team of experienced naval constructors and engineers which included such men as Captain W. I. "Andy" McKee, Captain J. W. "Joe" Fowler, Captain E. W. "Wally" Sylvester, Captain W. D. "Legs" Leggett, Jr., Captain Armand M. Morgan, Captain G. C. "Buck" Weaver and Captain W. T. "Bill" Jones. With such an array of talent in Washington or at building and repair yards it is small wonder that Bureau of Ships was generally way ahead of the ball.

Newly constructed submarines with trained crews were beginning to arrive at Pearl Harbor at the rate of four or five per month. During 1943, we received 52 of these fine new boats and three brand-new tenders: *Bushnell*, *Orion* and *Euryale*, plus the very old tender *Beaver*, which was transferred from the Atlantic to the Pacific. The *Otus*, which had started out the war with submarines, was transferred to the Southwest Pacific to act as a motor torpedo-boat tender. This left us nine submarine tenders in the Pacific, three in Australian waters.

Greatly interested in the new submarines, I was kept busy making training runs with them in the areas outside Pearl Harbor to observe new techniques and the operation of new equipment. Each submarine was assigned by the Commander Training Section to one particular division commander from the divisions based at Pearl. All division commanders were given this additional duty. Most of them were battle experienced and they took the particular submarine assigned to them through her entire training period of one or two weeks. Usually they made excellent elder-brother type instructors, but sometimes I heard rumors that they were too tough on the submarine captains.

One division commander, who was said to be very strict, and who, incidentally, had not made a war patrol, came to me and asked to be given command of a submarine and to take her on a war patrol. The matter was arranged and, I am happy to say, he made an excellent patrol and brought in a nice bag. The experience was excellent for him, I am sure, and for his subsequent trainees.

I was besieged with requests of a similar nature from division and squadron commanders, members of my Staff and even from Captain John Brown, boss of the Training Section. These requests I handled with sympathy, for I felt the experience would be of great value to themselves and to the Submarine Force. Most of them were granted in one way or another. I felt the lack of war patrol experience myself, and ventured a plea to Cincpac that I be allowed a shortened patrol as an observer, for, say, 40 days. Admiral Nimitz replied, in a very considerate note, that he wanted the Submarine Commander to be so situated that he could reach him on short notice and have him available for service to Cincpac. He concluded, "I appreciate your desire to see more active duty—a desire which I also share—but while we are in these billets we must remain close to our command posts."

However, from time to time, I was permitted to make the four-day trip to Midway via submarine. This gave me an excellent opportunity to check up on the state of training and material readiness of our ships, to judge the state of our morale—and to get a breath of salt air. I planned to avail myself of that opportunity frequently.

The particular operation which had brought about my request to Admiral Nimitz, was a foray into the Sea of Japan, which we were planning to make in the near future, with a force of three or four submarines.

During the spring months of 1943, plans had been made to recapture Kiska, but the target was later shifted to Attu. *Narwhal*, Lieutenant Commander F. D. Latta of Burlington, Iowa, and *Nautilus*, Lieutenant Commander W. H. Brockman, Jr., as I previously mentioned, were included in these plans. When D-Day was finally set for May 11, after postponement from May 7 and May 9, they embarked the Seventh Scout Company in rubber boats and headed them in for Scarlet Beach at 0309. *Nautilus* maintained her position for some time, showing an infrared light toward the landing place to assist the Scouts in holding the correct course. Both

submarines then retired toward Dutch Harbor, leaving the
surface forces free to attack any submarine sighted.
Transport of this large number of troops had not been accomplished without considerable discomfit.

The delay in landing operations and the extended periods submerged, sometimes from 0530 to 2300 on account of
the long daylight hours, put a severe drain on oxygen
reserves, for, with about 200 men aboard, the percentage of
CO_2 would rise to the top limit—3 per cent—about 1700 (5
P.M.). All CO_2 absorbent had been exhausted by the middle
of the long waiting period, so the submarines were forced to
surface sufficiently to get the engine induction valve out of
water and "blow out" the boat.

In waters being patrolled also by Japanese submarines,
this was not too safe a maneuver. The Army's appetite, however, was reported unimpaired by the discomforts of the trip.
One mess cook is said to have turned in his suit after feeding
72 hot cakes to six soldiers!

The *Tunny*, under Lieutenant Commander John Scott,
returned from a patrol in the Truk area, with an astonishing
story of an attack on a carrier formation. At this time the enemy were known to be ferrying many planes into Truk, for
use against our forces in the Solomons, hence constant patrol
of the area was maintained. At 2228 on the night of April 9,
Tunny, patrolling southwest of Truk, made radar contact
with a formation of ships at about 15,000-yards range. The
enemy's course was obtained and his speed plotted at 18
knots. This high speed made it seem probable that here was
an aircraft ferry trip. John Scott flooded down to an awash
condition to reduce his silhouette and bored in at full speed.
The convoy made his task easier by changing to a course
which put the submarine dead ahead. There his radar PPI
scope showed a large ship on his starboard bow, two lesser
ships in column on his port bow, and a destroyer on each
bow of the formation. *Tunny* was about to pass down between the two columns of what Scott believed to be a carrier
group—the realization of a submarine officer's dream!

All tubes were reported ready and John planned to
swing hard left and fire six torpedoes at the two-ship column,
at the same time firing four torpedoes from his stern tubes at
the single bigger carrier.

Suddenly three smaller craft, probably torpedo boats, appeared not more than 500 yards on his port bow. Swiftly

changing his plans and his torpedo set-up, Scott swung right and dived to 40 feet, which left his radar screen just above water. The seconds were packed with excitement and tension, yet not once did his fire control party get rattled.

The big ship, now presumably dead ahead, was hard to pick up by periscope but some thoughtful Jap on the target started sending with a signal lamp! That made everything perfect and at 2248, only 20 minutes from the beginning of the approach, *Tunny* fired four torpedoes from her stern tubes at the leading target of the two-ship column at a range of 880 yards and immediately afterward, six torpedoes from her bow tubes at the big carrier with a range of only 650 yards. Then *Tunny* headed for the depths. Four explosions were heard astern and three ahead—seven good hits presumably, but, alas, most of these explosions were prematures, for we know now that the escort carrier *Taiyo* was the only ship damaged. Her damage was not sufficient to interfere seriously with her schedule. Thus was a brilliant attack, perfectly executed with supreme daring, thwarted by a defective exploder mechanism.

To give the devil his due, I must admit that the Bureau of Ordnance was doing its level best to solve the exploder problem. About May 10, a leading radioman from the Alexandria torpedo factory arrived at Pearl with a new set of adjustments to be made to the Mark VI which theoretically would cure its defects.

He talked a good game and we watched his experiments and tests with greatest interest. They seemed to have promise and I decided we would give his conversions a test for perhaps a month and then, if percentage of prematures did not decrease, I would ask Cincpac to inactivate the magnetic feature.

By this time Captain S. S. Murray, who had been my able Chief of Staff in the Southwest Pacific, had arrived at Pearl and had taken over the same billet from Captain John Griggs, who went to command the new Submarine Squadron 12, which was just being organized.

The situation seemed to be as well in hand as could be expected, so I took passage in *Finback*, Lieutenant Commander John A. Tyree of Danville, Virginia, for Midway on May 12. These four-day sea trips to Midway were a great relaxation to me. We were under radio silence from the time the submarine left Pearl, therefore I could send no messages, except in case of great emergency. This left all responsibility in the hands of my Deputy, Captain Brown, and allowed me to enter into the life of the submarine in which I happened to be embarked; to wander around while ship drills were going on; to talk to members of the crew; to absorb the spirit (non-alcoholic) of the wardroom mess—in short, to imagine myself once more an operating submarine officer.

One of the new navigational techniques, which had grown up during the war, was the taking of star sights long after sunset. In my day as a navigator, if the sky was overcast so one couldn't get star sights at morning or evening twilight while the horizon was still visible, the opportunity was lost forever.

Now this new generation of navigators, who hardly knew one star from another, except as identified by declination and azimuth from the star tables, would come up on the cigarette deck long after twilight with a prepared list of stars they intended to "shoot." They would take a round of five or six widely separated stars and, by crossing their lines of position, come out with a very accurate fix.

One night watching this procedure, I waited to see if the navigator would take an altitude of Polaris, the North Star, which was looking him right in the eye. Finally he finished taking sights and, as he was heading for the hatch, I said, "Did you get Polaris?"

"No, sir," he said, "she isn't up tonight." Many ancient navigators probably turned over in their graves on that one.

We arrived at Midway at daylight on Sunday and I was disappointed to find that in so far as completion of submarine facilities at Midway was concerned, very little progress had been made. The Seabees, upon whom depended most of our construction projects, had ben engaged chiefly on work for the aviators. The dredges, which I needed so badly to clear shoal patches alongside the dock, where I wanted to put the new tender, *Sperry,* with a squadron of submarines, were still dredging the lagoon to make it suitable for anchorage of a cruiser task force. Not being a War College graduate, I couldn't see how aviation or a cruiser task force could win the war from Midway, but I could see that this base as a place to refit simultaneously from eight to 20 submarines, thus speeding up their return to operating areas, could aid vitally in the economic strangulation of Japan.

A sheltered, all-weather refit basin, in which I could put

tenders and submarines, was a "must" to me. The contractors, who were doing the dredging, were on my side, for they urgently needed such a refuge into which they could move their equipment on the approach of winter storms.

With these thoughts turning over in my mind like maggots in a cheese, I went into a huddle with Cincpac's staff when I got back to Pearl. Cincpac's Chief of Staff was adamant and I finally asked if I might present the case to Admiral Nimitz in person.

"All right," was the answer, "if you want to keep on butting your head into a stone wall, go see Admiral Nimitz."

"Well, sir," I said, "I've butted my head into a lot of stone walls and I've still got it with me." So, accompanied by my towering, top-level brain-trusters, Captain Brown and Captain Sunshine Murray, we went up to Admiral Nimitz's office.

Our presentation of the situation must have been convincing, and I am sure the conviction which each of us felt in the urgency of our need, must have shown in our faces. Admiral Nimitz is a man who can always listen to an argument with an open mind, no matter how much previously established policies may be affected. The upshot was that he said, "It looks as though the situation needs to be re-studied." The re-study resulted in a directive to develop the cruiser anchorage area and the submarine refit basin on a basis of equal priority.

With that directive in the hands of the contractors, I knew I couldn't lose—not did I. During the remainder of the war, no cruiser ever entered Midway lagoon, even after anchorages had been provided, but hundreds of submarines did enter for refueling and scores were refitted. One of the first steps I took was to send out the *Sperry*, tender and flagship for Commander Subron 10, Captain Styer. She immediately dug herself into the job of refitting submarines, bringing our continuous refitting capacity up to eight boats.

The sinking scores for May were beginning to come in and, in spite of our prematures and duds, the results were the best thus far in the war. JANAC lists 34 enemy vessels sunk for that month, 30 by submarines for a tonnage of 128,138 —accounted for by 16 different submarines. All patrol areas were active—Palau, Sulu Sea, East China Sea, Yellow Sea, the Marianas, New Guinea, the Marshalls, and the Empire —and each contributed a quota.

Saury, Lieutenant Commander A. H. "Tony" Dropp of Milwaukee, Wisconsin, had high score with four down—including one 10,000-ton tanker in the East China Sea.

Plunger, Lieutenant Commander R. H. "Benny" Bass of Freer, Texas, came in with a story of relentless determination during a patrol in the Truk-Marianas area. Toward evening of May 8 she had contacted, north of Truk, a convoy of five large marus and two escorts, heading for Japan.

He was unable to attain firing position at that time, but after dark he surfaced, got ahead of his quarry and at 0300 of May 9, made a night periscope attack, which he believed resulted in a sinking as the sound operators reported hearing "breaking-up noises," i.e., rush of water into compartments, collapse of bulkheads, etc. When he surfaced, an hour or so later, no wreck could be found.

Daylight found *Plunger* at full speed on surface, scratching for position ahead. In spite of the fact that the convoy was within 200 miles of Truk and only 390 miles from Saipan, no enemy planes arrived to spoil the game. At 1657, Bass was again in position. This time he divided his fire between the two largest targets and got two hits in each. The escorts counterattacked and held him down till sunset. On surfacing, three ships were in sight, two of them hull-down to the northwest and the third apparently sinking. Benny kept on after the two escapees and shortly before dawn fired four torpedoes for three hits.

At 0605 of May 10, from periscope depth Bass observed a large ship stopped, listing badly, while a small escort vessel stood by. With hope high in his heart, he stood in to finish off the cripple but, while maneuvering for position, he suddenly found that the last and biggest vessel of the convoy was lying to about 4,000 yards beyond the stricken ship. This seemed too good to be true and Benny immediately headed for this new target.

At 0825, when *Plunger* was still 3,000 yards away, the big passenger-cargo ship evidently realized the foolhardiness of her action and got underway. *Plunger* fired two torpedoes, both of which hit, and the ship started down immediately. Bass had now three torpedoes remaining, plus a determination to get that last ship. He had had no rest or sleep, and precious little food, for two days but he was too excited to think about such commonplace things. He had wiped out most of this convoy, but he had to make it a clean sweep, so he would be entitled to steam into Pearl Harbor flying a broom at the masthead.

Enemy planes arrived at 1020 in the morning to complicate the problem but, at 1245, Bass fired two torpedoes, heard both of them thud against the target's side—but no explosions! One torpedo remained. An hour later, *Plunger* came back to periscope depth to see what might be going on. The situation was much the same, except that the target appeared to be abandoned. At 1351 Benny fired his last torpedo and this time got an explosion under the smokestack. The escort vessel, evidently worn out or out of depth charges, dropped only one ash can and then retired to a safe distance.

Plunger kept the damaged ship under observation all day, but the escort also remained in the vicinity, so Bass could not surface and use his gun. However, that night he did surface and sent me a message asking if the submarine in the next area could come in and finish off his cripple.

Immediately we got off a message to the *Whale*, I think it was, but next morning had to cancel it. At daylight of May 11, *Plunger* had found the escort absent and proceeded to riddle the big ship with 180 rounds of 3-inch shell and 1,000 rounds of 20-mm ammunition. She was abandoned and burning. *Plunger* passed close under her stern and read her name —*Asaka Maru*.

May ended with a bang, about 200 yards from my office. A huge column of water rose from the midde of the crowded harbor and the accompanying detonation rattled our teeth. I was just leaving my office for Cincpac's daily morning conference, where I told Admiral Nimitz that it was probably a Jap torpedo war head, a relic of December 7, which somehow had been jarred into action. Imagine my embarrassment when I got back to my office and the bad news was definitely known; *Searaven* had accidentally fired a live torpedo from a stern tube! Fortunately it had hit bottom and exploded. Had it continued on its course, it would have blown up a dock in the Navy Yard; had it deviated slightly to the right, a nice new cargo ship would have lost her bow— and I could have lost my job! The *Searaven*'s torpedo crew had been drilling a new man in firing "water slugs," i.e., blowing out a tubeful of water from an empty tube in simulation of a war shot. By an almost unforgivable mistake, a tube containing a torpedo, complete with war head, was used.

No harm was done and we learned a good lesson very cheaply.

By this time submarines were doing all sorts of diversified duty. *Tautog*, Lieutenant Commander W. B. Sieglaff, contributed an interesting incident from "down under." On her seventh patrol she had been assigned the additional mission of landing two Javanese Mohammedans on the coast of Kabaena Island, off the Southern Celebes. One of the men was a well-to-do landowner from Java and his colleague was a teacher, high in standing in Moslem circles by virtue of 17 pilgrimages to Mecca. Their mission was to land on Kabaena Island, where an influential relative of the landed Javanese could furnish the necessary papers to permit them to travel from island to island and spread the word that relief from the Japanese occupation was coming.

Three times daily the couple prayed toward Mecca and it was necessary for the navigator or officer of the deck to furnish them with the relative bearing of that holy place on each occasion. At night, prayer rugs were brought topside to perform this ritual under the open skies.

The Moslems were very interested in American jazz and eagerly awaited surfacing at night, when the wardroom radio was turned on. They were so moved on one occasion that they asked if they might contribute a song of their own. Commander Sieglaff replied it would indeed be a pleasure to hear them, whereupon the two men broke into song—"From the Halls of Mon-te-zu-ma to the shores of Tripoli . . . !" It developed that they had lived in a Marine camp in Australia and they were very proud of their knowledge of fine American songs.

Canned tuna and salmon had been brought along as a principal and necessary ingredient of the Mohammedan diet but, as a variation, one day the mess treasurer offered some canned lobster at the wardroom table. The passengers gave every indication that this was the finest delicacy they had ever tasted. It was with reluctance, mutual respect, and admiration that *Tautog* parted with the two agents when they were put ashore.

My old friend and one time shipmate on the battleship *California*, Major General Holland M. Smith, arrived early in June fresh from Marine training activities at San Diego. I thought he had aged somewhat, which was not surprising in view of the years of struggle he had spent in the Caribbean and elsewhere, building up training for amphibious forces to a point where it was really effective.

That was the reason he had been ordered to the Pacific as Commander Fleet Marine Force, to plan and organize the amphibious part of our coming advance across the Pacific. His fighting spirit showed no sign of aging and he was as full of pep and ginger as ever—and not very happy about the part in which he had been cast. He wanted a corps of his own in the South Pacific and a more personal part in cleaning up the Japs.

General Smith, always a very forthright gentleman who called spades by their right name, said he had heard a rumor back in the States that we immediately detached from his ship any submarine commanding officer who came back without sinking enemy tonnage.

I was surprised and disturbed that such a rumor should be afloat, for we certainly leaned over backward in giving each skipper a chance to show his worth. If, after trials in different areas, including those normally highly productive, the submarine was still unlucky in the matter in making hits or in finding targets, I acted upon the advice of the division and squadron commanders and sometimes changed the quarterback just as a coach would in a football game.

The sinking scores for June kept rolling in and it began to look like a record month, but JANAC reports only 26 ships sunk for a total of 105,108 tons. Two of these were sunk by other forces—one by an "unknown agent"—however this nearly fulfilled the "one ship per day" schedule for which I had been striving for many moons.

The most exciting attack turned out to be no sinking at all, but it was a milestone in our war against our defective exploder mechanism. On June 11, *Trigger*, Commander Roy Benson of Concord, New Hampshire, patrolling 25 miles south of the entrance to Tokyo Bay, sighted a Jap carrier with two destroyers as escorts and some air cover, standing his way. The situation developed beautifully and *Trigger* bored in to an ideal position 1,200 yards on the target's starboard bow. Unfortunately, the destroyer on that side was behind the usual screening position, in fact, it was well back on the carrier's beam. This put *Trigger* in a dangerous position directly ahead of the destroyer, nevertheless, Benson commenced firing his six bow tubes and saw two explosions before he had to duck his periscope and head for deep submergence to escape the depth charges which rained down in his close vicinity from 2000 until 0100 the next morning.

Due to the early daybreak at that season, *Trigger* was able only to get about an hour's charge into her depleted battery before it was necessary to submerge.

Roy told me that the two explosions which he saw were at the correct time for his first two torpedoes. The plumes of water were forward of the carrier's bridge, but no debris went up in them, hence I felt certain they were prematures. He had heard the explosion of the next two torpedoes after ducking his periscope. These hits, if they were hits, should have been abaft the carrier's bridge. Presumably, torpedoes number five and six passed astern. We learned afterward that the 28,000-ton *Hitaka* was towed back to port badly down by the stern. Had all four explosions been under her hull, she probably would have sunk. As it was, she lived to fight again and was finally sunk by carrier planes from Admiral Spruance's Fifth Fleet in the First Battle of the Philippine Sea.

The question uppermost in all our minds was whether or not the Japs had devised some sort of equipment which detonated our torpedoes before they reached their mark. Were the hulls of their ships highly magnetized to induce explosions at a safe distance from their sides? Were their ships towing some sort of a paravane from their bows, which trailed an electrified wire and thus detonated our magnetic exploders? If they were employing such protective measures, certainly they would install them first in their most valuable ships—aircraft carriers—and here, in two recent attacks against carriers, *Tunny* and *Trigger* had suffered an almost unbelievable number of prematures.

The paravane theory appeared the more tenable. In *Trigger*'s attack, for instance, her first two torpedoes exploding near the device might have destroyed it, thus permitting the next two torpedoes to reach the target. In any case, it seemed that inactivation of the magnetic feature of our Mark VI exploder was an immediate must. I called a conference of all my top torpedo personnel and the vote was unanimous to issue orders to that effect.

First, however, I must have authority from Cincpac. I therefore went to see Cincpac's Gunnery Officer, Captain Tom Hill, who called in Lieutenant Commander Ellis A. Johnson (in civil life a mathematical physicist at the Carnegie Institute, Washington, D.C.). The latter had just returned from the Navy Department, bringing with him a copy of a rough-drafted letter which was "being processed" around the Bureau of Ordnance. This remarkable document, although not in final officially approved form, raised so many questions and was so full of qualifications as to the proper magnetic heading of the target and the magnetic latitude in which the exploder should be used, as to cast grave doubts on the feasibility of installing any type of magnetic exploder in torpedoes.

Tom Hill was highly in favor of deactivation, in fact, he had broached the subject to me before, but at that time I was reluctant to lose the value of the magnetic features—especially for down-the-throat shots—and had a hope its defects could be cured. Together, we went to Admiral Nimitz and after hearing our arguments, he directed me to issue the necessary orders for inactivation. I left his office feeling that a great weight had been lifted from my shoulders and from those of the Submarines Pacific Fleet.

Commander Submarines Southwest Pacific did not follow suit in this matter. Rear Admiral Christie was one of the fathers or godfathers of this exploder and was determined to make it work. Therefore, the submarines "down under" struggled along with it for about another year. At times their percentage of prematures was as high as 13.5.

A personal letter from Admiral Spike Blandy, placing a period at the end of this discouraging chapter, was typical of the forthright character of a damned fine officer. "Before signing off," he concluded, "I want to say once more that this Bureau is not a closed corporation. I wish the submariners would look on it as their bureau as much as the rest of the Navy's . . . Every other type of craft is well represented here: aircraft, carriers, battleships, destroyers—even PT boats and Marines, but you fellows have for the most part stayed on the outside and cussed. Come on in; the water may not be fine, but we'll share it with you." From then on, we did a great deal of sharing.

At long last, four exercise Mark XVIII torpedoes made their appearance in the Hawaiian area. This was the electric type manufactured by Westinghouse at Sharon, Pennsylvania, and was a "Chinese copy" of the German electric torpedo. Unfortunately, we had felt it necessary to improve on the model and, in so doing, had run into difficulties.

The first five "handmade" copies had been available to

the Bureau of Ordnance and the Torpedo Station, Newport for experiments in June, 1942. There the job had bogged down and it was not until a year later that the first four arrived at Submarine Base, Pearl. These torpedoes were slower than our "steam" types, but they left no trail of bubbles as did the others, a very important consideration to the submarine skipper, who wanted no telltale wake to lead antisubmarine craft to the spot from which the torpedo had been fired.

Hence, all hands eagerly awaited these new "fish." They were pretty much "raw material" when they arrived: the storage batteries generated hydrogen, for which there was no escape, thus causing explosions; the rudder posts were of steel, which corroded and produced erratic steering or circular runs; the space left for electrolyte over the tops of the storage battery plates was so shallow that frequent withdrawal from the tubes was necessary to permit watering batteries; and they frequently knocked their tail vanes off on the tube shutters when fired.

I was apprehensive about the effect of a heavy explosion of hydrogen in one of these Mark XVIII torpedoes fully ready for a war shot. Would the shock of such an explosion be sufficient to detonate the TNT (or Torpex, which was now being substituted for TNT) loaded war head? The best way to find out was to try it and see.

First, however, we decided to try an explosion without a war head, just to see what damage would be done to the torpedo. So we put a torpedo out in the middle of the baseball diamond, charged it with hydrogen, and then assembled behind some sandbags to observe the explosion.

I checked up on the arrangements and was informed by the lieutenant in charge, Lieutenant Leon I. Ross, USNR, of Newark, New Jersey, just what percentage of hydrogen the torpedo's battery compartment contained. He told me the percentage, 28, and added that such a percentage would produce an explosion of maximum violence.

I said jokingly, "What amateur chemist figured this out?"

He replied, "I did, but I'm not exactly an amateur. In normal times, I teach chemistry at Yale."

That seemed good enough, so we pushed the firing contact, but no explosion resulted. We tried again, checking the circuit, still no result.

Finally Lieutenant Ross said he would have to check the

whole thing over again, so I went back to my paper work. About an hour later I was informed all was ready and I went out to the ball park. "What was the matter, Lieutenant?" I asked. His head drooped, "Well, sir, the gas bottle was incorrectly marked. We had filled the torpedo with nitrogen!"

The explosion badly damaged the torpedo but it was not violent. However, the next day we took an old torpedo tube out into the algarroba thicket near Barbers' Point, put a torpedo into it, complete with war head, and charged the battery compartment with hydrogen. Then, from a safe distance, we pressed the firing key. The resulting explosion was hardly audible and, although the forward bulkhead of the battery compartment had been forced violently into the TNT of the war head, the shock had not been sufficient to detonate it. With this demonstration, I felt safe in sending the Mark XVIII out on patrol.

Our torpedo shop personnel designed a hydrogen eliminator, consisting of a red-hot nichrome wire, which burned up the hydrogen as it was generated. The other defects took longer to correct but, before the end of the war, fully 65 per cent of the torpedoes fired were Mark XVIII's. We allowed each skipper to select his own type of torpedoes and, despite its slower speed, the electric fish was the favorite weapon.

CHAPTER 7

The Sea of Japan was, we believed, crowded with enemy shipping. Early in July, *Permit, Plunger* and *Lapon* entered via La Perouse Strait, north of Japan, and took up widely separated stations. Where we had expected our submarines to find an abundance of targets, they found few worth the expenditure of a $10,000 torpedo.

Lapon, patrolling the Shimonoseki-Korea shipping lanes, encountered heavy fog and contacted only sampans. *Permit* and *Plunger* sank two cargo ships and a passenger-cargo vessel in the northern part of the Sea. By mistake, *Permit* also sunk a Russian trawler.

The scarcity of targets indicated that the Japanese had transferred most of their available bottoms from the Sea to ocean routes in order to loot as much oil, rubber, tin and other war supplies as possible from the Netherlands East Indies, Malaya and the Philippines before our inevitable counteroffensive. Therefore, I decided not to continue these operations in the Sea of Japan unless we had definite indications of better hunting.

After four days on station inside, the boats had orders to withdraw by the same route they had entered, before the enemy could organize effective countermeasures and perhaps block the exit. This withdrawal was timed for the date on which *Narwhal* was to create a diversion by making a surface bombardment of Matsuwa airfield, in the Kuriles.

Narwhal ran into difficulties at Matsuwa, where heavy fog conditions prevailed. On the afternoon of July 14, visibility bettered and despite the presence of a small patrol vessel close inshore, Commander Latta "battle surfaced" 7,000 yards from the airstrip, only to have the visibility drop to 2,000 yards before he could fire a shot. The next evening *Narwhal* again surfaced, this time at 14,000 yards, and opened fire with her two 6-inch guns. Hits were observed in the hangar area and one large fire was started. The enemy shore batteries returned heavy fire and Commander Latta broke off the action and submerged.

The mistake made by *Permit*, Lieutenant Commander W. G. "Moon" Chapple, which I mentioned above, was the sinking of a Russian seiner in the Sea of Japan on July 9 near the southwest tip of Karafuto. During the afternoon, *Permit* sighted a ship and dived to make an approach. Since Russian ships might be found in that vicinity, Chapple decided to look her over before attacking. He therefore passed her on an opposite course, at a range of 1,200 yards. The vessel appeared to be an unarmed trawler, radio-equipped. No flag could be seen and there were no special markings on the side. *Permit* battle surfaced 1,800 yards on the trawler's quarter and opened rapid fire with her 4-inch gun, closing the range as she fired. When about 800 yards distant, a man and a woman were seen in the bow waving a white flag.

Chapple ceased fire, closed in and discovered it was a Russian not a Japanese ship. He took off 13 survivors, one of whom died very soon after being brought aboard. Five of the Russians were women, three of whom had shrapnel wounds. The trawler had been holed in six or seven places and sank. Moon immediately reported the situation to me and stated that he proposed to land his passengers at Petropavlosk on

Kamchatka. I thought that Dutch Harbor would be a better place to leave them, thus avoiding any possible international argument. From there they could be transferred to a Russian ship passing through Cold Bay. The Russians might think differently about the sinking. I reported the matter to Admiral Nimitz and he concurred.

Chapple turned over the forward torpedo room to the women and made all as comfortable as possible. Moon, the six-foot-two, ex-wrestling champion at the Academy, told me that the women said good-bye to him at Dutch with tears in their eyes and that the Russian skipper in his official report did not say his ship had been sunk by an American submarine. He merely said the trawler had been shelled by an unidentified submarine and that an American sub had taken off the survivors. Certainly, Moon must have been a very charming host.

Up from the Southwest Pacific came reports of submarine activities in collaboration with guerrilla forces in the Philippines. *Trout*, Lieutenant Commander A. H. Clark, had evacuated Lieutenant Commander Charles "Chick" Parsons, USNR, and four officers from the south coast of Mindanao. *Thresher*, Lieutenant Commander H. Hull, landed a commando party of four, with 5,000 pounds of stores and 20,000 rounds each of 30- and 45-caliber ammunition, on the west coast of Negros. This very secret activity started in January, 1943, when *Gudgeon*, Lieutenant Commander W. S. Stovall, Jr., landed Major Villamor and five Filipinos, with a ton of special equipment, on the west coast of Negros. In March, *Tambor*, Lieutenant Commander S. H. Ambruster, landed "Chick" Parsons with thousands of rounds of rifle and pistol ammunition, plus $10,000 in currency, on the south coast of Mindanao. Parsons had been President of the Luzon Stevedoring Company and spoke the native dialects fluently. General MacArthur put him in charge of contacting and supplying the guerrillas and throughout the entire war he was in and out of the Philippines at will, in spite of the price which the Japs had put on his head.

With Midway developing nicely and a scheme being figured out for connecting it to Pearl by teletype, I considered the time ripe for requesting permission to shift my own headquarters to that base. Admiral Nimitz heard all my arguments courteously but did not agree with me. He felt that Midway's activities could be handled by one of my squadron

commanders and that my proper place was near his own
headquarters.

He said that the time would undoubtedly come when he
would want to move west, but he was not considering Midway in that connection. I was disappointed at the time, but
later was glad to be close to Cincpac—especially to his FRU-
PAC (Fleet Radio Unit Pacific), whose intelligence items,
hot off the air, were relayed by Captain W. J. "Jasper"
Holmes over a private wire to my Operations Room.

On July 20 the *Runner,* Lieutenant Commander J. H.
Bourland, was reported "overdue and presumed lost." She
had been assigned an area off the northeast coast of Honshu
and we know from postwar reports that she sank a cargo ship
and a passenger-cargo vessel. The cause of her loss is not
known even now. The areas on the east coast of Hokkaido
and the northeast coast of Honshu had been disappointing in
results and with two submarines lost there, we decided to
abandon them until we had better information on their antisubmarine defenses.

The sinkings for July showed a distinct drop, one gunboat, one submarine and 17 merchantmen constituted the
bag. Captain Frank Watkins, a division commander, had
taken out the *Flying Fish* while her regular skipper, Donk
Donaho, was making a speaking tour of the training centers
back in the U.S. Frank had few contacts and sank one ship
off Foochow.

I raised a question with the Bureau of Ordnance regarding the weight and type of explosive carried in Japanese
war heads. Enemy destroyer torpedoes were creating such
havoc with our destroyers and cruisers, whereas our submarines were lucky if one hit would blow a merchant ship in
two. Larger ships frequently got back to port after being hit
two or three times. Should the Bureau of Ordnance consider
increasing the size and power of our war heads? The Bureau's
reply to this question was that they were already carrying the
equivalent of 1,000 pounds of TNT—twice as much as they
contained when we began the war. Their new explosive admittedly was better, and we knew that tremendous heads
were planned for the newest type torpedo, but that fish was
always "just around the corner" and never got into the war.

Disturbing reports kept coming in of duds and suspected
duds with our long-accursed Mark VI exploder, whose magnetic feature was now deactivated. One skipper reported he

had hit a freighter "with two air flasks," meaning that the compressed air flasks, but not the war head, had exploded. Earlier in the war the *Salmon* actually punched a hole in a ship with a dud torpedo and sank her.

I am grateful that this trouble did not drag through long, weary months as the former trouble had done, but was brought quickly to a head by the astounding bad luck of the *Tinosa*, Lieutenant Commander L. R. "Dan" Daspit, of Houma, Louisiana, who returned from patrol on August 6.

Dan, while patrolling in the Truk area, encountered the 19,000-ton "whale factory" *Tonan Maru*, sailing alone, and attacked from periscope depth in broad daylight with a salvo of four torpedoes on a 95-degree track, i.e., practically perpendicular to the target's course. At least two of the torpedoes hit but failed to explode. The target put on speed and turned away but Daspit fired the remaining two torpedoes from his forward tube nest and got two good hits and explosions aft which stopped the tanker. These last two torpedoes had struck the target at an obtuse angle—and there was the key to the whole problem, had we but realized it. Those striking the target squarely, dudded; those which struck a glancing blow, exploded.

Dan, a careful observer whose calm is seldom ruffled, now proceeded with the job of sinking his quarry. He could not surface and use his gun, for the enemy also had guns, and Daspit did not want to waste torpedoes. He took a position 875 yards on the target's beam and fired one torpedo. It was heard to strike the enemy hull and the skipper observed a large splash at the point of aim—but no war head explosion. Then followed a heartbreaking series of eight more duds, all from carefully selected positions—positions we had always considered ideal. With 11 duds, Daspit naturally concluded there was something very rotten in the state of Denmark so he saved his remaining torpedo for us to examine and returned to Pearl.

When he arrived in my office, Dan was the nearest to being boiling mad I have ever seen him. I expected a torrent of cuss words, damning me, the Bureau of Ordnance, the Newport Torpedo Station and the Base Torpedo Shop, and I couldn't have blamed him—19,000-ton targets don't grow on bushes. I think Dan was so furious as to be practically speechless. His tale was almost unbelievable, but the evidence was undeniable. *Tinosa*'s last remaining torpedo was examined with the utmost care and no defect could be found. When tested, its detonator fired normally.

We wracked our collective brains over the problem and several theories were advanced, which were pretty close to the solution at which we arrived some days later. Meanwhile Captain C. B. "Swede" Momsen, inventor of the Momsen Lung for escape from a sunken submarine and always full of practical ideas, came to my office. He proposed that we take a load of torpedoes, all ready for war shots, down to the little island of Kahoolawe and shoot them against its vertical cliffs which rise sheer from the sea with perhaps 50 feet of water at their base. At the first dud, we would cease firing, recover it and see what we could find out. A thoroughly practical idea, but I suspected we would find ourselves shaking hands with St. Peter when we tried to examine a dud war head loaded with 685 pounds of TNT. However, Admiral Nimitz gave his permission and *Muskallunge* departed Pearl for Kahoolawe and fired three torpedoes against the cliffs. The first two exploded, the third dudded. Then Swede Momsen, Lieutenant Commander H. A. "Pie" Pieczentkowski and I, went down to the scene in the submarine rescue vessel *Widgeon*, with the *Chalcedony* as escort.

The entire crew of the escort apparently were expert "skin" divers from Oahu for, when we went aboard to ask for some assistance in locating this dud torpedo, the skipper, Lieutenant Commander Castle, the Executive, Lieutenant (jg) Love and the boatswain's mate, John Kelly, son of the Honolulu artist, got into their trunks and goggles and climbed into the dory with us. Then followed a delightful morning of swimming about in the surf at the foot of the cliffs until finally Kelly located the torpedo, and by some very expert diving—during which he went down to 55 feet without benefit of suit or helmet and shackled a line to the torpedo's tail—we got the dud aboard the *Widgeon*. The war head was crushed in at the forward end and, when we got the exploder mechanism out of it, we found the firing pin had actually traveled up its badly bent guides and hit the fulminate caps, but not hard enough to set them off.

With the trouble located, all hands turned to on the job of eliminating it. By dropping dummy war heads, with an exploder in them, 90 feet from a "cherry picker" onto a steel plate, (to approximate the speed of striking) we quickly found that every 90-degree impact resulted in a dud. If the plate were slanted at, say, a 45-degree angle, perhaps half were duds. This information was sent out immediately to the submarines at sea, urging them to fire their torpedoes at sharp or oblique angles to the path of the target—anything but a 90-degree track.

For weeks we ate, slept and dreamed exploders. Captain Perley Pendleton of the *Holland,* Commander Tom Eddy of the Base, Lieutenant Commander Johnson of the Service Force and many other officers and enlisted men contributed to the modifications which in three weeks' time produced an acceptable, safe and sure-fire contact exploder.

What a load of anxiety that lifted from all our shoulders! I felt that the dozen or so exploder mechanisms which we had wrecked—at about $830 each—had not been expended in vain.

Finally, when I was sure of my ground, I went to Admiral Nimitz, who had been following our experiments very closely, and asked permission to send a boatload of these modified exploders on patrol. He gave permission unhesitatingly. Cominch, Admiral King, who was making one of his periodic inspections of the Pacific, was with Cincpac at the time and both agreed we should go into large-scale production at once.

On September 30, 1943, *Barb,* Lieutenant Commander Johnny Waterman, left the Submarine Base at Pearl, with 20 torpedoes equipped with the new modified exploders, and all major exploder troubles suddenly ended.

August and September netted four men-of-war and 50 merchant ships, a total tonnage of 218,767. Thirty boats made these kills at points which covered the entire Pacific, Sea of Japan, Yellow Sea, East China Sea, Indo-China, Makassar Strait, Molucca Strait, Java Sea, Palau, Truk, Marshalls, Marianas and the Kuriles.

With less than 100 submarines in the Pacific, plus 18 S-type on patrol in the Kuriles or supplying services for training to escort vessels and using our new exploder, we made the Pacific a graveyard for enemy shipping.

Trigger, Lieutenant Commander R. E. "Dusty" Dornin of Mill Valley, California, sank two cargo ships and two tankers in the East China Sea for a total of 27,000 tons. Three of these Dusty sank in a single night. *Bonefish* and *Snook* each got a 10,000-ton transport, but, other than these, the victims were of moderate size. The *Harder,* Commander

Samuel D. "Sam" Dealey of Dallas, Texas, on her second patrol, in the areas south of Honshu, the main island of the Japanese Archipelago, sank five ships, including the 5,878-ton tanker *Daishin Maru*. Tankers were at the top of our priority list.

Two submarines were lost during this period: *Grayling,* Lieutenant Commander R. M. Brinker, and *Pompano*, Lieutenant Commander W. M. Thomas. How the *Grayling* was lost, we do not know, but postwar reports show she sank a 5,500-ton passenger-cargo ship near Verde Island Passage in the Philippines. The cause of *Pompano*'s loss is also unknown but it is believed she struck a mine in the area northeast of Honshu. She sank two cargo ships on that last fatal patrol.

During the first part of August, Captains Andy McKee and Armand Morgan, our top-notch submarine designers, paid us a visit at Pearl and continued on to Midway. They were full of useful ideas about increasing our fuel and torpedo capacity. Their stay was not of the "24-hour expert" type and we both benefited.

Commander Fred W. Beltz, of the Bureau of Ships, whose main job was locating and chasing submarine spare parts out to the Pacific, also paid us a visit during the very hectic autumn period. Spare parts were at such a premium that nothing was ever scrapped until the last possibility of repair, and use as a spare, had been exhausted.

Certainly the importance of spare parts in wartime should be inscribed indelibly on our memories.

Not so reassuring was the visit of another delegation from the Navy Department, whose mission was to impress us with the alleged fact that submarines needed formidable AA defenses. They pointed out that a German submarine had been encountered which was equipped with double-decked AA batteries of 11 guns, sized from 87 mm down. When Japanese air power grew to more formidable proportions, what were we going to do? A proposal had been made to us from the Navy Department, regarding installation of a "flower pot" on our decks aft. This eight-ton monstrosity was to fire a rocket into the blue, which would trail a wire intended to foul the propeller of an attacking plane. Naturally, by that time the plane already would have launched its weapon and the entangling wire would be merely revenge. In that I was not interested—besides, I had seen fields of these gadgets in England, designed to protect airstrips, and knew that the aviators reposed little confidence in them. Even the visiting delegation was not sold on this idea.

However, they did feel that we should have a 40-mm or 20-mm watertight turret on deck aft, which could defend the submarine from air attack, while in that critical condition between running on surface and running submerged. That also I did not want.

I still felt that the submarine's best defense against ships or aircraft was submergence and all we needed was a good radar to inform us when planes were approaching. If submarines were to be cluttered up with so much defensive gear that their torpedo-carrying capacity would be impaired and their silhouettes increased, then, having destroyed much of their offensive character, we might just as well keep them in port.

We were living in a period when Japanese air power had reached its peak and probably was on the decline. If we had not required such cumbersome defenses during that peak, why should we send submarines to navy yards for long installation jobs when the need for the proposed equipment was unlikely to arise? The services of all the submarines I could muster were urgently required "out front."

The upshot of the whole argument was that Admiral King ordered me to develop multiple barreled AA mounts which could be operated from the conning tower and directed through the periscope. The idea was excellent, but development ran into many snags and had not been completed when the war ended.

During the first part of August *Saury*, Lieutenant Commander A. H. "Tony" Dropp, returned to Pearl looking as though her periscope shears had run foul of a cyclone. On her previous patrol in the East China Sea she had piled up a fine score of 19,936 tons which included a big tanker, but this time misfortune overtook her. While making a night attack at periscope depth, a destroyer suddenly loomed up in the gloom, heading right for *Saury* and, before Tony could reach a safe depth, crashed into the shears. Evidently the Jap skipper did not realize he had struck a submarine for he dropped no depth charges.

A single ash can at that point might have ended *Saury*'s career.

So many things happened at this period, that I shall make no attempt to set them down in order of relative importance. The situation looked very rosy indeed with the increased effectiveness of our torpedo and the build-up of confidence in it. The resultant increase in sinkings put us all on the crest of a wave of enthusiasm such as I had never before witnessed.

Mush Morton of *Wahoo*, and Benny Bass of *Plunger* insisted that they be allowed to penetrate into the Sea of Japan again, via La Perouse Strait, even though not yet equipped with the new exploder. They entered without difficulty, following the route used by Russian shipping. Both ships reported poor torpedo performance but Bass managed to sink two cargo ships. These are included in my August-September summary. *Wahoo*'s luck was very bad and the performance of his torpedoes completely baffled Morton who, in desperation finally asked to come home for examination and checking of his fish.

Naturally, I granted permission and he arrived after a record-breaking 11-day run. Mush was boiling mad. He had found plenty of targets but a combination of deep running and duds had broken him down. His decision to return and make a new start with re-checked torpedoes was a wise one. All Morton wanted was a quick turn around, a load of our new torpedoes, the Mark XVIII electric, and an area in the Sea of Japan. The *Sawfish*, Lieutenant Commander E. T. "Gene" Sands of Texarkana, Texas, was almost ready for sailing and also wanted a crack at the Sea of Japan with the new torpedo. They entered that area in the last days of September.

Kiska was occupied on August 15, after extensive preparation, only to find that the Japanese had evacuated. There were a lot of red faces in both Army and Navy over that fiasco. This left our submarine squadron commander in Dutch Harbor, Commander F. O. Johnson, free to move out to the new base he had selected at Pyramid Cove, Attu. From there, operations in the Kuriles and the frigid Sea of Okhotsk would be greatly facilitated. Cincpac had directed that a new full-scale base, such as the one at Dutch Harbor, was not to be set up, therefore we pleaded for, and finally obtained, the old submarine tender *Beaver*.

With Commander Johnny Jaynes, of New York City, in command of the detachment, an advance base at Attu was established in October, 1943. A few quonset huts, with machine tools from our base at Kodiak, constituted a minimum shore establishment.

The radar PPI scope (Position Plan Indicator) made its appearance about this time and Cincpac very generously assigned to Subpac 12 radar specialists to operate and instruct submariners in the use of our new equipment. These new lads were excellent, many of them graduates of technological colleges, and all but one eventually became qualified submarine officers. Future supply of these specialists was insured by assignment of 25 to each class at the Submarine School in New London. I went out for exercises in *Snook,* Lieutenant Commander C. O. "Chuck" Triebel, on August 14, to see the radar operate and was delighted with its effectiveness. Triebel made excellent use of his new equipment on the patrol for which he was then training.

In the afternoon of September 20, Flight 321 arrived at Pearl from the South Pacific. Its distinguished passenger, about whose identity much secrecy had been observed, proved to be Mrs. Franklin D. Roosevelt. Admiral Nimitz had directed me to prepare quarters at the Royal Hawaiian Hotel and to see if I could find an Anglo-Saxon maid for her. The secrecy of the operation being what it was—although I heard various hints that indicated quite a lot of people were in the know—I had to make several discreet inquiries before a lucky tip put me on the right track. I manned the telephone and Walter Dillingham generously volunteered the services of Mrs. Dillingham's maid, a woman of Scotch ancestry. I sent my own steward to set up her mess, much to his pleasure. He had served Mrs. Hoover when she traveled on the *Maryland.* Our assistant operations officer, Lieutenant Larry Doheny, acted as her escort and guide.

Mrs. Roosevelt remained until the 22nd, when she took off for San Francisco. At the Royal Hawaiian she impressed all hands with her graciousness and charm. She carried a tray at the cafeteria and sat wherever her fancy inclined. At a quiet dinner for her at Admiral Nimitz's quarters on the eve of her departure, seven flag officers were present but no other ladies. She was much at ease and made us feel likewise. She said the hotel was fine and when I asked whether she considered the men had insufficient comforts or whether they were being pampered, she replied, "Neither," and amplified her remark to say they were getting just the right treatment.

The Royal Hawaiian was our most highly prized recuperation project. In early 1942 it had been leased from the Matson Company by authority of Admiral Nimitz and turned over to Comsubpac to staff and administer, Cincpac's directive assigned it as a recuperation center for submariners and aviators returning from combat operations. Naval Aviation officers had, in addition, a very comfortable residence on Kalakaua Avenue which had been loaned them by Mr. "Chris" Holmes, hence, not many of them made use of the Royal. The hotel had been arranged to accommodate about 150 officers and 1,000 enlisted men. Since there were seldom enough recuperating submariners or aviators at Pearl to fill all bunks, weekly quotas were made available to other seagoing forces present in the area. The Royal was organized as a part of the Submarine Base, Pearl and had an Officer in Charge, Lieutenant Commander F. A. McHugh, who had formerly been employed in large U.S. hotels.

A group of patriotic ladies of Honolulu, who called themselves the Waikiki Hostesses, had volunteered their assistance in adding the necessary feminine touches to our naval management to keep it from deteriorating into the class of a superbarracks. The original group, changes in which occurred as time went on, included, I believe: Mrs. Wayne Pflueger, Miss René Halbadl, Mrs. Forrest Pinkerton, Miss Wilhelmina Tenney, Mrs. Julie Weller, Mrs. A. Y. L. Ward, Mrs. Hazel Scott, and Mrs. Carl Allenbaugh. The Submarine Service deeply appreciated the thought and devotion they gave to our comfort.

Also of much importance to our efforts for personnel rehabilitation was the Honolulu Red Cross, of which Mrs. Herman Van Holt was the head. Hundreds of sweaters and other items of warm clothing were furnished by this very thoughtful organization to our submarines proceeding to frigid areas. Submarines scheduled to be on patrol during the Christmas season always received, before sailing, a box of presents plus small Christmas trees.

Lifeguarding—rescue of downed aviators by submarines —was born during August in a series of conferences during which training exercises for the coming Operation Galvanic, in the Gilbert Islands, were being planned. Rear Admiral Charles A. "Baldy" Pownall, then commanding carrier forces of the Pacific, was about to make a strike, chiefly for training purposes, on Marcus Island, some 1,100 miles southeast of Tokyo. The question was raised as to whether or not it would be possible to rescue his pilots, who might be downed at sea, rather than allow them to fall into the hands of the enemy. Hope of rescue would certainly add to the confidence and daring of the aviators in making their attacks. Baldy Pownall and I talked the thing over and decided that we could arrange a bit of cooperation.

Snook was about to sail from Midway en route to the Yellow Sea and could be diverted to a standby spot off Marcus. So it was scheduled, and, although *Snook* had no opportunity to pick up downed aviators, she was the first of scores to perform a like service for our brothers in the air.

The moving pictures of this strike taken with "gun cameras" by the flyers, were shown a few days later at Cincpac morning conference. Marcus certainly was caught with its pants down and took a severe pasting. *Steelhead* was on lifeguard station for the Gilberts strikes of September 20, but she also had no opportunity to effect rescues.

The first effective lifeguard duty was performed by *Skate*, Commander Gene McKinney, formerly of the *Salmon*, now enjoying the satisfaction of taking out a new ship. When Rear Admiral Montgomery's bombers and fighters struck Wake on October 6–7, *Skate* was on station so close to the beach that some of her rescues were performed under shellfire from shore batteries. Unfortunately, a Jap Zero caught her unawares by diving out of the overcast and *Skate*'s Executive Officer, Lieutenant (jg) W. E. Maxson, was wounded by a bullet in the back. By this time *Skate* had picked up two aviators. Upon being informed of Maxson's serious condition, Montgomery was asked by me to have a destroyer rendezvous with *Skate* and take off the wounded officer. *Skate* was informed of the rendezvous position and told that, in case a meeting was not effected, she was to proceed to Midway on completion of her special mission. The air strikes having been completed, and having been unable to contact the destroyer, *Skate* headed for Midway at best speed.

About this time, Admiral Montgomery radioed me giving the supposed position of nine aviators who had made forced landings. There was nothing for it but to send *Skate* back, a decision which was hard to make but which proved to be correct.

Lieutenant Maxson died of his wound the next morning, two days before the submarine could have reached Midway. *Skate,* combing the water about Wake on October 9 and 10, rescued four more Navy aviators. The last to be found was

Lieutenant Commander Mark A. Grant, an Air Group Commander.

Grant was perfectly sure he would be picked up and had amused himself planning his conversation with his rescuers. He decided the correct opening remark was, "Ah, Dr. Livingstone, I presume." However, when sighted, Grant was asleep in the bottom of his rubber boat. A hail from the sub aroused him and, in his excitement, he leaped overboard and swam to the *Skate*, leaving his shoes and a dental plate in the boat. On being helped up the side, his first remark was not the one he had rehearsed, but, "How are you boys fixed for water? I've still got half a canteenful!"

Somewhat later in the war his brother, Commodore Grant, was in command of the Naval Base at Majuro Atoll, where we established a submarine recuperation camp on Myrna Island. In the view of Commodore Grant, nothing was too good for submariners.

A similar thought was expressed by the *Lexington* to *Skate,* who had picked up some of the carrier's flyers. "Anything on the *Lexington* is yours for the asking," read the message. "If it's too big to carry away, we will cut it up into small parts!" From that time on, no important carrier strike was made without submarine lifeguards.

The *Puffer,* Lieutenant Commander M. J. Jensen of Sheboygan, Wisconsin, patrolling out of Fremantle, had a grueling depth charge experience in Makassar Strait on October 9–10. She submerged at daylight, 0525 on October 9, and conducted a submerged patrol in the narrow northern part of the strait. Later in the morning, a large merchantman with a Chidori-type destroyer escort came along and Jensen got two torpedo hits which stopped the cargo ship dead, but did not sink her. *Puffer* swung and fired two stern shots, one of which prematured. The other either missed or dudded.

About this time the Chidori got on the job and Jensen decided to haul clear and await a better opportunity. He did not go deep, which was unfortunate, for the escort laid a pattern of six charges close above him. Both the conning tower door and hatch were lifted off their seats by the explosions and admitted a terrifying amount of water before reseating. Several sea valves backed off their seats and the gaskets were blown out of the main engine air induction and ventilation valves. There was much minor damage to glass and cork insulation.

Puffer went deep but the Chidori was able to keep track of him, possibly because of oil leaks or by bubbles from the blown gaskets. Repeated attacks were made and at 1820 another escort vessel joined the party. By this time, *Puffer* was badly flooded, down by the stern and desperately struggling to keep depth control. Fortunately, all the depth charges exploded above her, but at times they forced the sub to dangerous depths. The last depth charges were dropped at 0115, October 10, but the destroyers, evidently having exhausted their supply, continued making "dry runs" above her until 1225 that afternoon, when they apparently withdrew, hoping, no doubt, that the submarine might surface or at least show a periscope.

Jensen wasn't taking any chances and it is lucky he did not, for no sooner had he emerged after dark, than *Puffer* made radar contact with a small vessel, probably a patrol boat still waiting for her. *Puffer,* however, was looking only for a bit of peace and quiet until she could re-charge the depleted storage battery and repair her damaged piping. Therefore, Jensen worked around behind the patrol until he reached a position where he had a land background against which the enemy radar would have difficulty in picking him up. This 31-hour working over of the *Puffer* is the most persistent depth charge attack of which we have record.

Wolf packs were the next order of business with us, now that we had sufficient numbers to cover most of the important trade routes and focal points. The size, protection, and defensive tactics of Japanese convoys were increasing to a point where a single submarine had not sufficient torpedoes to deal with the whole outfit—even if they stuck together—which they did not. At the first explosion the better-trained convoys scattered in every direction, which required endless high-speed chasing and many "end around" runs to pile up a respectable score. Three or four submarines acting together, after training in Babe Brown's "Convoy College," and equipped with radar, could handle such a situation.

Japanese convoys never approached the tremendous size of our own convoys to Europe, in which 80 or more ships might be assembled. The enemy convoys our submarines met probably never exceeded 15 ships—six or eight were the usual numbers. Hence, we did not need the huge wolf packs of 15 or 20 boats, which the Germans were employing. Besides, to my mind, a pack of that size was too unwieldy, especially if operated from a shore station, as the Germans attempted to do. The assembling of so large a number of submarines in one spot gave great advantage to our antisubmarine vessels and aircraft—the hunter-killer groups—and resulted in terrific losses to Admiral Doenitz.

As Admiral Dick Edwards, in a letter to me in August, 1943, summed it up in one of his typically cogent paragraphs, "Wolf packs are all right when used against sheep, but they are duck soup for the opposition if he is ready for them. Your old friend Doenitz lost most of his shirt last winter by sticking to that type of operation, in circumstances which he should have known were most inappropriate from his point of view." Doenitz was even then losing more of his wardrobe by continuing those tactics and by attempting to "shoot it out" with planes. I intended to adopt none of this technique.

One of Doenitz's chief handicaps was the fact that his submarine force was expanding so greatly and his boats were being expended so rapidly that his submarine crews were never able to achieve a high degree of perfection in training—and they got precious little rest and recuperation between patrols. Nor did we intend to attempt to direct our wolf-pack attacks from Pearl Harbor, beyond keeping them supplied with up-to-the-minute information on enemy movements.

Our wolf-pack leaders were sometimes division commanders seeking "the bubble reputation even at the cannon's mouth," plus relief from the daily grind of intensive training at our submarine bases. Usually, however, the senior submarine commander of the pack was given orders as "leader" and took charge when his submarines stood out for patrol. I expected pack leaders to carry out the doctrine learned at Convoy College and they acquitted themselves most creditably.

As I said back in April, 1943, in communications lay the key to this problem: all we required after that key had been provided was a sufficient number of submarines. We now had a sufficient number to initiate the operation. Convoys approaching Pearl were almost always attacked by our training wolf packs—after very definite warning. We attacked them to eastward of Oahu, because enemy periscopes were frequently sighted on the west side, sometimes in our training areas. There had been occasions on which a destroyer or escort vessel running as target for, say, three boats, had found that he was getting echo ranges from four. The order would then be given for all submarines to surface and when the three

Americans had surfaced the target vessel would proceed to depth charge the intruder.

Why these enemy submarines—for such they must have been in numerous instances—never fired torpedoes at anyone is a mystery to me, and a foolish mistake on their part. They were evidently sent there to observe movements in and out of Pearl and observe they did, for after the first few months of the war, no U.S. ship was ever fired at in the vicinity of Pearl Harbor or Midway.

Captain Swede Momsen was given command of the first wolf pack to leave Pearl. He had trained this particular pack and wanted a chance to prove the efficacy of his methods—a recognized procedure in the old peacetime target practice rules. How far away all those complicated rules seemed—war was much simpler! So we gave Swede orders and away he went, in *Cero,* which he had chosen as his command ship. *Shad* and *Grayback* completed the pack; the areas assigned were the East China and Yellow Seas, where good-sized convoys had been reported. The *Grayback,* Lieutenant Commander J. A. Moore, got two ships for a total of about 14,500 tons but the others, according to JANAC, drew blanks. The estimated kill of this pack, on return to Pearl, was five ships sunk and seven damaged. The three, which JANAC says did not sink, should be added to the damaged columns, making a final score of two sunk and nine damaged. Communications were still not good enough and simplification of code messages was initiated.

Repeated reports from submarines on patrol indicated that all was not lovely in the garden so far as our new Mark XVIII electric torpedo was concerned. Its teething troubles were not completely cured. In addition, its slow speed put it back in the class of the old Mark VIII, which I used to shoot in V-3 in 1928. With such slow speed, the data obtained by observation and tracking of the target needed to be very accurate. To skippers accustomed to the high-speed Mark XIV and to the wider margin of error permitted by that speed, this deficiency in the electric fish appeared almost unforgivable.

Erratic runs were reported which endangered the firing submarine; the handholes into its battery compartment were prone to leak; charging them, adding battery water to the cells and ventilating them was a man-killing job. A battery fire occurred in a torpedo in one tube of *Flying Fish,* which generated heat sufficient to melt the Torpex. The Torpedo Data

Computer was not designed for the slow speed of the Mark XVIII, so firing data had to be extrapolated.

The hair of our Base Torpedo Officer, Commander George K. Hodgkiss, which had almost returned to its normal color at the conclusion of the exploder troubles, again showed a tendency toward graying. It is no wonder that popularity for the electric fish came slowly. Nevertheless, we were determined to conquer this "mass of raw material," as we had conquered the Mark VI exploder—and eventually we did, largely by our own efforts.

My unscheduled, monthly trip to Midway had been delayed by the presence of top-command echelon personnel and numerous VIP's, including four U.S. Senators. A report came in from *Snook* that she would arrive at Midway about October 3, with several men wounded during a surface gun battle. There had been criticisms by old school submariners of our use of guns. These contended that putting a gun on a submarine encouraged her to take unwarranted chances. Perhaps this was true, but with torpedoes which would not perform well at shallow settings, the gun was the only means of destroying the numerous radio-equipped picket boats that formed a cordon about 600 miles off the Japanese Empire.

It seemed an opportune time for me to meet *Snook* on her arrival at Midway and get Triebel's story of the gunfight at first-hand. I therefore flew out in the regular bi-weekly NATS plane, past the towering cliffs of Kauai, and high over Nihau and French Frigate Shoals.

At Midway, *Snook* warped into her berth in a snappy fashion and Captain Triebel took us below to the wardroom. Over cups of coffee the skipper brought out his patrol report and ran through it with me. Only one of his men had been badly hurt—a broken femur—and arrangements had been made to send him immediately by plane to Pearl. As I surmised, the gun battle had been with an armed trawler which *Snook* had stopped with a 3-inch hit in the engine room. Sinking her with that small gun was a long job, and enemy aircraft might be expected to arrive shortly, so, when all return fire had been silenced, Triebel closed in the better to place his shots in the trawler's waterline. Thereupon a Jap, who had been playing possum, turned loose a burst from an automatic rifle. He was instantly mowed down but succeeded in wounding four of the gun's crew. I considered we had learned an excellent lesson fairly cheaply.

Snook was proceeding to Pearl the next noon, so I decided to take passage in her instead of returning by plane. The trip back was peaceful. The captain estimated they had sunk or damaged some 25,000 tons of enemy shipping—not a bad bag.

As we drew in to the dock at the Submarine Base at Pearl Harbor, the customary "Star Spangled Banner" flared forth from the band, then came three ruffles on the drums and three flourishes by the bugles—the honors due a Vice Admiral. This fanfare really didn't register beyond possibly a thought that the bandmaster and my Flag Lieutenant would have red faces when someone called their attention to their error. I climbed down from the bridge to meet Babe Brown, Sunshine Murray, Swede Momsen, Dick Voge and practically the entire Staff, all grinning and offering congratulations. Babe Brown handed me a dispatch which purported to come from Bupers, stating that the President had designated me as Commander Submarine Force, Pacific Fleet with the rank of Vice Admiral Raymond A. Spruance was designated to comshifted to some other job.

Actually I thought my Staff was pulling my leg—an exercise which I frequently applied to them—and it was not till I arrived at my desk in the bomb proof and found a congratulatory message from Admiral Nimitz, that I really believed this marvelous bit of good luck. That my promotion was just a way of commending the entire submarine force on their splendid performance, I knew full well. There was no real need for a Vice Admiral in submarines, as I had twice contended when the subject had been brought up in Washington correspondence. Unnecessary, perhaps, but damned pleasant to take!

CHAPTER 8

The Central Pacific war was now entering a period of island conquest. Our top priority project for October was planning Operation Galvanic—the invasion of the Gilbert Islands, Tarawa and Makin—with a target date of November 20. Vice Admiral Raymond A. Spruance was designated to command the Central Pacific Force; Rear Admiral Richmond

Kelly Turner was brought up from the South Pacific to command the amphibious forces, and Major General Holland M. Smith was to command the landing forces.

The submarines were to play an active part well ahead of the landing by photographing the principal objective, Betio Island in the Tarawa group; by obtaining current and tidal data there, and by landing a detachment of four Marine officers and 74 men at Apamama, some 90 miles south of Tarawa.

Nautilus, Lieutenant Commander W. D. "Bill" Irvin of Glenside, Pennsylvania, was assigned to this first job and, after conferences with Kelly Turner, Holland Smith and Captain Carl Moore, Spruance's Chief of Staff, we sent her off during the second week of October. Cameras for periscope work were scarce but fortunately Lieutenant Commander "Ozzie" Lynch, Executive Officer of *Nautilus*, had a Leica of his own, which did a fine job. This was the first time that panoramic views of landing beaches were made and, from then on, it was a standard operation prior to each new invasion.

When *Nautilus* finished her panoramic periscope pictures, she ran them back to Johnson Island whence they, and the technicians who took them, were flown back to Pearl and delivered to Cincpac's Photographic Section. One or two technicians from this Section always went on these photographic reconnaissance trips and some of the results achieved were remarkable. At Iwo Jima, for instance, one picture showed a squad of Japs digging a machine-gun emplacement on the beach. The faces of the individual men were almost clear enough to be placed in their family albums. *Nautilus* then returned to Pearl until the time arrived to pick up her Marine detachment and take station as a lifeguard at Tarawa on November 9.

The Japanese, slowly learning the lessons of their own shipping disasters, began to retaliate. Bad news came from the Seventh Fleet that *Cisco*, Lieutenant Commander J. W. Coe, was overdue, presumed lost on a patrol in the South China Sea. Postwar reports make it fairly certain that *Cisco* was sunk in the Sulu Sea on October 9, by air bombing and depth charges. In S-39 and in *Skipjack*, in the early part of the war, Jim Coe had piled up a fine record for himself and his ships. Additional bad news came from the North Pacific submarines, where the Japs claimed sinking of S-44 and capture of two prisoners, which proved to be true. Lieutenant

Commander F. E. Brown and all hands except E. A. Duve, CTM, and W. F. Whitemore, RM.3/c, were lost off Paramushiro.

Submarine losses in the Atlantic and Panama areas has been few. S-26 was sunk in January, 1942, as result of a collision with a PC boat, with the loss of all but three of her personnel. R-12 was sunk off Key West in an operational disaster from which there were only five survivors. The news, therefore, of the disappearance of the *Dorado*, Lieutenant Commander E. C. Schneider, in the Caribbean area, about October 12, was a considerable shock to us. Had the Germans waylaid her? She was a brand-new boat, en route to Pearl Harbor, and had sailed from New London on October 6, but never reached Panama. There was grave suspicion that she was sunk by one of our own patrol planes based at Guantanamo, which dropped three depth charges on an unidentified submarine during the evening of October 12.

A Court of Inquiry was convened in the case but, due to lack of evidence, was unable to reach definite conclusions. Numerous attacks had been made on our submarines in the Pacific by friendly planes, which totally disregarded instructions regarding safety lanes. The aviators concerned in the *Dorado* case had received faulty instructions as to the location of the bombing and attack restriction area surrounding the submarine. All such incidents pointed to the need for fewer trigger-happy aviators and a foolproof recognition system.

In view of these sinkings and to counter the threat posed by increased enemy antisubmarine measures, our efforts to achieve greater protection were intensified. One advance made during this period was in the matter of camouflage for our submarines. Originally, all boats had been painted black as this was found by many tests to be the best color for concealment from planes when submerged. Now, however, planes were not so great a menace as escort vessels and it was found that in making attacks on surface at night, submarines were frequently sighted by the enemy at fairly long ranges. Solid black on a starlit or moonlit night made too noticeable a spot on the sea.

Lieutenant Commander Dayton Brown, USNR, an artist of national reputation, was sent out to us by the Bureau of Ships. Experiments were undertaken to break up the solid lines of a submarine's silhouette and Commander Brown, with Joe Grenfell of my Staff, spent many nights out with our wolf packs in training. The final answer was a light gray color for use in tropical waters and a slightly darker gray for areas north of the tropics. These colors were applied to all vertical surfaces, while horizontal surfaces remained black. The result was a submarine which was invisible beyond 1,000 yards, even on a moonlit night, and there were instances wherein our boats approached within 700 yards of an enemy destroyer without being challenged.

On October 27, I began to fear that the death toll of submarines for the month was not complete. *Wahoo*, Lieutenant Commander D. W. Morton, should have reported in the night before but no word had been received. In fact, we had heard nothing from *Wahoo*, except in a Japanese broadcast, since she departed from Midway on September 13. Domei, the Japanese news agency, was quoted as saying that on October 5 a steamer was sunk by an American submarine off the west coast of Honshu, in the Sea of Japan near Tsushima Strait. The ship had sunk in a few seconds with the loss of 544 persons. *Wahoo* was the only American submarine in the Sea of Japan, so that scalp belonged to her.

Days dragged by and still no word came. The last time the Japanese had admitted a loss, they also had announced that the submarine had been sunk. That particular boat was the *Snook*, which had returned safely to give the lie to the Imperial Japanese Navy's Assessment Committee—if it had one. Regarding *Wahoo*, they had made no such claim. It just didn't seem possible that Morton and his fighting crew could be lost. I'd never have believed the Japs could be smart enough to get him.

As time went on—Admiral Nimitz allowed me a week's margin on reporting losses—I finally had to send the dispatch which added *Wahoo*'s name to the list of "overdue, presumed lost." The entire Submarine Force was saddened by the news that she, one of our most valuable units, would never come steaming in again with a broom at her masthead and Mush Morton's fighting face, with its wide grin, showing above the bridge rail.

JANAC credits *Wahoo* on this last fatal patrol, with the sinking of four ships in the Sea of Japan. This makes her final total 20 ships for a total of 60,038 tons. Postwar reports indicate she was sunk by depth charges from a plane in La Perouse Strait on October 11, 1943.

With revenge written grimly across his face, Captain Freddy Warder shoved off, on October 30, for a patrol in the Marianas, with a wolf pack consisting of *Harder, Pogy* and *Snook.* In the next month, we sank 232,000 tons of Japanese shipping.

The sinking score for October was very good—26 merchantmen, of the 39 merchant ships (158,093 tons) credited in JANAC to all forces, had been victims of submarines. The biggest bags were got by *Wahoo,* four in the Sea of Japan; *Silversides,* four south of the Carolines; *Rasher,* three in the Banda Sea. *Gurnard* got two big ones northwest of Luzon. In his patrol report, the skipper mentioned that while still cursing because he had suffered a dud on a nice big target, he watched, through his periscope, a Jap escort vessel, which evidently thought it was depth charging *Gurnard,* drop three ash cans. All were duds. The sight made him feel much better. *Bonefish* sank two in the South China Sea, one a 10,000-ton transport.

Our modified exploder—designated by Bureau of Ordnance as the Mark VI Mod. 4—was working perfectly. In fact, the first four submarines which took it on patrol reported better than 50 per cent hits, with no duds whatever. Roy Davenport, of the *Haddock,* reported four hits on 90-degree tracks, which sank two ships; Dusty Dornin, of the *Trigger,* reported eight hits, which sank three ships; and Slade Cutter, of the *Seahorse,* reported seven hits on approximately 90-degree tracks, which sank three ships. Business was really booming.

The Mark XVIII electric torpedo was still a headache, and a man-killer at sea, but we were not downhearted. We believed we could lick it, but we temporarily ceased issuing electric torpedoes to submarines going on patrol until the "bugs" had been worked out. Even in its imperfect condition, its big advantage was becoming evident. *Tinosa* reported that in one attack the escort vessel, with no bubble track to assist her, failed to locate the sub and dropped her depth charges 1,500 yards away. As a final bit of cheer, Captain W. A. "Hod" Gorry, out from Bureau of Ordnance to help with the electric fish troubles, told us the Bureau had a top-notch group of scientists at work on the problem of producing a reliable magnetic exploder.

In the first part of November, our submarines began taking their stations for the Tarawa-Makin operation. All plans had been completed and surface forces were assembling. Truk, usually a base for important units of the Japanese Fleet, had four main entrances and each was to be guarded by a submarine. If the enemy fleet sortied to go to the aid of Tarawa and Makin, these boats had orders to report the movement first and then attack if possible. The warning of our Central Pacific Force was considered more important than damage which might be inflicted by a single submarine. There was plenty of power in Admiral Spruance's Fifth Fleet and both he and Admiral Nimitz had expressed the hope that the enemy main body would try to interfere. It would be a grand opportunity to bring on a major naval engagement.

Plunger was to act as lifeguard off Mili, in the eastern Marshalls, for the carrier strikes preceding the amphibious assaults, while *Nautilus* was to perform a similar service at Tarawa. Three more submarines were stationed in or near the Marshalls, between Truk and Tarawa, organized as a wolf pack which was to rendezvous on call to oppose the advance of any enemy force. A fourth submarine had been warned that she, too, might be directed to rendezvous with this pack. The pack consisted of *Sculpin, Searaven* and *Apogon.* Captain John P. Cromwell, of Henry, Illinois, the pack leader, was embarked in *Sculpin,* whose commanding officer was Lieutenant Commander F. A. Connaway of Helena, Arkansas.

Before *Sculpin* shoved off from Pearl on November 5, John Cromwell came to my office to say good-bye and receive last-minute instructions. Commander Dick Voge, our Operations Officer, and I gave John an outline of the attacks which were about to be launched in the Gilberts, so he would have a clear picture of the situation and know where he might expect to encounter friendly naval forces in case dispositions had to be radically altered by dispatch.

In conclusion, I cautioned him not to impart this information to anyone, in order to lessen the danger of exposure of the plan of campaign, in case the submarine was sunk and prisoners taken. This was to be John's first war patrol and he was elated at the prospect. We wished him "good luck and good hunting" and a few minutes later the *Sculpin* backed away from the dock.

During the days immediately before the Tarawa and Makin landing, tension was terrific. This, our first big operation in the Central Pacific, was the trial by fire which was to establish the pattern for our advance across the Pacific. It had to be a success. Had we done everything humanly possible to insure that our part would be perfectly carried out? Had coordination with other surface forces, and with the air forces, been properly planned? I venture to say that Commander Dick Voge and I went over our directives from Cincpac and our own operation orders a dozen times, looking for flaws, and found none. Then came a shock: on the night of November 19–20 *Nautilus*, our lifeguard at Tarawa, carrying 78 Marines for the capture of Apamama, was shelled and badly damaged—in fact almost lost—when she encountered one of the bombardment groups approaching Betio Island.

The *Nautilus*'s dispatch said that after leaving her lifeguard station and proceeding to her new one, she had encountered surface forces which, at a range of 6,000 yards, opened fire. Before she could get under, one shell had hit her, a dud which struck under the bridge, pierced the main air induction pipe, dented the conning tower, ricocheted in the superstructure and finally came to rest.

Whose surface forces were they, we puzzled? Then we found out. In other dispatches, the destroyer *Ringgold* had claimed credit for sinking an enemy patrol boat and the light cruiser *San Juan* said she should have credit for an assist to the extent of having contributed seventy-six 6-inch shells toward this sinking. *Nautilus* had followed a prescribed route in order to avoid any interference, but, in spite of these precautions, our surface ships, with orders to attack no submarines unless attacked by one, had mistaken *Nautilus* for an enemy patrol boat and decided to shoot first and ask questions afterwards.

Despite her wounds, the *Nautilus* proceeded as per schedule and landed her Marines at Apamama, where she supported them with her 6-inch guns during their assaults. All of the enemy garrison were either killed or committed harikari in their trenches.

Plunger, Lieutenant Commander Benny Bass, who acted as lifeguard at Mili in the eastern Marshalls, where the Japs had considerable air strength, also had trouble. She rescued one aviator but her Executive Officer and five men were wounded by a Zero fighter, which dived on her from out of a cloud. Fortunately none were fatally injured. I visited the wounded in the hospital at Pearl. The Executive, Lieutenant George Brown, was in high spirits and proudly showed me a

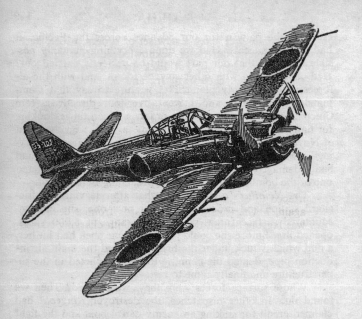

Zero

machine-gun bullet which the medicos had dug out of his backside.

"Well," said I, "you certainly have something to show your grandchildren, but how are you going to explain to them about being shot in the stern?" "Well, sir," said Brown, "I guess I'll just have to tell 'em I couldn't run fast enough to get out of the way!"

The quartermaster of the watch was hit five times, three wounds in the body and two in arms or legs. I asked if there were anything he wanted—someone to write letters for him, someone to read to him. "No, sir," he said, "there's only one thing I'd like to have and that's a bottle of bourbon." The doctor said it would do no harm—taken in small doses—so I sent a bottle over.

On the night of November 29, Captain Cromwell, wolf-pack leader in the Marshalls, who had left Pearl Harbor in the *Sculpin*, was ordered to assemble his pack for a sweep to northwestward. No orders were issued by *Sculpin* and, after 40 hours' waiting, another submarine was ordered to form the pack. *Sculpin* was given a new set of orders, which were sent out repeatedly, but never acknowledged. Not until the end of the war, when we got back from Japanese prison camps Lieutenant G. E. Brown, Jr., and 20 enlisted men of the *Sculpin*'s crew, did we learn the details of her loss.

During the night of November 18–19, *Sculpin* made a radar contact on a fast convoy, and made an end around at full power. Submerging on the enemy track for a dawn attack, *Sculpin* began what promised to be a successful approach. However, she was detected in the attack phase, and the convoy zigged toward her, forcing her deep. There was no depth charge attack at this time. About an hour later, the ship surfaced to begin another end around, but immediately dived again, having surfaced 6,000 yards from a destroyer, which was lagging behind the convoy. Depth charging started as soon as she dived.

Early in the ensuing attack, a string of depth charges did the ship minor damage. Lieutenant G. E. Brown, the engineer and only officer survivor, was relieved as diving officer to make an inspection and found her fundamentally sound. At this time, the submarine had succeeded in shaking the enemy, but before Brown returned to the control room the ship broached when the diving officer tried to bring her to periscope depth and the depth gauge stuck at 125 feet. The depth charge attack was renewed at once.

About noon on November 19, a close string of 18 depth charges threw *Sculpin,* already at deep depth, badly out of control. The pressure hull was distorted, she was leaking, her steering and diving plane gear were damaged, and she was badly out of trim. Commander Connaway decided to surface and fight clear with his gun, a desperate measure which he must have known had no chance of success. The ship was surfaced and manned all guns. During the battle, Commander Connaway and the Gunnery Officer were on the bridge, and the Executive Officer was in the conning tower. The destroyer placed a shell through the main induction, and one or more through the conning tower, killing these officers and several men.

Lieutenant Brown succeeded to command. He decided to scuttle the ship and gave the order "all hands abandon ship." After repeating the order several times, the ship was dived at emergency speed by opening all vents. And so the old *Sculpin* went down with engines running and colors flying. The men in the water said her last dive was as pretty as any she had ever made.

About 12 men rode the ship down, including Captain Cromwell and one other officer, both of whom refused to leave it. Captain Cromwell, being familiar with plans for our operations in the Gilberts and other areas, stayed with the ship to insure that the enemy could not gain any of the information he possessed. His last words to Lieutenant Brown were, "I can't go with you. I know too much." For this action, Comsubpac recommended that he be given the Congressional Medal of Honor. Ensign W. M. Fiedler, when told the ship was to be abandoned, went into the wardroom and was last seen laying out a hand of solitaire.

In all, 42 men were taken prisoner by the Japanese destroyer, but one was thrown over the side immediately because he was severely wounded. Another wounded man escaped being thrown overboard only by wrenching free of his captors and joining the other men.

The group of 38 enlisted men and three officers were taken to Truk, where they were questioned for 10 days. Then they were loaded on two carriers (21 on one, 20 on the other) and started for Japan. En route to its destination, the carrier *Chuyo,* carrying 21 *Sculpin* survivors, was torpedoed and sunk by *Sailfish* on December 4, 1943, and only one American was rescued. This was a particularly coincidental and tragic event since *Sculpin* stood by *Squalus* (later recommissioned as *Sailfish*) when she sank off Portsmouth, New Hampshire, in 1939.

The *Corvina,* Commander R. S. Rooney, was also lost during the Gilberts Operations. She left Pearl November 4, on her first war patrol and took station south of Truk to guard against exit of enemy forces through South Pass. At the end of her patrol, she was to report to Commodore Fife's command at Brisbane (Fife himself had recently moved up to his tender *Fulton* in Milne Bay, New Guinea). Enemy records indicate that *Corvina* met her doom on November 16. A Jap submarine reported having sighted a surfaced submarine southwest of Truk, three torpedoes were fired at the American, two of which hit, causing "a great explosion sound."

While preparing for our part in the great Central Pacific offensive, which got underway in the Gilberts, I also was working on other projects. For some time, I had been endeavoring to establish a separate training command. Training of new submarines and refresher training of the experienced boats fell to the lot of Comsubron 4, Captain John Brown, who was designated as Training Officer. Submarine Squadron 4 and Submarine Squadron 2, Captain C. B. Momsen, had no tenders assigned to them but they both used the Submarine Base at Pearl as a tender. Because of their more or less permanent station there, it was logical that they should take on this very important part of all submarine operations. Captain Momsen acted as chief staff officer for Captain Brown and all Division Commanders were assigned additional duty under the Training Officer. It was, however, a bit awkward having two squadrons on the Base and I desired to set up a separate Operational Training Command under John Brown and combine Subron 2 and Subron 4 under Swede Momsen. Certain economics in officers and staffs could in this way be effected. Approval of this plan was finally given by Cominch and the new organization placed in effect.

And that brings up the subject of New London, the Submarine School there, and Submarines Atlantic. Rear Admiral Freeland A. Daubin commanded Submarines Atlantic Fleet and Captain E. F. Cutts commanded the Submarine Base, which has been the site of the Submarine School since 1916. There, in times of peace, officers and enlisted men were given a fairly extended course of schooling in torpedoes, storage batteries, diesel engines and submarine operations before they were sent out to the fleet. A division of older boats was based there in order to give the students elementary training.

Now, with the nation at war, and the submarine force expanding at the rate of five to 10 ships per month, the school period had to be cut to three months for officers and one month for enlisted men. All hands were given a course in escape from a sunken submarine, using the 100-foot diving tank. New personnel were carefully screened by the medical officers, of whom Captain C. W. Schilling, Medical Corps, was an outstanding specialist, to insure that they had adequate night vision, were not claustrophobics and that they were mentally adaptable to life in the crowded quarters of a submarine. Several intensified courses were included to acquaint the students with special weapons then being introduced. There was also a Prospective Commanding Officers' School, in which submarine officers of rank sufficient to be eligible for command in the near future, were given realistic training by war-seasoned skippers in the art of making attacks and of evading enemy countermeasures.

Naturally, the School had grown like a mushroom and the proportion of veteran personnel to raw recruits was low. One of our jobs in the Pacific was to feed experienced personnel into the School and to the Commander Submarines Atlantic Fleet in order to provide instructors and nucleus crews for new boats.

It was heartbreaking to send back personnel whom we needed so badly, but there was no denying the necessity for keeping Sublant supplied. Inevitably, arguments arose in the process which the Bureau of Personnel had to referee but, in the main, we settled our differences out of court. Admiral Daubin's organization took over all new submarines as soon as they were commissioned, gave them about four weeks of training and sent them along to Pearl for final polishing up there. Sublant also made important contributions to solution of our torpedo troubles, notably the ventilation tube for the Mark XVIII electric torpedo. Another important step was taken by Admiral Daubin when he sent Captain Hod Gorry of his Staff, an experienced submariner and torpedo officer, to the Torpedo Station at Newport to assist in expediting the range trials and alterations necessary for the same fish. The excellent job done by Comsublant, the Submarine Base, New London, and the Submarine School in training personnel and in fitting out and training new boats was responsible for making effective combat operations possible within a minimum time after each new boat reported in at Pearl Harbor.

Another matter which had engrossed my attention was the need of a full-scale conference with the various building yards and bureaus which produced and equipped our submarines. When they visited us in midsummer, Captians Andy McKee and Armand Morgan had suggested a conference with the Bureau of Ships every six months, but now so many projects had arisen with other bureaus that a conference with all offices and bureaus concerned was imperative. Dozens of official letters were being exchanged monthly on various subjects and I believed that a three- or four-day meeting of my "brain-trust" with high-level representatives of the shore activities could eliminate the need for most of our correspondence and expedite the matters under discussion. A date immediately following the Gilberts operation seemed suitable and so I asked permission from Cincpac to make the neces-

Diving Tank, New London

sary requests. Admiral Nimitz gave the proposal his blessing and a date of December 10, at Navy Yard, Mare Island, was set.

Before Pearl Harbor Day, only three building yards were employed in the construction of submarines. The Electric Boat Company of Groton, Connecticut, had produced fine boats for many years, and, with the Lake Torpedo Boat Company at Bridgeport, Connecticut—which closed down about 1922—had been the pioneers in American undersea building. Then the Navy Yard, Portsmouth, New Hampshire, got into the game and finally Mare Island took up construction.

There had been other submarine building firms before and during World War I, but when our country started to gird its loins for World War II, only three yards were turning out submarines. The building capacity of these yards was, of course, greatly increased at the outbreak of war and, in addition, two other yards went into production; Cramp Shipbuilding Corporation at Philadelphia and the Manitowoc Shipbuilding Company on Lake Michigan, at Manitowoc, Wisconsin. The Cramp experiment was pretty much of a fizzle—the *Dragonet* was, I believe, the only boat they completed—but at Manitowoc, Mr. Charles West and his excellent organization turned out 28 beautiful submarines. These ships were built to Electric Boat Company plans and with guidance by some EB foremen, I believe. Whatever the arrangement was, the results were outstanding. Manitowoc itself won the high regard of submariners who served there, as a most desirable place to live.

Undersea craft built at this yard were floated down the Chicago Drainage Canal to the Mississippi and on to the Naval Station at New Orleans, where they were prepared for sea. Their training was obtained at Balboa under the able tutelage of Captain J. G. "Johnny" Johns.

I was anxious to get our electric torpedoes back into the picture as a Christmas present for Tojo. The Base Torpedo Shop and all the experts had been working unceasingly on the problems involved and believed they had all the answers. The exercise head—filled with water instead of explosive—was still a pain in the neck because of a Rube Goldberg-designed blowing system intended to rid the exercise head of its ballast water at the end of a practice shot, so the torpedo would acquire positive buoyancy and remain afloat. This arrangement was different from the very reliable blow used in the older torpedoes and was no doubt considered a boom to submariners by the Torpedo Station, Newport, but it cost us plenty in sinkers. It was very important that we be able to fire practice shots with these new electric fish in order to let the skippers and fire control parties become accustomed to their slow speed.

Finally, the Base Torpedo Officer, Commander M. P. Hottel, invited me to go out in *Haddo*, Commander John Corbus of Vallejo, California, at daylight on November 30. Hawaiian sunrises are usually things to write home about, gorgeous with flaming colors. This one, however, was overcast, and drizzling rain accompanied us down the channel and through the nets. An uncheerful beginning for an uncheerful day. The eight electric torpedoes, which we were to fire that day, had been prepared and adjusted by officers and torpedomen from the Base Shop, our most experienced personnel.

Two or three made good runs. We lost three out of the eight and Commander Hottel was ready to jump overboard. Newport's answer was that we did not know how to run them, but I noticed similar fiascos in the reports which our submarine representatives at Newport were sending me. There the torpedoes were adjusted by the same naval and civilian "plank-owners" who criticized our efforts. The difference was that they never made public their poor performances, a frank discussion of which might have been of great assistance to the forces at sea.

In spite of this very discouraging outing with the electric torpedo, the lads in the Torpedo Shop did not turn in their suits; they dug in their toes instead. Tojo's Christmas stocking did not have a Mark XVIII in it, as I had hoped, but mid-January saw plenty of them heading his way.

The sinking score for November, 1943, was the best thus far in the war. Seventy merchant vessels were sunk during that month for a total of 320,807 tons. Of these 232,333 tons, 48 merchant ships, were sunk by U.S. submarines. Three enemy men-of-war also were sunk by our boats and one, the big Jap submarine I-34, was sunk by a British submarine in Malacca Strait.

According to my bible, JANAC, the scores in order of tonnage were as follows:

Seahorse:
    1 tanker, 1 passenger-cargo, and
       3 cargo ships .... 27,579 tons
Bowfin:
    2 tankers, 1 passengr-cargo, and
       2 cargo ships .... 26,458 tons
Raton:
    3 cargo ships .... 18,801 tons
Harder:
    3 cargo ships .... 15,270 tons
Trigger:
    2 passenger-cargo and 2 cargo ships . 15,114 tons

Drum got the largest target, an 11,621-ton converted submarine tender, while *Bluefish* and *Searaven* each got a valuable 10,000-ton tanker.

The patrol of the *Seahorse*, Lieutenant Commander Slade D. Cutter of Oswego, Illinois, was particularly noteworthy in that this was Cutter's first patrol as a commanding officer. *Seahorse* was a brand-new boat, having made only one previous patrol on which she had no sinkings. Slade Cutter will be remembered by football and boxing fans of the early 1930's for his stellar performances in Naval Academy athletics. As a tackle and as a heavyweight boxer, he had few equals and no superiors, in my amateurish opinion. That same aggressiveness, which he had demonstrated in sport, he carried into war.

Cutter's first patrol began its action on October 29, south of the Empire, when he battle surfaced at 2,400-yard range from an armed trawler and sank her by gunfire. The next day, he stopped another by gunfire and while she was sinking, boarded her and recovered publications, charts and the log, for delivery to the intelligence section at Cincpac. On the following day, an intended trawler victim tried to ram but was thwarted in her attempt and joined the other two on the bottom via the gunfire route.

With this as a warming-up exercise, Slade got down to real business two nights later, when he contacted a 17-ship convoy, including several Chidori-type escort vessels. At dawn the next day he was in attack position, but escorts frustrated his approach. Heavy explosions indicated that another submarine was in action—undoubtedly the *Trigger*, captained by his teammate, Dusty Dornin. Determined not to let these beautiful targets escape, Cutter waited till they got over the horizon, then surfaced and at full speed made an end around, and got ahead of them for the third time. Shortly after midnight, his persistence was rewarded by three hits in a 5,859-ton passenger-cargo ship which he saw go down. Four hours later he got two hits each in a tanker and a freighter, but according to JANAC only the latter sank. Two Chidoris chased *Seahorse* but, with full speed, she was able to escape without resorting to diving.

Submarine skippers did not dive at night if they could possibly avoid it, for that meant losing the initiative and probably subjecting themselves to a pounding with depth charges. Nobody liked that—and who can blame them? Running away on surface was dangerous, too, especially after the Jap escorts were equipped with radar, and several narrow escapes resulted.

Cutter had several contacts in the next few days but got nothing except plentiful depth charging. One ship, contacted in low visibility, appeared to be stopped and Slade bored in submerged until his rapidly decreasing fathometer readings made him realize that the target was on a reef and that he would be similarly unfortunate in a matter of seconds. Finally, on November 22, *Seahorse* made a night periscope attack on what must have been a valuable convoy, for it consisted of only two freighters, with three destroyers as escorts. Half of whatever was being so carefully guarded went to the bottom when Cutter got two hits in the *Daishu Maru* and sank her to the accompaniment of many scattered depth charges, which did the submarine no harm.

Four days later, a night radar contact, near the mined areas of Tsushima Straits, developed into another long running fight. In desperation, lest the target escape through the swept channels, Slade took a long chance (he had taken long chances before on football fields, with place kicks at critical moments) and fired four torpedoes at a range of 3,750 yards. Luck—and a good fire control party—was with him and a 7,000-ton tanker went skyhigh in a brilliant blue-white flash.

Getting in and out of the East China Sea was something of a problem. Every pass between the islands of the Nansei Shoto chain was covered by patrol boats at night. One submarine, the *Whale,* reported a miracle had occurred to help her run through on a bright moonlit night. A full eclipse of the moon had supplied the necessary cover. As *Seahorse*

prepared to leave the Sea some remark was made in the
conning tower as to how tough it would be to get through the
pass, whereupon the helmsman, a signalman second class
named White, evidently thinking out loud, said he believed
they could get out on surface in broad daylight because the
Japs would not be expecting it.

That sounded reasonable. They chose the Tokara Kaikyo,
south of Yaku Shima, and went out at 12 knots between 8
and 10 A.M. The houses on the island were in plain sight and
a high-flying plane paid no attention to what he probably
thought was a fishing boat. Cutter added to the illusion by
flying a Japanese flag taken from a trawler earlier in the patrol. Everybody felt pretty good about the whole thing, especially the helmsman.

The patrol ended in a blaze of gunfire. There were only
four torpedoes left—all in the after torpedo room—when, on
November 30, he encountered three medium-sized cargo ships
with two small escorts. In a chasing action, use of the stern
tubes is sometimes difficult to manage. At 2240 that night,
Cutter got into position only to have the enemy make a wide
zig away from him and open fire. *Seahorse* persisted, however, and about an hour later gained position and fired her
last four fish. One torpedo prematured 50 seconds after firing.
This usually happened if a torpedo broached badly—or perhaps it had struck flotsom. In any case, it alerted the targets
and all opened fire. In the wild melee of explosions, Cutter
was unable to tell whether hits were made on the enemy, but
JANAC records no sinkings at that time and place.

This meteoric start, which earned a Presidential Citation
for *Seahorse*, did not slow down as long as Cutter remained
in command.

Bowfin, Lieutenant Commander W. T. "Walt" Griffith of
Mansfield, Louisiana, operating from Fremantle and using
Darwin as a refueling base, made a whirlwind patrol along
the Indo-China coast to pile up the score given above. In just
three days and nights, Griffith fired 24 torpedoes and got 19
hits. He celebrated Armistice Day by sinking two small tankers by gunfire in Sibutu Passage and, during the remainder of
his patrol, sank five more lesser craft, all of which must have
been too small to show on the record. In the South China
Sea, *Bowfin* ran into a typhoon with continuous heavy rain
and towering seas. Visibility was practically zero. The aircraft

warning radar was used to locate mountain peaks on the beach and thus keep the ship from getting into danger.

Shortly after midnight on November 26, the radar made contacts at one and two miles. At first Walt thought he had got tangled up in a group of islands, but he was apprised of the real situation when other close contacts and a near collision showed he was in the center of a five-ship convoy. After determining the convoy's course and speed, *Bowfin* planned to attack the two ships in the right column—neither of them yet visible. The explosion of two hits on the leading ship proved her to be a tanker, as gasoline fires spread on the water. The doomed ship turned on her floodlights and the crew could be seen abandoning ship. The second target was hit by only one torpedo. Tankers are hard to sink and Griffith decided to give her another salvo of three torpedoes. Two of them hit and the tanker sank.

After reloading torpedo tubes, *Bowfin* returned to the scene and, in the dim morning light, found that her second target had also gone down, leaving her bow sticking above the surface. About 0830 a medium-sized transport of this same convoy was picked up. That was a bit of luck, for visibility was still less than two miles. The submarine pulled ahead and submerged for the attack. Four torpedo hits sent the transport to the bottom. The next day, *Bowfin* sighted and tracked submerged a small coastal steamer, which flew a French flag and had *Van Vollenhoven* painted on her side. As the entire area was under Jap control, there could be no doubt this vessel also worked for our enemies, so Griffith sank her with three hits.

In the early morning hours of November 28, another five-ship convoy was contacted and, after tracking to ascertain course and speed, the leading ship was sunk with four hits. Two more hits were obtained in the second ship.

Bowfin was hit by a shell during her last attack and vital piping was punctured. However, the holes were patched up and she made her way back to Perth. The outstanding character of this patrol was soon recognized by the award of the Presidential Citation.

Harder, with Commander Sam Dealey still in command, was a member of Captain Freddy Warder's wolf pack, which went out to avenge our losses. Dealey followed up his September sweep with a nice bag picked up when his ship encountered a homeward-bound convoy north of the Marianas on November 19. All three of his kills were made that night and early the next morning. Sam had a positive genius for packing his action into the shortest possible space and he picked his targets with the coolness of a seasoned hunter.

Earlier in this same patrol *Harder* attacked a small freighter, escorted by a patrol vessel, and an armed trawler equipped with depth charges. Dealey approached submerged and fired three torpedoes, two of which hit and broke the cargo vessel in two.

The escort headed for *Harder*'s position and Dealey went deep, ordered "silent running," and rigged for depth charge attack. Two ash cans were dropped fairly close and then a distant, heavy explosion was heard. On returning to periscope depth about an hour later, a surprising sight met Dealey's eye. The trawler's stern was completely blown off and the escort vessel was circling around her. Had *Harder*'s No. 3 torpedo made an erratic run and hit her, or had her depth charges exploded in the racks? Dealey took pictures and then, at dusk, surfaced and pumped the wreck full of 20-mm and 3-inch holes. The escort vessel showed no desire to get into this show and preserved a discreet distance of about 4,000 yards. *Harder* departed unmolested.

One of the most-prized pictures in my war gallery is a snapshot of that modest, smiling Texan receiving a Navy Cross at the conclusion of these two excellent patrols.

Trigger, Lieutenant Commander Dusty Dornin, who had taken over command from Commander Roy Benson, turned in a brilliant patrol in keeping with the traditions of the ship. *Trigger* had a PPI scope, one of the first installed in submarines, and she used it to full advantage even though the radar ranges obtained were not as great as was later possible with more powerful transmitters. With this instrument, the position of the targets and their escorts was visible at all times.

The blacker the night, the more Dornin was pleased. During the night of November 1, she was in contact with a convoy of 10 or 12 ships, which was probably the same convoy that *Seahorse* was attacking, for the positions of the two submarines agree within 10 miles. Here, then, were two former football teammates—and keen rivals—working on the same targets. Each got two ships, so the score thus far was a tie.

All of Dornin's attacks were made at night and he specialized on keeping track of the escorts and dashing in through unguarded holes to attack. Dusty's long experience as an end had taught him how to elude interference and get in on the ball carrier. On one attack, however, he was spotted and forced to dive, whereupon two escorts saluted him ineffectively with 40 depth charges. On another occasion, after the convoy had scattered, *Trigger* came upon a lone freighter and stopped her with one hit. She did not appear to be sinking, so Dornin bored in to administer the coup de grace. The Jap, however, must have sighted the submarine, for he opened fire with two guns. Since none of the shots fell close, Dusty continued to close the range and downed the freighter with two more hits. *Trigger* was awarded the Presidential Citation.

CHAPTER 9

As our submarine offensive was stepped up, technical efforts to strengthen our fighting arm kept pace. We were constantly seeking and developing new weapons, new equipment and new techniques for outwitting the enemy.

The occasionally canny Japanese had some tricks of their own, too, which they continued to play until the very end of the war. A favorite was a radio campaign, which included ferreting out the frequencies on which our submarines transmitted their messages and then jamming it when one of our boats opened up. If the sub happened to be fairly close to a Jap station, the jamming could be pretty effective. I doubt if the Japanese ever realized that this trick wasn't much of a handicap, after the first week or so, for we merely assigned alternate frequency bands.

It was seldom really necessary for a boat to get a report back to Headquarters and communication between subs of a wolf pack was done by phone, radar or a special frequency. Hence, the Japs might just as well have spared themselves the effort. Their DFing (Direction Finding, i.e., locating a radio transmission by direction finding) was also ineffective, whereas the DFing employed by our antisubmarine forces in the Atlantic was one of our most valuable aids in destroying Hun submarines. Japanese radio and radar equipment and technique were always about a year behind our own.

At the beginning of the war, submarines used the radio with extreme caution, expecting an enemy plane on their necks immediately after any messages were transmitted. With experience they became bolder and, from the middle of the war onward, they talked freely, sending weather reports with impunity from positions just off enemy coasts so that bombing planes, landing forces and bombardment groups could be informed of terminal weather. Occasionally, an enemy plane showed up, possibly as the result of a DF-ed message, but, toward the end of the war, our own night-flying radar-equipped planes generally were much more of a mental hazard. Our skippers could never be sure these friendly planes had been properly briefed so, when they had reached a radar range of about five miles, the submarines usually slipped under and, to paraphrase Mr. Gray, "left the world to darkness and the fly-fly boys. . . ."

The need of a night periscope was well in the foreground, since visibility at night through our regular attack periscopes was much reduced, except on moonlit nights. Several foreign navies had such periscopes, but the nine-inch tube, in which they were encased, appeared to us a serious handicap, since its size precluded use as an emergency periscope in daytime. The matter had been preliminarily discussed with Captain Morgan in the Bureau of Ships and we felt sure a solution would be forthcoming. A periscope radar antenna, chiefly for range finding during daytime periscope approaches, had also been under discussion for several months and this need, too, had been taken up with the Bureau.

One project, on which I had placed considerable dependence and whose accomplishment I had endeavored to expedite, seemed to be dragging interminably. I refer to the supply of deception gear and noisemakers which we needed to throw enemy antisubmarine craft off the scent. Various devices had been proposed, but so far none had been delivered to forces afloat. We had heard that the king-sized Alka Seltzer tablets—a tube about two feet long—were excellent for creating a bubble screen behind which a submarine could maneuver to evade attacking surface craft and had been effectively used in the Atlantic by the Germans. If a simple device of that sort could confuse our own submarine hunters in the Battle of the Atlantic, even for a short period, I felt sure it would be useful against the Japanese until something more efficient could be devised. With our submarine losses steadily mounting, it appeared the matter should be given higher priority in the production schedules. This was another of the items I expected to take up at the approaching submarine conference at Mare Island.

Plans for this conference were now completed and on December 8 I sent Captain Momsen, Comsubron 2, and Commander Casey Hurd, Force Material Officer, on ahead by air and followed next day with Commander "Sparky" Woodruff, Flag Secretary, and Commander Freddy Warder, whose general background of experience was very great.

At Mare Island, I reported in to the Commandant, my old boss, Rear Admiral Friedell, and, with the help of the Commander, Submarine Administration, at the Yard, Captain "Shorty" Edmunds, got the conference organized. Much to my satisfaction, I found that the interested Bureaus and Offices in Washington had sent their best-qualified and best-informed officers to attack our problems. In addition, Captain Andy McKee was there from Portsmouth Navy Yard, plus Commander Saunders Bullard, USN, Rtd., who represented Mr. Spear, President of the Electric Boat Company.

After a short general meeting, the conference split into committees for a couple of days, after which each met with me and went over all business. Highly satisfactory agreements were reached, for all hands were animated by the same desire to get the war won. A night periscope, combined with an ST-type radar, was designed right there on a table, with a pencil and a sheet of foolscap. Captain Morgan spoke for the optical features and Commander Bennett, also of the Bureau of Ships, guaranteed the electronic commitments. They said they would have it in service for us in nine months and actually got the first one installed in *Sea Fox* in seven months. The size of the periscope head, an important feature from the point of view of concealment, was reduced to a very acceptable figure and the length of the tube was longer than had been considered feasible in earlier correspondence.

The Bureau of Ordnance representatives delighted us with the news that a 5-inch deck gun was practically ready for installation on all Fleet-type submarines. This was a real victory.

The only item which still hung fire was the prosubmarine program, deceptive devices for protection of submarines against antisubmarine craft. A new tube had to be designed

5" Gun

to eject these gadgets from the submarine, but this was being installed in all new construction and in each boat coming in for overhaul. I was told that the UCDWR at San Diego was progressing well on some special gear of this nature, which I would have an opportunity to see when I inspected our outfit at that place.

We needed this gear urgently, a fact emphasized by news that *Capelin*, Lieutenant Commander E. E. Marshall, was reported "overdue, presumed lost" in the Southwest Pacific, but even postwar reports contain no definite clue. Minefields existed there and may have been the cause of her loss.

After the conference adjourned, there were odd jobs to be cleared up at Mare Island, Hunters Point and Bethlehem Steel. These were our main dependences for repairs to submarines and, with experienced engineers and submariners such as Captain Joe Fowler, Captain "Rim" Rawlings, Captain "Dutch" Klein and Commander "Kraut" Dettmann, they were turning out excellent overhaul jobs. We could foresee that, as our force expanded, existing repair capacities in the San Francisco Area would be exceeded and plans had to be made to give a full overhaul to some submarines at the Submarine Base, Pearl, and to send all long jobs, such as badly damaged boats, all the way to Portsmouth, New Hampshire. We could not count on Navy Yard, Pearl, for it was constantly full of bomb damaged and torpedoed ships.

When these matters had been attended to, I proceeded to

San Diego, with a few members of my Staff, to look over the situation at the Repair Base and to visit Dr. Harnwell's workshops, where I saw that real progress was being made in pro-submarine deceptive gear. Most of this equipment is still on the secret list. These were things we needed desperately out in the patrol areas but their production involved problems in priorities and supply of critical electronic material, which could be handled only by the Navy Department. I pushed and pulled for them; pleaded and cajoled but, in spite of all I could do, it was the spring of 1945 before the last—and best—of them made its appearance at Pearl. The bottleneck in electrical supplies was terrific all through the war.

One new bit of equipment I did pick up, that was of great value to us. This was a silent fathometer, which Dr. Harnwell demonstrated for me, one that could be used for depth finding with perfect safety right in an enemy harbor. The type with which our boats were equipped was susceptible of detection by hostile listening gear, hence, when close in to the Japanese coast, just where they needed a fathometer most, submariners hesitated to use it. This silent type, known as "Susie," was soon installed in many boats.

The FM Sonar, which I had first seen back in April, was now ready for installation and a set was scheduled to be mounted in *Spadefish*. Its value as a mine detector had become apparent and I was anxious to witness sea trials when it arrived at Pearl.

Back at Pearl, I found much had happened in my absence—some of it good, some, tragic.

Captain Freddy Warder had returned with his wolf pack, claiming 57,000 tons sunk and 19,000 tons damaged. JANAC cuts the sinkings down to seven ships for a total of 33,620 tons. Damage figure should go up accordingly. This wolf pack was not fully equipped with all communication aids and Freddy's principal recommendations concerned the need for telephones and IFF (Identification, Friend, Foe), the latest identification gear.

Shortly thereafter we received our first IFF in the new submarine *Angler*. The supply of this gear for planes and ships came along smartly, but it was not a complete success. The switch which controlled it had to be turned on by hand, and this was frequently forgotten, either by the plane or by the submarine. We went through several night alerts at Pearl, merely because some incoming pilot had forgotten to turn on his IFF. Later in the war, the word got around that the Japs had captured some of this equipment and were using it against us. The sinking of the fleet repair tug *Extractor* by *Guardfish* in 1945 was brought about by this distrust.

From the Japanese Empire Area came the tale of a terrific battle between *Sailfish*, Lieutenant Commander R. E. M. "Bob" Ward of Antioch, California, and a Japanese carrier formation. Patrolling about 300 miles southeast of Tokyo Bay entrance, on the night of December 3, the *Sailfish* surfaced at dusk in typhoon weather. Tremendous seas, with a 40–50-knot wind and driving rain, made it just the kind of a night one would enjoy drowsing before an open fire and listening to the wind howl. Very little headway could be made against wind and sea and visibility was practically zero. The drenched, cold night wore on until just before midnight the radar operator reported contact. The fire control party sprang to its stations as radar picked up three more contacts. Two large and two small pips appeared on the scope.

Ward headed in at full speed, but was unable to make more than 12 knots into the gale, while his targets were apparently making about 18. He could see it was going to be a close thing, for the two big targets were still at long range. With a heavy sea running, torpedo performance was unlikely to be of the best, therefore the firing range should be as short as possible. Black water piled over the bow and the bridge was deluged with practically unbroken seas. At exactly midnight, 12 minutes after contact had been made, the nearest small target, evidently a destroyer, turned on a searchlight and began blinking at *Sailfish*. Evidently she, too, had radar and had picked up the submarine.

Ward wasted no time, as the destroyer was only 400 yards distant, and instantly "pulled the plug." He checked the dive expertly at 40 feet, so his radar antenna was still out of water between wave crests. Then, using radar bearings and ranges exclusively, he set up his torpedo spread for the nearer of the two big pips—range 2,100 yards—and commenced firing four torpedoes. The destroyer had just passed close ahead of the *Sailfish*, her skipper no doubt wondering what had happened to the pip on his radar scope, and probably mumbling in his beard about the unreliability of this new-fangled gadget and his radar operators. Less than two minutes later, two torpedoes were heard to hit. Then the destroyer realized her fatal mistake and wildly dropped 21 depth charges, none very close. Ward continued on at deep submergence to cross astern of his target, surfaced after the excitement had died down, and commenced running down the track of the convoy.

At 0230 he picked up his large radar pip at 8,400 yards and found that his target was steering in a circle and had a smaller pip, probably a destroyer, with her. Finally she settled down on a northwesterly course, at a speed from one to three knots. To the weary lads in the rolling, pitching submarine, this news was like a shot of oxygen. Here was a nice, big cripple to finish off and Ward quickly made his decision. With the rain stopped and visibility improving at the approach of morning twilight, things had to happen fast, so Bob planned to stand in on surface, as close as possible, and fire three bow tubes. If this proved insufficient to sink the enemy, he would then go in submerged and deliver the death blow.

At 0552, with a range of 3,200 yards, *Sailfish* fired three torpedoes and observed two hits—brilliant balls of fire in the darkness—but even with this illumination Ward still couldn't see his target. At 0748 Bob Ward finally saw his target, an aircraft carrier, dead in the water, with a destroyer standing by her. Telling me the story afterward, Bob could hardly stay in his chair, reliving the excitement of those minutes. Aircraft carriers didn't cross one's periscope wires every day. He was convinced that carrier was a dead duck, but he wanted to see her sink. It seemed hours to him before his torpedoes were checked and loaded and by this time the crews were dead on their feet.

At 0912 Ward stood in and passed along her port side, at a range of 1,700 yards. She seemed to be settling evenly, with only a slight list to port. There were a number of planes on deck and sufficient people running around to populate a small village. *Sailfish* swung around for a stern shot and at 0940 fired three torpedoes, from which she got two hits. The breaking-up noises of the sinking carrier could be heard plainly throughout the ship, without the aid of listening gear, and when the lone discouraged destroyer had finished dropping seven depth charges, *Sailfish* again came to periscope depth to find the flattop erased from the surface forever.

But imagine Ward's amazement to find, only 4,000 yards away, a Takao- or Nachi-class heavy cruiser. Where she came from was a mystery to Bob, but there she was, with three turrets forward and two turrets aft. In the heavy sea which was running, *Sailfish* started to broach and, in desperation, Ward ordered 90-foot depth, for the cruiser was heading almost directly at him and he didn't want to see his ship picked up on that forefoot, which was plowing through the waves at 18 knots. The cruiser had evidently been off on the opposite side of the carrier, but Bob blamed himself bitterly for not having found it somehow, so he could have sunk her first and then polished off the carrier. As it was she got clean away.

The tragic part of this sinking was that the flattop turned out to be *Chuyo,* which was carrying the prisoners from the *Sculpin.*

This attack, which lasted some 10 hours, was cited in a general order to his force by the Japanese Vice Admiral Miwa, Commander Sixth Fleet (the Submarine Force), as an example of what can be accomplished by persistent attacks. It was a great pleasure to me to recommend Bob Ward for a Navy Cross for that patrol. His score also included two cargo ships, for a grand total of 29,571 tons. For this outstandingly successful patrol, *Sailfish* was awarded the Presidential Citation.

Dispatch orders arrived detaching Captain Gin Styer, then at Midway, and ordering him to command the Submarine Base at New London. This was a fine job for him and for the Submarine Service, but involved a serious disappointment to Gin just at that time, for he had been training a wolf pack at Midway and had my permission to take it on patrol. Thus perished his hope for a combat pin.

On her seventh war patrol, *Gato,* Lieutenant Commander R. J. Foley, operating out of Brisbane, on December 20, had an experience which, I believe, establishes a first in world submarine history. After a depth charging, which followed an attack on a convoy, she surfaced with a live depth charge on deck. Foley's attack was quite normal, except that he had bad luck in the form of a last-moment zig by the convoy, which forced him to fire at a small target rather than the large one on which he had planned his approach. The *Tsuneshima Maru,* 2,926-ton naval-cargo carrier, was hit and sank immediately. Then the two escorts set to work on *Gato* and, while they dropped only 19 charges, their accuracy was remarkably good and seemed right on top of the sub, which was shaken violently with each explosion.

Two hours later, Foley surfaced at dusk during a heavy rain squall and, on coming to the course which might again put him in contact with the convoy, discovered two disturbing factors—two escort vessels, the nearest of which was only

1,500 yards distant, and an unexploded depth charge on deck. Foley turned away and went to flank speed as the escorts opened fire and by 2100 had gained sufficient lead to permit him to dispose of his unwelcome passenger. This he did by lashing it to a rubber boat, punctured to produce a slow leak, and setting it adrift in the path of his pursuers.

Seven days later *Gato* established another first in the U.S. Navy, which disturbed even Cominch. Her attack on a convoy had been frustrated by the intervention of an enemy float plane—the type we called a Jake—and, after the target was over the horizon, *Gato* surfaced and pursued. Ten minutes later the Jake reappeared and made a diving approach, evidently intending to drop depth charges.

"Jake"

Gato had manned her AA battery, consisting of two 20-mm and one 50-caliber, machine guns, and gave him a few bursts. The plane was soon enveloped in tracers and, well before the release point, pulled up in a steep climb and turned away. Four times the Jake threatened and each time was forced to change his mind by a rapid and accurate fire from the submarine, which punched several 20-mm holes in his wings and a strip of 50-caliber bullets in his starboard pontoon. All rounds were definitely won by *Gato,* which eventually submerged when the skipper felt he had opened the distance from the Admiralties sufficiently to preclude arrival of surface craft from that base in his area prior to daylight.

Gato was not under my command, but the example set was disturbing to me, for I did not want my submarines engaging in gun battles with planes. While I was considering a diplomatic way of protesting to her Force Commander, a dispatch came from Cominch taking a "poor view" of the affair. I doubt that Admiral King personally sent that dispatch, for he, only two months earlier, had been insistent we improve our AA defenses. Why improve them if there were no intention of using them?

As 1943 drew to a close, reports of returning submarines indicated another good month. Twenty-two submarines had accounted for 29 merchant ships, of 127,000 tons, and three men-of-war, for an additional 22,000 tons. This brought our sinking score for 1943 up to 308 merchant ships, for a tonnage of 1,366,962 tons, plus 22 men-of-war for a total of 43,597 tons.

Next to the *Sailfish*, the best tonnage score had been made by *Flying Fish*, under the redoubtable Commander Donk Donaho, who sank an 8,600-ton cargo ship in Luzon Strait and a 10,200-ton tanker in the South China Sea. Tankers—those were the ships we most wanted to sink.

Silversides, Lieutenant Commander J. S. Coye, Jr. of Berkeley, California, contributed a nice bag of three cargo ships, all sunk in a single night.

Christmas Day was not devoted "to peace on earth, good will toward men." Commanders Dick Voge and Joe Grenfell (respectively my Operations and Strategic Planning Officers) and I spent the morning with Admiral Spruance and his Staff, working out the preliminaries of the forthcoming Flintlock Operation—invasion of the Marshall Islands. Our arrangements this time were better, I felt, for we provided for no lifeguards in the vicinity of the main targets, where large numbers of surface craft would be present. From experience gained in the Gilberts operation, it appeared that our forces would have unquestioned air superiority and could do their own lifeguarding. Thus, we would avoid other *Nautilus* incidents, but outlying targets, which would be struck by bombing planes alone, were to have lifeguard submarines in attendance.

The target date for opening the ball for Operation Flintlock had been set for January 29, with the landings to be made on February 2. The basic plan for the taking of the Marshalls was bold in the extreme. The main stronghold, Kwajalein Atoll, which contained the heavily fortified islands of Roi-Namur and Kwajalein, had outlying air bases at Maloelap, Mili, Wotje and Jaluit. This outer ring was to be kept under subjection by our carrier aircraft, while our main forces struck at the center. Majuro Atoll was also to be taken for use as a fleet anchorage.

Our submarines were to cooperate by guarding the northern, eastern and southern exits from Truk and by stationing lifeguards at Ponape, Kusaie and Eniwetok. The primary mission of all submarines was to attack, except in case of contact with a large and hitherto unreported enemy force moving toward the Marshalls. In that case the orders were to report first and attack later, if possible. These became standard orders for all joint operations. The areas around the Empire and in the Marianas were to be patrolled in the normal manner, but special attention was to be paid to all exits from Japan through which the enemy fleet might sortie.

Alterations to the electric torpedo having been completed, *Seahorse* and *Angler* each went on patrol with eight of them in the after torpedo room. They planned to use the faster steam torpedoes in the forward torpedo room for night attacks, when the bubble tracks could not be seen. The electrics they intended using for daylight attacks in which their wakeless features would be of great advantage to the submarine.

The new Bureau-designed electric exploder, called the Mark VI Mod. 5, had arrived in Pearl but we found it very prone to flooding around the handhold plate gasket which sealed the exploder chamber. Admitting water into this compartment resulted in a premature as soon as the torpedo armed. There appeared to be no end to the variations which our torpedo troubles could assume. We therefore went on using our own exploder until the new "Hyseal" gaskets arrived months later.

On January 20, we had our final conferences on Operation Flintlock. The plans looked smarter at each presentation. We had learned a great deal from the Gilberts operation. The periscope panoramas, made by our submarines of the landing beaches, were excellent. We took two sets, because the first set was not close enough in to the shore line. The second was so close one could count the individual fronds on the coconut palms.

While we were preparing for this operation, plenty of good news was coming in almost nightly of successes in the patrol areas. The *Haddock* reported that on January 18 she got two hits in *Unyo,* a 20,000-ton escort carrier, off Guam;

Seawolf, Commander Roy Gross, a veteran of many undersea battles, sank four cargo ships in the East China Sea for 23,000 tons; *Kingfish,* Lieutenant Commander Rebel Lowrance, came in from "down under" during the last part of January with a fine score of three tankers, totaling 15,600 tons; *Skipjack,* Commander G. G. Molumphy of Berlin, Connecticut, reported having sunk, northeast of Truk, the 1,580-ton destroyer *Suzukaze* and a 6,700-ton converted seaplane tender, while *Guardfish,* Lieutenant Commander N. G. "Bub" Ward, also was credited with an assist to the Flintlock Operation by sinking the 1,580-ton destroyer *Umikaze* southwest of Truk.

I was deeply interested in the outcome of that particular invasion because I wanted to establish a refitting base and rest camp in the Marshalls, to serve as another Midway for submarines patrolling the areas down near the Line and thus add about 4,000 miles to their cruising endurance.

The sinkings for January were almost double those of December. JANAC shows that 35 submarines, including the British *Tallyho,* accounted for 53 merchant ships for a total of 154,400 tons, plus one light cruiser, two destroyers and a mine layer. Included in these kills were eight tankers, boosting our enemy tanker score up to 30. Those who know how seriously our own tanker losses embarrassed our operations in the Atlantic, felt that such losses could not fail badly to cripple the Japanese, whose tanker fleet was far less numberous.

The biggest target for the month, a 11,933-ton submarine tender, fell to Dusty Dornin in *Trigger,* which, with her new light gray camouflage, intercepted a convoy headed for Truk and closed in to about 700 yards on one of the escorting destroyers, which gave no sign of sighting her. The quartermaster on Dusty's bridge finally got worried and said, "Cap'n, don't you think we'd better tell him we're here?" Dusty did inform him a moment later by firing four torpedoes across his bow, so close they almost nicked his forefoot. Then, having fatally wounded his target, he swung away at full speed and fired his four stern tubes at the now alerted destroyer. The torpedoes missed, since the target presented by the charging enemy was very small, but it discouraged him so much that he turned tail, and *Trigger* steamed off untouched into the darkness.

The taking of Kwajalein was accomplished in record

time, with minimum losses. We had learned much from the Tarawa operation. When General Holland Smith, who had commanded the landing forces, came back to Pearl Harbor he said that, due to short-range bombardment by 12-, 14- and 16-inch battleship guns, "a midget with a popgun could have taken the first 400 yards of the beach at Kwajalein Island."

Majuro Atoll, a beautiful and ideal anchorage, had been found deserted and had been occupied immediately, when the preparatory bombardment developed no return fire. The result was a series of Hollywood South Sea settings intact, as opposed to the treeless wastes which our bombardments had produced at Kwajalein. This shorn appearance of the island was promptly dubbed a "Spruance Haircut."

Admiral Nimitz came back from a flying trip to our newly acquired possessions and gave me permission to fly down and pick out the site for our new submarine base. Admiral J. H. Towers, Commander Air Forces Pacific Fleet, was going down to pick out sites for his new bases in the Marshalls and offered me a ride in his plane.

From Tarawa, I took off in another plane to have a look at Majuro, while Admiral Towers inspected Tarawa. I shall never forget the magnificent sight which greeted our eyes as we neared Majuro Atoll. Literally hundreds of ships, everything from huge carriers and battleships to landing craft, were anchored in the jade green waters of the lagoon. Our chests probably expanded a foot.

I paid my respects to Admiral Spruance aboard his flagship, the *New Jersey,* which was commanded by Captain Carl Holden, an old friend. The Fleet had received little punishment in the conquest of Kwajalein and Majuro Atolls and Admiral Spruance was all set to push on and take Eniwetok, at the same time plastering Truk with a bombing and bombardment attack. In fact, sailing orders were for 1600 that afternoon. This move had been part of the original plan, in case the Marshalls job was finished promptly, hence I had disposed submarine lifeguards and patrols before leaving Pearl. There was just time to give my own operation order to Admiral Spruance and wish him luck before the Fleet got under way.

The novel feature of this combined maneuver was that a new provision was made for the safety of our submarines, as well as for alerting them in case the Fleet pursued enemy forces into areas not included originally. The agreement was

that no U.S. escort vessel would attack a submarine unless
the sub attacked first, or was in a position to attack a major
unit. Even then, if safety demanded an attack on a submarine, depth charges were not to be set deeper than 150 feet.

For warning the submarines that friendly forces might
appear in their areas, it was arranged that the Fleet Commander would send out a single word in plain English
addressed to all submarines. We had selected a series of odd
names such as "succotash," "Budweiser," "sycophant" and
so on, and had sent out test messages for several days in order to familiarize all hands with the procedure.

I looked over the chart to select a suitable island for my
rest camp in case Kwajalein had nothing to offer. There were
plenty of beautiful islands of just about the right size, but
Majuro was 240 miles further from Japan, hence I wanted to
get a more advanced location if possible.

On the way down from Pearl, Admiral Towers and I
had looked over the charts of Kwajalein carefully to deter-

U.S.S. Gato

mine where we wanted to locate our respective activities. Kwajalein Island was to be the site for the NOB (Naval Operating Base) but the next island north of it, Ebeye, appeared well suited for both of our purposes. However, Admiral Towers didn't seem to think it would be big enough for both of us. All I wanted was about 20 acres and Ebeye appeared spacious enough for me for both our outfits.

Kwajalein Atoll finally hove into view and Admiral Towers told the pilot to orbit Ebeye and Kwajalein Islands. What a picture of desolation spread below us. Ebeye, on which I had set my heart, was a pockmarked desert. It was obviously no place to locate a rest camp, where men were supposed to relax taut nerves and dispositions. I turned to Towers and said, "Admiral, please forget what I said about wanting part of Ebeye. She's all yours."

We sat down in the lagoon at 1015 and went aboard the *Rocky Mount*, one of the first of the new "command" ships, the flagship of Rear Admiral Kelly Turner, who gave us the latest information on the organizational set-up and space allocations and sent us ashore on Kwajalein Island to look over the terrain.

Captain Charlie Erck and I borrowed a subchaser and went 10 miles north to an unpronounceable island which had been renamed Bennett. Captain Erck had come down from Pearl with me to help select the location, because his squadron tender, the *Sperry*, was to be the one which established the new base. Bennett was only partly blasted but also was unsuitable.

Majuro Atoll looked better and better as time went on, but next morning we hiked over one more island before mak-

ing a decision. This one was practically untouched, but had a
poor anchorage for the tender and a poor beach for swimming.

On return to the *Rocky Mount* we went into a huddle
with Captain Johnson (CEC), Admiral Spruance's field
representative, and pored over the chart of Majuro Atoll. Finally, largely on his advice, we selected a little island whose
name was Myrna. The native name was too much for our
Anglo-Saxon tongues. We couldn't have made a better selection, for it proved to be a jewel of a place, right out of a
movie set—minus Dorothy Lamour.

The softening up bombardment of Eniwetok was well
under way when we arrived back at Pearl and our submarines were all in position for lifeguarding and heading off any
ships which might try to escape from Truk. It was expected
that Admiral Spruance's Fifth Fleet would certainly be
sighted prior to its arrival at Truk and that enemy shipping
would attempt to run out via the northern, western and
southern entrances. *Skate, Sunfish* and *Searaven* guarded the
northern exit; *Tang, Aspro* and *Burrfish* were disposed to
west and northwest; *Darter, Dace* and *Gato* from Rear Admiral Jimmy Fife's Brisbane Task Force took positions to south
and southwest. This plan for a beautiful reception of any
would-be deserters failed only because the Japanese got no
warning of Admiral Spruance's approach and, on February
17, were caught flat-footed by bombers and fighters from
Rear Admiral Mitscher's carriers.

However, submarines did get a little action, for just at
sunset on February 16, *Skate,* Lieutenant Commander W. P.
Gruner, Jr., of St. Louis, Missouri, sank the new light cruiser
Agano in a superbly executed submerged attack, with 100
per cent hits from four torpedoes. This was Gruner's first patrol as a commanding officer—a nice start. Next day the
destroyer *Maikaze,* transporting *Agano* survivors to Truk,
was sunk by planes and gunfire of the carrier task force.
Tang also sank a large freighter.

Some of our subs at Truk was close enough in to see
Admiral Spruance's Fifth Fleet as it circumnavigated the atoll
and what an inspiring sight it was to them to see our battleships and carriers in that part of the ocean. For 26 long
months submarines had been fighting a private war in the
lonesome reaches of the Pacific and it certainly was nice to
have other forces come out and share the water with us.

Upon my return to Pearl, I received permission to go ahead with my plan for putting a tender, a floating dry dock (ARD) and a quonset-hut rest camp at Myrna Island in Majuro. The ink was hardly dry on the operation order we wrote to start that ball rolling when a dispatch arrived from Admiral Spruance proposing that he strike Saipan, the enemy's strongest base in the Marianas, on February 23. The outstanding success of the Truk bombing had inspired him with the desire for an encore before taking a bit of rest and upkeep at Majuro.

Admiral Nimitz was highly pleased with the idea and his Chief of Staff, Rear Admiral C. H. "Soc" (short for Socrates) McMorris, called me to see what submarine cooperation we could give. Fortunately, we had plenty of boats available in that area, so Dick Voge and I got together with Cincpac's Staff and at midnight we gave the Admiral the final plan. With his approval the radio waves started buzzing to get our ships in position. Our plan was similar to that used at Truk. Since Fifth Fleet would strike from the east, we disposed *Apogon, Searaven, Sunfish* and *Skipjack* on the arc of a circle west of Saipan. *Tang* we put in the safety spot beyond this line, to intercept anything which broke through. *Sunfish* was given additional duty as a lifeguard during the strike.

Task Force 58—the carrier task force—did not reach Saipan undetected as was the case at Kwajalein and Truk. Enemy search planes sighted it on February 22 and Admiral Mitscher's ships fought off Jap bombers and torpedo planes before reaching a launching position. However, they suffered no damage, shot down a number of the attackers, and delivered their strike on schedule.

Sunfish, Lieutenant Commander E. E. Shelby of Cincinnati, Ohio, sank two good-sized ships which ran out of Tanapag Harbor during the night and early morning, before the fly-fly boys struck. In the darkness and drizzling rain, Shelby identified the first as an escort carrier, but JANAC lists both as freighters.

Tang, backing up the line, turned in another of Dick O'Kane's stellar performances by sinking one passenger-cargo and three cargo ships. He had already got a 6,800-ton freighter. This was O'Kane's first war patrol as a commanding officer. He received his earlier training in *Wahoo*, with Mush Morton, and appeared to have learned his lessons well.

Commander E. E. "Eddie" Peabody (The Banjo King), an old friend and shipmate, who had asked for duty with Submarines Pacific, arrived on February 17 with his "Tune Toppers." Eddie had been a QM2/c with me in S-14, back in 1919–20. He was a clever lad with a ukelele or a banjo and when paid off in Long Beach, just before we started for Manila, left a vacuum in our musical lives. There's nothing like a good musician in a submarine crew to effect cohesion and keep everyone in a good humor. When I had command of N-5, years before, I once offered to trade two top-notch torpedomen for a cook who played the accordion on the old K-8, but had no success. K-8's skipper wouldn't have traded that lad for my whole ship.

In the years between 1920 and 1944, Eddie Peabody had built himself a national reputation and worked his way up in the Naval Reserve. In the fall of '43, he asked if I could get him out to the Pacific, and Bupers heeded my request. Not only did Eddie bring his "Tune Toppers"—four musicians, with a marvelous magician and an excellent singer, John Carter—but later he also obtained for us two complete Navy bands, which he had recruited and trained at Great Lakes. This was indeed a boon, destined to bring pleasure to a lot of people at advance bases such as Midway, Majuro, Guam and Saipan.

Admiral Nimitz came down to the Submarine Base one Saturday morning in late February and presented 18 decorations to submarine officers and enlisted men. It was customary to hold these ceremonies aboard one of the subs and this time *Tullibee* and her crew did the honors. Work was not stopped on other ships, nor on the Base, but Admiral Nimitz's microphone was hooked up to the loud-speaker system so all hands could hear the citations. We enjoyed having the Big Boss make the awards, for he always gave us a short, pithy and inspiring talk and frequently added his latest funny story.

This particular day the Admiral was in excellent form and the awards recognized some especially fine performances. Mush Morton got two Navy Crosses—one of which had followed him up from the Southwest Pacific. When all scheduled citations had been read off, imagine my surprise to hear Admiral Nimitz read off my name and announce that I had been awarded the Legion of Merit—"For exceptionally meritorious conduct as Commander Submarine Force, Pacific Fleet. He initiated an experimental program of great importance to the prosecution of the war. The improved efficiency of submarines under his command, as a direct result of this program, has resulted in increased tonnage of enemy ships sunk and damaged."

Naturally, I was as pleased as I was surprised, for I had not thought of my part in solving our torpedo problems—which was the "experimental program" mentioned above—as being anything more than my obvious duty. Still, it was very gratifying to know that the Big Boss considered the job well done and that he had taken pains to add the element of surprise to the thrills of the occasion.

That our work on the exploder had done wonders for the resultant torpedo performance, as well as for the morale of the submariners, could not be denied, for even the percentage of hits had shot skyward. In December and January, for instance, Subpac had fired 482 torpedoes for 220 hits, a neat 45.6 per cent, as against about 20 per cent in the beginning of the war.

Our sinking scores for the month were excellent, practically identical with those of November, 1943, which was still our banner month. Fifty-one merchant ships, including nine vitally needed tankers—231,002 tons—carrying the lifeblood of the enemy economy, had been gathered into Davy Jones's locker, escorted by one light cruiser, two destroyers and one submarine. Twenty-three of our undersea boats participated in these kills.

Grayback, Commander J. A. Moore, lost with all hands on that patrol, stood first with a bag of four ships for a total of 21,594 tons; *Tang*, Lieutenant Commander R. H. O'Kane, stood second with five scalps totaling 21,429 tons; *Pogy*, Lieutenant Commander R. M. Metcalf, came third with five kills for a total of 21,152 tons, while *Jack*, Lieutenant Commander T. M. "Tommy" Dykers, got fourth place with an amazing score of four tankers, all sunk on February 19, in the South China Sea, north of Borneo.

Dykers, who comes from New Orleans, was on his first patrol as a Commanding Officer and his performance left nothing to be desired. *Jack* suffered damage to her main engine air induction piping, which resulted in bad leakage. Somehow that leak had to be located and stopped. Chief Machinist's Mate Earl M. Archer volunteered to crawl from the engine room up into the main induction piping, while the submarine was submerged, and locate the leak. It was a dangerous job, which might have resulted fatally for him, since the piping was barely large enough to permit him to squeeze through it. Blocking the passage completely would have dammed the flow of water and drowned Archer. Nevertheless, he squirmed through about 100 feet of this piping, found the leak and then wriggled backward into the engine room.

With the difficulty located, *Jack* took a chance on surfacing in daylight, even though she was in closely patrolled enemy waters, for it would have been hopeless to try to make the necessary repairs in the dark. Archer and his engine room crew worked swiftly and well and succeeded in stopping the leak. They were just in time, for, next day, *Jack* was subjected to another damaging depth charge attack. Had the weakened induction piping not been repaired, the *Jack* might not have survived.

February ended with the taking of the Admiralty Islands by forces of General MacArthur and Admiral Kinkaid, in an operation whose execution had been advanced one whole month. Rabaul, Kaviang and all points southeast were thus sealed off from effective aid from the Empire. From that time forward, they were just another set of by-passed bases, left to starve and serve as bombing targets, until the final collapse of the Japanese.

What with the loss of the Marshalls, Eniwetok, the Admiralty Islands, and the blasting of Truk and Saipan, the Japanese took a severe beating in the month of February, 1944. Our own war machine had shifted into high gear.

CHAPTER 10

We were beginning to worry about the increasing tempo of Japanese antisubmarine activities, which were costing us a disturbing number of boats. Obviously, the enemy was learning from experience, and the task of our submarines was becoming more difficult and hazardous. I got away for a hurried trip to Midway on the *Barb*, Commander J. R. "Johnny" Waterman of New Orleans, Louisiana, troubled by the probability that *Scorpion* was lost.

She was overdue but we hoped she might show up at

Midway. If a submarine returned from patrol with her radio out of commission, the standard procedure was for her to approach Midway at night and attract attention by rocket signals. This would avoid the possibility of being attacked by some trigger-happy "zoomie," since the aircraft patrols were discontinued at nightfall. We watched anxiously night after night, but had no such good fortune, and on March 6, *Scorpion* was declared "overdue, presumed lost."

Under command of Commander Max G. Schmidt, she had left Midway for patrol in the East China and Yellow Seas. Two days after her departure, she reported one of her crew had sustained a fracture of the upper arm. A rendezvous was arranged with *Herring,* which was returning from patrol, in order to send the injured man back to Midway. The two submarines effected a meeting but heavy seas made it impossible to transfer the patient. *Herring* informed us of this fact and added, "*Scorpion* reports case under control."

That was the last ever heard or seen of her. Japanese records show no attacks that are likely to have been made on her, but we learned later in the war that minefields had been laid across the Yellow Sea. It therefore appears probable *Scorpion* was lost due to an enemy mine. JANAC shows that she sank during previous patrols, four enemy vessels for a total of 18,316 tons.

By mid-March, I was becoming worried about the *Grayback,* Commander J. A. Moore. She was a ship which stood high on the productive list, with many sinkings to her credit and her captain was both resolute and experienced. During her final patrol in the Luzon Strait–South China Sea area, she had twice reported making successful attacks and in the second dispatch she stated that only two torpedoes remained aboard, one forward and one aft. This was a difficult set-up, so Moore was directed to return to Midway. This message was not acknowledged nor was a later one asking where she had found the best hunting. At long last, after hope had been abandoned, I reported to Cinpac that *Grayback* was overdue, presumed lost.

Japanese reports say that a carrier plane made a direct hit on a submarine in about the position where we expected *Grayback* to be on February 26. The sub, so the Japs alleged, exploded and sank at once, leaving a large pool of oil. JANAC credits *Grayback* with sinking 14 enemy vessels in

10 patrols, including a submarine, a destroyer and an ex-light cruiser.

Back in the fall of 1943 we had added a small section to our Headquarters Staff. The new outfit, headed by Dr. Rinehart, was named SORG (Submarine Operational Research Group). This addition represented a distinct departure from traditional naval organizational set-ups. Its mission was to study and analyze patrol reports and other forms of intelligence, to determine whether or not our operational methods were the most effective which could be employed, what enemy antisubmarine measures were most dangerous to our boats, what evasive tactics on our part led to best results, and so on. In short, Dr. Rinehart and his assistants were an unbiased, uninhibited, scientific group of kibitzers, who reduced everything we did to figures or graphs and showed us in black and white what was happening. They were in constant contact with ASWORG (Anti-Submarine Warfare Operational Research Group) in Admiral King's Tenth Fleet in Washington, from whom they got valuable tips based on the Battle of the Atlantic.

The results they produced were startling at times and always highly valuable in shaping the trend of our efforts. Before the war ended they could tell us—and prove their statements—what firing ranges produced best results, what type of torpedo spread got the most hits, what agencies probably caused our heaviest losses—there seemed to be nothing which they could not reduce to a punch card on an IBM machine. The results of their studies were published monthly or oftener, in our *Submarine Bulletin*.

SORG constantly emphasized the need for prosubmarine weapons and devices—deception gear for throwing antisubmarine vessels off the trail, and a new type of torpedo designed to destroy small, shallow-draft craft which were almost impossible to hit with our service torpedoes. This was not a new subject to me. On the contrary, it had been a matter of great concern for some time, with our submarine losses averaging about two a month and enemy patrol craft showing positive evidence of being equipped with radar. *Rock* reported that she had been chased at night by a destroyer undoubtedly equipped with radar, which landed a 4.7-inch shell in her periscope shears, wrecking both scopes and the radar mast. Fortunately, *Rock* was diving at the time, otherwise the shell would have hit her conning tower.

Although most of this gear was, and still is, secret, the knowledge that such equipment was in use by our enemies—notably the Germans—and by our own forces in the Atlantic, was not conducive to lessening our impatience at the constant delays in delivery which we encountered in the Pacific.

A case in point was *Tambor*'s night encounter with an enemy PC boat. Both ships were taken aback at finding themselves in close proximity and the Jap turned to ram. Luckily, *Tambor* had her 20-mm gun ready and as she desperately swung her stern out of the way, a steady stream of tracers into the enemy wiped out her guns' crews as they tried to get their weapons in action. The PC boat missed the submarine's stern by about 20 feet and by the time she could circle around and get in position for depth charging, *Tambor* was well on her way to deep submergence. However, the sub then had to take a pretty bad pounding which slammed her down to 300 feet and inflicted considerable damage, including cracks in her conning tower doorframe. Here was a beautiful opportunity to use the new secret weapons then in use in the Atlantic—if we had possessed them.

By March our Pearl Harbor-based Fleet boats had taken over the "Polar Circuit" from the S-boats which had been retired to training duties. *Sandlance,* Commander M. E. Garrison of Sioux City, Iowa, came in on March 23 from our first patrol in this new area. The Polar Circuit consisted of the Kuriles and the waters bordering them, with Paramushiro and Matsuwa Islands as the main points of interest to us because of sizable enemy bases thereon. Garrison had accumulated a nice bag of three cargo ships, one of them in February, for a total of 12,756 tons, plus the 3,300-ton light cruiser *Tatsuta* which he had correctly identified as being of the Tenyru-class. The last two victims *Sandlance* sank in the area south of Tokyo Bay after moving down from her frigid cruise in the Kuriles.

Garrison was patrolling on surface in bright moonlight in the first part of the midwatch of March 13, when a plane contact forced him to dive. At 0240 he ran up his periscope and found himself in the middle of a convoy of at least five merchantmen and three escorts. Things happened fast then, for Garrison decided to use his only remaining six torpedoes on three targets. The cruiser, hit by only one torpedo, sank, as did also one freighter. The third target, another freighter, was damaged but apparently made port. Following this attack, *Sandlance* received a 16-hour depth charging during which 102 ash cans were dropped. Miraculously she received only minor damage. For this outstanding first patrol, *Sandlance* received the Presidential Citation.

A carrier task force strike on Palau, Yap, Ulithi and Woleai had been in the planning stage ever since the Truk and Saipan bombings proved so successful.

Conferences with Admiral Spruance, Rear Admiral Mitscher, and Admiral Nimitz's Staff perfected plans for submarine lifeguards, and in addition, Palau, the only place at which any considerable shipping would be found, was blockaded on the west side by *Tullibee*, *Blackfish*, *Bashaw*, *Tang* and *Archerfish*. *Tunny*, close in to the targets at Babelthaup Island, and *Gar*, close to Peleliu Island, were to act as lifeguards. *Pampanito*, at Yap, and *Harder*, at Woleai, were also lifeguards.

Tullibee was lost at Palau. As we found out after the war, she was sunk by a circular run of one of her own torpedoes three days before the carrier planes struck. Only one man survived. Her sinking left an important spot unguarded at the northern end of the semicircular blockade, and it is evident that most of the enemy merchant shipping, which began running out the day before the strike, escaped through that hole in our line.

One important target, however, did not escape unscathed. *Tunny* had been on regular patrol at Palau, during which her skipper, John Scott, fired quite a lot of torpedoes and estimated he had sunk, among other things, a submarine and a destroyer. However, JANAC credits him only with the submarine I-42.

At sunset on the eve of the carrier strike, *Tunny* had a ringside seat close in to Tuagel Mlungi Passage, the main entrance into Palau on the western side. There, in the gathering dusk, Scott saw a big battleship standing out, escorted by a light cruiser and two destroyers. The battleship was the 63,000-ton *Musashi*, one of Japan's two supergiants. A bad zig on the part of the big target left John a long shot but at 2,500 yards he fired anyhow, hoping the *Musashi* could not dodge all six of his torpedoes. An alert destroyer saw the torpedoes coming and gave the alarm, with the result that the battleship was able to swing away and evade all but two torpedoes. These struck her well forward and she managed to make good her escape. Had she been hit aft, it is possible she might have been slowed down so other submarines or Mitscher's dive bombers could have sunk her next morning. Instead, she survived six months longer.

The following day *Tunny's* jinx caught up with her again. While on surface 30 miles west of Palau, waiting for calls to pick up downed aviators, and watching our planes bombing, she sighted a formation of nine torpedo bombers passing to westward. Suddenly, two of them peeled off and headed for *Tunny*. The leading plane turned away but the second came so low that U.S. wingmarkings were plainly visible and dropped a 2,000-pound bomb, which landed 30 feet from the starboard side and exploded abreast the maneuvering room. Scott had already "pulled the plug" and the submarine went deep to check damage. The shock of the explosion caused only a short and a fire in the main power control cubicle which was quickly extinguished. At the time of this attack, *Tunny* was well within the area where bombing of submarines was forbidden. Some trigger-happy fly-fly boy had again narrowly missed killing 80 of his countrymen and destroying a 10 million dollar ship stationed at that particular spot for the express purpose of saving his life.

Just how eager our lads were to save aviators' lives and what chances they took in doing so, was illustrated the next day at Woleai. Sam Dealey, captain of the *Harder,* lifeguard in that target area, was watching a show from two miles off the beach, which he said rivaled any Hollywood "colossal" he had ever seen. Bombs from our carrier planes rained on every structure on the island. Whole buildings appeared to be lifted and thrown high in the air, there to disintegrate into kindling wood. Fighters dove in from all directions, strafing the AA guns. Many looked as if they would go right on through the blanket of smoke and crash on the island, but all managed to pull out just above the palm trees.

Suddenly, a plane zoomed the submarine and told Sam by radio phone that a pilot was down on the second island to westward. *Harder* stood over at full speed to pick him up. The pilot was sighted standing on the beach about 1,500 yards inside the line of breakers. Dealey flooded his forward ballast tanks and nosed in until his bow was on the reef, meanwhile calling for volunteers to man his only rubber boat—which, it was discovered, had no paddles, Lieutenant Sam Logan, J. W. Thomason, Slc, and Francis X. Ryan,

MOM, were chosen from a large group of volunteers and over the side they went, swimming and pushing their boat.

Meanwhile, a plane had dropped a boat to the aviator, who tried to paddle out to the rescue party but succeeded only in drifting further away. Finally, after an hour and a half, two of the rescuers reached the aviator, who by then was completely exhausted. The rescue party, fighting the surf and with legs, hands and arms badly cut by coral, weren't feeling any too well either. Nevertheless, they got him in their own boat and out to the heavy breakers, where another volunteer, Freeman Pawnet, Jr., GM, swam a line in to them and the whole party was hauled aboard. During the entire time, fighter planes cooperated beautifully by strafing the island to keep down snipers who were continuously firing at the rescue party and the ship. That "zoomie," Ensign John R. Galvin, is certainly living on borrowed time.

During the lifeguarding off Palau, *Tunny* found two Jap aviators in the water. One came aboard but the other preferred to stay where he was. *Gar,* Lieutenant Commander G. W. Lautrup, Jr., picked up eight of our aviators off Peleliu.

JANAC records that, during March, 1944, 20 submarines sank 27 merchantmen for a total of 123,462 tons, plus one light cruiser, one destroyer, one submarine, one gunboat and one subchaser.

Tautog in the Kuriles and off Hokkaido, got the most numerous bag—four ships—but *Lapon,* one of Rear Admiral Christie's command, in the South China Sea sank three big ships which gave her the largest tonnage for the month. This score was far below that of February because many submarines had been doing lifeguard and other "standby" jobs in supporting the rapidly moving Fifth Fleet.

Immediately after the Palau strike was finished, Admiral Spruance's Fifth Fleet and Task Force 58—Rear Admiral Mitscher's big carrier force—set to work on plans for repeat bombing of Truk. Whether this plan had been made long in advance or "just grew," I am not sure, but it seemed a good idea to all of us. Captain Dick Voge and I spent several hours with Admiral Nimitz's Staff, working out the details of the general operation order and perfecting the coordination of subs with the surface and air forces. Twice, in previous operations with the Fleet, my submarines had been attacked by friendly forces and I wanted plenty of safeguards this time.

Admiral Nimitz asked me to fly down to Majuro with him and part of his Staff, in his plane *The Blue Goose*. The Fifth Fleet was heading back there after its scourging of the western Carolines and Cincpac wanted to check over the proposed new operation in person and hear at firsthand the full story of Admiral Spruance's most recent triumph.

Next afternoon we arrived at Majuro and went immediately aboard the *New Jersey,* where Admiral Spruance's flag was flying. A full-scale conference had been called which included Rear Admirals Marc Mitscher, Ike Giffen, Johnny Hoover, Swede Hanson. Ole Oldendorf and several others with their Staffs. Admiral Spruance's Operations Officer put on a very complete presentation of the projected strikes which made the whole thing look extremely simple.

Next day I spent aboard *Sperry* with Comsubron 10, Captain Charlie Erck and with Captain Frank Watkins, one of his Division Commanders. I inspected also our quonset-hut recuperation camp on Myrna. Admiral Nimitz and Admiral Spruance showed up about 1100 to inspect the recuperation center and we gave them the grand tour. The place was really beautiful and now being organized as a plantation, with two pigs and a small flock of chickens. The Seabees, in addition to doing a splendid job of making roads, running water lines, and so on, had blasted holes inside the reef to provide swimming pools. At the conclusion of the inspection, Admiral Nimitz proposed a dip in the lagoon. The suggestion was enthusiastically received and, there being no bathing suits at hand, the inspection party, led by Cincpac, piled its clothes on the sand and dived in "au naturel."

Our refitting activity at Majuro had already been initiated with *Kingfish* as the first customer. *Flying Fish* also came in for refit as I was about to take off. Her captain estimated that he had sunk three ships and damaged two others. Postwar reports show that his sinkings were correct as stated.

From Majuro, I took off for Eniwetok via Kwajalein to locate an anchorage for tenders and a site for a rest camp at the former place, just in case we might require it. I carried with me a notebook full of memos concerning personnel and material needed at Myrna. The requirements ranged all the way from garden seeds to a couple of athletic specialists. A baseball diamond, an aquarium and limited livestock installations were already in active operation. I only wished I could own a "Myrna" somewhere back near the U.S. As a winter resort it would have been worth a million dollars.

At Eniwetok, where I thought perhaps we might have a future interest, I found Captain E. A. "Batt" Cruise in command, with Commander Sam King, USNR, as Port Director. Sam was an old friend from the class of 1910, USNA, who, after World War I, resigned from the Navy, settled in Honolulu and later served for a number of years as the Hawaiian territorial representative in Congress.

I inspected the atoll and found that two of the nearby islands, Japtan and Runnitto, appeared suitable for an advance submarine base if we ever needed it. However, with the war galloping along as it was, I already had my eye on a location at Apra Harbor, Guam, but I kept these two islands in mind.

On the way back to Kwajalein, we touched down at RoiNamur where I found my old friend Captain Eddie Ewen in command. He had many interesting things to show me, including some Jap torpedoes and an oxygen compressor. The Japs used oxygen in their torpedoes instead of air, as we did, and kerosene instead of alcohol. Keeping oxygen and kerosene in close proximity could lead to violent explosions but a Jap naval officer later, at Sasebo, assured me that such casualties almost never occurred. I noted, however, that the space in which their torpedoes were charged to full pressure was surrounded by a thick concrete wall. Japanese torpedoes were long range, fast, and carried a terrific charge. We could well do some "Chinese copying" from them.

I arrived at my desk at Sub Base at Pearl to find it buried in the usual pile of papers. Otherwise business seemed to be pretty dull; it looked as though the Japs were keeping off the ocean. We had in Subpac 44 boats at sea, 26 of them actually on station, yet few reports of sinkings came in.

At Majuro I had received a report that *Scamp*, Lieutenant Commander J. C. Hollingsworth of Decatur, Georgia, had been badly damaged by a bomb from an enemy plane, and later the full story came in to Pearl. *Scamp*, which belonged to Seventh Fleet Submarines, during the morning of April 7, patrolling south of Davao Gulf in the Philippines, sighted an enemy task force of six cruisers, screened by destroyers and aircraft. Conditions for periscope attack were unfavorable because the sea was glassy calm and during her approach the sub was detected and ineffectively depth charged. She remained deep for several hours and then surfaced to get off a contact report.

She had difficulty in establishing communications and remained on surface, vainly trying to transmit her report. Suddenly at 1543 a float plane was sighted coming directly out of the sun and *Scamp* dived. As she passed 40 feet, an explosion occurred close to the port side of the forward engine room. Fortunately it was abreast the bulkhead between the engine room and after battery room, which lent added strength to the hull plating. Otherwise, I believe the plating would have ruptured.

Most of the crew were knocked off their feet, all power was lost and the ship started for bottom which was hundreds of fathoms away. Emergency lights were turned on and the diving officer battled to check the descent. Meanwhile the cry of "Fire in the maneuvering room" came from aft. The rudder was jammed at full left, the pressure hull was terrifyingly dished in, thick smoke began to fill the after compartments and the main engine air induction piping was ruptured outside the strength hull. This added about 20 tons negative buoyancy to the ship. The situation was desperate and the Commanding Officer thought at one time that nothing remained but to surface and try to fight their way out. The diving officer, Lieutenant P. A. Beshany, by blowing all ballast tanks, finally caught the boat at 330 feet. Aft, the situation was bad, for all hands were violently ill from the phenolic smoke; nevertheless, they stuck to their jobs until eventually the fire was entinguished and power restored to both shafts.

Particularly heroic work was done by Chief Electrician's Mate J. R. McNeill and Electrician's Mate second class W. R. Fleury (who finally was overcome by smoke) in accomplishing this feat. The diving officer did a splendid job in keeping the ship alternately from going to bottom and from broaching and the Captain, in his report, was emphatic in his praise of the conduct of his crew during those grim 15 minutes before the ship was got under control. The skipper himself, in the opinion of all, had been an inspiration to his men.

Seven thousand gallons of oil had been lost from *Scamp*'s ruptured tanks so, for a time, the enemy aviators probably believed she had sunk. Later, they undoubtedly picked up the trail of oil as she headed away at a fairly shallow depth and again commenced bombing. This continued until dark and about 2100 *Scamp* surfaced and headed for the nearest friendly base in the Admiralty Islands. The stout hulls of our submarines and the stout hearts of their crews were two of the reasons why many of our boats are afloat today.

On April 17, I was sorrowfully compelled to report *Trout*, Lieutenant Commander A. H. Clark, overdue, presumed lost. Both ship and her captain were veterans of many patrols during the Pacific war. From postwar reports we learn that *Trout* sank the *Sakito Maru*, on February 29, about 700 miles east by south of Formosa. She did not report this sinking, as was the usual custom, hence, it is believed she was lost during or shortly after that attack.

In her 11 patrols which covered practically the entire Pacific and Southwest Pacific areas, *Trout* sank, according to JANAC, 12 enemy ships, one of which was the submarine I-182. She was awarded the Presidential Citation for her second, third and fifth partols.

About this same time a party of torpedo experts arrived to discuss with my "brain-trust" electric torpedoes in general and the Mark XVIII in particular. This group included Captain Jiggs Rezner from Sublant, Commander Jacobs from the Bureau of Ordnance, Commander Sampson from Sublant, and Lieutenant Eyeman from Bureau of Ordnance, with two civilians, Mr. H. V. Putman, Vice-President of Westinghouse, and Mr. J. G. Ford, Assistant Works Manager of the Sharon, Pennsylvania, plant where our Mark XVIII was being manufactured.

Our representatives were Commander A. H. "Art" Taylor of Philadelphia, Pennsylvania, the Staff Torpedo and Gunnery Officer; and Commander Martin P. "Spike" Hottel of Annapolis, Maryland, the Base Torpedo Officer, plus several experienced submariners from boats in port. Art Taylor won his spurs in *Haddock* with two Navy Crosses and a Presidential Unit Citation. Spike Hottel was also a veteran skipper and torpedo expert. Hence, we were able to inject a wealth of experience and talent into our conferences.

We believed we had cured the teething troubles of the Mark XVIII and found that the visiting experts were under a misapprehension regarding our needs in the matter of eliminating the hydrogen problem. What we wanted was no more Rube Goldberg contraptions added to an already workable and highly valuable torpedo. We did receive complaints from the submarines about the fumes from the Mark XVIII storage batteries, which rendered the torpedo rooms undesirable as sleeping and living quarters, but we believed this defect could be cured by improvements in the submarine's ventilation system and by the use of a deodorizer. The new torpedo ventilating scheme which the visiting group proposed, we wanted no part of, because it depended on the use of high-pressure air from the already overworked ship's air compressors.

Mr. Putman himself proposed to me that all suggested alterations to the electric torpedo should first get an O.K. from us, since we were its best customers and had the only thoroughly practical knowledge of its workings. The conference broke up with a fine feeling of cooperation and arrangements for direct personal correspondence—which I have always believed to be the best method of settling points of difference.

Following this, came a very cheering letter from Rear Admiral George Hussey, Chief of Bureau of Ordnance, in which he told me that the new 5-inch, 25-caliber deck gun, specially designed for submarines, was to be installed on *Spadefish*, then completing at Mare Island. To add to the good news, Rear Admiral Ralph Christie, Commander Submarines Seventh Fleet, who had retained the capricious exploder long after we abandoned it, wrote saying, "We have definitely come to the end of the trail on the magnetic (exploder)." The redesign which they had tried, turned out to be a flop. Thus finally ended another noble experiment.

On April 21, dispatches from Admiral Kinkaid to Cincpac advised that the Hollandia landings on the northeast coast of New Guinea, supported by Rear Admiral Pete Mitscher's carrier task force, were proceeding splendidly and almost unopposed. This meant that the carrier strike on Truk during the return trip of Mitscher's task force would take place as scheduled. Our lifeguard submarines for that air show were accordingly alerted and directed to take their stations. Once again, when we thought all air-submarine cooperation had been perfected, we reckoned without the persistent spirit of "sighted submarine; sank same." *Seahorse*, proceeding at full speed for station off Satawan Island southeast of Truk, was bombed but not hit, while in a safety lane, by a B-24 from Kwajalein or Eniwetok. I was furious and in a mood to de-

mand the head of that aviator on a charger or turn in my
suit. The zoomie recognized *Seahorse* after bombs were away,
for his report stated he had "bombed a submarine, apparently
friendly."

Slade Cutter, captain of *Seahorse,* sent a forgiving
message saying it was his fault, which was generous of him
but did not excuse the aviator. Slade blamed his own Officer
of the Deck because he hadn't seen the plane until bombs began to fall, at which point diving could not have saved the
ship. Admiral Nimitz demanded action from Rear Admiral
Hoover under whose command the B-24 was, and I hope the
zoomie caught hell. Knowing Admiral Johnny Hoover, I estimate that he did.

Seahorse, making her third patrol under Slade Cutter,
had just finished a beautiful performance in the Marinas
wherein, according to JANAC, she sank three freighters, a
converted sub tender and the submarine RO-45.

Cutter was reputed to have some special rabbit's foot
which gave him uncanny luck in finding targets. Our Operations Officer, Commander Dick Voge, used to say we could
put Slade on patrol outside Pearl Harbor and he'd still find
Japs. Cutter disclaimed the credit. He said that he and his officers and crew off watch had a habit of sitting around in the
control room, figuring out what they would do if they were a
Jap convoy commander entering that particular area known
to contain American submarines. Kids who couldn't even
read a chart would have their say and frequently produced
ideas that deserved thought and exploration. Slade claimed
that these impromptu, "no table" conferences made each man
feel that *Seahorse* wasn't just the Navy's ship or the skipper's
ship but his ship. Whatever the method used, it certainly got
results.

After the bombing, *Seahorse* spent six days lifeguarding,
and then joyfully headed for refit at Brisbane, where the beer
and other attractions were said to be superior to Pearl and
Honolulu.

It was at the bombing of Truk by Pete Mitscher's carrier
aircraft on April 30 and May 1, that Dick O'Kane of the
Tang again proved his mettle and set a record of 22 aviators
rescued, which stood for many months. Several of these pick-
ups were made so close to the beach that enemy shore batteries opened up and *Tang* replied with her own guns. Dick
noted that when friendly planes were over *Tang,* the enemy

guns did not fire at him, evidently because they did not want to disclose their positions to strafing and bombing aircraft. With an idea born of this discovery, Dick began calling the reporting plane or the parent carrier asking for fighter cover while he effected the rescue. Protection was invariably supplied and thereby was initiated a system used effectively wherever possible for the remainder of the war.

Kingfisher

Another unusual phase of *Tang*'s rescues was the assistance given by a Kingfisher float plane from the battleship *North Carolina*. It had been sent out for the purpose of picking up downed aviators but when the pilot, Lieutenant Burns, set his airplane down to effect a rescue, he was unable to get her into the air again on account of the high seas. He therefore toured the vicinity, picked up eight flyers and came in to *Tang* with passengers riding on the wings. His plane was so badly damaged that it was necessary to sink it by gunfire.

The monthly score for April was low for the same reasons that March was low. I find that we predicted it would be in the neighborhood of 100,000 tons. JANAC credits 27 merchantmen for a total of 91,592 tons plus one light cruiser, two destroyers, two submarines, a gunboat and a mine layer.

The largest bag was acquired by Lieutenant Commander Cutter of the *Seahorse,* who sank five ships for a total of 19,375 tons.

The light cruiser was the *Yubari,* the only one of her class. She was frequently confused with destroyers or vice versa, because of her small size. She had been reported sunk many times but usually it was a destroyer which took the rap. Finally, on April 27, *Bluegill,* Lieutenant Commander Eric L. Barr, Jr., of Seattle, Washington—whose father was a World War I submariner—put her down for the count while reconnoitering Sonsorol Islands southwest of Palau. *Bluegill* was making her first war patrol and Eric Barr his first patrol as a commanding officer. The submarine sighted a cruiser and a destroyer, but the cruiser disappeared behind an island. *Bluegill* then began an approach on the destroyer but suddenly the cruiser reappeared, making high speed. It was a snap shot, for Barr had only time to make a quick set-up, swing to the firing course and fire six torpedoes. His "nautical eye" estimates were not too bad for he saw one hit abreast No. 1 fireroom and heard two more explosions after he had ducked his periscope. A nice beginning for an aggressive young officer who had won his spurs in previous war patrols.

At this time orders came from Admiral King to raise the priority of Japanese destroyers as targets for U.S. submarines to a position above merchant ships. Indications were that enemy destroyer losses had been so heavy that they were having difficulty in supplying escorts to protect major men-of-war and important convoys. This directive sealed the doom of many destroyers which, up to that time, were considered distinctly second-class targets. By the end of the war, our submarines had sunk more of this type than any other branch of the service had destroyed.

During a lull in the Battle of Pearl Harbor, I availed myself of transportation on *Gato,* Lieutenant Commander R. M. Farrell, and made a trip to Midway in the first week of May. She was carrying a load of electric torpedoes aft and steam torpedoes forward. This gave me my first opportunity to observe the upkeep and care which the Mark XVIII electric fish required—and it was not inconsiderable. *Gato* also carried for the first time, the new design of exploder which the Bureau of Ordnance had finally got out to us. I was eager to see how they worked in actual war shots.

Our refit basin at "Gooneyville," as Midway was coming

to be known, was a joy to look upon and I felt as proud as a father of his first child. It would solve the problem of refitting three squadrons there during the winter months. The tender docks were not quite completed, but the dredging was all finished, including a 40-foot hole at the east end for the 2,500-ton floating dry dock (ARD) scheduled to arrive there at the end of May.

My feeling of elation was further increased by a dispatch from *Silversides,* Lieutenant Commander F. J. Harlfinger of Albany, New York, reporting a bag of four merchantmen and one destroyer, plus two other messages from members of a wolf pack led by Captain Pete Peterson, reporting destruction of one tanker, seven merchantmen and a destroyer, with four other marus damaged.

The end of May found Subpac with tenders *Sperry, Bushnell* and ARD-18 at Majuro, and tenders *Holland* and *Proteus,* plus the ARD-8, at Midway. Subs Seventh Fleet had the newly arrived tender *Eurayle* at Seeadler Harbor in the Admiralty Islands, so now we were in excellent position to repair battle damaged submarines in any theater. Not only did our tenders repair and refit submarines but they performed literally thousands of jobs, large and small, for destroyers and light craft.

However, we still needed—both Subs Seventh Fleet and Subpac—bases further advanced toward our most profitable patrol areas around the Empire and along the China coast, in order to cut down the long unproductive run required to reach those areas. I was about to get my base, or so I hoped, and we were all much elated at the prospect.

We had other reasons for elation, for excellent sinking scores were pouring in. JANAC records that at the end of May 20 submarines of Subpac and 15 submarines of Subs Seventh Fleet, had together sunk 55 merchantmen for 236,882-tons, plus three destroyers, two frigates and a gunboat. This tonnage surpassed that of November, 1943, thus setting a new mark to shoot at.

Gurnard, Lieutenant Commander C. H. Andrews of Hamden, Connecticut, a Seventh Fleet submarine, got the most tonnage for the month—a cargo ship, two passenger-cargo ships and a big tanker, all in the Celebes Sea, for a total of 29,795. The first three of these, she sank in a single night. She also reported getting two hits in a light cruiser which evidently did not sink.

Another Seventh Fleet submarine, *Crevalle*, Lieutenant Commander F. D. Walker of North Vassalboro, Maine, in addition to sinking two large passenger-cargo ships northwest of Luzon, performed a daring transit of Karimata Strait. This strait was very shallow and appeared an obvious place for a mine plant. However, the enemy used it and probably just hadn't got around to laying a minefield there. They had mined Balabac Strait, which unfortunately we did not know, and that may be one reason why Karimata was left open. After *Crevalle*'s passage, it was continuously used for the remainder of the war.

Sandlance, who started her whirlwind career on the Polar Circuit in March, bettered her score by sinking five freighters or passenger-cargo ships west and northwest of Guam for a total of 18,328 tons. *Tautog*, a veteran of many patrols with her veteran skipper, Lieutenant Commander T. S. Baskett, raided the Polar Circuit and sank one small freighter and three medium-sized passenger-cargo ships for a total of 16,038 tons. *Silversides*, Lieutenant Commander J. S. Coye, Jr., continued her high-scoring tradition by sinking six ships in that same general location, three of them on the tenth of May. They were small, however, and the combined tonnage was only 13,150.

Enemy efforts to strengthen their positions at Truk and in the Marianas, certainly had severe setbacks during that month. Our concentration of 12 submarines in the area was designed to isolate those island groups and prevent arrival of any reinforcements or supplies, in order to make easier the task which our amphibious forces would have to do in Operation Forager—the invasion of Saipan and Tinian and the recapture of Guam in the Marianas, for which the final plans were taking shape. The evidence from prisoners taken during that epochal operation shows that our mission was effectively accomplished.

CHAPTER 11

Once we had amassed, through assembly line construction in shipyards at home, an adequate submarine strength in the Pacific and were able to intensify our wolf-pack attacks, not only did we take big bites out of Japan's naval and mercantile fleets, but also took our place as a powerful force in the Central Pacific land offensive.

Training for Operation Forager, the conquest of the Marianas, our packs roved far and wide, smashing into enemy convoys. In April, Captain George Peterson, Pete to most of us, took out a wolf pack consisting of *Bang*, Lieutenant Commander A. R. Gallaher, *Parche*, Lieutenant Commander L. P. Ramage, and *Tinosa*, Lieutenant Commander D. F. Weiss, which reported sinking or damaging in the neighborhood of 100,000 tons during May. JANAC does not allow Pete all the sinkings he claimed, but it does chronicle the very interesting fact that on May 4 all three of his pack got into a convoy and sank five freighters for a total of 30,000 tons.

We have no records as to how many others were damaged in this shooting match in the northern end of the South China Sea, in the rotating patrol area Dick Voge had named "Convoy College," in honor of John Brown's school for training wolf packs. That was always our best hunting ground, for practically all Jap shipping passed that way. The bottom there must be literally carpeted with rotting hulks.

The *Bang*, a brand-new ship, sank two small freighters in the last days of April, which gave the pack a respectable score of seven sunk and probably an equal number damaged.

Their battle on May 4 was typical of many other wolf-pack attacks. The submarines were disposed in a line, at 10-mile intervals, athwart the shipping lanes. *Tinosa* made first contact at noon May 3 and informed the two packmates, who immediately closed in, and by 2230 the masts of the enemy were in sight. *Parche*, which was the command ship of Cap-

169

tain Peterson, directed *Bang* to attack from the port flank and she began an "end around" to gain proper position. At 0210 explosions indicated attacks by *Parche* or *Tinosa*. The targets opened up with gunfire and one vessel stopped. At 0332 two marus and two escort vessels paraded past *Bang* and she opened fire with her stern tubes. With four torpedoes she got three hits, two in the leading merchantman and one in an escort. Both sank and the maru is identified as the *Kinrei*, 5,947 tons. The Japanese do not admit losing a destroyer at this point, so the escort vessel must have been one of the hundred or more minor naval craft with which submarines are credited. This attack exhausted the *Bang*'s already depleted torpedo supply, so she was ordered to return to Midway, while her packmates carried on to sink four more ships that same night.

"Blair's Blasters," a wolf pack composed of *Pilotfish*, Lieutenant Commander R. H. Close, *Pintado*, Lieutenant Commander B. A. "Chick" Clarey, and *Shark*, Commander E. N. Blakely, started the ball rolling on June 1 in a wild battle with four different successive convoys in the Marianas, north and west of Saipan.

Captain L. N. "Chief" Blair was pack commander. He had left Midway with orders to destroy enemy traffic in the Marianas, until our air and surface forces began the softening up of Saipan, and then proceed to "Convoy College" Area, between Formosa, Luzon and the South China coast. At 1900 on May 31, *Shark* made contact and informed her packmates, who took stations for attack. However, a radical zig by the enemy put them out of position and it was just after midnight before *Pintado* submerged to make a periscope attack, bright moonlight making a surface attack impossible. Again the convoy made a radical zig and threw her out of position. Meanwhile *Silversides*, in an adjacent area, reported another convoy. *Pilotfish* was in a position to attack this second group and proceeded to do so. *Shark* was about to stand in for an attack on the first convoy when she saw *Silversides* boring in and held off lest she hit her teammate. *Pintado* finally got in an attack at 0437 and fired six torpedoes for five hits.

About this time, *Shark* found herself in front of another convoy and dived to attack but failed to reach a firing position. *Pintado* made contact with this same formation, so, at daylight, she and *Shark* were chasing one convoy while *Pilot-fish* and *Silversides* were in contact with another.

This resulted in a three-ring circus, complicated by enemy planes, which frequently drove our boats under. As a result, contact was lost with the first two convoys, but *Pilot-fish* was still trailing convoy number three, which was in ballast, heading back for Japan.

By 2000 June 2, all three "Blasters" were in contact with this same group and at 2300 *Shark* got in an attack which sank one ship and damaged another. Then at 1700 on June 3, *Pintado* sighted a fourth convoy, fully loaded and headed for Saipan. Blair immediately ceased chasing the third and ordered his boats to attack the fourth. *Shark* got in an attack the next afternoon, which sank a large ship, and from that time on, disaster after disaster struck the Japs. *Shark* and *Pintado* made repeated attacks, sank a total of seven ships and damaged several others. *Pilotfish* had the enemy zig away just at the wrong moment half a dozen times and is credited with none down.

The diary of a Japanese officer captured on Saipan records that this convoy, listed as cargo ships by JANAC, was carrying 10,000 troops, 6,000 of whom were lost, with their arms, ammunition and artillery. We credited Chief Blair's Blasters with an "assist" to General Holland Smith's Marines and Army ground forces in the subsequent taking of Saipan.

Against these successes, we had our own losses. On June 7, I had the sad duty of reporting *Gudgeon*, Lieutenant Commander R. A. Bonin, overdue, presumed lost. Her assigned area was in the northern Marianas from which *Gudgeon* was told to shift to another location on May 11. This message was not acknowledged nor were others, sent later.

The Japanese report that on April 18 planes succeeded in making two hits on a submarine. "The center of the submarine burst open and oil pillars rose," states the report, which seems quite definite.

Later, on May 12, several submarines in adjacent areas heard about 40 depth charge explosions, which are not accounted for by attacks on any of them. This depth charging conceivably could have sunk *Gudgeon*. In absence of definite evidence we can only say that the cause of *Gudgeon's* loss is not known.

She was a veteran of 11 war patrols. While under Captain Joe Grenfell's command, her sinking of the Jap submarine, I-173, in January, 1942, made her the first American submarine in history to sink an enemy combatant ship. Captain Bill Post also added to her laurels while he commanded her and her sinkings amounted to 12 enemy vessels for a total of 71,047 tons. She also was famous for her coat of arms, which contained a shamrock, a kangaroo and a Buddha with a motto, "Find 'Em, Chase 'Em, Sink 'Em." The Buddha on her escutcheon referred to the brass lucky piece of the forward torpedo room which sat between the tubes.

Another submarine was lost in June. This was *Herring*, Lieutenant Commander Dave Sabriskie, Jr. The enemy radio announced the sinking of an American submarine by gunfire which, according to postwar reports, was probably correct. The Japanese say that two ships anchored in the harbor of Matsuwa, in the Kurile Islands, were sunk by torpedoes during a surface attack by an American submarine which was, in turn, sunk by shore batteries, with two direct hits on the conning tower. "Bubbles covered an area about five meters wide and heavy oil covered an area of approximately 15 miles," says the report.

Herring was a veteran of war patrols in European waters, where she sunk a Nazi submarine and a freighter. On her fatal eighth patrol, JANAC credits her with sinking a Japanese frigate, two freighters and a passenger-cargo ship.

Plans were now in the final stages for Operation Forager. Admirals Halsey, Spruance and Turner and General Holland Smith were in frequent conferences at which Voge and I supplied the submarine picture.

As the date approached the first phase of the operation—the invasion of Saipan—our dispositions were made with a view to clearing the area of U.S. submarines before the actual assault, in order to give free reign to antisubmarine measures of the Fifth Fleet. I felt sure that it would encounter enemy undersea boats in considerable numbers, hence the presence of our customary lifeguards might hinder the operations of destroyers and other light craft. Our submarines, therefore, withdrew to north, west and south in order to be in position to intercept any enemy forces approaching from the Philippines, Formosa or the Empire.

There were about 48 Subpac submarines at sea when Forager broke. Those not in transit were off Truk, in the

western Carolines, off Palau, in Surigao Strait, in San Bernadino Strait, in Luzon Strait, off Okinawa and the Bonin Islands. All exits from the Inland Sea and Tokyo Bay were
covered, as well as normal areas along the coasts of the Empire. Comsub Seventh Fleet had three submarines in the vicinity of Tawi-Tawi, in the Sulu Sea, where a strong force of
the Japanese Fleet was known to be based, and three
southeast of Mindanao. The set-up looked excellent and we
sat back to admire it.

The Japanese believed we would strike next in the Marianas and their uneasiness was reflected in a movement of part
of the main fleet out of Tawi-Tawi, in the extreme south end
of the Philippine Archipelago, which *Harder,* Commander
Sam Dealey, observed on June 10. She was approaching the
anchorage to reconnoiter when, at 0910, two echo-ranging
destroyers were sighted, in all probability the advance screen
for larger ships. Dealey kept out of range and waited. Later
that afternoon, his patience was rewarded by sound contact
on light and heavy screws and masts appeared on the horizon. Three battleships, one unmistakably of the giant
Musashi-class, four or more cruisers and eight to 10 destroyers at a range of about eight miles were approaching on a
course which would not bring them close enough for a shot.
However, a lucky zig might give him a chance, so *Harder*
bored in.

The sea was glassy smooth and float planes were in the
air, so it is not remarkable that her periscope was sighted a
few minutes later. Undoubtedly, a plane dropped a smoke
float near the sub, for, instantly, the nearest destroyer began
belching a heavy black smoke to hide the battleships, dropped
three "scare" depth charges, and headed straight for *Harder*.
Dealey's sound operator counted the destroyer's propeller
beat and reported, "Thirty-five knots, sir." Sam, figuring, in
his quiet Texas way, that they were in for a beating anyhow,
decided not to go deep, but to keep his periscope up and give
her a down-the-throat treatment. He had sunk three destroyers in the last four days, so Sam's cool nerves probably never
even flickered as the destoyer, loaded with depth charges,
rushed at his periscope.

With the range down to 1,500 yards, Dealey fired three
bow tubes and ordered, "All ahead full; right full rudder;
take 'er deep!" Fifty-five seconds later the first of two torpedoes hit with a detonation that was far worse than depth

charging. By that time, *Harder* was passing 80 feet and was evidently nearly beneath the destroyer, when all hell broke loose above her. Dealey's patrol report says, "It (the explosion) was not from her depth charges, for if they had been dropped, this report would not have been completed, but were a deafening series of rumblings that seemed to blend with each other. Either his boilers or his magazines, or both, had exploded and it's a lucky thing that ship explosions are vented upward and not down."

After a two-hour pounding from depth charges and aerial bombs, the enemy lost him, and Dealey surfaced to send out the contact report for which our entire Pacific forces had been waiting. The Japanese fleet was on the move.

The next report came from *Redfin,* Lieutenant Commander M. H. Austin of Aetus, Oklahoma, also off Tawi-Tawi. At 0616 on June 13, *Redfin* made contact with a task force which consisted of six carriers, four battleships, five heavy cruisers, one light cruiser and six destroyers. It will be noted both of these big task groups were dangerously shy of destroyers. At that point, the Imperial Japanese Navy had lost 29 destroyers and 10 frigates to our submarines. *Redfin* was unable to get in an attack but she got off a contact report, which left no doubt in Admiral Spruance's mind that this time the enemy intended an all-out naval battle to contest our further advance.

We had not long to wait for further news of the enemy fleet. *Flying Fish,* Lieutenant Commander R. D. "Bob" Risser of Chariton, Iowa, guarding San Bernadino Strait on June 15, sighted an enemy task force coming out into the Pacific (this area, lying between the Philippines and the Marianas, was later named the Philippine Sea). She was never able to get closer than 11 miles, but she reported most of the ships already seen by *Redfin* and tracked them until contact was lost. Their course headed them directly for the Saipan area.

At 1411 on June 15 *Seahorse,* with Lieutenant Commander Slade Cutter in command, sighted smoke and a forest of masts about 200 miles east of Surigao Strait. Coming up from the south, these were evidently the ships seen by *Harder* and their course indicated a rendezvous with the force sighted by *Flying Fish,* at a point about halfway across the Philippine Sea.

Cincpac was instantly informed of these reports, which had come in to me, and he in turn passed the word to Admiral Spruance at Saipan, where our forces had landed. The stir caused there can well be imagined, with a desperate struggle going on ashore and an urgent need for supplies and fire support to our ground forces.

I thanked my lucky stars that I had plenty of submarines available to be thrown into the threatened area. A hasty conference, between Rear Admiral McMorris and Cincpac's Operations Staff on the one hand, and Commander Dick Voge and myself on the other, resulted in stationing submarines around the area to keep clear of Admiral Spruance but, at the same time, to harass the enemy's advance or retreat.

While these dispositions were being made, *Cavalla*, a new submarine on her first patrol, commanded by Lieutenant Commander Herman J. Kossler of Portsmouth, Virginia, at 2330 of that important 15th day of June, made contact with a convoy consisting of two tankers and two destroyers. *Cavalla* was on her way to relieve *Flying Fish* at San Bernadino Strait and her arrival there was urgent, since Risser had reported his fuel supply was running low. However, she couldn't pass up a chance like this, so Kossler raced for position ahead and, at 0315 June 16 took his ship to radar depth (with radar screen just above the water) and headed in for the firing position. The sub was nearly ready to launch her salvo of torpedoes when suddenly the nearer destroyer headed straight for her. Naturally she had to get down—and fast. As she was passing 75 feet, the destroyer crossed above her engine room, not pinging, and dropped no ash cans. Obviously, he had not contacted the submarine and his change of course was just a zig—lucky for the Japs but unlucky for Kossler. By the time *Cavalla* got back to radar depth, the targets were out of range.

Kossler surfaced and got off his contact report to me at 0545, stating he was continuing on to relieve *Flying Fish*. To us, however, it appeared most important to chase those tankers; they undoubtedly had a fueling rendezvous with the enemy fleet. Big game might be brought to bag by following them, whereas *Flying Fish*'s job was done. Hence, we fired a dispatch right back, telling Kossler those tankers were important and that he should "trail, attack, report." We also informed three other nearby submarines of the situation.

The next day, however, we slowed *Cavalla* down to normal speed lest her fuel become exhausted and, at 2015 June 17, the southern Japanese task force overtook and literally ran over her. Here was a problem in fidelity to orders, for, not knowing that *Seahorse* had already reported this major enemy group heading for the Marianas, Kossler's duty was to report first and attack afterward. It was a tough decision to make, but he made it, held his fire, did his best to count the number of heavy and light screws and surfaced after the last had passed. His contact report, sent at 2225, was of great importance, confirming the course and rate of advance of the enemy. On receipt of his message, we told all submarines that both Japanese forces had been reported and added instructions to shoot first and report afterward.

Virtue, however, as in all good stories, was to win its reward. At 1012 on the morning of June 19, planes were picked up on *Cavalla*'s radar screen and she dived to escape detection. At 1039 she could see planes circling and the masts of a ship. This looked distinctly interesting and, as the approach developed, it looked even better. By 1100 Kossler could see the whole group of four ships, the carrier *Shokaku*, two cruisers ahead and to port of the carrier, and one lonesome destroyer on her starboard beam. Since *Cavalla* was on the target's starboard bow, it was evident to her skipper that the escort was in an extremely menacing position.

No one could pass up such a chance, for here was a submariner's dream target: a carrier taking on planes, which meant she had to hold a steady course, and the range shortening by the moment until she filled the whole of his periscope field. At 1118, Kossler began firing a salvo of six torpedoes, and then headed for the depths, for his last periscope had shown the destroyer heading directly at him, range 1,500 yards. The first three torpedoes hit with terrific detonations and, four minutes after firing the first shot, depth charges began to rain down. In the next three hours, *Cavalla* received 105 depth charges, 56 of them close enough to wreck the sonar gear and the air induction pipe lines. At dusk Kossler surfaced his ship, reported the attack, his own damage, which he said they could handle, and added, "Believe that baby sank." "That baby," veteran of the Pearl Harbor attack, the Coral Sea battle and other actions, did sink, but we were not sure until so informed by prisoners toward the end of the war.

When we received *Cavalla*'s contact report of the tankers, which she had not succeeded in attacking, we moved *Finback*, *Bang*, *Stingray* and *Albacore* into positions along a line north of Yap, which we estimated might be the refueling area. Except for many plane contacts, nothing seemed to happen until the morning of June 19, when *Albacore*, Commander J. W. Blanchard, dived to avoid discovery by a Japanese plane.

At 0750 she sighted an aircraft carrier, a cruiser and the tops of several ships over the horizon. The range was 13,000 yards and the sub was almost on the carrier's port beam, a hopeless position. However, Blanchard rang up full speed and swung toward his target, but, even while swinging, a second group, consisting of a carrier, a cruiser and several destroyers, appeared out of nowhere. Best of all, he was only 10 degrees on the carrier's starboard bow at a range of about 10,000 yards.

The approach developed beautifully; a cruiser which might have interfered, generously crossed well clear, astern of *Albacore*, and a destroyer was deftly avoided by paralleling her course until she drew ahead. The carrier was making 27 knots. The firing range was going to be about 1,500 yards. Blanchard didn't know it, but that was the first day of the Battle of the Philippine Sea. This carrier was an important target. Her planes were even then on their way to attack the Fifth Fleet. Blanchard made a final periscope exposure to check data and found all correct. Then, at 0808, he gave the order, "Up periscope; stand by number one tube."

At that instant it was noted that something had gone wrong with the Torpedo Data Computer. With the target rushing by him at point-blank range, Blanchard did the only thing he could do—fired all six tubes. The one explosion which the submarine heard on her way to deep submergence—and a depth charge hammering—was timed correctly for the sixth torpedo. All the others missed astern.

Albacore, in his rueful report that night, claimed only damage and it was not till almost a year later that a prisoner admitted the *Taiho*, a new carrier, had been sunk by a submarine torpedo in the Battle of the Philippine Sea. That one torpedo had started gasoline fires and explosions which eventually caused her sinking. Most of the *Albacore*'s crew never heard this good news for she was lost on her next patrol.

I feel that we may chalk up an "assist" for *Cavalla* and *Albacore* to Fifth Fleet in winning the Battle of the Philippine Sea, which came to a climax on June 19 when, in battles between Japanese carrier-based planes and our own, the enemy fleet lost practically all its planes and pilots. On the next day, Rear Admiral Mitscher was able to get in a long-range attack with our aircraft which sank the carrier *Hitaka* and two fleet oilers. The carrier *Junyo* and one fleet tanker were damaged. The Japanese Fleet, what was left of it, fled homeward.

The perfect coordination between our Fleet and our submarines during the 11 days required to set up and fight the Battle of the Philippine Sea was the result of lessons we had learned in earlier operations and it was something of which the Submarine Forces will always be proud.

After the air battles were over, our submarines searched the area but found only six of the lads who were shot down while putting on that beautiful "Marianas Turkey Shoot."

As we closed the books for June there was a general feeling of satisfaction with our support of the Fleet and our knocking off of enemy tonnage. We didn't know until near the end of the war how well the efforts of our submarines had paid off. JANAC credits us with sinking 42 merchantmen for a total of 176,550 tons and 11 men-of-war, including two carriers, one mine layer, five destroyers, and three frigates for a total of 76,570 additional tons. Thirty submarines shared the credit.

Top scores went to *Albacore* and *Cavalla,* who sank the big carriers. *Harder* deserves very honorable mention for her three destroyers. Among the merchant-shipping scores *Tang,* Lieutenant Commander Dick O'Kane,* was high gun with five ships sunk southwest of Kyushu for a total of 21,997 tons. *Shark II,* Lieutenant Commander E. N. Blakely, stood second with four ships down in the Marianas area for a total of 21,672 tons.

At the suggestion of Admiral Nimitz, arrangements had been made for a conference between Rear Admiral Christie, Comsub Seventh Fleet, and his Staff, with my Staff and myself at Brisbane for July 6. So, at noon on July 2, I took off by air, accompanied by Commander Bud Yeomans, Strategic Planning Officer; Commander W. E. Ferrall, Material Officer; and Commander Sparky Woodruff, Force Personnel Officer.

Admiral Christie had already arrived and together we went in to pay our respects to Vice Admiral Kinkaid, Commander Seventh Fleet, at his Brisbane Headquarters. Rear Admiral C. E. Van Hook, an old friend with whom I had served in the Naval Mission to Brazil, was Chief of Staff to

* For Commander O'Kane's own story read *Clear the Bridge* another volume in The Bantam War Book Series.

Admiral Kinkaid, and several others of his staff were friends
or acquaintances.

There were many problems to be ironed out between our
two Submarine Forces and amicable solutions were arrived at
in most cases. Christie felt that he should have more submarines in the Seventh Fleet. I had felt the same way when I had
his job, but the distribution was made by Cominch, so there
was little I could do about the matter. As the land forces advanced northward it was inevitable that our two forces would
draw closer together and all areas would become crowded
with submarines. The general opinion was that, prior to invasion, a close blockade of Japan would be necessary, in which
case there would be no jobs for submarines except lifeguarding and special missions.

In the meanwhile, there were still plenty of targets for
both forces and our chief interest centered in expediting delivery of night periscopes, prosubmarine gear to lessen the
growing threat of enemy antisubmarine vessels and aircraft,
plus new torpedoes in the secret weapon category.

I found out that the guerrillas in the Philippines had two
radio stations, which guarded two different frequencies, and
talked to Australian stations whenever necessary to arrange
for supplies or rendezvous with Seventh Fleet's "guerrilla line"
submarines, "Spyron," as they were unofficially labeled. I believed it would be valuable for our Subpac boats to be able to
talk to those stations, and I contacted the lad who handled all
the guerilla details, Commander Chick Parsons.

I had heard practically unbelievable tales of Parson's ad-
ventures, hence I welcomed a chance for a conference. He
was in Brisbane momentarily, between trips to the Islands.
Seemingly there was no place in the Philippines that he did
not visit when occasion demanded, even though the Japs had
put a price of 100,000 yen on his head. Chick said he felt
flattered by the amount.

Commander Parsons had organized the Spyron activity
early in 1943 and had been placed by General MacArthur in
charge of contacting, organizing and supplying the American
and Filipino guerrillas. At first his operations were handled by
means of special missions assigned to various submarines.
Then, as the business grew, our two largest submarines, Narwhal and Nautilus, were detailed to Spyron and made more
or less regular trips. Other submarines were added until, at
the end of the war, statistics showed that 19 different U.S.

submarines had undertaken 42 missions in Spyron, only one of which failed—when *Seawolf* was lost.

Parsons, then a naval reserve lieutenant and part-time consular agent for Panama, had been captured by the Japanese in Manila, tortured by them in old Fort Santiago, and exchanged via *Gripsholm* as Panamanian consul. Finally, he was sent by the Navy Department to Australia to work out plans for re-entering the Philippines. All resistance had not been crushed by the Japs and it was important for us to ascertain the extent of any guerilla activity and to establish coast-watcher stations to report enemy ship movements.

Hundreds of tons of supplies were delivered and hundreds of persons exchanged by submarines between Australia and the Philippines. About 120 radio sets were furnished to coast watchers and others. It was one of his coast watchers at San Bernadino Strait who sent a warning, paralleling that of *Flying Fish*, advising of the sortie of the northern Japanese task force just prior to the Battle of the Philippine Sea.

Aside from arms and ammunition, the Spyron cargoes consisted of medicines, sewing kits, cigarettes (with the box bearing the promise, "I shall return"), shoes and hundreds of thousands of counterfeit Japanese yen. Submarines made landings in practically all parts of the Islands and even occasionally came alongside a dock in Mindanao to the music of "Anchors Aweigh," by a bamboo band.

Chick Parsons, now back at his old job in Manila, was awarded the Navy Cross with two stars, each of which he may wear with the consciousness that he won them the hard way.

Our Brisbane conference completed, I returned to Pearl, where I was greeted with the bad news that S-28, Lieutenant Commander J. G. Campbell, had been lost in training operations on July 4. S-28 had been brought out from San Diego for the purpose of rendering services to Destroyer Force Pacific (Despac) for training sonar operators. In company with the U.S. Coast Guard cutter *Reliance* she operated in the Pearl training area on July 3 and 4.

Her last run was begun at 1730, about four miles from *Reliance*. The scheme was that she should make a normal approach as for firing a torpedo, while the trainees on *Reliance* endeavored to maintain contact with her by sonar. S-28 submerged and came in toward the target, until the range by sonar decreased to about 1,700 yards. Then the bearing of the submarine drifted aft and the range gradually increased to 4,700 yards, when *Reliance* lost contact and never regained it, even though she reversed course and tried to communicate by means of her supersonic gear. No distress or other signals were heard. What accident or casualty led to her loss will never be known for the depth of water, 1,400 fathoms, precluded any possibility of salvage.

Before going to Brisbane I had requested permission to send the *Holland*, Commander C. Q. Wright, from Midway to Saipan, in order to act as a refueling and rearming base for our submarines on patrol. She carried 100 or more torpedoes and could fuel about eight submarines. Our boats in the Convoy College area between Luzon, Formosa and South China were finding so many targets that their torpedo supply was soon exhausted. Then they had to come all the way back to Midway to rearm. Cincpac's Staff, as usual, took a "poor view" of the proposition and said the harbor was too jammed with shipping to squeeze in any more until after Labor Day. This was a big disappointment to me, so I obtained permission from the Big Boss to write direct to Admiral Spruance and get his reaction. I felt sure he would find a space somewhere, for vessels with her repair facilities should have been mighty welcome in the forward area. As I expected, the reply came back in the affirmative, and on July 29 *Holland* dropped her hook in Tanapag Harbor.

The heavy resistance on Saipan and the sortie of the enemy fleet, plus bad weather, forced a delay in the invasion of Guam, the second phase of Operation Forager. However, this same delay permitted an excellent amount of softening up by Rear Admiral Mitscher's bombers and surface ships, before our amphibious forces hit the beaches July 21.

During the initial stages of the air attacks, *Stingray*, Lieutenant Commander S. C. Loomis, Jr., of Aurora, Illinois, staged our first periscope rescue of a downed aviator. Loomis received word that a pilot was down in a position about 40 miles from *Stingray*. He rang up full speed and headed in. As he closed Orote Point, the shore batteries opened up and when shell splashes got uncomfortably close, he dived. The pilot was still not in sight, but Loomis observed a plane drop a rubber boat, and a few minutes later the pilot was seen in it. Splashes were all around the unfortunate aviator, for he was not more than a mile from the batteries. He could be seen ducking as the shells landed.

Stingray had to make three passes at the zoomie before he finally got the idea and, on the fourth approach, looped his towline around the extended scope. He had a badly cut left hand, which he kept holding up before the object glass, but there was nothing Loomis could do about his wound at that time, for splashes were still rising all about them. One hour later it seemed safe to surface and Ensign Donald C. Brandt was taken aboard. He had been briefed on the possibility of this type of rescue, but evidently the experience of being shot out of the air at 14,000 feet and falling upside down in his parachute from 12,000 feet had confused him a bit.

An account of *Stingray*'s feat was found in a captured Jap diary on Guam. The writer averred that the submarine had entered the harbor to make this rescue—not bad publicity for our side.

Tragedy again struck when, on July 26, I was forced to report *Golet,* Lieutenant Commander J. S. Clark, overdue, presumed lost. She was a new submarine, on her second war patrol, assigned to the entire area along the northeast coast of Honshu. Japanese postwar reports record that on July 4 an antisubmarine attack was made which brought up cork, a raft and a heavy pool of oil. Thus *Golet* probably met her fate.

Our losses had been heavy during June and July but the Japanese had also taken serious losses in shipping and men-of-war. For July, JANAC records that 29 submarines sank 47 merchantmen, among them six irreplaceable tankers, for a total of 202,433 tons, plus one light cruiser, three destroyers, one submarine, a mine sweeper and a subchaser.

Tang, in the Yellow Sea in the first days of July, continued her amazing record by sinking five medium-sized ships. O'Kane, her skipper, celebrated July 4 with traditional fireworks, but enemy ships were on the receiving end of the explosions. She began the day with an end around run on a maru, whose mast could be seen over the horizon. The target was identified by O'Kane as a seaplane tender. *Tang*'s approach led her into water so shallow that she finally had to back down to keep from hitting bottom. This, however, did not distract the skipper, who fired two torpedoes, both of which hit and sank the target. The submarine then surfaced and cleared the area through a swarm of fishing boats. From postwar reports it appears that this victim was the 6,932-ton freighter *Yamaoka.*

Later that afternoon, *Tang* sighted smoke and closed in to make a fairly routine sinking of another freighter, the 6,886-ton *Asukazan Maru*. This was the tail end of a patrol begun on June 8, but all *Tang*'s attacks were concentrated in a period of 13 days, when she sank 10 ships for a grand total of 39,160 tons, the highest single patrol score against merchant-ship tonnage. No less remarkable on this patrol, was *Tang*'s torpedo shooting. Ten ships sunk with only 24 torpedoes is a top-notch performance.

Seahorse, Commander Cutter, also continued her high-scoring streak by sinking three ships in two days in Convoy College Area. Since she had sunk another in June on this same patrol, this brought her total bag up to four marus.

As *Seahorse* surfaced at dusk of the 3rd, the Officer of the Deck thought he saw a puff of smoke to westward. It proved to be a convoy. Bright moonlight forced a submerged attack. There were six escorts with five sizable ships in two columns and before midnight *Seahorse* was in beautiful position between the two. With this set-up it was fairly simple to sink one ship in each column, using bow and stern tubes, but evasion of the counterattack by the swarming escorts was not so successful. The depth charging ("death charging," as Slade's wardroom steward always called it) resulted in damage to the very important SJ radar installation. Repairs to this required three hours after surfacing, during which time Cutter was trying to locate the remainder of the convoy. He knew that his packmate, *Bang,* was closing to attack when he went in to fire and he heard distant depth charging, which might have given a clue but the direction was undetermined. Finally, on a hunch, he headed northwest trying to think as a Jap might think and select the course which a southbound convoy would be most unlikely to take.

The reasoning worked and, at 0630 on the Fourth of July, *Seahorse* was again in contact. There they were, the three remaining merchantmen, with only one escort, but two planes were circling over them. It required a wide end around to get in position ahead but Cutter finally made it and came in submerged. The first of the three he passed up because she looked small. *Seahorse* had torpedoes only for two ships and the other two looked larger. However, in crossing under her stern, he passed so close he said he could have recognized the Jap soldiers hanging their feet over the side if he had ever seen them before. Slade noted on his report that she looked top-heavy and had a 10-degree list to port. Maybe she would capsize anyhow, before she reached Manila.

Getting into firing position for the other two had its complications, however, when they zigged just as *Seahorse* was practically in position. The sonar operator, Chief Radioman Roy Hoffman, was a wizard at his job and reported hearing the leading ship put her rudder over. Sure enough, next time when Slade stuck his scope up, the targets were on a new course, requiring a rapid change in the firing plan. From her last seven torpedoes, *Seahorse* got five hits in the two targets, but somehow, if JANAC is correct, one ship escaped.

Guardfish, Lieutenant Commander N. G. "Bub" Ward of Indian Head, Maryland, patrolling the newly created Convoy College Area between Luzon, Formosa and the Chinese island of Hainan, slashed into the enemy shipping which streamed through that bottleneck toward the Philippines.

The Japs were desperately trying to re-enforce that sector of their crumbling empire against the expected onslaught of our amphibious forces. Ward, patrolling alone, received, on July 16, a contact report from a submarine about 100 miles distant and immediately headed in to intercept the enemy.

By 1130 that night Ward, running on surface, had worked himself into excellent position on the port bow of a convoy, which consisted of 10 ships and four escorts. The group formed an almost completely overlapping target and Bub fired his six bow torpedoes at the two largest, then swung at full speed to get his stern tubes into action. All six of his first salvo hit in the four nearest ships. The leading vessel, a tanker, evidently loaded with gasoline, blew up, sending flames thousands of feet into the air. Her next astern, a large freighter, loaded with ammunition, caught fire aft and later exploded with a tremendous roar. The third ship in the column, also a freighter, broke in two and sank, while the fourth, hit forward, settled rapidly, bow first.

In a wild scramble, the next group of ships scattered in all directions, so Ward held his fire and reloaded forward tubes. Later that night he sank one ship and hit another with two torpedoes, but did not see it go down. As dawn broke on July 17, *Guardfish* sank her sixth victim and received in return a series of tooth-rattling depth charge attacks, which kept her down for several hours. When he finally got back to surface, Ward continued the chase and on the 19th sank two more ships. In a period of 56 hours, according to Bub's estimates, *Guardfish* had sunk eight ships and damaged one.

Flasher, a Seventh Fleet submarine on her third war patrol, made a very pleasing contribution of four ships, one sunk in June and the others in July. Her skipper, Commander Reuben T. Whitaker, started *Flasher* on her way to becoming the highest-scoring submarine of the war. One of Whitaker's victims was a tanker sunk northwest of Manila but the most pleasing item in his bag was a light cruiser, later found to be the 5,700-ton *Oi,* downed about the middle of the South China Sea on July 19.

On his first attack Reuben got two hits out of four shots and stopped the *Oi* in her tracks. Her mainmast went over the side, she listed to port and settled by the stern but apparently did not intend to sink. The escorting destroyer gave *Flasher* a working over which did some small damage, and then returned to her crippled companion. So did the submarine, but this time all his torpedoes missed, due probably to faulty data, hastily collected just ahead of another counterattack. Whitaker, however, was determined to finish off his victim and two hours later when the destroyer had again stopped her depth charging, he came up for a periscope look. The cruiser was still afloat and the submarine went deep to reload torpedoes. Sometime during this reload the *Oi* went down, for when Whitaker came up for another look, the cruiser was gone and the destroyer hastily departing.

The Jap submarine included in our July bag was contributed by *Sawfish,* Lieutenant Commander A. B. Banister of Madison, Connecticut. She was part of a wolf pack in which *Rock* and *Tilefish* were also members. Captain Warren D. Wilkin, a division commander, was the pack leader. Subpac received a contact report on an enemy submarine which was evidently heading for Balintang Channel north of Luzon. One of Admiral Fife's boats had fired at it but missed. We passed the word to "Wilkie" and he laid a trap on the morning of July 26. *Sawfish* was first to sight the enemy running at good speed on the surface through waters which the Japs should have known were swarming with American submarines. Banister bored in, fired four torpedoes and got three hits, which on such a small target is perfection. *Tilefish* had actually started her approach on the enemy when *Sawfish*'s torpedoes hit and *Rock* was close enough to see the columns of water thrown by the explosions. The poor Jap never had a chance. We learned that she was loaded with German radar and technicians brought to Penang by one of Doenitz's submarines. There were no survivors.

Commander L. P. "Red" Ramage, of the *Parche,* staged a whirlwind battle in this same area on July 31. Red had been rewarded for his good work in *Trout* with command of a new boat.

Parche, with *Steelhead* and *Hammerhead,* had been formed as a wolf pack to operate in Convoy College, but for 30 days Lady Luck did not smile upon them. *Parche* had been unable to close a fast unescorted aircraft carrier and had been thwarted by the radar of a cruiser-destroyer force which she attempted to attack on surface at night. Red's approach was interrupted at long range by a hail of well-directed gunfire, which forced him to get under. Enemy aircraft from Formosa had been a constant menace. Nerves in the boat were getting edgy.

Finally, in pitch darkness, of the graveyard hours of July 31, *Parche* hit the enemy with a vengeance in 46 minutes of fighting that was outstanding in the annals of submarine warfare. Ramage had worked his ship on surface into the middle of a large, heavily escorted convoy and from that position commenced firing torpedoes. The hell that broke loose with his first hit can well be imagined: escorts fired flares, stricken ships fired distress rockets and everything with a gun aboard, opened up—sometimes at the submarine, sometimes at one another. Red calmly cleared the bridge of all except himself and the quartermaster. At times, he told me, he was so close under the sides of ships that they couldn't depress their guns to hit him.

It seems impossible that *Parche* could have survived those shell-and-machine-gun-packed minutes but she did. Twice, ramming was narrowly avoided, but Ramage stuck to the surface until the false dawn made it foolhardy to take further chances. By that time, *Parche* had fired 19 torpedoes for 15 hits. JANAC cuts the estimated sinkings, but whether or not all the ships sank, no one can discount the terrific damage caused by a torpedo hit—flooded holds, ruined ammunition and food supplies, jettisoned deck cargo.

Subpac Board of Awards recommended Commander Lawson P. Ramage for the Congressional Medal of Honor.

To our great satisfaction, this award was eventually given Red by President Roosevelt himself, who arrived at Pearl on July 26 aboard the cruiser *Indianapolis*. All flag officers were presented to him, as he sat in a big chair on the bridge deck. The President's appearance was distressing to me; he looked in extremely bad health. His skin had that grayish tinge one often sees in the very ill.

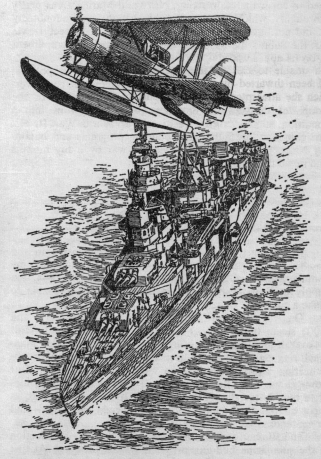

U.S.S. Indianapolis

Admiral King was out from Washington and General MacArthur had come up from New Guinea to meet the President, who took up his quarters in the Chris Holmes house, from which the aviators had been temporarily removed and on which Sub Base repair gangs had been working for a week to get it back into shape. Almost continuous top-level conferences occupied most of his time, but he managed to cover the main Army, Navy and Marine areas pretty thoroughly which, in view of his health, he undoubtedly should not have done. He did us the honor of inspecting, via car, the Submarine Base and was kind enough to compliment us on its appearance.

Regardless of differences which may exist in political faiths, the Navy will always have a great respect and reverence for Franklin D. Roosevelt, who pulled us out of the slough of despond in the early '30's, and got us into a condition of approximate readiness for World War II. His farsightedness, in authorizing building programs and obtaining bases, undoubtedly shortened the war by many months and saved thousands of American lives.

CHAPTER 12

In the early days of the submarine offensive in the Pacific, the shortage of torpedoes was so chronic that my commanders were frantic. But, by the middle of 1944, the supply at Pearl Harbor was so large that we were able to make a cut back.

On August 1, we had 200 electrics (Mark XVIII) and 1,005 steam types (Marks XIV and XXIII) on hand. With an overall monthly expenditure of 350, I recommended manufacturing only enough to keep the pipe line filled and concentrating excess facilities on new secret weapons. Our stowages were overflowing and great piles of boxed torpedoes grew outside the Base Torpedo Shop. It was obvious that, as surface and amphibious forces advanced, we would find fewer targets and shoot fewer torpedoes.

The Bureau of Ships also informed me that a reduction in the submarine building program was in prospect. At first consideration, this seemed a blow but realistic examination of this further indication of the healthy state of our armament production showed we could take a cut without curtailing our ever-increasing activities. With the submarines then in the Pacific—approximately 140—we had the situation well in hand, and dozens more were so far along in construction that they would have to be completed and sent out to us.

Secret weapons were beginning to come along and the Training Command was bending every effort to instruct submariners in their adjustment and use. The first night periscope with built-in radar, had been installed in *Sea Fox* but had not yet arrived at Pearl. Our two new ultra-short-wave radars for surface targets and for early warning of the approach of aircraft were still delayed. To my pleas that these be expedited, I got only sympathy and a reply that the Amphibious Forces had the top priority on electronics of all types and we would have to wait.

We know now that many of our submarines were sunk by enemy planes which surprised them, probably at a time when the submarine had its old type SD radar turned off. There were recurrent indications that Japanese planes could home on the beam sent out from the SD, hence most skippers used it only intermittently. We urgently needed something better and more secure.

While Admiral King, and his Chief of Plans, Rear Admiral C. M. Cooke, were in Pearl during July, frequent references had been made by them to the need for our use of midget submarines. This was an idea I had been battling all during the war. The Japs had midgets, the Germans had midgets, the Italians had midgets and now the British had used XE craft, four-man submarines, to attack the *Tirpitz* at Alten Fjord in Norway, therefore we should have midgets.

I wanted no part of it and said so quite frankly. In the first place, the production of such craft would reduce construction of our standard submarines which were doing such a good job of chasing Japanese shipping off the seas. After we had chased them all into port, they presented no great menace and could be destroyed by bombing or could be mined in by submarines or aircraft. The waters in the harbors of the Japanese homeland are so shallow that entrance of midgets therein, I felt, would result in their certain destruction, and I did not want to send men on suicide missions no matter how keen they were to go. Everyone should be assured of a fair chance of survival, and the loss of men daring enough to undertake suicide missions would rob us of personnel who could be more profitably employed.

Admiral Cooke said that, whether we liked it or not, we were going to have to take over a couple of the British XE craft and learn how to run them. That was slightly different, for it meant no reduction in building programs for Fleet-type submarines. When the proposition came up to send them in to Yokosuka or elsewhere, I would try to deal with the situation then. What ever happened to the idea, I don't know, but we never built any midgets and we never got any XE craft.

As to the very hush-hush prosubmarine gear which we so urgently needed and which was so slow in arriving at Pearl, I learned that Commander Dan Daspit of *Tinosa* fame, had been assigned as project officer to keep the production pushing as rapidly as possible. An additional officer, Lieutenant Fagan, had been ordered to San Diego to help the University of California Division of War Research boost their operations. With electronics priorities as they were, that seemed to be all I could do about the matter. Dr. Harnwell succeeded in obtaining release on 11 more FM Sonar installations which had been intended for mine sweepers. It was found they could not be used effectively by surface craft. I was sorry about the sweepers' hard luck, but I was overjoyed to have those sets fall into our laps. We could really use them.

Business appeared to be brisk in our Convoy College area at the top of the South China Sea. A Subpac coordinated attack group operating in that area on August 17, sighted a convoy heading south before daylight but was unable to get in an attack. One vessel of this group was the escort carrier, *Otaka*. The enemy had begun using such vessels with convoys much as U.S. forces were employing them in the Atlantic. Their reason for this was not clear because it would have appeared more economical and safer to furnish air cover to their convoys from Formosa, China or the Philippines. The escort carriers could then have been devoted entirely to carrying freight and ferrying planes. However, their error was all to our advantage.

Redfish, which made contact with this carrier escorted convoy, reported same to her packmates and also notified a two-boat pack from Seventh Fleet, which was patrolling in the next area to southward. This group consisted of *Bluefish*,

Commander C. M. "Charlie" Henderson, and *Rasher*, Commander H. G. "Hank" Munson, who was also pack leader.

Rasher, heading up toward Cape Bojeador, made radar contact at 15,000 yards. The enemy force appeared to consist of 13 ships and six escorts steaming in parallel columns with escorts in an arc across the front and several trailing astern. Intense air activity preceding its passage made it apparent this was an important convoy. Munson took a position on the starboard bow of the targets, about 1,500 yards ahead of the nearest escort, and opened the battle with a trial salvo of two torpedoes from stern tubes aimed at a large tanker. One torpedo hit and created an appalling explosion with flames at least 1,000 feet high—probably from aviation gas.

The starboard escort opened fire in all directions then turned and raced astern to drop depth charges on something two miles distant from *Rasher*. Other ships opened fire, two of them apparently at each other. Some turned on their running lights. Munson made an end around and took position 5,000 yards ahead and studied the radar picture. Finally he had the solution and eased in astern of the starboard bow escort. At 2211 he fired six bow tubes at the nearest big target. Swinging rapidly, he then fired his stern tubes at a big ship astern of the first one. Eight of the torpedoes hit in four different targets. Pandemonium broke out again with signaling, firing, and depth charging but still no one located *Rasher*. One ship was burning while another, believed to be a transport, dropped out of formation, accompanied by two escorts. Gradually her pip disappeared from the screen. Later that night, blinking white lights of lifeboats were seen in the area. Apparently, that target sank. A lake of heavy oil was also encountered, probably from the tanker.

About this time, the convoy split into two groups and headed west. *Rasher* kept tracking the leading outfit. The other section about five miles to the northward, later that night became targets for the *Spadefish,* one of *Redfish*'s pack, which was still pursuing.

Rasher then took position on the port bow of her quarry, tracked for a few minutes and headed in and, at 2330, fired her remaining four bow torpedoes at the leading ship. Again she swung at full speed and fired her last two stern torpedoes at a second target. All of these fish hit, one of them in a ship beyond the first target.

Spadefish got a passenger-cargo ship and, on August 22, a tanker which might have been one of Munson's cripples, while *Redfish* got a freighter. *Rasher*, with 15 hits out of 18 shots, had, in 150 minutes, sunk an escort carrier—probably on her third attack—a tanker, a transport and two freighters. Three other ships slipped away, damaged. Thus in one fateful night, the Japanese had lost a 20,000-ton carrier and 38,547 tons of shipping.

Croaker, Commander J. E. "Jack" Lee of Wilmington, Delaware, made her first war patrol in the East China Sea and brought back a nice bag, which included the light cruiser *Nagara*. On the morning of August 7, just south of Nagasaki, Lee encountered a cruiser escorted by a subchaser and a plane. The target was zigzagging radically and there was no time in which to determine her zig plan, so Lee got a hasty set-up and fired four torpedoes. Just at that instant the target zigged away from the sub. This might have been sufficient to cause all torpedoes to miss but for some reason the unfortunate captain, at the end of two minutes, made an equally radical zag back toward *Croaker* and received one torpedo hit aft. Lee remained at periscope depth, let his entire control party watch her death struggles, and took excellent color movies of the sinking.

In preparation for the next big push which was to follow the Marianas invasion, we were requested to make photographic mosaics of several specified islands, and a reconnaissance of beaches on Peleliu and Yap by means of landing parties. The Amphibious Forces were in great need of information as to depth of water on the reefs at various stages of the tide, entrances through the reefs and so on, in order to determine whether it was practical to use Higgins boats, DUKW's, LST's and Alligator tanks on any particular beach. Lack of such detailed knowledge at Tarawa had proved an almost fatal handicap to that assault.*

There was only one way to get such data and that was by landing parties in rubber boats operating from a submarine. The hazards of such operations were naturally very great. It was imperative that landing parties be undetected since their discovery on a particular beach would constitute advance notice to the enemy of our intentions.

---

* For a complete firsthand account of this battle read *Tarawa* by Robert Sherrod, another volume in the Bantam War Book Series.

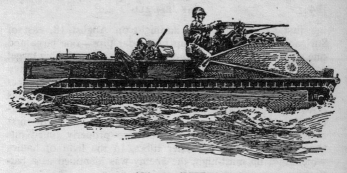

Alligator (LVT)

Burrfish, Lieutenant Commander W. B. Perkins of Bon Air, Virginia, was assigned the job of making the photographic mosaics at Palau and Yap and of basing the landing party which was supplied by Commander Amphibious Forces. This group, commanded by Lieutenant C. E. Kirkpatrick, USNR, consisted of one other officer and nine men, all highly trained in boat work and scouting. Their landing on Peleliu was entirely successful and valuable information was obtained. Further attempts to land in that vicinity and at Angaur were abandoned after several night approaches. The intensity of enemy radar activity made it practically certain that the submarine would be detected and thereby expose Cincpac's plan.

Burrfish then moved to Yap and on the night of August 16 a landing was made on the south tip of the island. The beach was found to be satisfactory for all types of amphibious craft. On the night of August 18, a landing was attempted on the nearby island of Gagil Tomil. Five men went through the surf in a rubber boat and after anchoring safely inside the reef, four went to explore the beach; one returned. The other three, we learned later, were captured. The appointed hour for return to the submarine came and went; the two men in the rubber boat manned the oars and searched within 100 yards of the beach but without result. The plan to invade Yap was abandoned, possibly because of the exposure of our intentions. In any case, by-passing of that island seemed a good idea to me, just as in the case of Truk, for it had little strategic value.

Hardhead, Commander F. McMasters of York, Pennsylvania, was fortunate in bagging the light cruiser *Natori* on her first patrol. Just after midnight on August 18, east of Surigao Strait, she picked up two radar pips—one large and one small—and began an approach. Eventually, the big target could be seen through binoculars and appeared to be a heavy cruiser or battleship. McMasters intended to take no chances on letting her escape so he fired five steam torpedos from his bow tubes, then swung and fired four electric fish from his after tubes. It is lucky that he did so, for not one of his first salvo was heard to hit. However, two properly timed hits were obtained from the after tubes. In the light of flames which shot up mast-high, the enemy was identified as a battleship.

Hardhead headed out and reloaded her tubes and then returned to the scene. The target was picked up by radar and attacked with six torpedoes, all of which exploded at the proper times but at dawn the target was still afloat. McMasters then approached submerged but the Jap sank just before he reached firing position.

Reports of sinkings indicated that August would be another record month. We estimated the score would be about 300,000 tons. JANAC, however, records that 30 submarines sank 41 merchant ships, including nine tankers, for a total of 215,657 tons. Sinking of men-of-war totaled 14 vessels of 41,089 tons. Included in these latter were one escort carrier, two light cruisers, two destroyers, four frigates and five auxiliary craft. The south coast of Japan, the Yellow Sea, the East China Sea, the Convoy College area and the South China Sea had become the best hunting grounds for subs. The best focal point was, of course, the Convoy College area which yielded more than one-third of the total tonnage sunk for August.

As soon as Guam had been reported secured, Rear Admiral John Brown, as my deputy, flew down there to stake out a claim for a submarine rest camp. The site of the base naturally had to be in Apra Harbor and was intended to consist of nothing more than piers for mooring three or four tenders, plus a HQ building for my office and perhaps a torpedo shop. The Recuperation Center, however, we wanted located on the east coast so as to have the advantage of the trade wind. I had been in Apra Harbor twice before and knew "the steaming stillness of that orchid-scented glade," as Mr. Kipling might have said.

When John got to Guam he found that nothing less than a tank could have got to the locality we had tentatively picked out on the chart. He finally selected, from the air, a coconut grove, just north of the Talofofo River.

Admiral Nimitz announced that he would shift his head-quarters to Guam and immediately there followed a mad scramble of all branches of the Service to obtain space there. However, Cincpac held the gold rush back and limited the new bases to those whose presence on Guam was vitally necessary. Even I, who had helped plan a submarine base on Guam in 1922, was held up by Cincpac's Staff—I fought more battles with that Staff than I ever fought against the Japanese—but, as usual, direct appeal to the Big Boss won my point, and I flew down from Pearl to make final plans. With me went Commander Joe Thew, Captain of the *Sperry*, whom I expected to send to Guam to set up the new advance base. En route I spent the second night aboard *Holland* in Tanapag Harbor, Saipan. Seven submarines were alongside reloading with torpedoes. They were wolf packs which had expended all torpedoes in a matter of days in Luzon Strait and were shoving off, three that afternoon and four next morning, to go back into the battle. It didn't require a sooth-sayer to foretell that September would be one of the most productive months.

I called on Vice Admiral Johnny Hoover aboard the destroyer tender *Curtis*. His title was Commander Marianas and as may be imagined, he had problems galore, some of which were being solved by the presence of the old *Holland* at Saipan. Her port side was stacked with submarines and on her starboard side were four light surface craft receiving re-pairs from her well-equipped workship. Just as I had fore-seen, *Holland* was a most welcome addition to the working forces at that advance base. Admiral Hoover told me that he would leave Saipan shortly for Guam and would take the *Curtis* with him, and I was invited to send another submarine tender to take her berth. This, naturally, I was delighted to promise for I had an ambition to move a submarine tender to Guam as soon as possible and get my own advance refitting base started.

At Guam, with General Henry Larsen, USMC, Island Commander, I took a jeep ride across the island to settle defi-nitely on the location of our rest camp. We took a tommy gunner with us because hundreds of Japanese had taken to the jungle. The site we selected was an abandoned coconut grove which sloped down to a good beach. With a bit of blast-

ing, swimming pools could be made inside the barrier reef.
There had been no artillery preparation on the east side of
the island. It looked ideal and later became—next to Myrna,
our camp at Majuro in the Marshalls—the prettiest rest camp
we had.

Admiral Nimitz arrived after me and, at a conference
with him, I asked permission to send a tender down and get
started immediately. This was objected to by his Planning Officer, who insisted the harbor was already too crowded. I
pointed out that while Apra Harbor might be a bit crowded,
the patrol areas out along the Asiatic coasts were not as
crowded with subs as I wanted them to be. By squeezing one
more ship into Guam, thus shortening the nonproductive distance to those areas, I could increase the density of our submarine coverage. Admiral Nimitz agreed and gave me the
green light. On consulting Captain Becker, the Port Director,
I found that he had already planned to berth a submarine
tender and a destroyer tender, and had a third berth available
for another tender if I wanted it. The advance base I had had
my eye on for months was now a reality.

After a short stay at Myrna, where I had the pleasure of
pinning a Navy Cross on Captain G. E. "Pete" Peterson, for
his excellent work as leader of a most productive wolf pack,
and a Silver Star on Lieutenant Commander Franklin G.
Hess of Sacramento, California, CO of the *Saury*, for his
work in a submarine to which he had formerly been attached,
I caught a plane for Pearl.

There I found that plans made last month for submarine
participation in the invasion of Palau (Operation Stalemate)
were being put into effect and submarines were en route to
their stations.

The Third Fleet under Admiral Halsey was ranging the
western Carolines, and planes from Vice Admiral Marc Mitscher's Task Force 38 were attacking Mindanao and the southern Philippines. Carrier strikes had already been made on the
Bonins and on Yap.

For the invasion of Peleliu and Angaur, set for September 15, Admiral Halsey had requested a reconnaissance line
of nine submarines about 400 miles northwest of Palau. This
group was intended to guard Third Fleet from surprise. Captain C. W. "Weary" Wilkins in *Seahorse* was in command of
this special detail. The usual lifeguards were provided at
Palau and Yap.

When the Fleet was no longer required at Palau, Admiral Halsey moved northward to strike Manila on September 21 and 22, and the Formosa-Ryuku area later. The "Zoo," as we designated the reconnaissance group, was therefore moved up to eastward of the top of Formosa and eventually it was dispersed to regular patrol stations. None of its members had opportunity to make an attack. We considered that this scheme was not profitable and it was not used again. The submarines composing the "Zoo" could have been better employed off ports from which enemy naval units might have sortied or along the trade routes.

The grand task of sinking Japan's naval and mercantile fleets was progressing rapidly. By September, more than 4,000,000 tons of Japanese shipping had gone to the bottom, representing about two-thirds of the enemy's total tonnage. However, in performing this feat, our losses had not been inconsiderable. The enemy had been responsible for the destruction of 28 of our submarines, and accidents had claimed six more. September brought more lost submarines.

From Submarines Seventh Fleet came the bad news that *Robalo*, Commander M. M. Kimmel, son of Admiral Husband E. Kimmel, was overdue, presumed lost. There was no clue as to the cause, but later word was received via the Philippine guerrillas and a U.S. Navy enlisted man, who was a prisoner of war at Puerto Princessa Prison Camp, Palawan Island, which gave all the facts thus far uncovered.

On August 2, 1944, a note dropped from the window of a prison cell in which the survivors from *Robalo* were held, was picked up by an American soldier in a work detail and given to H. D. Hough, Y2/c, another prisoner. Two days later Hough contacted Mrs. Trinidad Mendosa, wife of guerrilla leader, Dr. Mendosa, who furnished further information on the survivors. From these sources, we put together the following facts.

Robalo was sunk July 26, 1944, two miles off the western coast of Palawan Islands as a result of an explosion of her after battery. Four men swam ashore, an officer and three enlisted men: Samuel L. Tucker, Ensign; Floyd G. Laughlin, QM1/c; Wallace K. Martin, SM3/c; and Mason C. Poston, EM2/c. They made their way through the jungles to a small barrio northwest of the Puerto Princessa Camp. They were captured there by Japanese military police, and confined in the jail. They were held for guerrilla activities rather than as

prisoners of war, it is said. On August 15, they were taken off
by a Jap destroyer, and no other information is known regarding their destination or whereabouts. It is possible that
they were executed by the Japanese or that the destroyer in
which they were embarked was sunk. At any rate, they were
never recovered, and their note stated that there were no
other survivors.

It is doubted that a battery explosion could be sufficiently violent to cause the sinking of the ship and it is expected that the loss of *Robalo* was caused by an enemy mine.

Flier, also of Seventh Fleet, commanded by Commander
J. D. Crowley of Springfield, Massachusetts, was lost on August 13, while on surface transiting Balabac Strait south of
Palawan Island, the same locality in which *Robalo* had been
sunk.

Commander Crowley told me the story as he passed
through Pearl, en route home a couple of months later. The
submarine was blasted by a terrific explosion on the starboard
side forward, shortly before midnight. Several of the men on
the bridge were injured. Lieutenant Liddell, the Executive Officer, had stepped below the hatch to speak to Commander
Crowley; he was blown through it, and men poured out behind him. Within 20 or 30 seconds, *Flier* sank while still
making 15 knots through the water. The skipper's opinion is
that the explosion was caused by striking a mine.

Survivors stated that the following men were seen in
the water after the ship went down: Commander J. D.
Crowley; Lieutenant J. W. Liddell, Jr.; Ensign A. E. Jacob-
son; A. G. Howell, CRT; D. P. Tremaine, FCR3/c; W. B.
Miller, MoMM3/c; J. D. Russo, QM3/c; E. R. Baumgart,
McMM3/c; Lieutenant P. Knapp; Lieutenant J. E. Casey;
Lieutenant (jg) W. L. Reynolds; Ensign P. S. Mayer; C. D.
Pope, CGM; E. W. Hudson, CMoMM; G. F. Madeo, F2/c.
Lieutenant Reynolds was wounded, as was Hudson, and when
the word was passed for all survivors to gather together, they
and Pope did not reappear. Ensign Mayer was being assisted
by Howell, but after about 20 minutes he was unconscious
and had to be abandoned.

The first impulse was to swim to Comeran Island, but
when the question was weighed, and the possibility of falling
into Japanese hands was considered, Crowley decided to
strike out for the coral reefs to the northwestward. Mean-

while, Lieutenant Knapp became separated from the group and was not seen or heard again.

All this time Lieutenant Casey had been unable to see, having been partially blinded by oil. He became exhausted and the others were forced to leave him. Commander Crowley realized that the only hope for anyone lay in swimming at best speed, and all hands were told to do the best they could toward land, which was now in sight. Madeo now began to fall behind, and was not seen again.

At 1330 five of the group, Commander Crowley, Lieutenant Liddell, Ensign Jacobson, Howell and Baumgart reached a floating palm tree and used this to aid themselves in remaining afloat while pushing on toward land. This group came ashore on Bantangule Island at 1530 and were met there by Russo, who swam the entire distance. At 1700 Tremaine was found on the eastern end of the island. A lean-to was constructed and the night was spent on the beach.

A raft was made of drifted bamboo lashed together, and the party began working from island to island, with Palawan the ultimate objective. On August 19, they contacted natives who led them to a U.S. Army Coast Watcher Unit on Palawan. This unit made its communication facilities available to the group, and arrangements were made for evacuation by submarine. On the night of August 30, the survivors from *Flier* embarked in two small boats, and were picked up by *Redfin* early next morning.

Thus ends the tragic story of the *Flier*, first stranded at Midway and got off just by the grace of God. It is not surprising that with those two terrific experiences behind him, Crowley, when he lunched with me in Pearl a month or so later, though of powerful build, looked ready for a rest and a change at home. *Flier* was on her second war patrol when lost, but she had contributed a useful bit of work in her short life by sinking a 10,380-ton transport.

Another loss was *Harder*. On the night of September 15, an intercepted dispatch from *Haddo* to Comsubs Seventh Fleet expressed grave concern for the safety of *Harder*, and, later, Seventh Fleet confirmed the news that *Harder*, with Commander Sam Dealey and that fighting crew of his, was overdue, presumed lost.

Hake, Lieutenant Commander F. E. Haylor of Muncie, Indiana, with *Haddo*, Lieutenant Commander C. W. Nimitz, Jr., of Washington, D.C., and *Harder* set out as a wolf pack from Fremantle on August 5. Commander Sam Dealey, heroic veteran of many successful battles, was the pack leader. On the afternoon of August 20, *Ray*, patrolling the same area, tracked a large convoy into Paluan Bay on the northwestern coast of Mindoro. An hour after surfacing, she contacted *Harder* just outside the bay and Dealey formulated a plan for a concentrated dawn wolf-pack attack on the convoy of at least 16 ships, holed up in the bay.

When the convoy made its exit at dawn, *Ray* was to approach from the northwest, *Haddo* from the west, and *Harder* from the southwest. *Guitarro* also had been drafted by Dealey, and was to attack from the northwest near Cape Calavite Lighthouse. During the attacks which ensued, four ships, totaling 22,000 tons, were sunk. It is thought likely that *Harder* sank one of them.

The following day, *Haddo* and *Harder* conducted a combined attack on three small vessels off Bataan. All three were sunk; these were the coast defense vessels *Matsuwa*, *Sado* and *Hiburi*.

The morning of August 23 *Haddo* contacted a tanker escorted by a destroyer, and blew the bow off the latter in a down-the-throat shot. She fired her last torpedo in this attack, and in response to urgent calls for assistance, *Hake* and *Harder* rendezvoused with her. *Haddo*, being out of torpedoes, "received Sam's blessing" and left his wolf pack, heading south. *Hake* and *Harder* discussed plans for finishing off the damaged destroyer and then departed for their common objective off Caiman Point.

Early next morning *Hake* dived not far from Caiman Point and about four miles off Hermana Major Island, west coast of Luzon, with *Harder* in sight 4,500 yards south of her. *Hake* heard echo ranging to the south and soon sighted two ships which were identified as a three-stack Thailand destroyer (the *Phra Ruang*, of 1,035 tons) and a mine sweeper of less than 1,000 tons. At 0647 Haylor sighted *Harder*'s periscope about 700 yards ahead of him so turned away to avoid possible collision. Shortly thereafter the mine sweeper bore down on the two submarines and *Hake* went deep. At 0728, *Hake* heard 15 rapid depth charges, none close to her. Two sets of screws were heard by *Hake* as she evaded to the westward. By 0955 all was quiet.

Harder never was heard from again. Japanese records reveal that an antisubmarine attack with 440-pound depth charges was made on August 24, in the locality where *Harder* was last seen. The enemy said, "much oil, wood chips and cork floated in the neighborhood." Presumably *Harder* perished in this depth charge attack.

Harder was given the Presidential Citation for her first five patrols, and Commander Dealey was posthumously awarded the Congressional Medal of Honor for his outstanding contribution to the war effort on *Harder*'s fifth patrol. The ship's slogan was "Hit 'em again, *Harder*." Ten enemy merchantmen, four destroyers and two frigates know how fully she lived up to the letter of that slogan.

September was a month of tragedy in another respect. It brought the most heart-rending incident in the entire submarine war in the Pacific, resulting from a combination of circumstances which only prescience denied to man could have avoided, though it brought life and freedom to scores of our Allies.

In the predawn hours of September 12, a wolf pack (Ben's Busters) consisting of *Growler*, Commander T. B. "Ben" Oakley of Los Angeles, California; *Sealion*, Commander Eli T. Reich of New York City; and *Pampanito*, Lieutenant Commander P. E. Summers of Lexington, Tennessee, contacted a nine-ship convoy with seven escorts in the Convoy College area.

In this group was the *Rakuyo Maru*, which was transporting 1,350 English and Australian prisoners of war from Singapore to Japan. These prisoners were the hardiest of the original 90,000 that the Japs had taken in Malaya. They had been working on a railroad construction job from Mandalay to Saigon and were intended for work in factories and mines in Japan.

In the attacks which followed this encounter, four ships and two escorts were sunk and several others damaged, the *Rakuyo* being among those who went down. She sank slowly, giving the Japanese crew and guards ample time to make off in the lifeboats, leaving the prisoners to shift for themselves. By the time the *Rakuyo* took her final plunge, the POW's had constructed rafts and got off the doomed vessel. The Japanese survivors were picked up by various escort vessels but the English and Australians were held at bay at gun point and left to the mercy of the elements.

The submarines, totally unconscious of what had happened, pursued the remnants of the convoy until it took refuge in Hongkong, then they returned to station. On September 15, in late afternoon, *Pampanito* sighted a raft full of people. She went alongside to take a few prisoners as per standard instructions. To her consternation she found them to be Allies so covered with crude oil as to be unrecognizable as white men. She sent a message to *Sealion* asking for help (*Growler* had departed for home), and when the flash reached Pearl we directed two nearby submarines, *Barb* and *Queenfish,* to assist. They raced to the area and by the afternoon of the 17th it was believed all remaining survivors had been picked up.

Rescue parties consisting of strong swimmers went overboard dozens of times to bring in men who were too weak to hold on to a line. When they were got on deck, other parties removed their oil-soaked and louse-infected clothing, and carried them below. There they were cleansed of oil and stowed into improvised bunks. All this had to be done rapidly as the threat of enemy air attack was ever present.

The rescued men were in pitiable condition after three years of captivity and exposure to the ravages of tropical diseases. In all 150 men were saved by the four submarines, which then raced back to Saipan.

Commander Summers of the *Pampanito* said:

> The problem of habitability was an acute problem with the 73 survivors aboard plus our complement of 89 officers and men, but by careful planning and supervision the situation was kept under control and all hands fared very well.
>
> All survivors, except six of the most critical cases, were berthed in the After Torpedo Room. This required ingenuity in devising bunks from torpedo racks and deck space, but with two in each bunk and three or four in each torpedo rack most of them made out better than you might imagine.
>
> All men were infected to various extents with beriberi, scurvy, malaria, and skin irritations. Strict segregation from the crew was necessary. Two officers were assigned to manage the problems and a two-man "nursemaid" watch was kept in the After Torpedo Room in addition to the Pharmacist's Mate and two volunteer assistants (one Ship's Cook and one Seaman) who were working continuously.

The first problem was getting the men on board. In their weakened condition and due to the fact that they were covered with heavy crude oil, actual recovery was quite a task. Many of the men could help themselves but the majority had to be lifted bodily on board.

The next problem was to clean some of the oil off. While still topside, their clothes were cut away and they were given a diesel-oil sponge bath to remove most of the heavy crude oil. Getting the weakened ones down the hatch was quite a job until in the middle of one recovery operation, three planes were reported. You should have seen them run for the hatch when the word "Jap planes" was passed. Once below, the main problem was further examination to determine their injures and sicknesses. Water was their most acute need and they were given plenty, in small amounts at first. Hot soup, tea, and broth followed, and they were soon sleeping the sound sleep of thoroughly exhausted men.

En route to the rescue area *Barb*, Commander E. B. "Gene" Fluckey of Washington, D.C., and *Queenfish*, Commander C. Elliott Loughlin of North Wales, Pennsylvania, made a contact on the night of September 16. They were part of a wolf pack (Ed's Eradicators) commanded by Captain E. R. Swinburne. *Tunny*, Commander George Ellis Pierce of Tullahoma, Tennessee, was the third member, but had been damaged and was on her way to Pearl.

Queenfish told *Barb* she had encountered a five-ship convoy with six escorts and was attacking. By 2254 she had completed her attack so *Barb* stood in on surface. Closing for shots at the leading tanker, Fluckey made out the largest ship in the convoy to be a flattop and immediately shifted his target set-up. He maneuvered to get an overlap of the carrier with a large tanker and, with the nearest Chidori torpedo boat 750 yards away and closing rapidly, opened fire with his bow tubes. Gene then swung with full rudder and tried to bring his stern tubes to bear, however collision with the Chidori was imminent so he was forced to dive. On the way down, five hits were heard, three of which the sound operators said were in the carrier and two in the tanker. Loud breaking-up noises were heard and we now know that the escort carrier *Unyo* of 20,000 tons and the big tanker *Azusa* went down.

The depth charge counterattack was ineffective and shortly after midnight *Barb* surfaced and continued at full speed to the rescue area, where she immediately began picking up survivors.

Fluckey reported:

> They had been in the water or on their small wooden life rafts for a period of five days before being rescued. The, at first, dubious, then amazed, and finally hysterically thankful look on their faces, from the time they first sighted us approaching them, is one we shall never forget.
>
> Several of them were too weak to take the lines thrown them. These were rescued by the valiant efforts of Lieutenant Commander R. W. McNitt, Lieutenant J. G. Lanier, and C. S. Houston, McMM2/c, who dived in after them. The crew formed a production line which took the rescued men as they were got aboard, stripped them, and passed them on to the transportation gang to get them below, where they were received by the cleaners who removed the oil and grease, then on to the "doctors" and "nurses" for treatment, thence to the feeders, and finally to the sleepers who carried them off and tucked them in their bunks.
>
> The appreciation of the survivors was unbounded. Even those who couldn't talk expressed themselves tearfully through their glazed, oil-soaked eyes. We regret there were no more, for we had found it possible, by taking over every square foot of space aboard ship, sleeping three to a torpedo rack, etc., to accommodate a hundred.

The American rescue teams received quaintly phrased but nonetheless genuine compliments from the former prisoners. "I'll take back all I ever said about the Yanks," one of them remarked. Another said: "As soon as I can get back I'm going to write my wife to kick the Yankee out; I'm coming home." Fluckey also reported one saying, "Three bloody years without a drink of brandy. Please give me another," while one of the starved men remarked, "Be sure to wake me for chow."

It is sad to think of the many Allied lives that were lost in the sinking of the *Rakuyo*—and in other sinkings later in the war—but there was no way in which our submarines could have known of the presence of POW's in enemy ships. Had the Japanese so desired, diplomatic arrangements could have been made to permit such transfers in the name of humanity. The barbarous unconcern of our enemy for the lives of prisoners is now so well known that his failure to make any such attempt is not surprising.

Hardly had we got these liberated prisoners back to our base when trouble came from another quarter. Intercepted dispatches from Comsubs Seventh Fleet advised us of the desperate plight of *Nautilus,* Commander C. G. Sharp of Mystic, Connecticut, which was aground off Cebu, Philippine Islands.

On the night of September 26, she had approached the beach to 600 yards and delivered her cargo to the guerrillas but, on heading out for deeper water, just before midnight, she grounded on Luisan Shoal with only 18 feet of water at the bow. The ship had to be got off before daylight, otherwise there she would be, a sitting duck for enemy planes or patrol boats. The tide would be high about four in the morning but the rise too slight for much assistance. The Captain, therefore, lightened ship by sending about 40 tons of cargo ashore, jettisoning all the six-inch ammunition from the forward magazine and blowing all gasoline, plus 5,900 gallons of reserve diesel oil, overboard. Meanwhile all secret and confidential papers were burned. He also flooded his forward main ballast tanks to hold her on bottom and prevent her being carried higher on the reef as the tide came in.

At 0330 it was apparent that the tide was actually going out. The situation was desperate: *Nautilus* must be got off now or never, so Sharp blew all ballast tanks and back full speed. She came clear. Then with only three hours till sunrise, the problem was to flood the gas tanks, which normally required about five hours, compensate for the other losses of ballast and make a trim dive. They accomplished the seemingly impossible task by removing a manhole plate on the gas tanks and flooding with a hose. Six-inch shells had to be shifted from the after magazine to the forward torpedo room.

In the dive which followed, by a serious miscalculation, 45 tons of excess ballast water had been taken aboard, which led to a spirited battle on the part of the diving officer to keep *Nautilus* from plunging straight to bottom.

A comforting report was *Growler*'s sinking of the Japanese destroyer *Shikinami* during the midwatch of September 12, showing how our submarines dealt with their arch enemies. Just after midnight, patrolling east of Hainan Island on the South China coast, she made a radar contact and closed in. She was ready to fire at a good-sized target, when the skipper, Commander Ben Oakley, observed the starboard screening vessel bearing down on him. He immediately shifted his torpedo control set-up from the convoy to the on-rushing destroyer and commenced firing his bow tubes.

By the time he had got off three torpedoes, the range was down to 1,150 yards and closing so rapidly that sound judgment led Oakley to swing away with full rudder at full speed. A few seconds later, the first torpedo hit the destroyer, possibly in her war-head locker, for the explosion was terrific and shot flame so high into the midnight sky that the inside of *Growler*'s darkened conning tower was lighted by the glare. Nothing daunted by this interruption of his original plan, and in spite of 40-mm fire from a patrol boat only 1,200 yards away, Oakley steadied on the most promising target in the convoy, two overlapping freighters, and fired his stern tubes.

JANAC does not record that he sank any merchantmen during this attack, although hits were seen, but evidently one of his stray torpedoes found a more vulnerable target, for *Growler* is credited with destroying also the frigate *Hirado*.

The sinking score for September was good but not sensational, due to diversion of many submarines to other activities. JANAC credits 31 submarines with sinking 164,650 tons of merchant shipping (41 vessels) plus 30,285 tons of men-of-war. Among the former were seven tankers and among the latter was an escort carrier, a destroyer, three frigates, a submarine and four miscellaneous craft.

CHAPTER 13

Plans for the next big invasion, the Leyte campaign, designated as Operation King Two—the long-awaited "Return to the Philippines"—had been stepped up about two months. The target date was set for October 20. Abandonment of the plan to take Yap, at the same time that Palau was invaded, with the unopposed occupation of Ulithi Atoll, had left two fresh amphibious groups available. Admiral Halsey's blasting of the Philippine air defenses had exposed unexpected weakness and, to the high command, the time appeared ripe to strike. In the original scheme, General MacArthur had intended landing on Mindanao, but the plan was quickly changed, to by-pass Mindanao completely and concentrate on Leyte Gulf.

By this time, it was known that most of the Japanese Fleet was based on Singapore, Lingga Anchorage near the tip of Malaya, at Tawi-Tawi, and in Brunei Bay, Borneo. It was believed that the enemy had been forced to make this disposition of his forces by lack of tankers to service them in Empire waters. Our submarines could have told where 73 of the Japanese tanker fleet had gone.

King Two was entirely a Southwest Pacific operation, supported by the Third Fleet, under Admiral Halsey. Hence, it was the Submarines Seventh Fleet, based in Australia, which supplied most of the covering and reconnaissance services. Subpack boats, from Pearl Harbor, were covering the sortie routes from enemy home ports and the focal shipping points.

When plans were all agreed upon, I climbed aboard *Sea Fox,* for a bit of salt air and an inspection of operations at Midway. *Sea Fox*, Commander R. C. Klinker of Sebastopol, California, was the first submarine into which the combined night periscope and the ST periscope radar had been installed. According to the experts, the radar installation was not satisfactory and it had been removed at Panama for alterations. This practically broke the skipper's heart, for he was entirely satisfied with it. However, he still had the night

periscope and I was anxious to see how this new addition to
our arsenal for democracy would work. Every day and every
night on the trip to Midway, the destroyer *Litchfield*, which
accompanied us, made target runs while we attacked, using
the large-headed night periscope only. Results were highly
satisfactory. Even my eyes could pick up the target at 2,500
yards on a dark night.

I found Midway refreshing as ever, with two tenders and
the ARD-8 moored in the Refit Basin. Business was slack,
due to a gap in our refit program, but training, with submarine rescue vessels or patrol craft as targets, was in full swing.

Some concern still existed at Midway regarding the
safety of tenders and the ARD inside the Refit Basin during a
severe easterly or southeasterly blow because of the heavy
swell, which could still find its way in through the entrance.
It had even been suggested that we retire all tenders to Pearl
during the four worst winter months. This idea seemed a bit
fainthearted to me and its acceptance would have jammed
Pearl Harbor with tenders and refitting subs. Hence, I had

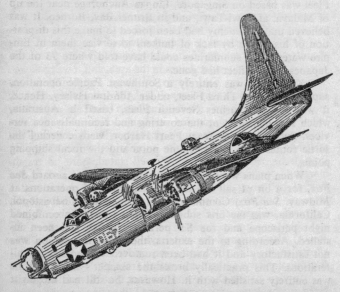

PBY4Y2

given instructions as to methods of mooring and laying out anchors to insure greater security. These, I found, had been well executed.

I flew back to Pearl in a new Navy Liberator, a PBY4Y2 with the long nose and single tail, which the pilot said was the first of its type to leave the U.S.

Back at my desk I found disturbing news from Subs Seventh Fleet that *Seawolf* was believed to be lost, possibly due to attacks by our own planes and surface craft. A Board of Investigation was convened and eventually the few known facts were given out. Beginning her 5th patrol, *Seawolf*, Lieutenant Commander A. L. Bontier, left Brisbane on September 21 and arrived at Manus on September 29. Leaving Manus the same day, *Seawolf* was directed to carry certain stores and Army personnel to the east coast of Samar.

On October 3, *Seawolf* and *Narwhal* exchanged radar recognition signals at 0756. Later the same day, an enemy submarine attack was made which resulted in the sinking of U.S.S. *Shelton*. Since there were four friendly submarines in the vicinity of this attack, they were directed to give their positions, and the other three did, but *Seawolf* was not heard from. On October 4, *Seawolf* again was directed to report her position, and again she failed to do so.

U.S.S. *Rowell* and an aircraft attacked a submarine in the vicinity of the attack on *Shelton,* having at that time no knowledge of any friendly submarines in the area, and it was believed *Seawolf* was being held down by these antisubmarine activities. It is possible that *Seawolf* was the submarine attacked.

The report from *Rowell* indicates that an apparently lethal attack was conducted in conjunction with a plane which marked the submarine's position with dye. *Rowell* established sound contact on the submarine, which then sent long dashes and dots. These, *Rowell* stated, bore no resemblance to the existing recognition signals. After one of the several hedgehog attacks, a small amount of debris and a large air bubble were seen. It has been established that the Japanese submarine RO-41 sank *Shelton* on October 3, and was able to return to Japan. The Commanding Officer of the *Rowell* was censured for not having made definite, positive efforts to identify the submarine under attack when sound transmissions were heard emanating from it.

In view of the above, and the fact that there is no attack listed in the Japanese report of antisubmarine attacks which could account for the loss of *Seawolf*, it appears probable she was sunk by friendly forces in an antisubmarine operation on October 3, about 200 miles north of New Guinea. It is, of course, possible that she was lost due to an operational casualty or as a result of an unrecorded enemy attack.

Seawolf had a long and distinguished career from the very beginning of the war. Her first seven patrols, under Lieutenant Commander Freddy Warder, were packed with thrills, daring undertakings, and narrow escapes and her next five, under Lieutenant Commander Roy Gross, sank 12 ships for a total of 53,000 tons. In August, 1944, when some of the older boats were being withdrawn from the most active patrol duties, *Seawolf* was shifted to duty with Spyron. She was thus engaged when lost. Lieutenant Commander Bontier, her commanding officer, had long experience in submarines, and, on her 14th patrol, successfully completed a similar supply mission into the Philippines.

Preparatory to the Philippines landing, Admiral Halsey and Vice Admiral Mitscher's fast carriers raided a series of targets including Marcus, Okinawa, Formosa, Pescadores, and northern Luzon. They finally concentrated on the Philippines and the Leyte Gulf region.

It was during these carrier strikes that *Trigger* contributed a courageous bit of lifesaving. About 1100 on October 12, a burning fighter plane from the *Bunker Hill* made a forced landing about 300 yards ahead of *Trigger*. The surface was rough and the fighter broke in two and sank. The dazed aviator, seen to be in trouble, disappeared several times beneath the water. Wind and combers were sweeping him away from the submarine when Lieutenant (jg) C. J. Roberts, of Chicago, Illinois, dived into the heavy seas and swam to the rescue. His action was one of particular gallantry, for not only were sea conditions hazardous in the extreme, but the arrival of enemy planes from their nearby bases might force *Trigger* to dive at any moment, leaving Roberts and the aviator to their fate.

In the months that followed a great many more such rescues were effected than it will be possible to recount. Lifeguard submarines formed teams of strong swimmers to assist aviators struggling in the water, dazed by the shock of landing, and often suffering from wounds. These were the same teams which had frequently been called upon to drag unwilling Japs aboard.

In spite of the alarm these carrier strikes must have caused in Japanese naval and shipping circles, targets continued to pour down through the East China Sea, through Formosa and Luzon Straits and into the South China Sea. The enemy's need for reinforcing the Philippines was desperate, and he paid a terrific price for every ton of cargo he got through. Of the 68 ships sunk during October, 44 of them were destroyed in the Convoy College area and in the South China Sea.

On October 14, *Besugo*, Commander Tommy Wogan, patrolling south of Japan, sighted three heavy cruisers, one light cruiser and several destroyers heading southward, intending, we hoped, to attempt interference with Admiral Halsey's strikes. The power contained in the Third Fleet was tremendous and "Uncle Bill's" boys were really looking for a fight. With the Jap Fleet beginning to move, another major naval engagement might develop.

In preparation for this biggest show of all, Rear Admiral Christie stationed *Darter*, *Dace*, *Rock* and *Bergall* in the Palawan Passage area, *Blackfin* west of northern Palawan and *Gurnard* off Brunei Bay, a big oil port in Borneo. *Cobia* was at the north end of Makassar Strait and *Batfish* was in the Sulu Sea, covering the inner end of Surigao Strait. *Guitarro* and *Angler* were off Manila and *Bream*, *Cero*, *Nautilus*, and *Cod* were strung along the northwest coast of Luzon as a reception committee for visitors approaching from the Empire. These ships, added to the 26 subs which Subpac had concentrated in the areas between Japan and the Philippines, constituted what we believed was an airtight blockade—or perhaps I should say—a "watertight" blockade.

After General MacArthur's Amphibious Forces were definitely committed to Leyte Gulf, events moved rapidly to a climax. *Darter*, Commander D. H. McClintock of Marquette, Michigan, was patrolling on October 21, west of Palawan, in cooperation with *Dace*, Commander B. D. Claggett of Baltimore, Maryland. The radio announced our landings on Leyte and Claggett, estimating that enemy forces from Singapore and Lingga Anchorage might use Balabac Strait to reach that area, headed south to rendezvous with *Dace*. A few minutes before midnight, she made radar contact with three large, high-speed ships. She tracked them for hours and made a contact report, but was unable to attain an attack position.

Finally, at daylight of October 22, Claggett abandoned the chase and again headed for a rendezvous. At midnight he contacted *Dace* and, while the two skippers were discussing patrol plans by megaphone, *Darter*'s radar operator picked up a contact at 30,000 yards. What followed will be written large in history as one of the deciding factors of the impending major naval engagements. The enemy task force which they contacted was heading northeastward up Palawan Passage. Both submarines raced to get ahead of the targets, and each obtained a beautiful attack position.

At 0517 October 23, *Darter* submerged ahead of the western column of heavy Japanese ships and began opening out to obtain proper firing range. A small zig of the targets away from her assisted in this maneuver. At 0532 McClintock, with a range of only 980 yards, commenced firing his six bow tubes at the leading cruiser. Instantly, when the last torpedo was fired, he swung with full rudder to bring his stern tubes to bear on the second cruiser and, about one minute later, fired four torpedoes at her. By this time his first salvo was hitting and five explosions were counted. The skipper swung his periscope for a quick look at his leading target and found her a mass of smoke and flames from No. 1 turret aft. As he headed for the depths, four hits were counted in the second target. A rain of depth charges began and it was 0820 before *Darter* dared again to show her periscope.

Meanwhile, *Dace* had not been idle. She submerged ahead of the eastern enemy column, also at 0517, but was not yet in firing position when she heard the thunder of *Darter*'s hits. The enemy task force went wild; destroyers raced hither and yon, and even the heavy units seemed to be milling about. In the dim morning light, Claggett could make out two enemy cruisers approaching and beyond them was a huge shape that he believed to be a battleship.

There was no time to mull this problem over and arrive at an orderly decision whether to shoot at a cruiser or wait for the battleship, that goal of all submariners' ambitions. Time and the targets were racing toward him and all his after torpedoes had been expended. He could certainly destroy one target, but if he held his fire and waited for the battleship, who could say what might intervene.

Most of us would have been too importunate to wait for the big target. We would have fired at the cruisers, but not Claggett, he steadied down and waited for what he believed

was a Kongo-class battleship. At 0554, he began firing his six
bow tubes, at a range of 1,800 yards, and got four hits. At
0601, there were two thunderous explosions, probably her
magazines, and the breaking-up noises were so loud that
Claggett ordered all compartments checked. To his relief he
found his own ship was all right, but it sounded as though the
victim might be coming down on top of *Dace*. "We better get
the hell out of here," the diving officer suggested, and the
skipper considered the advice sound. The depth charging received by both submarines was sustained and much too close
for comfort.

It was nothing short of a minor tragedy for Claggett to
find that his target was the heavy cruiser *Maya*, not a battleship. *Darter* sank the heavy cruiser *Atago* and badly damaged the heavy cruiser *Takao*. *Atago* was the flagship of
Admiral Kurita, who was transferred by destroyer to the battleship *Yamato*. Subsequent bad judgment displayed by that
officer might indicate he had been considerably shaken by his
perilous experience.

On the eve of a great battle, the Japanese Commander
in Chief had lost the services of three major units. He lost another that same day when *Bream*, Commander W. G.
"Moon" Chapple, formerly of *Permit*, contacted the two
heavy cruisers and escort first reported on October 21 by
Darter. Moon fired six torpedoes at the second cruiser, got
two hits, and so severely damaged the *Aoba* that she took no
further part in the operation.

But *Darter* and *Dace* had not finished their battle. There
remained the cruiser *Atago*, stopped, and guarded by three
escorts. She had to be finished off. After depth charging
ceased, both subs returned to periscope depth to consider the
situation. The destroyers were on the alert and throughout the
day kept the submarines out of range. However, at 1915,
they were both on surface and McClintock, the senior officer, directed *Dace* to take a position to southward of the
cripple, while *Darter* took a corresponding position to northward. With this disposition, one of them should be able to attack in whichever direction she moved. He expected that a
destroyer would take the cruiser in tow but at 2200 that
night she got under way at about five knots, under her own
power. Her course, evidently heading back for Singapore, was
erratic, as though she were forced to use her main engines for
steering. McClintock informed *Dace* that he was attacking

from the target's starboard quarter and began closing in.
However, he picked up two enemy radars sweeping toward
him and, anticipating that he would be detected if *Darter* remained on surface, decided to make an end around and attack submerged from ahead.

At midnight, he was about one hour from the desired position. *Darter* was logging 17 knots. There had been no opportunity to obtain a navigational fix in the past 30 hours and the
area through which the submarine was passing is one of the
most dangerous in the world. For centuries its name has been
shown on the charts as "Dangerous Ground"—and for good
reason, for hundreds of rocks and shoals are scattered about in
that portion of the South China Sea, many named for ships that
left their bones on them. Five minutes after midnight, *Darter*
hit Bombay Shoal with a tremendous crash and rode up until
there was only nine feet of water under her bow.

With no possibility of a tide high enough to float her
and a Japanese destroyer 18,000 yards away and closing,
McClintock began burning all classified papers and destroyed
his secret fire control gear, meanwhile manning all guns. Desperately, *Darter* informed *Dace* of her plight. The radar
range to the enemy destroyer closed to 12,000 yards and then
began to open. With sighs of relief, all hands leaped to the
task of throwing everything movable overboard in order to
lighten ship. At 0140, *Dace* came close in to the reef and
shortly thereafter, at high tide, futile efforts were made to
back the stranded ship off the shoal.

The situation was hopeless. She was perched up on the
coral heads like a lighthouse, and salvage would require weeks
of work with dredges and powerful tugs. *Dace* took off the

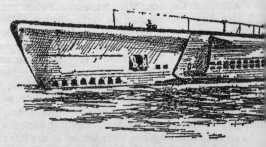

U.S.S. Tang

crew, demolition charges were set and at 0435 her Commanding
Officer left the *Darter*. Reliance has been placed on the detonation of the torpedo war heads when the demolition charges exploded to destroy the submarine; however, it was obvious this
did not occur. Claggett, therefore, set his few remaining torpedoes to run at minimum depths and attempted to blow her up.

When this scheme failed, due to the torpedoes striking the
reef and exploding short of the target, *Dace* manned the gun
and fired 30 rounds of four-inch ammunition into her erstwhile
teammate. At this point, a Jap plane caught *Dace* lying to with
25 men on deck. A mad scramble ensued to get down but the
enemy zoomie evidently misunderstood the situation and
dropped her bombs on the stranded *Darter*. After a day of frustrated attempts to get her own demolition charges into *Darter*,
Dace finally abandoned the attempt and headed back for her
base. We learned from captured documents that the enemy
did obtain some papers of limited value from the unfortunate
submarine, but these were chiefly blueprints of engines and
motors which it would require years to copy and build.

While all hands regretted the loss of *Darter*, we felt that
exchange of one submarine for two cruisers and a lot of enemy lives was not too bad. Her officers and crew were transferred in a body to the new submarine *Menhaden*, building at
Manitowoc, Wisconsin.

The intelligence transmitted by these submarines to the Seventh Fleet at Leyte Gulf was the first tangible evidence of the magnitude of the forces which the enemy was assembling to dislodge us. Its early receipt enabled our Fleet commanders to put into execution the countermeasures which resulted in a major disaster for the Imperial Japanese Navy. Supplementing this information was a report from *Seadragon*, Commander Ashley, that she had sighted on October 21, off the southern tip of Formosa, a carrier, two heavy cruisers and six destroyers, heading south.

The ensuing naval engagements, now known as the Battles for Leyte Gulf, were fought on October 24, 25 and 26. The area designated as the Philippine Sea had been entirely cleared of submarines as far north as our safety lane, which ran from Saipan to Luzon Strait, in order to give Third Fleet free rein in dealing with any submarines encountered. As three separate naval battles developed, in Surigao Strait, off Samar and off Cape Engano, we halted two wolf packs bound for the Convoy College area, in this safety lane, in order to head off enemy ships which might retreat northward. We also stationed a line of subs from Formosa to Luzon to attack ships retiring in that direction.

The wolf packs, "Roach's Raiders," consisting of *Haddock*, *Halibut* and *Tuna* under Commander J. L. "Beetle" Roach in *Haddock*, and "Clarey's Crushers," the *Pintado*, *Jallao* and *Atule* under Commander B. A. "Chick" Clarey in *Pintado*, were so close to the battle, which Pete Mitscher's planes were waging with a Jap task force off Cape Engano, that the thunder of bombs could be heard and occasional flashes seen. It was maddening to our lads to just sit and watch, so, with Admiral Nimitz's permission, I sent an urgent dispatch to Mitscher asking if we might join the party. Pete, always a good friend of submarines, radioed back, "Come on in," but, unfortunately, the air was so full of urgent messages we did not receive his O.K. for hours afterward and the opportunity was lost.

However, *Halibut*, Commander I. J. Galantin of Des Plaines, Illinois, fired six electric torpedoes at 4,000 yards at a fleeing battleship of the Ise-class, screened by a light cruiser and a destroyer. Five heavy explosions, correctly timed for hits, were heard but no sinking is recorded by JANAC. That night another attack was made at 2301 on a would-be escapee, the new light cruiser *Tama*. This time we did better.

Jallao, Commander J. B. Icenhower, of Parkersburg, West Virginia, fired three torpedoes from her bow tubes at the cruiser but missed, due to a radical zig toward the submarine. Icenhower swung away, brought his stern tubes to bear and, at a range of 700 yards, fired four more torpedoes, three of which hit and ended the Jap's short career.

While the terrific battles for Leyte Gulf were raging, another epic battle was being fought by *Tang* at the north end of Formosa Strait. All of *Tang*'s patrols were made under the leadership of Commander R. H. "Dick" O'Kane, and all were remarkable for determination, daring and excellent torpedo shooting. Dick's third patrol produced a tonnage score which, considering merchant shipping only, is the highest of any recorded in JANAC for a single patrol. His fifth patrol surpassed all others but it was his last, for his 24th torpedo, fired at an easy target, circled and hit the submarine, sending it plunging to the bottom.

Dick O'Kane was taken prisoner by the Japanese and his postwar report tells the story of *Tang*'s final patrol so simply, yet so vividly, that I quote parts with only slight changes to make them more understandable to lay readers:

> At 0030 of October 23rd, we made the first trial of our newly repaired radar and the operator reported land at 14,000 yards, where no land should have been. Commenced tracking, immediately discovering a small pip moving out in our direction. Put him astern and bent on the turns. He evidently lost his original contact on us for he changed course and commenced a wide sweep about the convoy which was now also in sight. A submariner's dream quickly developed as we were able to assume the original position of this destroyer just ahead of the convoy while he went on a 20-mile inspection tour. The convoy was composed of three large modern tankers in column, a transport on the starboard hand, a freighter on the port hand, flanked by escorts on both beams and quarters.

Dick, zigging with the convoy, dropped back between the tanker column and the freighter, carefully selected his position and fired five bow torpedoes at the tankers. He aimed deliberately for engine and boiler room spaces. With a maximum range of only 800 yards, in a matter of seconds, the missiles reached their marks, a series of terrific explosions blasted the night and three blazing ships started settling toward their graves. He had no time to watch them go, for the freighter was in position for shots from the stern tubes. Just as he was about to fire, Leibold, *Tang*'s Chief Boatswain's Mate, whose sharp eyesight had helped O'Kane in many a night attack, pointing to the transport, shouted, "She's coming in to ram!"

The situation was desperate. Boxed in by the blazing tankers and with the transport so close there was no time to escape her by diving, Dick had to get across that bow which already towered over them.

Dick wrote:

It was really a thriller diller, with the *Tang* barely getting on the inside of his turning circle and saving the stern with full left rudder in the last seconds. The transport commenced firing with large- and small-caliber stuff so cleared the bridge before realizing it was all above our heads. A quick glance aft, however, showed the tables were again turned for the transport was forced to continue her swing in an attempt to avoid colliding with the freighter which had also been coming in to ram. The freighter struck the transport's starboard quarter shortly after we commenced firing four stern torpedoes spread along their double length. At a range of 400 yards the crash, coupled with the four torpedo explosions, was terrific, sinking the freighter nose-down almost instantly while the transport hung with a 30-degree up-angle.

With a destroyer 1,300 yards away on *Tang*'s starboard quarter and an escort vessel on port bow and port beam, the situation was still critical. The destroyer was the most dangerous opponent, so Dick put her astern and headed for the smaller vessel on his port bow. That warrior, however, had evidently seen enough of *Tang*'s punches and rapidly swung away. *Tang*, emitting clouds of exhaust smoke, sped into the welcome outer darkness, to the accompaniment of gunfire and loud explosions as the transport's bow sank.

The ship's log showed that from the firing of *Tang*'s first torpedo to the last explosion on the transport, only 10 minutes had elapsed.

October 24th brought more targets. On surfacing at dark, O'Kane headed in for Turnabout Island, feeling assured that the best hunting would be found close inshore. Shallow water made operations there doubly hazardous but considerations of that sort had long since ceased to daunt our maru hunters.

Very soon radar contact was reported from the conning tower and, as the range shortened, the PPI scope was saturated with pips. The Leyte campaign had just begun and the enemy was evidently sending every available ship to bolster the defense of the Philippines.

After tracking the convoy for a short time to obtain its course and speed, O'Kane bored in. Random gunfire came from the escort vessels, perhaps just on suspicion or for "scare" purposes, for nothing landed near *Tang*.

O'Kane said:

> As we continued to close the leading ships, the escort commander obligingly illuminated the column with a 36-inch searchlight, using this for signaling. It gave us a perfect view of our first selected target, a three-deck, two-stack transport; of the second target, a three-deck, one-stacker; and of the third, a large modern tanker. With ranges from 1,400 yards on the first transport to 900 yards on the tanker, fired two Mk. 18 torpedoes each, in slow deliberate salvoes, to pass under the foremast and mainmast of the first two vessels and under the middle and stack of the tanker. In spite of the early warning and the sporadic shooting, no evasive tactics were employed by any of the ships. The torpedoes commenced hitting as we paralleled the convoy to search out our next two targets.

> Our love for electric torpedoes after the disappointing cruiser experience of October 20, was again restored as all torpedoes hit nicely. We passed the next ship, a medium freighter, abeam at 600 yards and then turned for a stern shot at another tanker and transport astern of her. Fired a single stern torpedo under the tanker's stack and one at

the foremast and one at the mainmast of the transport. The ranges were between 600 and 700 yards. Things were anything but calm and peaceful now, for the escorts had stopped their warning tactics and were directing good salvoes at us and at the blotches of smoke we left behind on going to full power. Just after firing at the transport, a full-fledged destroyer charged under her stern and headed for us. What took place in the following seconds will never be determined, but the tanker was hit nicely and blew up, apparently a gasoline-loaded job. At least one torpedo was observed to hit the transport and an instant later the destroyer blew up, either intercepting our third torpedo or possibly the 40-mm fire from the two escort vessels bearing down on our beam. In any case, the result was the same for, of the big targets, only the transport remained afloat and she apparently stopped.

Tang hauled clear at flank speed behind a screen of her own exhaust smoke, absolutely untouched by the hurricane of gunfire that had swept over her.

At 10,000 yards from the scene of battle, all pursuit had ceased, so O'Kane stopped and ordered the last two torpedoes, which had been loaded into the bow tubes, withdrawn and checked. About half an hour was spent on each torpedo, then, with all in readiness, the submarine stood back to finish off the crippled transport. This promised to be a typical *Tang* patrol—three or four weeks packed with thrills and action and, then, "Course 090" (the compass course back to Pearl) with empty torpedo tubes and a full bag.

The approach was made with great care, avoiding the two escort vessels. At a range of 900 yards O'Kane fired one torpedo. It ran straight and true for the target. Then the 24th fish was fired. As it left the tube, a voice in the forward room was heard to shout, "Course Zero Nine Zero!" But on the bridge, Dick O'Kane saw that fatal last torpedo broach and curve sharply to the left. He rang up emergency full speed and commenced a fishtail maneuver to escape its erratic, circular run, but in vain. Its phosphorescent wake streaked out and around and back toward the ship, death riding the war head. It struck abreast the after torpedo room with a terrific explosion, flooding the three after compartments and undoubtedly killing instantly all personnel therein.

Tang's stern sank so swiftly to bottom that there was not even time to close the conning tower hatch before the sea swept over it. Of the nine officers and men who were swept off the bridge, three were able to swim throughout the night. Lieutenant Savadkin, who escaped from the conning tower, saved himself by converting his trousers into a life belt.

Inside the ship, those remaining alive were able to isolate the after part of the ship and work their way forward. In the control room they leveled the ship off so she rested flat on the bottom at a depth of 180 feet. Conscious of their responsibilities to the last, they destroyed secret publications, and went on to the forward torpedo room. There they found the Torpedo Officer, Lieutenant James H. Flanagan, with several other men, bringing the total to about 30. The watertight door was secured behind them, for a fire had broken out in the forward battery and smoke was filling the torpedo room. All were issued life jackets and Momsen Lungs.

When the Japs ceased depth charging about 0600, Lieutenant Flanagan manned the escape trunk and sent the first party of three men up the ascending line to the buoy. Ensign B. C. Pearce, Jr., sent up the second party. Much time was lost due to men becoming unconscious in the escape trunk because of the 90-pound sea pressure, which they had to withstand. In all, four parties left the ship. Lieutenant Flanagan, who left with the last party known to have escaped, said the paint on the after bulkhead was melting and acrid smoke was seeping past the gaskets. Breathing was becoming difficult. It is believed that subsequently an explosion of the battery blew out the gaskets and asphyxiated the remaining personnel.

"When I reached the surface," said Flanagan, "four men were hanging onto the buoy. We were all that remained of the 13 who left the escape trunk. Maybe some tried to swim to the China coast, five or 10 miles away. There was a Jap freighter's bow sticking up about 500 yards from the buoy. We decided to wait till the tide changed, then salvage a boat or raft and make for the coast under cover of darkness."

That plan was spoiled when an enemy escort lowered a boat and picked up all nine survivors, including those who escaped from the conning tower and bridge. The prisoners were kicked and clubbed in approved Japanese style but, as Dick

O'Kane said, "When we realized these brutalities were being administered by the burned, mutilated survivors of our handiwork, we found we could take them with less prejudice."

JANAC has cut down the estimates of sinkings turned in by the *Tang*, but on her last patrol, she still is credited with seven ships, which brings her score for the short eight months of her life up to 24 ships, for a total of 93,284 tons. This score in number of ships sunk is exceeded only by *Flasher* who downed 26.

Commander Dick O'Kane was awarded the Congressional Medal of Honor "for conspicuous gallantry and intrepidity in combat with the enemy at the risk of his life above and beyond the call of duty and without detriment to the mission of his command." I had the pleasure of seeing this award presented by President Truman.

Another example of stout hearts in a stout ship occurred on October 31, about 100 miles south of Japan. After a successful attack on a huge tanker, *Salmon*, Commander H. K. "Ken" Nauman of Pelham Manor, New York, was caught by four close patterns of depth charges, about 30 in all. The charges exploded above her, driving her down, down, far below her test depth, off the scale of her depth gauges. Steering gear and stern planes went out of commission and water was coming in at a rate much beyond the capacity of her pumps. The strength hull was dished in over the engine room and forward battery and the 31-inch main engine induction piping was crushed flat. Her after torpedo room hatch was blown open and the ship was saved only by the fact that a bottom plate had been bolted onto the inner end of the hatch trunk.

Except at high speed, depth control could not be maintained and Nauman knew that would be fatal because, with high-speed running, his propellers could so easily be heard by the escorts. There was nothing for it but to surface and shoot his way out. Fortunately, by this time it was getting dark; however, there was a moon to be taken into consideration. *Salmon* surfaced, with a heavy list, and manned all guns, while the engine crews fought to get jammed exhaust valves open and the Chief of the Boat strove to get the ship on an even keel.

After a wait that seemed hours, engines were started and the *Salmon* headed for Saipan. All this while the nearest enemy, lying some 7,000 yards up-moon, had made no move. Finally, at 2100, she turned on her searchlight and opened a wild burst of firing. At 2130, Nauman called his packmates and then sent out a number of plain English messages purporting to come from other ships in the hope the Japs might think themselves outnumbered.

For three hours the nearest escort tried at long range to get a hit on *Salmon*. She would close in to about 2,000 yards, firing as she came, and then sheer out to avoid the sub's 20-mm fire. Then *Salmon* saw a "seagoing fox hole"—a rain squall—and headed for it. The enemy tried to head her off, converging on the submarine's port bow. This was the move Ken had hoped for. A champion middleweight boxer at the Naval Academy, he itched to get to close quarters. He swung hard left and headed in to ram, at the same time pouring everything he had into the escort vessel, including two coke bottles which an excited seaman hove at her. The Jap skipper evaded the ram but a 4-inch hit in the bridge structure and a withering 20-mm fusillade left his ship stopped, silenced and burning. Another escort came in and opened fire, but several near misses with the 4-inch gun and some smaller-caliber hits turned her back, and *Salmon* raced into the comforting obscurity of the rain squall.

Trigger, *Sterlet* and *Silversides* joined up that night and together they headed for Saipan. We asked Admiral Hoover to give her some air cover—which shot down one Japanese bomber as it was about to start a run—and on November 3, she moored to our tender at Tanapag to receive a hero's welcome. Nauman and his boys just didn't know when they were licked. Perhaps we should teach more boxing at the Academy.

The thing which perhaps pleased me most in this incident was the desire of that fighting *Salmon* crew to stick together. Their ship was beyond economical repair and normally they would have gone as replacements to other submarines. But the *Salmon* lads had a bond of comradeship that meant something very important to them, and Nauman radioed, asking for a transfer of all hands to a new boat. So, with the blessing of the Department, when that tired old warrior, *Salmon*, arrived at Mare Island, we transferred the officers and crew, lock, stock and barrel, to the brand-new *Stickleback*. At the end of the war, Commander Ken Nauman and his lads, equipped with mine-detection gear, were in that last bit of enemy-controlled waters, the Sea of Japan, looking for more Japs.

Two more losses must be recorded before the toll of the fatal month of October, 1944, is complete. To the names of *Seawolf, Darter* and *Tang,* we must add those of *Shark II* and *Escolar*—the heaviest loss of any month of the war.

The sinking of *Shark* was related to another tragedy involving prisoners of war being transported to Japan without our knowledge. In this case, the prisoners and victims of our own torpedoes were Americans. *Shark,* Commander E. N. Blakely, led *Seadragon* and *Blackfish* in the Luzon Strait (Convoy College) area in mid-October for a standard wolf-pack patrol. On October 22, *Shark* reported having contacted four large enemy vessels. She still had her full load of torpedoes aboard, so had not made an attack. *Shark* addressed no further messages to bases, but on October 24, *Seadragon* received a message stating that she had made radar contact with a single freighter, and that she was going in to attack. This was the last message from *Shark.*

However, on November 13, a dispatch originated by Commander Naval Unit, Fourteenth U.S. Army Air Force, stated that a Japanese ship en route from Manila to Japan, with 1,800 American prisoners of war, had been sunk on October 24 by an American submarine in a torpedo attack. No other submarine reported the attack, and since *Shark* had given *Seadragon* a contact report only a few hours before the sinking, and could not be raised by radio after it, it can only be assumed that *Shark* made the attack described, and perished during or after it.

Five prisoners, who survived and subsequently reached China, stated that conditions on the prison ship were so intolerable that the men prayed for deliverance from their misery by a torpedo or bomb. Because many prisoners of war had been rescued from the water by submarines, after the sinking of vessels in which they were being transported, U.S. submarines had been instructed to search for Allied survivors in the vicinity of all sinkings of Empire-bound Japanese ships. *Shark* may well have been sunk trying to rescue American prisoners of war.

A report from the Japanese, received after the close of the war, records the attack made by *Shark* on October 24. During the counterattack by escorts, depth charges were dropped 17 times, and the enemy reports having seen "bubbles, and heavy oil, clothes, cork, etc." Several American submarines report having been attacked on this date near the position given, but in view of the fact that none reported the attack on the convoy cited above, this attack is considered the most probable cause of *Shark*'s loss.

It is notable that JANAC, which lists seven ships sunk in Convoy College on October 24, does not credit any of them to *Shark*. Perhaps *Shark* was not the unwitting agent of destruction of American lives. JANAC does record that *Shark* sank four ships for a total of 21,672 tons, all of them in June, 1944.

Escolar, Commander W. J. Millican, departed Pearl Harbor on September 18 to proceed to Midway to top off with fuel. There she joined *Croaker* and *Perch* and left on September 23, to conduct a coordinated patrol, *Escolar*'s first, in the Yellow Sea. Commander Millican was in command of this coordinated attack group, which was designated "Millican's Marauders."

On September 30, when *Escolar* was estimated to be about north of the Bonin Islands, the following partial message was received from her, "This from *Escolar* X attacked with deck gun, boat similar to ex-Italian *Peter George V Otyi*. . . ." Although no further transmissions have ever been received by bases from *Escolar*, who was forced to break off the transmission and the engagement with the gunboat at this time, the Commander Officer of *Croaker* has stated that she suffered no damage and was in frequent communication with *Perch* and *Croaker* until October 17.

Perch reported that, on October 17, she had received a message from *Escolar* stating she was about 60 miles west of Sasebo and heading in toward that base. Neither *Perch* nor *Croaker* could raise *Escolar* by radio after this transmission was received.

Postwar information from the Japanese gives no clue as to cause of her loss. However, there were minefields in the general area of *Escolar*'s predicted position, which fact she knew. It is possible that she unknowingly got into a minefield or struck a floating mine, of which many were sighted in those days.

Commander Millican was a veteran of the *Thresher*, whom I knew well down in Australia in the early days of the War, and for whose cool courage and determination I had the greatest admiration. His loss was hard to accept.

The month of October ended with a small surprise for our side. On the 29th, a Japanese submarine sank a U.S. merchant ship about half way between San Francisco and Hawaii and shot up a lifeboat. The last did not surprise us; there had been plenty of that sort of barbarity in the Indian Ocean, perpetrated by Japanese submarines and commerce raiders, but a shipping raid on our home waters, after almost three years of inactivity along that line, was a surprise indeed. The disturbance it caused, and the consequent dislocation of traffic, showed just how much the enemy could have embarrassed us by more of the same.

On the other hand, we added a little variety by sinking the German submarine, U-168. She was sunk by a Dutch submarine, the *Zwaardvisch*, Lieutenant Commander H. A. W. Gossens, making her first patrol, and operating under Commander Submarines Seventh Fleet. The German sub was sighted in the Java Sea in the early morning of October 6 and, 13 minutes after contact, Commander Gossens launched six torpedoes. He obtained three hits, but only one torpedo, the one which hit furthest forward, exploded. The other two dudded. One good hit was sufficient, however, and U-168 slid bow first to her watery grave.

Zwaardvisch approached the wreckage submerged and could see six men in the water but, on surfacing, she found that 21 more had joined them. The water was only 120 feet deep and some had come up, using the German "gengenlunge," similar to our Momsen lung. Most, however, had made the ascent without it. The Dutchman took them all aboard, but later transferred 22 to a native fishing boat. The captain, three officers and an injured enlisted man were retained on *Zwaardvisch*, which proudly bore them back to Fremantle. The Japs ashore probably did not receive their shipwrecked allies with much enthusiasm for, so we had been told by rescued Australian prisoners of war, there had been evidence at Penang of bad blood between the Germans and the Japanese.

Another bit of variety which occurred during September-October, 1944, contributed not only an amusing note, but a note of inspiration as well.

My first information regarding this incident came through an intercepted radio message from *Snapper* reporting that Mo.-MM2/c H. H. "Hank" Quanstrom, a member of the

refit crews at Midway, had stowed away on that vessel. The
Snapper had left Midway the previous day for a war patrol
in the Bonins area.

Quanstrom had formerly served in S-31, patrolling out
of Dutch Harbor. In the only patrol he made on that station,
an area in which the aged S-boats battled the elements as
much as they battled the Japanese, bad luck perched on the
periscope. The submarine was bombed, but not hit, by one of
our own patrol planes, Quanstrom's left arm was badly
chewed up in a gear train and his skipper was fatally injured
by the premature explosion of an identification rocket.

After hospitalization, which put him back in good
condition except for two fingers on his left hand that ob-
stinately refused to function, Quanstrom was sent to Pearl
Harbor and, in course of time, found himself as a member of
the refit crews at Submarine Base, Midway.

He did his best to get back to sea but without success.
Perhaps he could not be spared, perhaps his injury was
considered as disqualifying him, but after seven months at
"Gooneyville," Quanstrom couldn't wait any longer. Almost
daily submarines were dropping in at Midway to refit or re-
fuel and their tales of adventure and battle fired his blood.
He just had to make a war patrol and win one of those
coveted submarine combat pins.

And so, one night in September at a farewell beer party
for *Snapper,* he enlisted the sympathy and aid of one of her
engine room crew. Next morning, with a handful of personal
effects, he boarded the ship and sat himself down in the engine room bilges. There he remained until nightfall when he
emerged and gave himself up. He figured that if he gave himself up during daylight, the skipper might call for a PBY to
take him back to Midway, but if he waited till dark, the next
daylight would find the *Snapper* too far from Midway to
make such a transfer economical.

He figured right, for the C.O., Commander W. W.
Walker, merely gave him hell for making it necessary to
break radio silence to report his presence aboard, and put
him to work as a lookout with additional duty scrubbing
clothes for the crew. Eventually he was given duty in the engine room and found such favor with his skipper that on return to Midway, when charges of "jumping ship" were
preferred against him, Walker gave him a deck court-

martial—the mildest form of court—and sentenced him to ten days restriction.

Even that might seem an excessive penalization of fighting spirit but, as Quanstrom says: "We were going back to Mare Island for overhaul anyhow, so my restriction was all served at sea!"

Today Hank Quanstrom, back in civil life, proudly wears the submarine combat pin won during his stowaway patrol, when the *Snapper* sank two enemy vessels in the vicinity of that well-known Pacific landmark, Lot's Wife,—an area in which two, possibly three, of our submarines were lost with all on board.

The sinking scores for October set a new high record for merchant shipping. JANAC records that 33 submarines sank 50 merchantmen—seven of them tankers—a total of 275,809 tons. Allied submarines also sank nine men-of-war for a total of 37,220 tons.

CHAPTER 14

With *Salmon* safely back in Saipan on November 3, after her broken date with destruction, we took time out to lick our wounds. October had been a tough month, with five submarines lost, *Salmon* damaged beyond repair, and *Crevalle* laid up temporarily, due to a serious flooding accident, which cost the life of one officer. And there were more losses in November.

The desperate resistance of the Japanese on Leyte still continued and the Third Fleet was constantly on duty, furnishing air coverage for General MacArthur's troops. Delays had been encountered by the Army Air Force in getting airstrips ready as planned at Leyte Gulf, hence the carriers of Task Force 38, then under Vice Admiral J. S. McCain, stood a "heel and toe" watch to keep enemy air installations in the Philippines beaten down to their tail skids.

Our submarines kept clear of areas used by the Third Fleet and patrolled further north and west. Hunting was still good close to the Asiatic coast, but these operations had become fairly routine and much of the time at Subpac HQ was spent planning for the next operation then in prospect. Admiral Spruance and his Staff were in Pearl getting ready for the show.

Meanwhile, I was increasingly preoccupied with new equipment. *Spikefish,* Lieutenant Commander N. J. Nicholas of Portland, Maine, came along with the first ST (periscope type) radar installation to arrive at Pearl and I played hookey from the desk to make a training trip with her. The skipper was delighted with his new combined night periscope and radar, as were all of us observers after testing it out. This would permit us to outwit the enemy's rapidly multiplying, radar-equipped escorts at night and would greatly assist periscope approaches in daylight. The ranges obtained were highly satisfactory.

As another bit of relaxation from the grind at my desk, I went out in *Tinosa,* Commander R. C. Latham of New London, Connecticut, to participate in what was becoming my favorite hobby—locating mines with the FM Sonar. Entry into the Sea of Japan, which was protected by extensive minefields, was a challenge that could not be refused and, in FM Sonar we had, I believed, the key that would unlock that closed entrance. I missed no opportunity to observe this equipment in operation and to study its capabilities. *Tinosa*'s performance that day was excellent and, beaten down though I was with worry over our losses and how to stop them, I went back to Base with a song in my heart. Eventually we would break through the Tsushima minefields and complete the strangulation of Japanese shipping, thereby forcing our enemy to surrender or starve, thus saving thousands of American lives.

Commander Harry Hull, our Staff Torpedo and Gunnery Officer, invited me to see some of the new secret weapons perform. Early on November 15, we stood out for the training area in a new submarine, the *Sea Owl,* Commander Carter L. Bennett of Nashville, Tennessee. She was an excellent example of the fine boats which Portsmouth Navy Yard was turning out in record building time. Admiral Withers, the Commandant there, had written me a short time before that they expected to build 36 in the next calendar year. That, for a yard which normally built three submarines in two years, was a tremendous advance.

We observed the first three submerged firing runs aboard the submarine and were considerably discouraged to learn, on surfacing, that only one run had been good. The other two units had never been sighted, had not hit the target and were lost. The curse of torpedo troubles still pursued us. Observers then shifted to the target vessel and again watched three runs of our new hush-hush gadget, not one of which hit. To us who were expecting miracles from this long-awaited prosubmarine gear, this performance was heartbreaking. Poor electrical gear was at the bottom of most of the failures, for a great amount of jerry-built equipment was being turned out. Several more weeks of exhaustive tests and alterations were required before these weapons were considered sufficiently reliable for issue to submarines. Torpedo history seemed determined to repeat itself.

Rear Admiral George Hussey, Chief of Bureau of Ordnance, was with me on this entire observation trip. I feel sure that he went back to Washington resolved to find out just what was so rotten in the secret weapons program and what could be done about it. Certainly some heads should have rolled in the sand.

News came in that a wolf pack from the Seventh Fleet Submarines, patrolling the South China Sea had made an important contribution by putting the heavy cruiser *Kumano* out of action. This pack consisted of *Guitarro*, Commander E. D. Haskins of Brooklyn, New York; *Raton*, Commander W. W. "Mike" Shea of Cleveland, Ohio; and *Bream*, Commander "Moon" Chapple, formerly of the *Permit*, who was OTC (Officer in Tactical Command) of the group.

At 0718 of November 6, *Guitarro*, patrolling off Cape Bolinao, Luzon, sighted a convoy consisting of two heavy cruisers, seven cargo ships and several escorts, approaching from the south. The submarine fired nine torpedoes at one of these cruisers, six from bow tubes, three from stern tubes, in the amazingly short space of 46 seconds. Three properly timed hits were heard. A few minutes later, *Bream* sighted this same convoy and fired four torpedoes at one of the cruisers. This time two hits were heard.

Thirty-five minutes later, *Raton* sighted the group still coming on and fired six torpedoes at the *Kumano*. Shea claimed three hits. This last salvo of torpedoes passed directly over the *Ray*, which had rushed in from a neighboring area, as she stood in for an attack. The deadly whirr of their propellers was distinctly heard through the hull of the ship. Our areas were really getting filled up with submarines.

At 0946 *Ray*, Commander W. T. Kinsella of Wilkes-Barre, Pennsylvania, fired four electric torpedoes at this same cruiser. At 1041, she observed the target with its bow blown off, being towed to a nearby beach.

On November 18, we received news from *Spadefish*, Commander "Judge" Underwood, that she had sunk a carrier in the Yellow Sea northeast of Shanghai. She, with *Sunfish* and *Peto*, had been assigned that area, with Underwood as pack leader. After sinking a freighter off the mouth of the Yangtze, *Spadefish* moved up north and, at 1434 on November 17, sighted smoke northeastward of her position. Soon there were five distinct columns of smoke, and eventually masts came in sight. The Judge decided that, since sunset was approaching, he would let this convoy pass over him and then attack on surface at night. In that way, he would have greater speed at his command for evasion in the darkness, instead of having to sit on bottom in shallow water and take a depth charge beating. He therefore dived and ran at 150 feet to avoid being picked up by aircraft, which sometimes spot a sub at 120 feet. The convoy passed right over *Spadefish* but, in spite of numerous echo-ranging escorts, she was not detected.

At 1734, Underwood came back to periscope depth and looked over his targets. There were five big ships, with numerous escorts, trailed by an escort carrier. An explosion was heard, followed by billowing smoke, from a ship ahead of the CVE (escort carrier), then came a string of depth charges. Perhaps another member of the pack had attacked.

At 1834, *Spadefish* went to battle stations, surfaced and began tracking the convoy. Two escorts had remained behind to work over the submarine that had recently attacked, but Underwood ran by them at 10,000 yards without being detected, even though they were sweeping toward him with their radars. *Sunfish* opened up and told Judge that she was preparing to attack an eight-ship convoy about three hours astern of the one *Spadefish* was tracking. One of our China-based Navy planes reported the convoy, which contained the CVE, had five destroyer escorts and nine other ships. Contact reports from our Navgroup China planes were by this time becoming a standard and very useful service.

Some months earlier we had detached Commander Wally Ebert from the *Scamp* and sent him down to Burma to act as Liaison Officer with Commodore Miles, who commanded Navgroup China.

At 2119, *Spadefish* was in position to attack the CVE at long range (4,600 yards) from the starboard side when she suddenly zigged away. Underwood hauled out, therefore, and came in again from further ahead. The convoy was steaming at not more than 14 knots, which made an end around in a moderate seaway fairly simple. While regaining attack position, Underwood heard from *Sunfish* that she had attacked her convoy and sunk one big freighter.

Spadefish headed in for another try, passing astern of the escort vessel. There was considerable radar interference, coming evidently from enemy escorts, but no one picked her up. At 2303, Underwood commenced firing six torpedoes at the CVE at a range of 4,100 yards, then swung with full rudder and fired his stern tubes at the leading ship, a tanker.

One torpedo hit in the stern of the carrier, followed by three more hits spread along her length. She burst into flames and started settling by the stern. One of the torpedoes from the stern tubes was heard to hit but no one saw the explosion; all eyes were glued on that burning carrier. She took a heavy list to starboard and the planes with which her flight deck was loaded could be seen sliding over the side. Rapidly she sank by the stern and when last seen, the bow, still burning, was sticking up in the air.

This victim was the escort carrier *Jinyo*, 21,000 tons. Japan had built five escort carriers. Four were lost to our submarines. Tucked away in the Inland Sea, the *Kaiyo*, last of her class, was later destroyed by carrier-based planes from Vice Admiral McCain's task force.

Judge Underwood stood in to attack again, just after the 18th of November had been ushered in. This time an escort spotted him, challenged, and then opened fire with a 40-mm gun. *Spadefish* raced away and the Judge cleared the bridge, not intending to dive but to get all personnel except himself under cover. Before she could get up to full speed, the Jap had closed to 970 yards and was pouring in 20-mm and 40-mm tracers, with a few heavier-caliber shells. The Judge zigzagged desperately, like a rising jacksnipe, not daring to dive in such shallow water, and eventually outran his pursuer. The Jap then dropped a string of face-saving depth charges and turned back.

Spadefish and her pack roved the Yellow Sea for 22 days and got a fair bag. Several of those they estimated sunk are not credited by JANAC, hence must be added to their damaged column. In addition to those already mentioned, *Spadefish* sank another freighter, which gave her four ships and 30,421 tons. Her companions, *Sunfish,* Commander E. E. Shelby of Cincinnati, Ohio, sank a freighter, a passenger-cargo ship and a transport for a total of 16,179 tons; and *Peto*, Commander R. H. Caldwell, Jr., of Atlanta, Georgia, sank three cargo ships for a total of 12,572. The pack's total of over 59,000 tons was one of the outstanding scores for the war.

During the first part of November we extended our versatility by what was originally intended as a picket-boat destroying show. Admiral Spruance asked us to sweep an area 180 miles wide, through which a carrier task force could pass for the first full-scale carrier aircraft attack on the Japanese homeland. It was believed that enemy picket boats could be eliminated by submarines without causing as much of an alert as destroyers would have stirred up. With pickets out of the way, our carriers would have a much better chance to achieve tactical surprise.

At the time our plans were made and certain submarines returning from patrol were ordered to assemble at Saipan, it was expected Admiral Spruance's strike would take place in November. However, the retention of Third Fleet to furnish air cover at Leyte compelled us to abandon the operation for the moment. With the submarines available at Saipan, it nevertheless seemed a good idea to carry our part of the scheme into execution to provide experience on which to base similar sweeps later.

A group of seven submarines, *Ronquil, Burrfish, Sterlet, Silversides* (flagship), *Trigger, Tambor* and *Saury* (listed in order from west to east on the initial sweep line) were organized into a wolf pack. Commander T. B. "Burt" Klakring, hero of the famous "race track" story, was placed in charge of the pack and in his honor the group was labeled "Burt's Brooms." They left Saipan on November 10; with orders to sweep an area approximately 180 miles wide, with certain specified boundaries, southeast of Japan. They were directed to sink every picket boat encountered and "to leave no holidays in the area."

The story of Burt's Brooms is a saga. Heavy weather made submarine gunfire inaccurate if not almost impossible—the low freeboard of a submarine permits firing of the deck gun only in comparatively calm water. A total of four picket boats were sunk, but a most valuable lesson was learned: instead of the sweep having the desired effect, it achieved the opposite. The enemy, to assist his pickets, sent all available planes and patrol craft in the vicinity, and the operation, intended to clear the area, actually would have lessened the chances of a Task Force getting through undetected.

During this sweep, *Ronquil* personnel furnished a stirring example of great courage under fire. While exchanging gunfire with two picket boats, *Ronquil* was holed in two places through the pressure hull into the after torpedo room. After the Executive Officer had made an examination and determined the extent of the damage, Chief Motor Machinist's Mate William S. Bellows volunteered to bring up a welding outfit and make temporary repairs. In order to accomplish this, it was necessary to place himself far aft on the sea-swept deck of the ship, exposed to continuing enemy gunfire. Arrival of enemy planes was imminent and actually occurred within an hour after *Ronquil* was hit. Had the submarine been forced to dive, it might have been necessary to abandon Bellows and the Executive Officer who worked with him, and take a chance on picking them up later. Nevertheless, Bellows proceeded with this vitally important work and successfully completed it. In the course of the repairs he was swept overboard, but when rescued, seized his equipment and completed the job.

Halibut, Commander I. J. Galantin, took an almost fatal beating at the hands of Japanese antisubmarine craft. As a member of a wolf pack attacking a convoy off the southern tip of Formosa, she was jumped by the escorts just after she had fired four bow torpedoes. Galantin headed for the depths but the enemy had long since got the word that U.S. subs evaded at deep depths, so they set their charges accordingly. Two escorts were conducting the counterattack, one on either quarter of the submarine. The "pings" of their echoranging gear were loud enough to be heard throughout the boat and there could be no doubt they had *Halibut* located. While one remained on the quarter and maintained contact by means of his "pinger," the other made runs over the sub.

Terrific explosions occurred in such rapid succession that exact count of them was lost. The conning tower was dished in along the port side, one periscope had all its insides torn loose, the strength hull was dimpled all along the after battery compartment, and the compartments were littered with cork insulation and broken glass. Some charges were so close above the ship that she was forced down far below her test depth.

The forward torpedo room caught a particular amount of hell when a close pattern made the torpedo skids, each carrying a 3,000-pound torpedo, leap a foot off their supporting beams. The floor plates were blown up and the torpedo crew flung into the bilges. One man was sure he was going through the bottom of the boat. All sea valves spun open, the escape trunk began leaking and the hull and tank tops were wrinkled. To add to an already terrifying situation, a high-pressure air line ruptured in the forward battery tank. The rush of air and the combined odors of hair tonic and shaving lotions, from shattered bottles, led the personnel in the forward battery compartment to believe it was flooding and that chlorine gas was being generated. The chaotic conditions existing inside the *Halibut* can be well imagined. The ship noises which existed were such that no antisubmarine vessel could have failed to hear them, yet for some unaccountable reason the depth charging ceased. As the Commanding Officer said later, "For some reason the Japs shoved off. A little persistence would have paid off handsomely."

Galantin swore to me, when *Halibut* arrived back at Pearl, that one of this last batch of depth charges, which wrecked the ship forward, had been heard to land on deck before it exploded. As proof he pointed out that the 4-inch gun's breech cover, a thick brass casting, had a hole punched in it and that the chamber of the gun had been pushed bodily to port. Certainly some powerful explosion took place very close to that gun. *Halibut*, veteran of many battles, with a record of 12 ships sunk for a total of 45,257 tons, was retired from active service.

Two unexpected changes in top-level submarine commands occurred at this time. Rear Admiral Ralph Christie, Comsubs Seventh Fleet in Australia, was relieved by Rear Admiral Jimmie Fife and Rear Admiral Freeland Daubin, Comsublant, was relieved by Rear Admiral C. W. Styer, newly promoted to flag rank. Those relieved fleeted up to command of important naval districts.

Again I seemed to feel the cold breath of transfer orders blowing down my neck. Therefore, in discussing these changes with Admiral Nimitz next day, I asked his aid in getting an amphibious job when and if my transfer was in prospect. I had fought so many battles with his Staff that I thought perhaps the Admiral might be getting a little weary of having me around. The Big Boss, however, stepped on any itching foot that I might have had by answering that he had no intention of moving me, unless I specially requested a change.

Plans for shifting Cincpac's Headquarters to Guam were complete and construction of offices and quarters on "Cincpac Hill," a high ridge in about the center of the island, had already begun. *Sperry,* Commander Joe Thew, tender for Subron 10, flagship of Captain George Russell, the squadron commander, moved out from Majuro and started setting up our quonset-hut Recuperation Center in Guam at the spot John Brown had selected. We named it "Camp Dealey" in honor of the heroic captain of the *Harder.*

I planned to quarter my own Staff and myself on a submarine tender in Apra Harbor, while waiting for our HQ quonset hut to be erected. However, there was insufficient room on any of our new tenders for accommodating more than three or four extra officers and, in addition, their radio facilities would in no way suffice to handle our large communication problem. Hence the decision was made to convert *Holland,* not then assigned to any squadron, into a command ship, without disturbing her machine or other shops. She would thus remain available to make "voyage repairs" for submarines and assist in caring for the scores of small craft, with which our advance bases swarmed. *Holland,* having been relieved at Saipan by Fulton, therefore was rushed back to Pearl, where a full-scale radio "shack" was added to her superstructure. The naval constructors took a dim view of the proceedings and entertained grave doubts as to her stability but she has, so far as I know, managed to remain right side up until the present day.

November 21 was a red-letter day, for on that day an American submarine sank the 31,000-ton Japanese battleship *Kongo*—the first battleship in history ever sunk by one of our submarines. Responsible for this exploit was *Sealion II,* Commander Eli T. Reich, of New York City. The news electrified us. We had received reports of battleship sinkings before, which turned out to be overestimates, but the evidence in this case was too conclusive to permit much doubt that Eli had really done it. *Skate* had got two hits in *Yamato*, and *Tunny*, two in *Musashi*, but saw their targets steam away. This time *Sealion* had watched her victim sink.

Eli Reich had been an officer in the first *Sealion*, bombed and sunk at Cavite on December 10, 1941. *Sealion* had lost four men killed and three wounded and *Seadragon*, lying alongside, lost an officer killed by fragments from the bombs which hit her teammate. The desire for revenge had lived long in Eli's heart and he made several successful patrols in other submarines. Finally, just as he reached command rank, the new *Sealion II* was nearing completion.

He came to me and asked if he might have command of that particular ship and I was glad to arrange the assignment. Eli is a live wire of the type everyone likes to help. He got back with his new boat at a time when enemy shipping was being crowded over to the China coast and hurried out to get into the fight.

During the three patrols on which he had command, he sank nine enemy vessels, for a total of 59,839 tons, climaxed by his epic battle with the enemy battleship-cruiser group, in the early morning hours of November 21. *Sealion* was patrolling the East China Sea, northwest of Formosa, when her radar operator reported contact at the unusually long range of 44,000 yards. This indicated a very large target, or the existence of a sort of radar mirage. Such phenomena were frequently encountered in those areas, especially in the Yellow Sea, where a freak distance of 60,000 yards had been reported on a target no larger than a good-sized junk. On this particular occasion, however, the submarine's radar turned in a beautifully consistent performance. The night was almost perfect for making a surface attack: sky overcast, no moon, the sea calm and visibility about 1,500 yards, hence Eli decided to remain on surface as long as possible. Against naval vessels equipped with radar, this plan might not work. However, he determined to make the attempt in order to retain the advantage of his surface speed and maneuverability.

By this time, the Japanese force had been identified as four ships in column: cruiser, battleship, battleship, cruiser, with a destroyer on either bow and one on the starboard beam. *Sealion* was on the port bow of the formation, the best possible position. The enemy was heading about northeast at 16 knots and not zigzagging—a fatal omission against a radar-equipped submarine. As the range shortened, Reich kept his bow pointed directly at the nearest destroyer, so as to present the smallest possible target, but, finding that he was getting closer than he wanted to be, put his helm over and made a complete circle.

He picked the first battleship as his target and set his electric torpedoes at eight feet, just in case a destroyer might get in the line of fire. The Japanese gave no evidence of concern, just plowed steadily on into the disaster which awaited them. Reich could hardly believe his astounding good luck. He had dreamed of such a situation ever since that ill-fated day in December, 1941. At 0256, his sights came on and he commenced firing his six bow tubes.

It was customary in the boats to mark a name on the head of each torpedo as it was loaded into the tube nest. They usually bore the names of the torpedo crews' wives or best girls. Some, made at the Sharon works, carried the names of the employee who had sold the most war bonds during a given period. That night, however, four of Eli's fish, as they raced out of the tubes, were stamped with the names Foster, O'Connell, Paul and Ogilvie—the men who had been killed in the bombing of *Sealion I*. Swift vengeance was on its way.

Reich wasted no time in reminiscences, however, but put his rudder hard right and swung the stern tubes onto the second battleship. At 0259 he stopped his engines, lest swirls from the propellers roll his torpedoes, and fired three stern shots.

Eli said that the four minutes required for his first salvo to reach the target seemed endless. All sorts of doubts assailed him. Had his set-up been correct? Had he underestimated the enemy's speed? Had his whole spread missed? Suddenly, the low clouds were lighted by the brilliant flames of three explosions along the length of the leading battleship. One minute later a violent explosion and sudden rise of flame lighted his second target.

By this time *Sealion* was racing at highest possible speed for the obscurity to westward. The Japs had not discovered her, and one escort was observed by radar to dash out to eastward, where she dropped a string of depth charges. Not a very sharp outfit.

Meanwhile, Reich paralleled the formation at 8,000 yards, continued tracking and reloaded his tubes. He found to his dismay that the target group had speeded up to 18 knots despite the hits it had absorbed. Evidently, his eight-foot torpedo setting had been wrong and the explosions had merely dented their armor-plated sides. Next time he would follow the book instructions. The increased speed introduced difficulties, for the sea had begun kicking up and the wind was dead ahead. Even with his engines running at a 25 per cent overload, he could make only about 17 knots. Seas were piling over the bow and coming solid over the bridge. The conning tower gratings were awash with water pouring down the hatch and the engine rooms were pumping vigorously to keep down water in the bilges. From a high of elation, spirits had dropped to below zero.

Then, at 0450, came a break. The enemy formation split in two. The PPI scope showed three heavy ships holding their course and speed while one heavy ship—*Sealion*'s first target—slowed to 11 knots and dropped astern with two destroyers as escorts. The third destroyer was nowhere to be seen. This is not remarkable for, as we now know, she was on the bottom of the East China Sea, sunk by the torpedo which Reich thought hit the second battleship.

Eli immediately decided to attack this slower group. By 0512, he had attained position ahead of his target, slowed and turned in for a second attack. A few minutes later his tracking party reported the target had stopped, then, at 0524, there was a tremendous explosion. The sky was brilliantly illuminated.

"It was like a sunset at midnight," Reich told me later.

Slowly the target's pip disappeared forever from the radar screen. This was the end of *Kongo*. *Sealion*'s dead were avenged.

These victories were not achieved without losses. All during October and November we had been making silent prayers for the safety of submarines which did not answer to their calls. It is a terribly helpless feeling to know that something must have gone wrong, that a ship may be in desperate straits and that nothing can be done about it.

The slayer of the big Japanese carrier *Taiho*, *Albacore*, Lieutenant Commander H. R. Rimmer, was lost, we believed, somewhere off the northeast coast of Honshu. Because of the danger of mines in shallow waters, she had been ordered not to go inside the 100-fathom curve. Postwar enemy reports state that, on November 7, a patrol boat witnessed an explosion in the approaches of Tsugaru Strait which might have been caused by a mine. After the explosion, bubbles, much heavy oil, cork, bedding and provisions came to surface. The assumption is that *Albacore,* by some mischance, had got into a minefield and was lost therein.

Albacore had been a very successful submarine and served both in Subsowestpac and Subpac. She sank 10 vessels for a total of 49,861 tons. Her score in naval vessels sunk was higher than any other submarine and included a big aircraft carrier, a light cruiser, two destroyers, a frigate and a submarine chaser. She took plenty of the enemy to light her way into paradise.

Growler, Commander T. B. Oakley, made famous by Commander Howard Gilmore's unforgettable sacrifice of his own life to save his ship, was next to be reported "overdue, presumed lost." She was working, on November 8, west of

U.S.S. Growler

Mindoro with a wolf pack consisting of herself, *Hake* and *Hardhead*. Commander Oakley was pack leader. *Growler* had been having trouble with her radar and had arranged a future rendezvous with *Bream* to obtain a few spare parts.

In the early morning hours, *Growler* made contact with a convoy, ordered her packmates to take certain positions and herself attacked. After about an hour had passed, *Hake* heard two distant explosions and *Hardhead* heard one which sounded like a torpedo. At the same time, the targets zigged away from the position *Growler* occupied and, shortly thereafter, *Hardhead* heard three distant depth charges explode. *Hardhead* then proceeded with her own attack. *Growler* was never contacted after that and her rendezvous with *Bream* was not kept. While enemy reports mention antisubmarine attacks at this time and place, no claim was made as to bringing up oil or debris. Was she sunk as *Tullibee* and *Tang* had been, by a circular run of her own torpedo? Did depth charges destroy her? We will never know; none survived her loss.

Her captain was an excellent and war-experienced officer, then making his third patrol in her. *Growler's* service extended over two-and-one-half years; she sank 10 enemy ships for a total of 32,607 tons. One of her victims was a frigate and two were our most-hated adversaries, destroyers.

Scamp, Commander J. C. Hollingsworth, we believe was lost in November, but we did not actually declare her overdue until the following month. Her assigned area was in the vicinity of the Bonin Islands, north of the Marianas Group, then held by our own forces. On November 8, her area was changed to the vicinity of Lot's Wife, a desolate pillar of rocks 500 miles south of Tokyo Bay. Next day, she acknowledged a dispatch telling her to keep clear of the Bonins while the B-29's were bombing them, but that was the last ever heard from her. Later, in order to provide rescue services for downed aviators from Saipan-based B-29's, she was ordered to a station just east of the Tokyo Bay approachs, but she acknowledged no messages after November 9.

Japanese postwar reports state that, on November 11, a patrol plane bombed what appeared to be oil trails left by a submarine, near *Scamp's* lifeguard station. A coast guard vessel was led to the scene and dropped some 70 depth charges, whereupon a large pool of oil appeared. Two other attacks were made on November 16, one about 120 miles south of her lifeguard station and the other back in the vicinity of Lot's Wife. From the last one resulted "great explosive sounds." Was she damaged while on lifeguard station and finally sunk while trying to make her way south—possibly to Saipan? Again we will never know. Her score included five vessels, one of them the big submarine I-24, for a total of 34,000 tons.

Another big triumph brightened the end of the month when *Archerfish*, Commander J. F. "Joe" Enright of Fargo, North Dakota, reported he had put six torpedoes into a carrier of the Hayataka- (Junyo) class and claimed that it had sunk. And so it had, though we couldn't be sure for months afterward. On November 29, *Archerfish* was assigned to a station near Hachijo Jima, an island about 150 miles south of Tokyo. In view of the scarcity of targets, her primary mission was lifeguarding for the B-29's, flying out of Tinian for bombing missions over Japan.

Early in the morning of November 28, she received word that the air strike for that day was canceled, hence she might operate at discretion until the next day. Accordingly, Enright moved up closer to Honshu and that evening found him off Inamba Shima, an islet about 90 miles south of the entrance to Tokyo Bay. At 2048, radar contact was made at 24,700 yards on something coming out from the north. Within an hour the target was identified as a carrier on a southwesterly course, zigzagging at 20 knots. The sky was overcast, but a bright moon at times gave a visibility of 15,000 yards. The northern horizon was dark, so Enright chose the starboard side of the enemy group for his position. By 2230, it was clear that the carrier had four escorts and that *Archerfish* was too far from her track to be able to submerge and get into firing range. There was nothing to do but parallel her course at full speed and pray for a break of luck.

The target's superior speed was slowly but surely removing her from danger of attack and Enright sent out a contact report, hoping some other submarine might be in better position. Unless the carrier made a decided change of course, the submarine had no chance.

At 0300 the break came: the Jap swung back and the range began closing rapidly. *Archerfish* was actually ahead of her quarry and bored in, submerged, for the kill. As the moment for firing approached, it looked as though the escort on the near side would be in the way but luckily it passed clear,

400 yards ahead of the periscope. The sub's position was ideal—1,400-yards range almost on the target's starboard beam so, at 0317, she commenced firing six "steam" torpedoes set for 10-foot depth. Just 57 seconds after firing, the first fish hit close to the stern and a ball of flame climbed the target's side. Ten seconds later Enright saw the second hit, then ducked his scope and went deep to sweat out the expected beating. On the way down he counted four more properly timed hits. Loud breaking-up noises began immediately, for some two-and-a-half tons of Torpex had registered on the luckless carrier. No wonder Joe jubilantly claimed a sinking.

Postwar reports inform us that instead of a 29,000-ton Hayataka class carrier, *Archerfish's* victim was the giant *Shinano*, 59,000 tons. A sistership of *Yamato* and *Musashi*, she had been converted to a supercarrier, and was on a trial trip when torpedoed. She sank several hours later, probably about the time Enright heard a distant heavy explosion. *Archerfish* had set a new world's record for tonnage of a single kill.

During the court martial of the Commanding Officer which followed *Shinano's* loss, it was revealed that the ship was not in a good state of watertight integrity. Yard workmen were still completing her and various openings existed in watertight bulkheads. Destroyers rescued most of the personnel, plus the Emperor's picture.

Sinkings of merchantmen for November were not up to the record set in October. JANAC tells us that 27 submarines sank 46 of these vessels—seven of them tankers—for a total of 211,855 tons. Thirteen submarines, eight included in the 27 mentioned above, sank 127,119 tons of men-of-war, an all-time high. Among these latter victims were one battleship, one carrier, one escort carrier, five destroyers, one frigate, one submarine, and seven other assorted naval craft.

In addition to those already mentioned, high tonnage scores were obtained by *Atule*, Commander J. H. Maurer of Washington, D.C., four ships, 25,691 tons, and *Picuda*, Commander E. T. "Ty" Shepard of Glens Falls, New York, three ships, 21,657 tons.

Pintado, Commander B. A. "Chick" Clarey, came in from patrol with the skipper cursing his luck. He had a unique experience with a big carrier which got away. While on patrol in the South China Sea on November 3, Chick sighted and made an approach on a flattop escorted by destroyers. The attack developed nicely but just as he fired a six-torpedo spread, the port screening destroyer steamed directly into the path of the torpedoes. The resulting explosions blew the destroyer *Akikaze* to bits but the carrier legged it over the horizon untouched.

CHAPTER 15

For some months our antiaircraft guns had been using a new type of shell, with what was known as a proximity fuse, and clearing the skies of Japanese planes. The action and use of the shell had been kept very quiet, in hopes that the enemy would not discover its secrets and introduce a similar type. The important feature of this fuse was a tiny electronic device that triggered off the shell at a specified distance in front of the target, thus making it particularly deadly against aircraft or exposed personnel. Strict orders had been issued that they should not be used where possible duds might fall in enemy territory.

We were eager to obtain some of this ammunition for our new 5-inch deck guns. It would be just the trick for annihilating gun crews and bridge personnel of patrol and picket boats. Those types were usually too shallow draft to be hit by a torpedo, and at that time our special torpedoes, designed to do this job, were not sufficiently reliable for issue—nor did we have enough of them.

I put in a plea for help to Cincpac's Gunnery Officer, Captain Tom Hill, and, after I had promised we would not shoot them into enemy territory, he came across with a generous supply. We loaded a dozen or so in the *Balao*, Commander C. C. "Cy" Cole of San Diego, California, and stood out to the training area, where a stationary target was rigged.

The first string of five looked like another Gun Club fizzle: four did not explode at all and one prematured about halfway to the target. The next string of 15, at a towed target, looked better. Four prematured, one was a dud and three did not explode until they hit the water. The remainder, seven out of 15, functioned as designed and evidently burst into hundreds of fragments, for the spray kicked up often completely obscured the target.

As this looked like something the boats could use, we asked for a complete allowance of them. Two weeks later, I went out in the *Charr*, Commander F. D. Boyle of Everett, Washington, and observed firing at a drifting LCVP (a small landing boat), which was about to be scrapped. A string of nine dummies hung on a wire between two masts, to represent a gun's crew. At first, our shooting and spotting was not good and shells passed so far above the target that the fuse mechanism was not activated. Then our gunners and spotters steadied down and got off about 15 shots at rapid fire, in which there were no duds or prematures. *Charr*, which had been firing at 5,000 yards, then began to close the target, which was threatening to sink. We reached the spot just as it sank, but we could see that four of the dummies were riddled with shrapnel and all the others appeared to have been hit. It was not long before another anti-picket-boat sweep was organized and gave the submarines an opportunity to try this new ammunition on live targets.

My usual trip to Midway this time had to be made by plane instead of via submarine, due to press of work. The regular plane schedule didn't fit my plans and so Admiral Nimitz kindly loaned me his *Blue Goose* to make the trip. Captain Cliff Crawford had recently relieved Captain Dutch Will as squadron commander there and the latter was on his way to Guam in the brand new *Apollo*, his squadron's tender. Things were busier at the Base this time. I found five submarines under refit in addition to the *Ray*, Commander Kinsella, which had stopped in for fuel en route to Pearl. She had taken part in the disabling of the heavy cruiser *Kumano*, related in the previous chapter. In addition she sank a freighter and a frigate and picked up two Navy aviators and two Army sergeants at a secret guerrilla rendezvous in the Philippines. The aviators had been shot down in a carrier strike on the Manila Bay area and landed in the water where they were picked up by fishermen, taken ashore to the guerrillas and eventually put aboard *Ray*. The two Army fliers were technical sergeants, captured when Corregidor fell. The Japs retained them to run the power installation at Fort Drum, but their captors grew careless and the soldiers ecsaped by swimming, with the aid of fuel drums, to the south shore of the bay. All of these escapees said that Jap coverage of Luzon was very sketchy, with garrisons of a sort only in the towns.

Linked with the need for new weapons and equipment was the overall problem of the part played by the Submarine Service in our national defense. I had an opportunity to express myself on this subject when I was summoned to appear before a board of which Admiral J. O. Richardson was Senior Member. This board, composed of Army and Navy members, desired the opinion of all flag officers regarding the reorganization of national defense on a one, two or three department basis.

When questioned, I frankly said I favored a two-department system, each with its own air arm, combined at the top by an all-powerful Chiefs of Staff Committee. With this the Army Air Force representative, Major General George, took issue.

"Why," he demanded, "do you feel that the Air Forces should be subordinate? Can't you conceive a separate strategic mission for Air, independent of the Army or Navy?"

"No," I answered.

"What about the destruction of the German Air Force in Europe by our Air Force, without which, most people admit, the landings in Normandy could not have been made?" he countered.

"That," I replied, "I consider a parallel to the work of the Submarine Forces in the Pacific which, fighting single-handed for two years, as a part of the overall campaign, have destroyed enemy supply lines to such an extent as to make possible the conquest of Japan's outlying bases with minimum loss of American lives. And," I added, "we don't want a separate Submarine Force."

Perhaps my manner was a little brusque, but frequent bombings of our submarines by "friendly" planes had not impressed me with the earnest desire of the Army Air Force to cooperate with other forces.

We snatched two more boats from death. The first was *Bergall*, Commander J. M. "Johnny" Hyde, of Flushing, New York. She was crossing the mouth of the Gulf of Siam, bound on a special mission. Late in the afternoon of December 13, she made contact with a ship to eastward of her, at a range of 35,000 yards. Tracking was begun and the engine room told to "pour on the coal" in order to gain position ahead. The target was making 15 knots, and the course headed her for the south tip of Indo-China, an area of shoal water in which it would be necessary for *Bergall* to act the role of a

PT boat in a night surface radar attack. The weather was favorable to the plan; the sea was glassy and there would be no moon.

As the range closed to 9,000 yards and the submarine drew ahead of her enemy, it was evident that she was tracking a large man-of-war. At 6,000 yards, they could clearly make out the oversize stack of a heavy cruiser, with extensive bridge superstructure—the "pagoda," as it was commonly called—and a second small stack of searchlight tower at the base of the mainmast. She was escorted by another vessel, which appeared to be either a light cruiser or a destroyer. The enemy's new destroyers were about 2,100 tons and were frequently mistaken for cruisers. Gradually, *Bergall* crept up to firing position and at 2037, with a range of about 3,500 yards, commenced firing six bow tubes. At the instant of firing the heavy cruiser and the escort were overlapping, furnishing a beautiful target.

Two terrific explosions were seen with flames spread along the entire length of the enemy ship, leaping hundreds of feet up into the darkness. By this time, *Bergall* was racing away, reloading tubes and anticipating hot pursuit, but the escort remained with her charge, which appeared to have broken in two. The radar had three pips instead of two and both sections of the ill-fated cruiser were in flames.

Johnny Hyde believed the cruiser was finished, but now he wanted a clean sweep—he wanted that escort—but it almost cost him his ship and his own life too. As *Bergall*, at 2100, closed the range slowly toward the escort, lying dead in the water, two gun flashes were seen and two shots landed— one in her wake, the other piercing the forward torpedo loading hatch. Hyde turned away and put on speed as a second salvo landed 200 yards short and a third, 300 yards off the starboard bow. Luckily the escort did not pursue, for, with an undetermined amount of damage forward (small fires and the lights in the torpedo room could be seen from the bridge) the skipper could not take a chance on flooding his torpedo room by running at full speed. Once again a little persistence would have paid dividends to the enemy.

Hyde's immediate problem was to put as much distance between himself and the scene of the attack as possible before daylight, then he could start worrying about how to get back to the nearest base, Exmouth Gulf, Australia, 2,000 miles away.

In the meantime, there were electrical fires to combat, wreckage and debris to be cleared, gear to be moved away from the shot hole, and repairs to be effected. The first step in accomplishing this last, most important item was to stuff the hole with mattresses to keep out spray, They could dive, but with the two forward compartments flooded she could never get up again. The next step was to mount all machine guns to fight off aircraft while the "black gang" made repairs. They performed miracles of improvisation, using whatever materials and means were practical. A repair yard might have raised eyebrows at this job but, for a ship in dire straits, it served the purpose and showed what resourcefulness and desperation can do.

Next morning *Angler*, Commander H. Bissel, Jr., of Buffalo, New York, was contacted. She had just come up via Karimata Strait and reported enemy aircraft covering the shipping routes in the Java Sea, but no patrols in the important Lombok Strait area. That night she took one officer and 54 men from *Bergall*, leaving eight officers and 21 men to run the gantlet.

By adjusting speed to pass through Karimata at night, to cross the Surabaya-Balikpapan shipping lane after dark, and similarly to run Lombok Strait into the Indian Ocean, Hyde figured he could make it back to base. To him, scuttling his ship and taking refuge on *Angler* was unthinkable. He was going to have a try at bringing her home. Unbelievable as it may seem, he did it—steamed 2,000 miles through enemy waters, without being sighted. *Angler* followed all the way, in case air or surface attacks should force Johnny to open the sea valves and swim for it.

The Japanese heavy cruiser, *Myoko*, which was *Bergall*'s target, managed to get back to Singapore, where she remained for the duration. She had the dubious distinction of being one of the targets for British XE boats that penetrated the defenses of that harbor in the last stages of the war.

Strangely, an almost exactly parallel case occurred 4,000 miles northward in the icy waters of the Kurile Islands, only two days after *Bergall*'s near fatality. On December 15 *Dragonet*, Commander J. H. "Jack" Lewis of Hillsboro, Texas, was patrolling submerged in the early forenoon, six miles south of Matsuwa Island, where we lost the *Herring* in June. There were planes in the air and therefore Lewis was running at 100 feet, rising to periscope depth to take frequent looks.

Returning to the 100-foot level after one of these periscope exposures, while passing 70 feet a slight jar was felt and the ship came to 58 feet. At first, this was believed to have been a small aircraft bomb. The idea of having hit bottom did not occur at once, for the chart showed 70 fathoms. However, on attempting to take her down with increased power, heavy grinding and bumps convinced Jack he was aground. Even while he was damning the ancestors of the man who made that chart, the squawk box announced, "Torpedo room flooding!" No one who hasn't heard such a report can fully realize the cold terror it injects into one's bloodstream. Many years ago, in the old R-25 off Panama, my chief engineer came dashing into the control room, his eyes fairly popping from his head, shouting, "Engine room flooding!" I haven't forgotten. It's a situation I could not wish upon my worst enemy.

Lewis did all the right things, automatically, as a result of years of drill. The torpedo room was abandoned and flooded completely before he could build up pressure through the salvage line and start forcing the water out. The ship was pounding badly and the captain felt he must get her off bottom before other compartments were holed. There was, in his opinion, nothing to be done but surface and run for it—slip away to eastward where, some 2,400 miles away, lay Midway Islands and safety. After getting the forward torpedo room fairly well under control, *Dragonet* blew all ballast tanks and surfaced, exchanging, as Lewis said, "a feeling of temporary relief for one of shameful nakedness." They could feel the eyes of every Jap on Matsuwa staring at them. After days of low visibility, this one had to be clear as a bell. They got away clean, but their troubles were not over, for next day the barometer started dropping and by nightfall they were in a cyclonic storm, with heavy seas from ahead and wind blowing a gale. Speed was slowed to steerage-way and course changed frequently to ease the ship. Tons of free water in the torpedo room were causing terrific rolling and leaks around wiring into the forward battery compartment. The weary crew experienced many of those heart-stopping moments when the ship hung at the end of a roll and seemed to be trying to decide whether to right herself or roll on over.

In the midwatch of December 18, the ship gave a violent roll to 63 degrees, from which she nearly did not return. Personnel were flung from their bunks and the mercury out of the gyro compass, which promptly went out of commis-

sion. At eight that morning, three officers and two enlisted
men sealed themselves in the forward battery room and put
pressure on the compartment, so as to keep sea water down
to the holes in the hull of the torpedo room, then opened the
torpedo room door and went in to make what repairs were
possible.

Meanwhile wind and seas had worked around to westward and were definitely abating. About four o'clock that afternoon that most welcome sight in the world met their
eyes—the patrol boat *Beryl,* which we had sent out from
Midway to meet them. It had been a bad four days, but by
their exertions and good seamanship, *Dragonet* lived to fight
again.

With these disappointments and near disasters, there
should have been some compensating triumph and it remained for Sandy McGregor, Commander L. D. McGregor,
of the *Redfish,* to have the honor of providing one.

At this point, the war was going pretty well for our side.
Leyte was practically in the bag and Army troops had landed
unopposed—except by enemy air—to establish aviation facilities at San Jose, Mindoro. Third fleet fighters and bombers, in
a series of strikes on Luzon in mid-December, had swept all
before them and destroyed some 269 enemy planes. The
Japanese were in desperate need of aircraft in their southern
holdings.

Redfish, on patrol on December 9 in the East China Sea,
south of Nagasaki, had, in collaboration with *Devilfish,* Commander R. E. Styles of Ashville, North Carolina, hit the carrier *Junyo* so hard she never operated again. Aside from this,
Redfish's luck had been bad. There was, reportedly, a gremlin
in her Torpedo Data Computer and only the *Hozan Maru,* a
2,345-ton transport, had succumbed to her fire. But Sandy,
with his Highland ancestry, was not a man to be easily discouraged. On the afternoon of December 15, running submerged, he sighted the mast of a supposed patrol boat and
swiftly moved in to investigate. A few minutes later a second
patrol boat came over the horizon. Finally four ships were in
sight—three destroyers in an inverted V, ahead of a flattop.
The carrier, which was headed to pass him at long range,
suddenly zigged 30 degrees toward the sub and, at 1635, just
eight minutes after sighting the big target, *Redfish* commenced firing the last four torpedoes which remained forward. The gremlin was still in the TDC, for there was only

one hit, but that was well aft and the target stopped, evidently with propelling gear wrecked. Instantly, the starboard screening destroyer charged down on the sub's periscope from a range of 1,700 yards and Sandy let her have four stern tube shots. They evidently missed, but there were so many explosions going on at the time it was hard to tell. At any rate, they caused the destroyer to turn away and leave *Redfish* alone for the next few vital minutes.

The flattop, meanwhile, had listed 20 degrees to starboard and was burning aft. The planes, with which her flight deck was loaded, began sliding over the side. It was a beautiful sight but not good enough. Sandy wanted to see her sink. Three torpedoes were all that remained in the ship. The carrier was wildly firing all her starboard guns and the destroyers were dropping scare depth charges indiscriminately, but Sandy didn't scare easily. Finally, one tube was reported ready and, at a range of 1,100 yards, McGregor fired, aiming just abaft the amidships structure. The torpedo hit as aimed, tremendous explosions followed, and the vessel began to capsize. Even then *Redfish* did not try to escape; instead she took periscope pictures of the sinking carrier and set up her TDC for a shot at the nearest destroyer.

Unfortunately, at this point, the destroyer evidently sighted her scope and charged down "looking like she was all bow wave." Sandy rang up full speed and headed for 200 feet, which is about all the water to be found in the East China Sea. At 150 feet, to quote the skipper, "All hell broke loose as a salvo of seven well-placed depth charges exploded alongside the starboard bow." They seemed to shove the ship down, and bodily to port, and she wound up on bottom at 232 feet, with dozens of material casualties such as a crack in the forward torpedo room hull plating, 12 broken battery jars, bow and stern plane gear out of commission, gyro compass 50 degrees off its proper heading, and one man's ear nearly severed by a watertight door which escaped from its fastenings. To make their misery even more complete, one of their two remaining torpedoes was running hot in a stern tube.

But did the McGregor or any of his troops crack under this treatment? Not those boys. After two hours more punishment, Sandy surfaced and headed for home, badly battered but still in the ring, with the consolation of knowing his opponent was on bottom and would never surface. Best of all, the battered enemy forces in the south received no carrier re-enforcements.

On Christmas Day, while nearing Midway, he entered in the patrol log: "All hands enjoyed a delicious Christmas dinner and have now begun to breathe easier; it's been pretty tough going since the attack on that carrier."

Admiral Sir Bruce Fraser, RN, Commander in Chief of the British Eastern Fleet based at Trincomalee, Ceylon, arrived in Pearl in December for conferences with Admiral Nimitz. His Fleet was about to move round to the east coast of Australia and was intent on getting into the scrap. I had known Admiral Fraser as Third Sea Lord (Chief of Bureau of Ships in our parlance) while I was on duty in London in 1941. He had a fine sense of humor and was an enthusiastic helper in passing along to our fleet and Navy Department everything the British had learned in two years of war. For instance, I had been permitted to ship back to the United States 52 sets of radar—which the British badly needed for themselves—one four-barreled pompom (antiaircraft gun), one air and one electric German submarine torpedo. In the hullabaloo of postwar arguments, we are prone to forget such important evidence of goodwill and cooperation.

My plan this year was to spend Christmas at Guam. Each year I got depressed about Christmas time: so many people had wives, mothers, whole families on the verge of dying, which made their presence in the States a vital necessity. These tragedies always happened just before the holidays. It's very disillusioning to the man who has to read such alibis, and I hoped to avoid the gloom by getting away from it all. Admiral Nimitz must have felt a smiliar urge, for I found that he planned to spend Christmas with the Third Fleet in Ulithi.

Commander Bud Yeomans (the And So Forth Officer) and I flew down to Guam, arriving on the 23rd. We found *Sperry* and *Apollo* berthed in Apra Harbor, which looked like the East River on a busy day. Admiral Nimitz arrived in the *Blue Goose* two hours later and there followed a series of conferences with Admiral Hoover, General Larsen, Commodore Hiltabidle, Captain Becker and many others. We all sat in on Admiral Nimitz's press conference and then I went out to see the "Harbor Stretchers," headed by Commodore Fiske and Commander Hines, CEC (late of Midway), who were responsible for dredging, berthing of ships, etc. Their plans for Apra Harbor were amazing. It was to have an area larger than Pearl Harbor with practically all the facilities of that Base. They pointed out to me on the chart a small island surrounded by swamps at the southwest end of Apra Harbor, which was just about the size which we required for tender piers and an HQ set-up. A tremendous amount of dredging, filling, and road making would have to be done, but I had seen these lads in action before and had no doubt they could produce.

"Coconut Island," as we named it, was the best site in view and I accepted with alacrity. Awaiting completion of piers there, we would refit subs alongside their tenders at berths assigned in the harbor. Already four submarines, just in from patrol, were alongside and their crews were recuperating at Camp Dealey.

Bud Yeomans and I were assigned quarters at the Recuperation Center in the "Visiting Fireman's" hut, complete with fire buckets and a picture of a fireman's hat. Camp Dealey had developed rapidly since I last saw it. The quonsets were set under the coconut trees end-on to the beach, so the trade wind blew right through them. Two swimming pools had been blasted in the coral, a softball field, a volleyball court and other recreational features were in constant operation. The next project was to get the existing country road to Agana improved and led around the camp rather than through it, thus eliminating the dust nuisance. Altogether, the camp was almost as pretty as Myrna.

On Christmas Eve, I was too weary to stay up with the lads at the Officers' Mess at Camp Dealey, named "Trader Vic's," next door to my quonset. At intervals throughout the night I could hear carols and old Navy songs keeping alive the holiday spirit in this particular end of the earth. I noted that "Sink 'Em All" was a prime favorite here, as it had been in Australia. By this time it had been added to the repertoire of bands welcoming our returning boats.

Christmas morning we were invited by Captain Schwartz, USMC, the Administrative Officer of Talofofo village to join his people in a celebration. This village was a resettlement area for Guamanians about two miles from Camp Dealey, where perhaps 500 people were quartered and rationed by the Island Commander. Several of us drove up in a couple of jeeps and had our first close view of the native population. We were introduced to all the dignitaries and given ringside seats. The first event was a "stick dance" by two small boys. Each had a bamboo stick and they put on a novel sort of "peas porridge hot" performance after the fashion of sword dances one sees in some countries. Then came a hula by "three little girls from Guam," aged about 10 or 12. We had to leave before the athletic events began but we gained a very favorable impression of a fine people—people who evidently were glad to see us back in Guam.

Yeomans and I flew up to Saipan for a visit to Fulton and her rearming activities. Peterson, the squadron commander, met us at Isley Field, as did also Brigadier General Hansell, Commander Bomber Command 21. The General invited me to inspect one of the B-29's parked alongside the runway, and I accepted with pleasure. It was my first look inside one of these superforts and I was much impressed with their armament and bomb load. However, I thought I'd rather stick to subs—not enough gadgets in aircraft to absorb one's whole attention. The field had been raided the night before by a small flight, probably from Iwo Jima, which came in low and thus evaded our radar. One B-29 had been burned and two damaged. One bomb had landed in a barracks at the Naval Base, killing three and wounding 34.

Our lifeguarding missions were growing more and more numerous and the year drew to a close with a pleasing report of the courageous rescue of an injured aviator by Clyde L. Reese of Blue Diamond, Nevada, QM1/c, serving aboard the *Sea Fox*. On December 27, an Army B-24, returning from a bombing mission, spotted the submarine on lifeguard duty in that area and came in low for a forced landing. The pilot pancaked down nicely but, due to heavy seas, the plane was badly broken up and the pilot, Flight Officer Sachs, was thrown clear of the wreckage. The bomber's crew succeeded in launching two rubber boats but the pilot, one arm broken and encumbered with heavy clothing, was being rapidly swept away. Reese, on the bridge of the submarine, instantly sized up the situation and, though realizing that a rescue attempt would be extremely hazardous because of the heavy seas, dived in and struck out for the drowning aviator. Reese reached Sachs in time, towed him back alongside and, although himself exhausted, helped lift him aboard. Artificial respiration was successful in reviving the half-drowned pilot and he was taken below for treatment. The quick action and courage of Reese was undoubtedly responsible for saving Sach's life and recommendations were made for suitable recognition of his praiseworthy deed.

The sinking score for December was low. Targets had been few and of small size. The Japanese seemed to be giving up the seagoing way of life. JANAC records that 13 submarines sank 14 merchant ships for a total of 86,611 tons, plus nine men-of-war totaling 29,387 tons.

One tremendous bag was turned in by *Flasher*, a Seventh Fleet submarine, commanded by Commander G. W. Grider of Charlottesville, Virginia. *Flasher*, on December 4, got into an important convoy southwest of Manila and sank two big destroyers and a big tanker. Not content, Grider on December 22, contacted another convoy off the coast of Indo-China and sank three more large tankers. His score in merchant tonnage was 38,668 tons, almost equal to *Tang's* record breaker. At this phase of the war, loss of tankers and their cargoes was a crushing blow to the Japanese. Grider's name was added to our list of submarine greats. *Seadevil*, Commander R. E. Styles, added 16,326 tons in two nice targets sunk in the East China Sea. *Trepang*, under Roy Davenport, contributed 13,073 tons in three ships, sunk in a single night in the Convoy College area.

We came to the end of 1944 with a great feeling of accomplishment. It had been a tremendously successful year. JANAC records that during 1944, Submarines Pacific together with Submarines Seventh Fleet, sank one battleship; seven carriers (plus one so badly damaged she never fought again); two heavy cruisers (plus four so badly damaged they never fought again); seven light cruisers (plus one sunk by a British submarine); 30 destroyers and seven submarines (plus one sunk by a British submarine and one German sunk by a Dutch submarine). Scores of naval auxiliaries and light craft are omitted from this summary.

In merchant ships, they sank, in the same period, 548 for a total of 2,451,914 tons. Seventy-two of those merchantmen were tankers, carrying the lifeblood of a navy and of a nation. At the end of 1944, Japanese shipping, which once dominated the carrying trade of the Pacific, dared only to slink along the shallow coasts of China and Korea and to navigate the supposedly safe waters of the Sea of Japan. And we had plans in the making which would render even that

area unsafe. The enemy, whose domestic economy and power
to make war depended upon oversea supplies, could not long
endure such severance of her life lines.

These victories had not been won without sacrifices and
heartbreaking losses for, in that crucial year, 19 submarines,
with about 1,500 officers and men, were reported "overdue,
presumed lost."

CHAPTER 16

The year 1945 opened with plenty of stir and bustle,
preparatory to our move to Guam. Cincpac was timing his
move for the last week of January and I wanted to arrive at
about the same time. I planned to take with me only an operating staff, leaving the administration at Pearl to the Chief of
Staff, Commodore Merrill Comstock. Rear Admiral John
Brown, who ran our Training Command, was designated as
Deputy Comsubpac so that, in my absence, he had the top responsibility of both jobs.

Captain Dick Voge, Operations Officer, and Captain Bill
Irvin, Communications Officer, were to set up their offices at
Subpac HQ on *Holland* in Apra Harbor, but all other Staff
members—except the Flag Lieutenant, Bob Vaughan—would
remain at Pearl. The other Staff Officers would maintain
contact by occasional trips to Guam and personal letters to
me. Later in the war, we held a Staff radio-phone conference
once a week.

There were several Fleet plans in the making with which
we had to effect coordination but, in each, the Subpac part
amounted chiefly to making photographic mosaics and lifeguarding. Our patrols were so numeous that all possible enemy sortie routes were covered and a number of submarines
were left over for lifeguarding jobs. The landing at Lingayen
Gulf was scheduled for January 9, and target dates had already been set for the assault on Iwo Jima and Okinawa.
Photographic and mine-searching missions for the last two
were already under way.

As for the Submarine Forces of the entire Pacific, the
changing strategic situation called for a re-examination of our
major and minor missions and for a reorientation of our

concepts. The transition of the submarine, from a more or less independent unit to a unit that must cooperate closely with the fleet was approaching completion. Our patrol areas were being cut down by each advance of the Army and Marine Amphibious Forces and sinking scores dwindled as Japan's navy and merchant marine tottered toward collapse. The Japanese were scraping the bottom of their shipping barrel.

Specifically, our plans for the next five months were shaped toward the accomplishment of three minor missions, which had moved into the major league:

First, to educate ourselves and train our officers and crews in the use of the secret weapons which, in driblets, had begun to reach Pearl. With this new equipment, designed to facilitate evasion of depth charge attacks and to destroy antisubmarine craft, I hoped to save submarines and the lives of their crews. We had been kept waiting far too long.

Second, to improve our methods and techniques in lifeguarding. Closer liaison with bomber commands was urgently needed. Better communication facilities between submarines and planes were imperative. Scores of lives already had been saved (140 aviators had been rescued in 1943-44), but we felt that the percentage rescued was not as high as it could be. With the improvements which we had in prospect, we believed that this percentage would be substantially increased.

Third, to perfect our mine-detection gear and our training in its use, in order that we might accurately locate known or suspected minefields, search for mines in waters about to be used by our invasion forces and, finally, to penetrate the mine barriers into the Sea of Japan. That last thought was uppermost in many minds and we demanded that the Sea of Japan be cracked as insistently, perhaps, as Cicero demanded the destruction of Carthage. And like that worthy Roman senator, we eventually won our demand.

The first five months of 1945 were devoted chiefly to intensive and vigorous pursuit of these objectives, while still maintaining a throttling grasp upon enemy supply lines.

Holland's transformation was finally completed. On January 14, carrying about half our office files, all our personal baggage, and rows of seedling royal palms waving from the upper deck, she set sail for Guam. Chief Ship's Clerk Vestergaard, our office manager, and some others of the office force rode down with her. Dick Voge was anxious to get his new, and very fancy, operations board working. The back of a vertically mounted chart board was sheet steel and the markers used to represent ships were magnetized steel dots. The parcel post shipment containing his precious markers came just before she sailed. Dick had worried about them and wanted to delay sailing if necessary to await their arrival.

Tunny, Commander George E. Pierce of Tullahoma, Tennessee, arrived fresh from overhaul on the Coast, bringing with her the newest version of an FM Sonar. All these sets were more or less "handmade," so we expected each one to be better than the last. In this I was disappointed, for when I went out with her to a dummy minefield off Pearl her set was temperamental. Sometimes we got mines and sometimes we passed them close aboard with no results. This was a setback, and we immediately radioed San Diego to send out a field representative from UCDWR. I told Pierce that as soon as he got to Saipan I would make more runs with him. That gadget just had to work.

Few radio reports came in from the patrol areas. Most Subpac targets were deep in the Yellow Sea or right on the coast of China. Rear Admiral Jimmie Fife's boys were finding them in the Java Sea, the Gulf of Siam and hugging the Indo-China coast.

Targets were becoming scarce elsewhere, but *Spot*, Commander Bill Post, returned from a patrol on the China coast during which she sank no ships, even though she expended all torpedoes. She managed to save a little face and introduce a novelty by boarding an enemy ship. Early on the morning of January 20, she conducted a gun engagement with an estimated 800-ton auxiliary patrol vessel. The accurate fire from the *Spot*, raking it fore and aft, stopped the vessel dead in the water, caused very extensive damage, and drove the few surviving Japs to cover. Although badly damaged, the vessel appeared not to be in a sinking condition, so the Commanding Officer decided to send a search and demolition party aboard.

The boarding party, under the command of Lieutenant A. H. Clark, Jr., boarded the vessel and conducted a thorough search, uncovering numerous books, instruments, charts, and other valuable intelligence booty. While they were below decks, the Commanding Officer observed that the vessel was settling in the water and was in imminent danger of sinking. He gave the signal to discontinue the search, but the noise made by escaping steam from the badly holed boilers made it inaudible to the boarding party. Suddenly, without warning to those below, the vessel heeled down by the stern and sank in a few seconds.

Four members of the party managed to scramble back to the *Spot*. The other three escaped to the topside, just as the vessel sank, and managed to float clear. One prisoner was taken for intelligence purposes.

Through a combination of unfortunate circumstances, we lost the *Extractor*, a fleet salvage tug, northwest of Guam and blotted our own escutcheon. The *Extractor* had been sent out from Guam into a joint safety zone to pick up a damaged vessel. Sometime after she left port, her orders were canceled and she was directed to return to Apra Harbor. This radio message, however, was garbled and could not be deciphered by *Extractor*. Her skipper did not dare break radio silence to ask for a repeat, hence continued on his way, expecting a repetition of the message. Meanwhile *Guardfish*, Commander D. T. Hammond of Stephens, Arkansas, returning from patrol through this same safety lane, picked up a night contact. She had no information of a friendly force in that area and so sent a message to Comsubpac and the Squadron Commander in Guam explaining the situation.

By Comsubpac, Hammond was advised that there were no known friendly submarines in that vicinity and that if it were a surface ship, she was probably friendly. He was warned that his contact was in a safety zone and that enemy identification was essential. By the Squadron Commander in Guam, after consultation with the operational authorities there, he was informed that no known friendly forces were in the vicinity and again was reminded that he was in a joint safety zone. The Operations Officer on Guam evidently believed that *Extractor* had changed course and was returning to Apra.

On just such lack of imagination depended six lives. *Guardfish*, herself, was not blameless in what followed. She had not attempted to use her IFF (Identification Friend or Foe), because the enemy was known to have used IFF for deception purposes on occasions. She dived before daybreak and approached her target on opposite courses. In the half-light of dawn, from a position well up on the bow, she identified *Extractor* as an I-365-class submarine and fired four torpedoes. Two hit and, as she sank by the bow, her stern came out of water, proving to *Guardfish* that her victim was no submarine. Hammond surfaced and picked up 73 survivors. Six men were lost.

To me three people were guilty of negligence: the CO of the *Extractor,* who took no action on a dispatch addressed to him which he could not read; the Operations Officer on Guam, who probably never considered the possibility that the contact picked up by *Guardfish* might be the ship he had sent to that area; and the CO of the *Guardfish,* because he had not taken all possible means to identify his target.

It was our first accident of this sort and I felt very depressed by it. Plenty of people had attacked submarines by mistake, but this was the first slip on our part.

On January 24, Dick Voge, Bill Irvin, Bob Vaughan, Lieutenant Commander E. L. Hynes, Flag Secretary, and I flew down to Guam, complete with piles of office work and several yeomen. Commander Carter Bennett was also a passenger on this trip. He had left his submarine, the *Sea Owl,* in Guam and flown up to Pearl to tell us the results of his attacks on enemy patrol craft with "Cuties," as we called our newest secret weapon. His was the first employment of this new gadget and he had sunk two patrol boats. The chief of our SORG unit, Dr. Rinehart, went with Bennett on this exploratory patrol "to accumulate background," and, according to the doctor, he had accumulated quite a lot. We sat down in Apra Harbor and found *Holland* moored among the coral heads, deep in the inner anchorage. It was good to live aboard ship once more, where everything necessary to one's occupation—office, communications, mess, bunk—was right at hand.

Swordfish, Commander K. E. Montross, was lost sometime during January, on a special mission to make a periscope photographic mosaic of the beaches on Okinawa, which had been selected for Army and Marine landings. This was a routine service, which we performed for the Amphibious Forces prior to each invasion, and *Swordfish* had on board two photographers from Cincpac's organization to insure a professional job. These mosaics, combined with oblique pictures taken from planes, were used to construct scale models of the islands, especially the beaches which were to be stormed.

On January 2, we gave Montross orders to keep clear of the Okinawa area, because our carriers were attacking, but on January 9 he was directed to proceed with his mission. *Swordfish* acknowledged her first set of orders and on the second set no acknowledgment was requested by Subpac. It was expected the job would require about a week. No further communication was ever received from her, in spite of repeated attempts to raise her by radio.

In the report of her loss, mention was made that *Kete*, which at the time was patrolling the vicinity of Okinawa, reported that before daylight of January 12 she had contacted a submarine by radar. It was believed this contact was with *Swordfish*, since it was in her assigned area. Four hours later, *Kete* heard heavy depth charging from that area, and it was believed this attack might have been the cause of *Swordfish's* loss.

Japanese information on antisubmarine attacks records no operation of which *Swordfish* is likely to have been the victim. However, it is now known that there were many mines planted around Okinawa, since the Japanese were expecting an Allied invasion of that island. The majority of the mines were planted close in. It is considered about equally likely that *Swordfish* was sunk by depth charge attack before she reached Okinawa for her special mission or that she was lost to a mine.

Swordfish won fame early in the war as the first American submarine to sink an enemy ship and as the war machine of Commander Chet Smith which dealt many severe blows to the enemy. She ran the blockade into Corregidor with 40 tons of supplies and brought out President Quezon, Vice-President Osmena, Chief Justice Santos and many other Filipino officials. She was awarded the Navy Unit Citation for the period of her first, second and fourth patrols. JANAC credits her with sinking 12 ships, for a total of 47,928 tons, and it is estimated that she damnaged 17 other vessels.

The sinking scores for January were very small: 18 merchant ships, three of them tankers, totaling 84,185 tons, were sunk by submarines. We also sank six men-of-war, including one destroyer and two frigates, for a total of 5,674 tons.

Barb, Commander Gene Fluckey, was high gun for the month with a bag of four ships, garnered in the East China Sea or Formosa Strait, for a total of 23,246 tons. She also contributed one of the most stirring incidents of sheer daring and courage in the annals of U.S. submarine history. *Barb*'s first kills during that patrol were made during the night of January 8, when, in a series of attacks in the north end of Formosa Strait, she sank a freighter, a passenger-cargo ship and a tanker. After this promising start, however, the hunting became poor. With the carriers hammering at Formosa, all shipping avoided that side of the Strait and hugged the China coast.

Fluckey observed that no lights showed on the coast—a stretch so dangerous that nothing bigger than a sampan could have negotiated it at night without the aid of navigational lights. This meant the ships were running the inshore route by day and holing up at night. This belief was confirmed by coast-watcher reports, transmitted direct to our submarines by Commodore Miles's Navgroup China. From them, Gene got word of a convoy proceeding up the coast and decided to locate it. His plan was to close the coast and mingle with the junk fleet which fished those waters. With it as cover, he could approach near enough to observe the passage of the convoy he sought and make an estimate as to where it would anchor for the night. This involved going some 10 miles inside the 10-fathom curve, a position in which it would be fatal to dive if attacked, since there was barely enough water to cover the submarine.

From this vantage point Gene sighted smoke of three to six ships, moving in column along the coast, tracked them, and estimated they would anchor in Wenchow Harbor that night. Acting on this information, *Barb*, at 0300 January 23, poked her nose around Incog Island, made radar contact with a large group of anchored ships in the lower reaches of Namkwan Harbor and slowed to take stock of the situation.

In this estimate Gene included the possibility that a minefield might lie between *Barb* and her targets. His radar told him of the presence of three enemy patrol vessels which are also equipped with radar.

His charts showed him a large area to northward marked "unexplored" which contained sufficient "rocks awash" and "rocks, position doubtful" to make any overambitious patrol boat think twice before crossing it at night. Fluckey decided this would be the ideal line of retreat, since the mass of junks fishing there would also serve to impede pursuit. For his own part he would have to rely on his radar and his fathometer. Since *Barb* was 19 miles inside the 20-

fathom curve, she would need an hour's run at full speed before she could reach diving water, therefore must take advantage of any obstacles which could be thrown into the path of possible pursuers. A speedy, darting knife thrust and a full speed withdrawal were vital to success.

Weighing all these factors, Gene estimated the odds were 10 to 1 in *Barb*'s favor! He manned all battle stations, took station in the conning tower, sent another officer to take his place on the bridge and started the approach.

Shifting the captain to the conning tower reminds me of the first time I heard of this new technique from Slade Cutter—or perhaps it was from Dusty Dornin. Traditionally, the captain's proper station in any type of ship is on the bridge, so, when in the course of describing a night surface attack, this particular skipper said he had run the attack from the conning tower, I asked the purpose of this departure from standard practice.

"Well," he said, "I found that if I stayed on the bridge, those ships out there in the dark looked awfully close and I usually got scared and fired at too long range. However, if I stay in the conning tower where the range and bearing of every target shows right on the PPI scope, the Exec. up on the bridge can get scared and squawk as much as he likes, but I don't fire until we are at the proper range."

Fluckey evidently had adopted the same procedure. As *Barb* drew nearer and nearer to her firing position Gene reported, "Seriously considering placing crew in life jackets, but the atmosphere throughout the boat is electric. The men are more tense that I've ever seen them. Save for an occasional report of 'single ping sounding, 6 fathoms,' the control room is so quiet the proverbial pin would have sounded like a depth charge. Discarded the idea of life jackets as definitely alarmist, with so many hearts doing flip-flops."

I quote his story of the attack:

Range 6,000 yards. Made ready all tubes. Ships are anchored, in three columns about 500 yards apart, with a few scattered ships farther inshore. This, frankly, must be the most beautiful target of the war. Actual measurement of target length is 4,200 yards. Ships are banked three deep. Even an erratic torpedo can't miss. Radar officer counts

12 ships on one bearing. Estimate at least 30 ships present. Our biggest job will be to prevent too many torpedoes from hitting one ship. For purposes of set-up, chose one of the large ships to left of center of the near column as target. Fired tubes 1, 2, 3, 4. Range 3,225.

Right full rudder, all ahead standard. Sounding 5 fathoms.

Shifted target to right for ships ahead in near column.

Fired tubes 7, 8, 9, 10. Range 3,020.

This was the result:

Main target of attack a large freighter, in first column, was hit by torpedoes 2 and 3. Target observed to settle and undoubtedly sink. Unidentified ship in second column was hit by first torpedo. Damaged. Large cargo-carrier, in third column, hit by fourth torpedo; shortly thereafter caught on fire. Probably sunk. Torpedo 6 hit in the first column. Believed to have hit in main target of attack or ship close to this target. Observation not sufficiently accurate to claim additional damage. Large freighter, in first column, to right of main target of attack, hit by torpedo 8. Damaged. Unidentified ship, in second column hit by torpedo 5. Ship sank. Large ammunition ship, in third column, hit by torpedo 7. Ship sank.

Taking one last look around as the smoke from vessels hit, on fire, and exploding completely obscured all ships, preventing any further observation of other damage, Fluckey went on to tell his own story:

The *Barb* is now highballing it for the 20-fathom curve at 21.6 knots, broken field running through the junk fleet. With the radar sweeping rapidly 30 degrees either side of the bow—wildly maneuvering when some of the junks are inside the sea return. Expect to see a junk piled up on the boat at any second. Gunfire from well astern. Some poor junks getting it.

The Galloping Ghost of the China coast
crossed the 20-fathom curve with a sigh. Never realized how much water that was before. However,
life begins at forty, so keep going.

JANAC cuts down on the number of ships Gene sank
that night, but it was still a beautiful attack, superb in its
planning, daring and execution. The China radio reported
that a major naval engagement had taken place at Namkwan!

Subpac Board of Awards recommended redheaded,
smiling Gene Fluckey for a Congressional Medal of Honor
and his ship for the coveted Presidential Citation, both of
which were granted.

The next few months passed with amazing swiftness. At
Guam, one felt so much closer to the war and consequently
of more use to the war effort. Digging ourselves in at first occupied much of our time. Communication teething troubles
were legion. *Holland,* moored bow and stern deep in the
eastern part of Apra Harbor, had a telephone-teletype cable
running from one of her buoys along the bottom to the
nearest point on the shore line. From there it was buried in a
shallow trench and ran inland to join the main circuits. It
seemed to me that hardly a week went by without some wan-
dering LST anchoring over our cable and breaking it when
she weighed anchor, or some dodgasted bulldozer plowing
through it on the beach.

Liaison with Major General Curtis Le May, who had the
Twenty-first Bomber Command on Guam, was initiated immediately. He had recently moved down from Chungking
and was familiar with our lifeguarding activities, since we
had set up lifeguard submarines for his first strike on Kyushu
in June, 1944. His staff included a very lively young naval
reserve, Lieutenant Wm. H. McGhee, who facilitated our efforts in every way.

Rescue of downed aviators at this time was absorbing a
considerable amount of our attention and effort. The frequent
requirements of our carrier forces for submarines stationed in
the vicinity of their targets had been increased in November,
1944, by services furnished to the AAF. Representatives of
the Twentieth Bomber Command called on me at that time
and requested stationing of submarines for air-sea rescue
work, during the first B-29 strike on the Japanese home islands from the Marianas. Four submarines were placed on

the approach and retirement routes of the B-29's and thereafter four or more boats were constantly employed in what was dubbed the "Lifeguard League."

Immediately after setting up our Lifeguard League, I called on General Le May to arrange Staff conferences for ironing out the many difficulties which prevented proper communication between submarines and B-29's. Even our own "Dumbos"—Navy seaplanes assigned to rescue duties—had difficulty in contacting rescue submarines, because of differences in radio and radio phone frequencies. We also needed equipment in submarines for sending out a beam on which damaged planes could home.

To say that the Lifeguard League met with immediate success would be at variance with the truth. At first, the same difficulties that had been experienced with other land-based bombers were encountered, and the aviators had to be educated to the possibilities of rescue by submarine. Submarines were an unknown and uncertain factor to the Army aviators, and one that inspired little confidence in the uninitiated. The

U.S.S. Wasp

B-29 pilot would take his chance on bringing his damaged plane home, rather than ditch in the vicinity of those little gray ships that might or might not be there when he wanted them.

In addition, a rescue by submarine didn't necessarily mean that the fliers were completely out of danger; frequently the rescues would be effected at the start of the submarine's patrol and the fliers would accompany their rescue ship to the patrol area, to be introduced to many thrills and hazards not included in the curriculum of Pensacola or Kelly Field. On June 2, 1945, the *Tinosa,* en route to patrol area, recovered 10 aircrewmen from a ditched B-29 just south of Kyushu. When Latham, the Captain, informed the survivors that he was en route to underrun the Tsushima Strait minefields for a patrol in the Sea of Japan, they were unanimous in their desire to climb back into their rubber boat to wait for another submarine to come along. This drastic action was unnecessary. Arrangements were made for the *Tinosa* to transfer the survivors to the *Scabbardfish,* which returned them to Guam.

A naval aviator, Lieutenant (jg) Jack Heath, of the carrier *Wasp,* had experiences aboard the submarine *Ray* which are fairly typical of what might happen if picked up by a submarine on regular patrol, as distinguished from one assigned solely to lifeguard duty. Heath's plane had been damaged

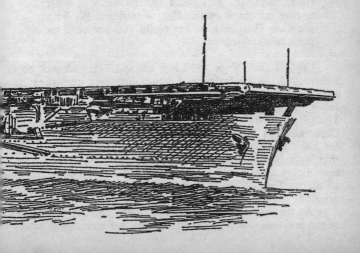

during an attack on shipping in Manila Bay on September 21, 1944. He attempted to reach the lifeguard submarine stationed near Subic Bay, but was unable to make it, and ditched his plane a short distance from the Cavite shore. With the aid of Filipino fishermen, and, later, of Filipino guerrillas, he made his way southward across Luzon, and eventually reached the island of Mindoro, from which he was evacuated by the *Ray*.

In recording his experience, Lieutenant Heath stated:

> We rendezvoused with the *Ray* just after dark one evening. We were in a launch and the *Ray* surfaced. We spotted her, started up our outboard motor, went on over to her, got aboard, and I thought that I had been rescued. I say I thought I had been rescued, but a few times later I had my doubts. Captain Kinsella took me out and got me bombed, depth charged, had me aboard 34 days and practically made a submariner out of me. Finally got me into Midway and I was flown back to Pearl.
>
> While we were aboard, we had lifeguard duty off Lingayen and picked up another "zoomie," Lieutenant James Brice, a fighter pilot from the Cowpens, who had been shot down. We picked him up after he had been in the water about two days. He came aboard, so I had a little company in order to take our stand against the submariners. We both got back O.K. and we are really 100 per cent for these submarine men.

Captain Dick Voge and I flew out to Ulithi and back on February 5, to confer with Admiral Spruance regarding a submarine sweep he wanted arranged in connection with his full-scale carrier strike on Tokyo, scheduled for February 16. The plan was to send *Sterlet*, *Pomfret*, *Piper* (flagship of Commander B. C. McMahon), *Trepang* and *Bowfin* ahead of the Fifth Fleet, armed with our secret torpedo. We believed that, by making submerged attacks with this new weapon, enemy picket boats could be destroyed before they could give an alarm. Thus the Fleet might be able to attain tactical surprise.

At the same time, making use of the reaction obtained in the previous sweep by Burt's Brooms, we intended to send

Sennet, Haddock and *Lagarto* (flagship of Commander F. D. Latta of Burlington, Iowa), known as Latta's Lancers, to create a diversion some 200 miles to westward of Mac's Mops, by attacking picket boats with gunfire. The entire show was a preliminary to the assault on Iwo Jima, which was set for February 19. Iwo, with Chichi Jima and HaHa Jima, in the Bonins, had been under attack by aircraft and surface units of the Fleet so consistently since early December that our submarine patrols kept clear of the area, seldom operating south of Lot's Wife.

Our plane landed at Falalop, one of the several islands that fringed Ulithi lagoon, about 400 miles southeast of Guam, where an old friend, Captain "Scrappy" Kessing, was in command of the Base. Dick and I found Admiral Spruance aboard his flagship, the *Indianapolis*, Captain C. B. McVey, Jr., and there, with his Chief of Staff, Captain Carl Moore, we quickly put the finishing touches to our plans. Doing business with Admiral Spruance and his team was always a pleasure. He never failed to inject his quiet, modest spirit into the work, so no matter what he asked—and it was never exhorbitant—we felt it a privilege to comply. Our subs were assembled at Saipan, ready to proceed to their stations. A day or so later, Dick Voge and I flew up to Saipan to brief them on their missions.

The Fifth Fleet sailed shortly thereafter and made a wide detour to eastward of the Marianas, in the hope of deceiving any snooping planes or submarines. Complete tactical surprise was attained—due principally to unfavorable weather, which kept the Japs out of the air—and Admiral Spruance told me afterward that, when Task Force 38 planes swept into the Tokyo area, they found the enemy having morning setting-up drills on their parade grounds.

Neither Mac's Mops nor the Fifth Fleet sighted any picket boats, but Latta's Lancers, off to westward, had a series of stirring gun battles, which evidently absorbed the attention of the entire area. These boats had been specially fitted out, each with two 5-inch guns and two 40-mm guns. Some "proximity" fuses had been issued for their 5-inch battery and an improved type of voice radio had been installed. They were really "loaded for bear."

They started their sweep at daylight of February 11, but at first found nothing. Even picket boats appeared to be getting scarce. Finally a B-29, flying over, gave them a contact report on a couple of small vessels. The leader made his plans for attack at daylight and informed his pack by radio phone. Fire was opened by *Haddock* (then under command of Bill Brockman, who originally had *Nautilus*) followed by *Lagarto,* Commander Latta, and *Sennet,* Commander George E. Porter of Oakmont, Pennsylvania. After a spirited gun battle, both pickets were sunk. The proximity fuses performed nicely in annihilating the enemy's gun crews. That same night, *Haddock* made contact with two more pickets, but next morning both submarine gunboats ran out of ammunition and *Haddock* missed with her torpedo, so the badly scared picket boats escaped.

Two shore projects concerned us very much. One was an AA Training Center, commanded by Lientenant Commander R. H. "Dick" Walker, USNR, of San Mateo, California, where our submarine crews could obtain training in 5-inch guns, 40 mm and 20 mm. A similar range near Pearl, run by Lieutenant Commander Kirkpatrick, USNR, had done wonders for our shooting up there and we needed more of the same in Guam.

The other project was the building of a Fleet Recreation Center, where the enlisted men of our tenders and repair crews, who were not entitled to use Camp Dealey, could swim, play softball, relax on the beach and obtain a bottle of beer. With Guam on a permanent basis and crowded with ships, the thousands of men aboard them badly needed something of this sort. Two locations existed but bathhouses, etc., were slow in getting built. One of our submarine tenders had, with a commendable spirit of enterprise, built an attractive but inexpensive shack for her people, when suddenly the Commander Marianas decreed there should be no private clubs and commandeered our prize exhibit. The indignation this caused can well be imagined and I endeavored to obtain a more just viewing of the situation, for I felt that ships' initiative should be encouraged rather than penalized. We eventually lost the battle, but the publicity our struggle attracted showed up the lack of push and progress on the part of those who should have had the matter better in hand and resulted in giving the project a much needed boost in the sternsheets.

February 13 brought a needless tragedy to Camp Dealey. Seven men of the *Sea Fox* crew, with one Chamorro constabulary man, were ambushed on a jungle trail about one mile from the camp. Six were killed. The remaining two—wounded—managed to crawl back to Dealey.

The bosque was known to harbor many fugitive Japs, in fact the Marines, in a drive just a few days before, had killed 47 and captured eight. Strict instructions existed forbidding anyone to go into the jungle but these lads, recuperating at Camp Dealey, had somehow got to know a member of the native constabulary, who went with them. The two men who escaped said about 30 Japanese had ambushed them and everyone in their group was evidently hit at the first volley. The enemy were shooting the men on the ground as these two *Sea Fox* crewmen crawled away into the jungle.

Immediately upon their return to camp, an armed party was organized, which went in and brought out the dead. Powder burns showed some had been shot as they lay wounded on the ground. The Chamorro's throat had been cut. All their shoes and some clothing had been looted. The camp was wild to arm two or three hundred men and go in after the Japs, but that would have been foolish, and the Island Commander certainly would have forbidden the expedition. To send inexperienced men into the jungle was to invite greater disaster. Instead we strengthened our patrols and sentries; tightened our regulations, and next day buried our dead amid the white crosses of the Marine cemetery back of Agat beach. Thereafter, we carried side arms and armed our drivers when traveling in isolated parties along the road.

Word came in from Admiral Fife that a force consisting of two Japanese battleships, one armored cruiser and a destroyer had been sighted headed up from Singapore, evidently making a run for home. Apparently, they had slipped past his patrols and the weather was too bad for the zoomies to find them. Dick Voge and I hastily planted the 11 submarines available on the China coast, in spots which it seemed they must pass but, by holing up for a time in the Saddle Islands and using unpredictable routes, they managed to get back to Japan untouched.

Our faces were very red for a few days until news from *Batfish*, Commander J. K. Fyfe of Seneca Falls, New York, salved our damaged feelings. His targets didn't get away. *Batfish* was one of three submarines which we had spotted on a line between Aparri, on the north end of Luzon, and Takao, on the southwest end of Formosa. General MacArthur's troops were steadily forcing the Japanese into the mountain provinces of northern Luzon and, with their air and sea communications cut, we rightly suspected night reinforcement activity or evacuation of pilots and other personnel, whose jobs had folded up. Such operations had taken place at Guadalcanal and Leyte and this time we wanted to be ready for them.

Batfish was nearest to Aparri and on February 9, her first night on station, she picked up on the radar search receiver indications of an enemy radar, north bound. She closed in and tracked the unknown ship, until finally she sighted a dark shape identified as a Jap submarine. The intensity of the radar emanations, known to be on a Japanese frequency, satisfied Fyfe that he had found his quarry. The silhouette of our submarines differs greatly from those of the Japanese and the Germans, hence he was sure she was not American.

Fyfe closed to 1,850 yards and fired four torpedoes, all of which missed. The *Batfish* hauled out to reload and check data, to find out why she had missed. The night was dark, with a low ceiling and no moon, so Fyfe moved in next time to 900 yards without the target giving any evidence of being alerted. He fired three torpedoes, one of which struck the enemy, which sank instantly to the accompaniment of loud breaking-up noises.

The next night, a few miles north of the spot where he had encountered the first enemy submarine, Captain Fyfe again picked up Japanese radar emanations and closed in on his target. At a range of 1,300 yards, a submarine identified as enemy was plainly visible, but just as he was about to shoot, the target dived. Somewhat disturbed and feeling he had muffed his attack, Commander Fyfe hauled off in order to avoid enemy torpedoes if they should be fired.

Whether the target heard *Batfish* or merely made a short routine dive, we will never know, but one-half hour later the sonar operator reported, "Captain, I can hear someone blowing ballast tanks," and in a few moments enemy radar emanations again were picked up on the receiver. *Batfish* immediately dived, started closing the range and, when only 880 yards distant, fired four forward tubes. The first torpedo hit and literally blew the target apart. The next two torpedoes evidently struck debris in the water, for they also exploded, and, as the ship went down, two more loud explosions oc

curred, which were believed to be her own war heads deto-
nating.

The next morning at 0230 *Batfish*, in about the same
position, again picked up the now familiar enemy radar indications. This time it wasn't so simple, for the Jap, for no apparent reason, dived while the *Batfish* was 7,000 yards away.
Fyfe, undismayed, plotted the enemy along at estimated submerged speed, following the course that he had been steering.
At the end of half an hour, his patience was rewarded by
again receiving enemy radar emanations. He dived and closed
in toward his target. The Jap came plowing merrily along
and *Batfish* blew him sky-high with one hit. On surfacing to
look for survivors, *Batfish* found nothing but a large amount
of debris among which was a midshipman's navigation log-
book. The book indicated this particular midshipman could
not have been a very enthusiastic nagivator, since the last entry had been made some two months before.

Thus, in the space of 76 hours, *Batfish* bagged I-141,
RO-112 and RO-113, plus, undoubtedly, a goodly store of
much needed supplies.

One of Seventh Fleet's submarines, the *Barbel*, Lieutenant Commander C. L. Raguet, was lost during the month
of February. Patrolling out of Fremantle, she had been sent
to cover the western approaches to Balabac Strait, at the
north end of Borneo, in conjunction with combinations of
other submarines.

On February 3, *Barbel* sent a message to *Tuna, Blackfin*
and *Gabilan,* reporting numerous daily aircraft contacts. *Barbel* said she had been attacked by aircraft three times, with
depth charges, and would transmit a message "tomorrow
night" giving information. This was the last word from her.
On February 6, *Tuna* reported that she had been unable to
contact *Barbel* for 48 hours, and that she had ordered her to
rendezvous west of Jesselton, Borneo, on February 7. The
rendezvous was not accomplished, and *Tuna*'s search was unsuccessful.

Japanese records indicate that, on February 4, a plane
attacked a submarine north of Jesselton, scoring one hit near
the bridge, with one of two bombs dropped. It appears almost
certain that this attack sank *Barbel*. JANAC gives her credit
for having sunk six ships for a total of 15,263 tons. In addition, it is believed she damaged four others. When lost *Barbel*
was on her fourth patrol.

Just before the assault on Iwo Jima, the Secretary of the Navy, James Forrestal, showed up at Guam, looking perhaps a bit more tense, but otherwise bearing his tremendous responsibilities well. I saw him at dinner at Admiral Nimitz's quarters, where he talked to me at some length regarding our public relations.

I told him briefly the stories of the recent exploits of *Barb* and *Batfish*, explaining that *Barb*'s story, judiciously edited, could be told without harming submarine security, but that *Batfish*'s sinking of three enemy subs was too packed with secret information to permit release. Actually, with the war drawing toward its end, I was anxious to release as much submarine publicity as could be done with safety. I felt that our lads, who were doing such a splendid job, should get a bit of recognition now and then; otherwise the country, by reading the press releases, might gain the impression that the zoomies were winning this war singlehanded.

There were a large number of forces fighting in the Pacific at that time, each as part of a splendid team, and I was loath to see anyone pose as the "Winner of the War." World War I wound up in that sort of an undignified scramble. This time we should be able to handle the situation more intelligently—like adults.

The sinking score for February was a mere shadow of our former records. Fourteen merchantmen and 14 men-of-war were sunk by 19 submarines. The total merchant tonnage was 54,761 and the other 11,397. Notable targets sunk included four tankers, five frigates, one destroyer, and four submarines. To this score, *Guavina,* Commander Ralph H. Lockwood of Glendale, California, contributed the most, by sinking a freighter and a tanker off the coast of Indo-China, for a total of 15,565 tons.

Something really unusual occurred at the end of February. *Hoe,* Commander Miles P. Refo III, of Norfolk, Virginia, and *Flounder,* Commander J. E. Stevens of Ridgefield Park, New Jersey, had a collision submerged off the coast of Indo-China. Their areas were adjoining and, due to miscalculation of existing currents, one encroached on the other's territory. *Hoe* was running submerged at 60 feet, on a course north, while *Flounder* was running submerged at 65 feet on course east.

Suddenly, *Hoe* felt a slight bump and was forced upward; *Flounder* gave a shudder and was forced down. *Hoe* had passed over *Flounder,* just forward of the periscope shears (supports extending up above the conning tower), and only superficial damage was done. This was the first and only—so far as we know—submerged collision of the war.

CHAPTER 17

March, 1945, was an almost continuous workout on training FM Sonar-equipped submarines for mine-detection jobs, in preparation for one of the greatest undertakings of the war—underrunning the mine barrier in Tsushima Strait, blocking the entrance to the Sea of Japan.

On March 2, I flew up to Saipan to brief *Grouper* for her patrol, and remained to observe training of *Tunny,* Commander George Pierce, to westward of Tanapag Harbor, where a mine sweeper laid three dummies for us. Since the water was much too deep for anchoring these dummies, we suspended them from buoys, which held them at a depth of about 42 feet below the surface. The submarine then made runs under these mines for training of officers and operators.

The first day's runs on *Tunny* were most discouraging. The gear was temperamental and occasionally gave an echo, more frequently did not. Professor Malcolm Henderson, of UCDWR at San Diego, assisted in all these tests and even he was discouraged. When we returned to port that night, I was about ready to tear up *Tunny*'s secret directive. We had written orders for her, to be opened after leaving port, which instructed her to make a run through a certain area, which we believed contained two lines of mines. It looked as if she could never undertake such a job.

Professor Henderson sat up most of the night with the sonar set, and next day the performance was much better. Like most electrical gear, this system depended on adjustment of condensers, relays and other equipment, best known to electrical engineers—and Malcolm Henderson and his helpers were the lads who knew how to humor those gadgets.

On our return from exercises, I sent a dispatch to Cincpac, reporting tests completed satisfactory (I had previously discussed the whole proposition with the Big Boss), and asking permission to accompany *Tunny* on a short run into the East China Sea, in order to try out her gear against a suspected enemy minefield. I promised to be back in 10 or 12 days. The Watch Officer called me in the middle of the night to give me a message which said, "Sorry that answer must be, No." I felt badly about the refusal because, after all, the installation was temperamental, and I wanted to lend moral support in this our first FM Sonar mission. Secondly—and selfishly—I wanted to be in the first U.S. submarine to penetrate an enemy minefield. The negative answer was not sent by Admiral Nimitz, who was away on a sudden trip to Washington. I believe he would have understood my position in the matter and granted my request.

Next morning, I went with *Tunny* for a half day of training, and said good-bye to Pierce and his "troops" at noon, feeling worse than I had in the morning. *Tunny*'s gear was working perfectly—but if she did not come back, at whose door lay the blame?

I had received word that Rear Admiral George Creasy, Royal Navy, Flag Officer Submarines, with his Chief of Staff, Captain G. C. Phillips, and the Flag Lieutenant, Lieutenant Commander M. R. G. Wingfield, were making a tour of all British submarine bases and would arrive in Guam for a conference with me and to pay respects to Admiral Nimitz. I was delighted with the news for I had known Admiral Creasy, then a Captain, at the Admiralty in London. He was at that time head of the antisubmarine organization and did a colossal job, but he was not a submariner. It was rather surprising, therefore, that he should have been put in command of all British submarines, but I knew it would not take him long to learn the "drill."

Admiral Creasy and his Staff arrived on Guam on the night of March 10, with but one piece of baggage among them. His Flag Lieutenant had entrusted their bags to some other Flag Lieutenant at Kwajalein while the Admiral went to lunch with the Island Commander and, somewhere in the shuffle, the baggage missed the NATS plane to Guam. The Admiral himself carried a musette bag containing his shaving kit, but the rest were destitute. For the next few days, until their luggage caught up, they had to reconcile themselves to American uniforms. That was not difficult for, led by Admiral Nimitz, we had all stripped down to short-sleeved khaki shirts, short khaki pants, socks and field shoes.

When we first arrived on Guam in January, orders from Commander Marianas were that complete uniforms were to be worn. Many of our submariners were sent back to their ships by shore patrols for being out of uniform. With the advent of the Big Boss, who wore full uniform only on occasions of ceremony, the order fell into the discard, to our great satisfaction and greater comfort. However, the Island Commander, General Larsen, never wore shorts and looked askance at those who did.

One morning before Cincpac's conference, I saw the General carrying two swagger sticks (one, I learned later, he was going to present to Admiral Nimitz).

"Henry," I said, "I've always seen you with one swagger stick but never before with two. What would happen to a Marine General if he were caught without any swagger stick at all?"

"I don't know, Charlie," he said, glancing at my knobby knees, "maybe they'd make him wear short pants."

We showed the visiting British submarine delegation everything there was to be seen and outlined our future plans. They were able to help us in our quest for an effective mine detector, for they had equipment, a type of "Asdic," as they call their supersonic echo-ranging gear, which had been used by British submarines for locating Italian minefields off Sicily, before our Amphibious Forces hit the beaches. Rear Admiral Jimmy Hall, who had commanded a force in the Mediterranean, first told me about these gadgets and I had been trying to run them down ever since. They were not, I considered, as good as our FM Sonar, since they could be overheard by the enemy and showed on the sonar scope only a spark, which might have been anything from a ship to a floating log. When we picked up a mine on the FM Sonar, there was no mistaking its identity.

At that time, a flotilla of British submarines, with their tender, *Maidstone,* had been serving for some months with Admiral Fife's command at Fremantle, and was expected to move up with him in April to his new base in Subic Bay. Another flotilla of midget XE boats, loaded on their tender, *Bonaventure,* was heading west from Pearl Harbor. The British standard-size boats were smaller than ours, hence their people led a much more rugged life and made shorter patrols. I had seen a good deal of these lads, while on duty in England in 1941, and had gained great respect for their ability and daring. The entente between our two submarine services was cordial indeed. Admiral Creasy and his Staff departed by plane for Pearl on March 13, leaving goodwill and comradeship behind them.

With the big job in mind, I took off that same afternoon for training runs with *Spadefish,* Commander W. J. Germershausen. I had been aboard this submarine for mine-gear tests, while "Judge" Underwood had command, but I wanted to be sure she was still operating properly. The story was much the same as on *Tunny.* The 14th and 15th were replete with disappointment, adjustments and cussing, but on the 16th, with a rough sea, when sonar conditions could be expected to be unfavorable, we got good ranges, actually, the best we had ever got.

After completing tests on *Spadefish,* Professor Henderson and I shifted immediately to *Tinosa,* Commander R. C. Latham, and worked with her on the 17th. Her set was much better adjusted and, by 1235 of the first day, we had her ready to sail.

During these trials, a message came in from *Tunny* reporting that she had successfully penetrated the area assigned in her secret orders and had charted 222 mines. This was indeed good news and gave a tremendous boost to our spirits. Later, when *Tunny* returned to port, examination of her plot led us to believe that a number of the mines she had located were not mines at all, but must be a cargo of oil drums from some sunken freighter, heaped on the bottom of the East China Sea. However, the rows of mines for which we were looking were definitely there and, after the taking of Okinawa, hundreds were swept up by the Mine Force.

Tunny's skipper, George Pierce, was jubilant over having penetrated and located the lines of mines, in which we believed at least one of our submarines had been lost. Admiral Nimitz sent him a message of congratulations. I immediately got orders for Pierce to return to the Sound Laboratory in San Diego, tell them of his success, and give them a pep talk about getting more sets of the gear out to us.

Since our mine-detection training program was reaching large proportions and absorbing a considerable portion of my time, I decided to shift the scene to Guam, to eliminate the trips to Saipan and the long absences from my HQ. We rigged suspended mines about 10 miles off the entrance to Apra Harbor and, on March 27, took *Crevalle,* Commander E. H. "Steiny" Steinmetz of Rockville Center, Long Island, out for a check. She had already been put through her paces at the Penguin Bank dummy minefield, southeast of Pearl Harbor. Sound conditions were ideal, as the water was iso-thermal and about 1,600 fathoms deep. Sometimes, when using high power, we could pick up large blobs which, by the peculiar tone of their echo and the swiftness of their move-ments, were evidently schools of fish or perhaps whales.

Many runs were made at 100 and 150 feet to simulate underrunning a deep-laid minefield—of the type used by all navies to trap submarines. *Crevalle*'s gear was not up to snuff and we returned to port after a long day, somewhat beaten down. That was typical of FM Sonar operations: one day we would be sunk in a slough of despond; the next, on the crest of the wave.

At about this point Commander Barney Sieglaff, ex-skip-per of *Tautog* and *Tench,* came to Comsubpac Staff as an Assistant Operations Officer. However, we made a quick shift and put him in charge of the FM Sonar training, to take some of the weight off my shoulders and to get the operation properly organized. It was a happy selection, for Barney soon had things humming. Professor Henderson came out from the Coast every time we had a large batch of subs on our hands for training and two of his field assistants—one of them Lieu-tenant (jg) "Dinky" Dye of Santa Cruz, California—were constantly on the job. Confidence improved and boats fitted with FM Sonar began to feel less and less like expendibles.

Underrunning minefields was not a new stunt. In World War I, the British submarines had done quite a lot of such work, notably in penetrating the Dardanelles. But their trips had been made blindly and the scraping of mine cables along their sides was a frequent occurrence. We wanted our sub-marines to be able to see the mines they were dodging and avoid their anchor cables. To make doubly sure, "rope guards" were placed around bow planes, stern planes, and propellers so they would not be fouled by mine anchor cables. These rope guards, made of wire, were not too satis-factory at first. Several of them were carried away in heavy seas. In *Seahorse,* on March 26, one of these cables became fouled with the bow planes, preventing their operation and necessitating a hazardous clearing job in heavy seas.

March was replete with thrills and narrow escapes. *Rock*, Commander R. A. Keating of Wollaston, Massachusetts, was proceeding westward through the Java Sea toward Karimata Strait on March 18. In the midwatch, the Captain, sleeping in the conning tower, was awakened by a heavy jar aft. The after torpedo room reported some heavy object had struck the ship in that vicinity. The thud of the blow was accompanied by a whirring sound, such as might have been made by a torpedo's propellers. Subsequent dry-docking tended to confirm that *Rock* had been hit by a dud torpedo, which tried to climb her side, as our skippers had often seen their own torpedoes behave in the days of our exploder troubles.

The most unusual escape was reported by *Devilfish*, Lieutenant Commander S. S. Mann, Jr., of Baltimore, Maryland. She was proceeding to her patrol station, up near the Empire when, west of Iwo Jima, the Officer of the Deck sighted a Japanese plane diving at them from the clouds about five miles distant, and instantly "pulled the plug." As *Devilfish* was passing 50 feet, at which depth the top of the periscope shears is just going under, a shock, as of a near explosion, was felt and water began pouring in through the bottom of the radar mast and the search receiver lead-in. Things looked pretty grim for a few minutes until it was found the pumps could control the flooding. Both periscopes and his radar were out of commission so Mann did not surface until dark. Then he found on the bridge, bits of wreckage and a name plate which indicated a *kamikaze* plane had dived into them. That was the first and, so far as we know, the last instance of this sort.

Spot, Commander Bill Post, had a bad time off the China coast on the morning of St. Patrick's Day. In consideration of the shamrock Bill had put on the escutcheon of *Gudgeon*, it might appear that the revered gentleman gave him a hand that day. The sub had closed the coast at night looking for enemy shipping, made several attacks and expended all torpedoes. At daylight, *Spot*, legging it for deep water, found herself pursued by a patrol boat. Post was determined to get off his request for a reload of torpedoes at Saipan, and he was even more determined not to let this Jap skipper force *Spot* to dive in shallow water, where chances for successful evasion of depth charges were practically nil. He decided, therefore, to run for it and hold the enemy off with the 5-inch gun mounted aft.

The Japanese—a new mine layer—opened fire first and Bill returned the fire, first with his 40 mm and then his 5 inch. After the first 5-inch shot was fired, a heavy sea knocked down the gun's crew. All were able to scramble back to their gun and, after several more salvoes, got a hit at the base of the enemy's forward gun, which put that menace out of action.

Another huge wave sent the gun's crew sprawling. The danger of losing his gun crew overboard was too great, so the skipper secured the gun, but kept up the fight with his after 40 mm, until a heavy sea climbed the cigarette deck and jammed its loading mechanism. The range was then down to 2,100 yards and the urgent message still had not been cleared.

Bill next took a long chance by swinging right, so his forward 40 mm could be brought to bear. His shells poured into the Jap, but the range was decreasing at terrific speed, and the mine layer was evidently intent on ramming. The 40-mm pointer received a bad leg wound and *Spot* secured the gun and the crew tumbled below. With the range down to 350 yards and machine-gun bullets bouncing off the super-structure, Post had one hand on the diving alarm, the other on the collision alarm. Fortunately, at that critical point the radio shack reported the message was cleared to Subpac and the enemy lost his nerve. He swung left and crossed the submarine's stern, at a range of about 100 yards. As he slid by, it could be seen that he had suffered considerable damage, whereas *Spot* was hardly scratched. Bill thanked his lucky stars for that hit on the Jap's big forward gun, pulled the diving alarm and headed for bottom—a totally inadequate 30 fathoms.

Our next move was to establish Commander Charlie M. Henderson in Okinawa as a member of Real Admiral John Dale Price's Staff, in order to coordinate our lifeguard service with Navy and Army units operating out of Okinawa against Kyushu. There, Commander Henderson's job was not too simple. Admiral Price was extremely helpful, but the Army Air Force commander evidently considered our arrangements for rescuing his pilots unnecessary, and obviously his airmen were not properly briefed, for shortly thereafter a lifeguard, operating on surface south of Kyushu, was bombed—and missed—by a B-25. Naturally, I complained to Admiral Nimitz, who repeated the protest to the commanding general on Okinawa. No acknowledgment was ever received to Cincpac's message, nor was our Commander Henderson able to obtain an audience with this Air Force autocrat. My first impulse was to recall the lifeguard submarine on that station. However, more considered thought made me realize that this isolated case of bad manners did not entitle me to withdraw protection from pilots, who possibly did not share the self-sufficient views of their chief.

Two months later, we ordered Commander J. A. "Caddy" Adkins to temporary duty with the Air-Sea Rescue Unit at Iwo Jima, in order to supply lifeguard information direct to the submarines in the National League. (The "Lifeguard League" had been split into the "Texas League," operated from Okinawa, and the "National League," operated from Iwo.)

When Lieutenant General Barney Giles assumed command of the Army Air Forces, Pacific Ocean Areas, with headquarters at Guam, I immediately made contact with him in order to promote the lifeguard business. A series of round-table conferences were arranged, attended by the General and myself, with our Staffs and skippers of submarines recently returned from lifeguard duty. On one occasion, we had Commander Hiram Cassedy of *Tigrone,* who had broken all records by rescuing 31 Army flyers in one patrol. These meetings were productive of many excellent ideas for improving our methods and communications. They also produced a spirit of comradeship, which worked wonders in our everyday relations. B-29 crews, resting after a certain number of missions, were invited to make use of quarters at our Camp Dealey. Aviators were taken out for training dives in submarines, and submariners were given rides in B-29's, during their training flights. This last, however, led to several young daredevils making bombing runs on Tokyo. Naturally, I had to insist on stopping that phase of the "training," since it involved unnecessarily hazarding the lives of our always barely sufficient personnel.

Equally vigorous efforts were being made in Admiral Jimmie Fife's command to effect all possible rescues of downed airmen. Opportunities for lifesaving by his submarines were fewer, but the resourcefulness and daring of his skippers left nothing to be desired.

The Submarine Forces are very proud of the fact that, during World War II, 86 submarines rescued a total of 504 aviators of Army, Navy, Marine and British forces. The value of lifeguarding cannot be measured alone in terms of lives saved, important though that factor is. Actually, its effect on the morale of the air forces was of much greater moment. No one, not even the most courageous, relishes the idea of making a "one way" flight. The thought that, if shot down, he might be tortured or murdered by a barbarous enemy, or serve as live bait for sharks and barracuda, could not be too comforting to an aviator, and conceivably might influence him to pull his punches. The confidence with which Air-Sea Rescue and submarine lifeguard services were able to inspire flying personnel undoubtedly had a great and beneficial effect upon the fighting spirit of that heroic arm of the Services.

The folloiwng dispatches are typical of many received and illustrate the reaction of various commands to the lifeguard operations of submarines:—

From General MacArthur
To: *Sea Robin* and Crew
   I wish to extend my sincere appreciation for your efforts in effecting the rescue of Lieutenant Alfred N. Royal. The presence of submarines adds materially to the morale of the Far East Air Forces combat crews, and has resulted in increased effectiveness of our operations.

From: Commdr. Task Force 93 and Deputy Commander 20th Army Air Force
To: All Submarines
   The courage, cooperation, and untiring efforts of the officers and men in submarines on lifeguard duty has contributed immeasurably to the morale of combat crews and to the success of our superfortress and Mustang operations over the Empire. To all, a well done. Good luck in our continued operations.

Two submarines, *Kete*, a new boat on her second patrol, and the battle-tested *Trigger*, on her 12th, were lost during the month of March. In neither case are we sure as to the cause.

Kete, Lieutenant Commander Edward Ackerman, left Guam on March 1 for patrol in the Nansei Shoto area. As additional duty she made special weather reports, for the use of our aviators, and furnished lifeguard services. On the night of March 10, *Kete* reported having sunk three medium-sized freighters on the previous night. She reported, on the night of March 14, that she had fired four torpedoes, which missed a small enemy cable laying vessel, and that she had only three torpedoes remaining aboard. In view of the small number of torpedoes left, *Kete* was directed to depart her area and proceed to Pearl for refit, stopping at Midway en route for fuel. On March 19, she acknowledged receipt of these orders. Next day, she sent in a special weather report from a position just east of the Nansei Shoto chain. This was the last message received from her. At normal cruising speed, she should have arrived at Midway about March 31 where watch was kept for her until hope was abandoned.

P-51 Mustang

The second loss was *Trigger*, Commander D. R. Connole. She left Guam on March 11, also bound for the Nansei Shoto area, with orders similar to those given *Kete*, regarding weather reports and lifeguarding. After having sent several routine messages en route to her area, *Trigger* reported her first action on March 18. She stated that she had made a seven-hour end around on a convoy she had previously reported, and had attacked. She sank one freighter and damaged another.

On March 26, *Trigger* was told to proceed to rendezvous southeast of Kyushu, with a wolf pack whose other members were *Seadog* (pack leader) and *Threadfin*. This message required an acknowledgment, but none was ever received. However, on that same date she did make a special weather report. Two days later, by which time she should have reached the wolf-pack rendezvous, *Seadog* reported she had been unable to communicate with *Trigger*. Many attempts were made thereafter to raise *Trigger* by radio, but none was successful. On the afternoon of March 28, Japanese planes and ships conducted a two-hour depth charge attack just south of Kyushu, which was heard by four other submarines in nearby areas. It is considered that *Trigger* was, in all probability, lost during this attack.

Trigger had a long and illustrious career in World War II, and twice was awarded the Presidential Citation. Her attack on the Japanese carrier *Hitaka* was the spark which set off a train of events leading to the eventual solving of our torpedo exploder difficulties. JANAC credits her with sinking 18 vessels, for a total of 86,552 tons. It is estimated that she damaged about 22 other enemy ships. One of her victims, the *Odate*, a Japanese naval repair ship, was sunk on March 27, just the day before *Trigger* was herself lost.

Our sinking score for March was only slightly better than February. Eighteen submarines sank 24 merchantmen (including six tankers), for a total of 59,755 tons, and five men-of-war (including two frigates), for a total of 5,456 tons.

Balao, Commander R. K. Worthington of Oakmont, Pennsylvania, contributed the most tonnage by sinking a transport and a freighter in the Yellow Sea, for a total of 11,293 tons. *Sea Robin*, Commander P. C. Stimson of Santa Monica, California, one of Admiral Fife's command, was high gun with a clean-up in the Java Sea of three freighters and an ex-gunboat. During the last one-third of the war, it is remarkable how many ex-men-of-war we find listed as merchantmen. The need for tonnage to carry food and raw materials back to the Empire forced many such conversions of naval vessels.

April opened with the biggest error in the history of American submarine operations, one which could have brought serious reprisals. *Queenfish*, a brand-new boat commanded by Commander C. Elliott Loughlin, of North Wales, Pennsylvania, torpedoed and sank the *Awa Maru*, a Japanese vessel carrying Red Cross officials and Japanese wreck survivors, which had been accorded safe-conduct through international arrangements, to which the United States had agreed.

Queenfish, under Commander Loughlin, had made an outstandingly aggressive and successful first patrol in August and September, 1944, and followed it in November with one even more productive. For these meritorious performances, she was awarded the Presidential Citation. While on her first patrol, she had the remarkable experience of being fired at three times in the same day by enemy submarines. Each time the wakes were sighted in time to permit the Officer of the Deck to take effective evasive action, which speaks well for the training and alertness of her lookouts, as well as of her officers of the deck.

Loughlin, an experienced submariner, was in his first fleet command, but had made four patrols in the Atlantic as captain of the old S-14, which I put in commission at Bridgeport, Connecticut, in 1921, and took out to the Philippines. He was not only an excellent officer, but had been for several years the Submarine Force's representative in Fleet championship tennis matches. *Queenfish,* it will be remembered, was rushed in to search for survivors, after *Sealion* sank an enemy ship packed with Allied POW's, and had rescued 18 of them.

When the Staff Duty Officer called me, in the early morning hours of April 2, with *Queenfish*'s dispatch reporting the sinking of the *Awa Maru* and recovery of only one survivor, we immediately ordered *Sea Fox,* who was patrolling close by, to assist *Queenfish* in rescuing all possible survivors. I was gravely concerned about the view the Japanese might take of our apparent breach of faith in sinking a vessel to which full immunity had been accorded and I was deeply concerned, also, that so fine an officer as Elliott Loughlin had made such a serious and fatal mistake. However, my chief worry was occasioned by the fear that the Japanese might wreak barbarous reprisals upon submarine prisoners, whom they had captured or might later capture.

The sinking of the *Awa Maru* was a mistake, brought on by fog and errors in communication, for which latter I was partly responsible.

Queenfish was patrolling off the China coast, at the north end of Formosa Strait, when at 2200 on April 1, radar contact was made on a single ship, at a range of 17,000 yards. Loughlin said in his patrol report:

> All radar contacts previously made on own and enemy ships indicated this contact should be the size of a destroyer or DE and the approach was made with this identification in mind. This belief seemed to be substantiated by:
>
> 1. High speed of 16–18 knots in fog
> 2. Proximity to position of *Seafox* attack nine hours earlier
> 3. Track was on only route used by enemy shipping along this portion of China coast.
>
> Position was obtained 1,000 yards off contact's track on parallel course, until the range was closed to 3,600 yards. Slowed to 4 knots, then swung right for stern tube shot on 90-degree starboard track and torpedo run of 1,200 yards. Surface visibility was reduced to 200 yards by the existing fog with night dark, sky partially overcast, and the moon breaking through at intermittent intervals. Although sea condition was choppy, decided upon three-foot depth setting with small spread as set-up checked perfectly.
>
> At 2300, with torpedo run 1,200 yards and the bridge watch, including Commanding Officer, straining to get a glimpse of the ship, commenced firing four torpedoes from stern tubes using radar ranges and bearings. Four hits resulted at the proper time intervals with the flash of the torpedo explosions discernible although the ship itself was never sighted.
>
> 2303: Increased speed and turned to head back to the attack position with the pip on the radar screen disappearing before we could get turned around.

Fifteen or 20 survivors were sighted in the water clinging to wreckage, but only one could be induced to come aboard. Later interrogation of the prisoner revealed that the ship sunk was the *Awa Maru*.

Commencing in the morning of the following day, *Queenfish* conducted an intensive search for survivors, which lasted until about noon of April 3. *Sea Fox* joined the search on the afternoon of April 2, but departed the area because of injury to a crew member, while *Queenfish* continued the search until evening. Each submarine reported sighting an estimated 2,000 bales of rubber floating on the surface, beside many tins of an unidentified granulated substance. Four bales of rubber and two of these tins were recovered by *Queenfish,* but no other survivors were sighted.

The Commanding Officer of *Queenfish* was tried by General Court Martial and found guilty of Negligence in Obeying Orders, for having neglected and failed to proceed with due caution and circumspection in the identification of a ship, as a result of which the *Awa Maru* was attacked and sunk. It was proven that *Queenfish* had received three dispatches concerning *Awa Maru* on that patrol. The first one was received in early March, from the Commander in Chief U.S. Fleet, and stated that the *Awa Maru* would sail from Moji and return with relief supplies for U.S. POW's, for which voyage the U.S. Government had guaranteed safe conduct. It described the ship and her itinerary. The second dispatch amended the route of the ship and her sailing dates, and was also received in early March from the Commander in Chief. The third dispatch was received on about March 30, from Comsubpac, and stated that the *Awa Maru* would pass through *Queenfish's* area between March 30 and April 4, 1945, lighted at night and plastered with white crosses, and to "let her pass safely."

This third dispatch contained an error, for which I was responsible, in that it was addressed to "All Submarines," whereas the part concerning the *Awa Maru* was of interest only to the submarines through whose areas she would pass. A member of the Court Martial told me afterward the evidence at the trial of Loughlin led to the conclusion that the Communication Officer of the submarine had not shown the earlier plain language dispatches to his commanding officer, therefore Loughlin was not aware of the particular significance of our last dispatch. The Captain's sense of loyalty did not permit him to "pass the buck" to his junior.

We obtained excellent legal counsel for Commander Loughlin—Captain Chester Bruton and Lieutenant Colonel Coffman of the Marines, both trained in naval law. Knowing that I would be absent in the U.S. for an electronics conference at the time of the trial, I sent an official dispatch to Cincpac, pointing out that the tragedy was due partly to my own error and asking that I be held equally responsible. While in Washington in April, I paid my respects to Secretary Forrestal and Fleet Admiral King, explained the situation to them, and asked that Loughlin be given every possible consideration and clemency. In spite of all we could do, Loughlin was given a reprimand by the Secretary. From information which reached us after the *Awa* was sunk, it appears Loughlin should have been awarded a commendation instead of a reprimand.

Intelligence sources told us that *Awa Maru*, on her trip south, engaged in what was supposedly an errand of mercy, had carried, in addition to her 11-pound Red Cross gift packages to Allied POW's, 500 tons of ammunition, about 2,000 bombs and 20 crated planes, which she unloaded at Saigon. The pity is that some submarine did not sink her on that leg of the voyage. Those 11-pound packages couldn't do much toward saving the lives of our starving POW's, but the remainder of the *Awa*'s cargo could deal out death to thousands of able-bodied Allied fighting men.

The lone survivor of the *Awa*'s sinking testified that the ship was lighted with seven white crosses at 2200 on April 1, when he took a walk around deck, and that he had heard no fog signals sounded up to that time. Had *Awa Maru* been sounding fog signals, as required by International Law, it is very likely *Queenfish* would have heard them and undoubtedly *Awa Maru* would have been saved. At the time of her sinking she was carrying a cargo of rubber, lead, tin, and sugar. Seventeen hundred merchant seaman and 80 first-class passengers, all survivors of ship sinkings, were being transported from Singapore to Japan. The first-class passengers included Captains, Chief Engineers and Foreign Department officials, on board to administer Red Cross supplies. At the time of her sinking the survivor said no Red Cross supplies were aboard, they having been previously unloaded.

The danger inherent in this error was the possibility of Japanese reprisals. The enemy made charges earlier in the war that U.S. submarines had violated the Geneva Convention by firing upon and sinking properly registered and marked hospital ships.

The allegations were untrue except that on one occasion, by mistake a hospital ship was the target for submarine torpedoes. This incident occurred in a rain squall, when the target could be seen only dimly. Fortunately, the torpedoes missed and when the visibility improved, showing the enemy vessel to be a hospital ship, no further pursuit or attack was made.

In 1942, *Skipjack* fired at and missed, unfortunately, an armed, zigzagging transport showing a red cross on the end of her bridge wing. Another similarly marked and armed

U.S.S. Skipjack

transport was in company with her. The target fired with her forward gun in the direction of the submarine for about 15 minutes.

In July, 1943, the Japanese complained we had hit a 2500-ton hospital ship near Palau. *Gurnard* attacked a convoy sortieing from Babelthaup Harbor on the date mentioned and fired torpedoes at an aircraft carrier. The Captain did not even see the alleged hospital ship but she must have been a part of the convoy, and stopped a torpedo intended for the flattop. The enemy also claimed that a submarine sank a hospital ship off Hongkong. This ship, however, must have been the victim of mines, which we laid along the China coast, for no submarine was in the vicinity at the time.

Submarine commanders often asked permission to stop and search hospital ships, because of the suspicious-looking deck cargoes carried, and I recall that Admiral Halsey made a similar proposal to Cincpac, but none of these requests were granted. Toward the end of the war, a hospital ship proceeding to Wake was intercepted and searched by a destroyer as she approached the island and as she departed therefrom. No fault was found with her. Most of her patients were neither wounded nor diseased, but were obviously suffering from starvation.

The large number of hospital ships which the Japanese employed—about 25—looked suspicious and we had been told by Allied POW's, rescued by submarines in the South China Sea, that they, as dock labor parties, had often unloaded ammunition from hospital ships.

Naturally, the Japanese protested the *Awa Maru* incident violently, but no reprisals followed. For me, I sincerely hope that the career of Charles Elliott Loughlin—a damned fine officer—will not be harmed by this tragic mistake. My own sorrow at our violation of *Awa Maru*'s immunity is tempered somewhat by the conviction that she finally got just what she deserved.

In the first part of April, administrative command of Submarines Seventh Fleet was given to Comsubpac. This made no change in our actual operations. Admiral Jimmie Fife and I had worked together very closely, at all times, and this change was intended merely to facilitate handling our overlapping commands, as the ground forces moved up closer to the Empire. Jimmie had already folded up submarine activities at Brisbane and Mios Woendi, and was in process of closing out his headquarters, repair, fueling and rearming facilities at Perth, Fremantle, Exmouth Gulf and Darwin. Everything in his command, including the British flotillas, was being concentrated at the new submarine base in Subic Bay. Cooperation between his submarines and Rear Admiral F. D. "Honus" Wagner's planes, operating out of the Philippines, had completed the strangulation of enemy traffic along the Indo-China coast. Only occasionally were targets found running between Singapore and Saigon or between other Japanese-held ports in the Netherlands Indies. Our once rich Convoy College area was now destitute of enemy ships and was used chiefly by submarines lifeguarding for Luzon-based planes, which hammered Hongkong and Formosa. We reassigned it to Admiral Fife to simplify control of his lifeguard stations.

On April 6, there were indications, reported by bombers over the Empire, that remnants of the enemy fleet were about to make a move. With the Okinawa battle raging right at her doorstep, it was to be expected Japan would make some sort of a *banzai* charge with her few remaining men-of-war, to support the all-out attacks being made by her air forces against our invasion fleet. Our submarine dispositions had been made with this very possibility in view and every exit from Japanese home waters was heavily patrolled.

We alerted all submarines and, shortly before midnight of that same day, I was awakened with the news that *Threadfin*, Commander J. J. Foote of Brooklyn, New York, had made contact in Bungo Suido, the southwestern exit from the Inland Sea, with a force which she reported as two battleships and eight destroyers. The first battleship was the giant *Yamato*, but the other turned out to be the light cruiser *Yahagi*. Foote had been in excellent position to attack, but sacrificed his chance to write his name large in the Hall of Fame as the annihilator of an enemy battleship by carrying out his orders to report first and attack afterward. *Hackleback*, Commander F. E. Janney of Winnetka, Illinois, also made contact, but due to the high speed of the enemy could not attain attack position. We vainly endeavored to vector a third submarine into position, but the Japanese force escaped to southwestward.

However, *Threadfin*'s sacrifice was not in vain, for all her contact reports, as well as those of *Hackleback*, were passed along to Commander Fifth Fleet, Admiral Spruance. Next morning, Vice Admiral Pete Mitscher's fighters, dive bombers and torpedo planes swarmed into the air and caught the luckless Japanese in the East China Sea, southwest of Kyushu, where the *Yamato*, *Yahagi* and four destroyers were torpedoed and bombed to death. *Skate* had hit *Yamato* on Christmas Day, 1943, with two torpedoes, but that was not enough. The aviators said it took six or eight torpedoes, plus as many more bomb hits, to put her down for the count. Thus ended, for all practical purposes, the meteoric career of the Imperial Japanese Navy.

Submarines combed the waters where this latest battle was fought and *Seadevil* picked up three Marine flyers from the *Essex*. Admiral Mitscher's gratitude was expressed in one of his typically laconic dispatches—"Maybe it is routine for you fellows but your rescue of our Marines is considered quite extraordinary in this force."

After the liberation of the Philippines, Japan had garrisons cut off in many places throughout the Netherlands East Indies. In order to supply and consolidate these scattered forces, she had to use whatever shipping was available. Frequently combatant vessels, because of their speed and better antisubmarine defenses, were pressed into service. In early April, a wolf pack consisting of *Besugo,* Commander H. E. Miller, *Gabilan,* Commander W. B. Parham, and *Charr,* Commander F. D. Boyle, was patrolling off Paternoster and Postilyon Islands, in the Java Sea area, under tactical command of Commander Boyle.

During the forenoon of April 4, contact was made with the light cruiser *Izuzu,* bound on a transport mission. *Besugo,* after a night transit of the dangerous Sape Strait, succeeded in sinking one of the escorts, a mine sweeper. During the afternoon of April 6, *Charr* saw the cruiser enter Bima Bay and passed the word to *Gabilan,* which attacked and damaged her. After this attack, *Izuzu's* low speed of 10 knots made *Charr's* approach quite simple and at 0724 she fired six bow torpedoes, three of which hit and sank the cruiser. This was the last of nine light cruisers sunk by U.S. submarines. The *Kuma,* sunk by a British submarine off Penang, gave Allied subs a good round score of 10 for that class of difficult targets.

We added two more enemy submarines to our bag. *Sea Owl,* Commander Carter Bennett, returning to Pearl under orders to reconnoiter Wake Island en route, decided to picket the place after sighting a submarine periscope. He and his adversary played hide and seek for a couple of days, when the Jap evidently thought the American had departed, for he anchored one night and signaled shore boats to come out. Carter waited until the launches got alongside, then hit the enemy with one torpedo, sinking the RO-56.

Besugo, Commander H. E. Miller, a Seventh Fleet submarine, added the German submarine, U-183. Intelligence said the Germans were running a regular submarine ferry and freight line into Penang where the cargo was transshipped into Japanese submarines. U-183 never reached her rendezvous and Miller brought in her navigator to prove the identity of his victim.

Only one boat was lost during the month of April. *Snook,* Commander J. F. Walling, in company with *Burrfish* and *Bang,* departed Guam on March 25, with the CO of

Snook in command of the pack. Their assigned area was Convoy College. Later, the other two submarines were assigned lifeguard stations and *Snook* was ordered to join *Tigrone,* under Commander Hiram Cassedy. When *Tigrone* came back from patrol, Cassedy told me that, on April 8, he had been fired at by an unseen opponent and had dodged two torpedoes. At first, he suspected that *Snook* might have fired at him but, on contacting her by radio that night, *Snook* said she had fired no torpedoes. Hiram then warned Walling to be on his guard against the Jap which had fired at *Tigrone.* Next day Cassedy could not raise *Snook* by radio, and on April 12 she was ordered to a lifeguard station at Sakeshima Gunto, with the British carrier squadron, but did not acknowledge her orders. She was never heard from again.

No Japanese report of antisubmarine attacks appears to account for the loss of *Snook* and it seems unlikely that she hit a mine. It is therefore probable she was sunk by an enemy submarine, which was in turn destroyed. JANAC credits her with sinking 17 vessels for a total of 75,473 tons. It is estimated that she damaged 15 other ships.

Sinking scores for April were little better than for the previous month. JANAC shows that 19 submarines shared in the sinking of 18 merchantmen, 66,352 tons, and 10 men-of-war, 13,651 tons. Included in the latter category were one light cruiser, two frigates and two submarines, one of them a German.

Sunfish, Commander J. W. Reed of Sharon, Pennsylvania, and *Tirante* were tied for high score, with four ships each, while the unfortunate *Queenfish* sank the most tonnage, the 11,600-ton *Awa Maru,* however, the patrol of *Tirante,* Commander George L. Street III, of Richmond, Virginia, had begun in March, during which she sank two ships. These, added to her four April sinkings, gave *Tirante* an outstanding bag for that period of the war.

Lieutenant Commander Street, on his first patrol in this new boat, had really beat his targets "out of the bushes," as Captain Tex McLean would have said. The scarcity of good torpedo targets forced our submarines to hunt in extremely dangerous waters—the shallow reaches of the Yellow Sea, along the Manchurian and Korean coasts and in enemy harbors. The story of *Tirante*'s maiden patrol is the saga of a courageous, daring and sagacious commanding officer, backed by the skill and devotion of a fighting crew.

Her assigned area was in the East China and Yellow Seas, both shallow. En route to his station, Commander Street had made a careful study of sailing directions and of the contracts reported by submarines, who had previously hunted these waters. His conclusion was that enemy shipping was hugging the coast in water too shallow for a submarine to operate submerged. His decision was to go in after that shipping.

In the first part of his patrol, Street made four torpedo attacks, penetrating strong escort screens in shallow waters. In these attacks he estimated that he had sunk two freighters, a tanker and a troop-laden transport. According to JANAC's report, only three ships were sunk, hence one of the cargo ships must have been damaged only.

After her attack on the transport, *Tirante* received a terrific beating with depth charges, some so close they bounced her off the bottom, where she was lying doggo in a futile evasion attempt. Finally Street, fighting for the life of his ship, came up to periscope depth and, in a brilliantly executed torpedo attack, sank one of his tormentors.

Although by this time *Tirante* had rolled up a creditable score and might with good grace have retired to less dangerous waters for a breather, Street would not consider leaving until he had inflicted maximum damage upon the enemy. He had noted a convoy or so passing just out of range, headed toward Quelpart Island or Saishu To, as the Japanese call it, and this evidently set him to studying that Gibraltar of the Yellow Sea as a source from which he might extract some enemy tonnage.

This high rocky island, which lies at the southern tip of Korea, was reported to be held in great strength and Cincpac's planners were already considering it as an objective for Operation Olympic, the invasion of Japan. It had long been a source of interest to submarines, because of its air base, from which flew obnoxious patrol planes. It was reported to have huge underground hangars, whose entrances could be seen from seaward. We anticipated that it would be a tough nut for the Amphibious Forces to crack. It had two anchorages, but the one on the northwest side appeared to be used the more. There a small outlying island offered shelter to ships anchored behind it. Undoubtedly mines had been laid thereabouts for protection of a harbor. Captured notices to mariners showed a large section north of Saishu To to be

"Restricted." However, Commander Street believed that, by approaching from the northeastward—from the direction of the Empire—the protecting minefields could be avoided and entry made into the anchorage. Street had five torpedoes remaining and was determined to use them.

Proceeding according to this plan, *Tirante* approached the harbor on surface at night, with gun crews in stations. The water was too shallow for diving, therefore, if detected, it would be necessary to shoot her way out. Street's decision to carry out this raid, like that of Gene Fluckey at Namkwan, was strongly flavored with recklessness, a recklessness born of confidence in their ships, their crews, their weapons—and in themselves.

As *Tirante* slipped silently into the Quelpart anchorage, several shore radar emanations, and at least two radar-equipped patrol vessels, were detected. Street kept as close under the cliffs as he dared, so that radar echoes obtained from the sub might be lost in the shore background. Once in the inner harbor, the force of the current was checked and a rapid set-up made on a nearby tanker. Two torpedoes were fired and the resulting terrific explosions and blast of flame nearly flattened the men on *Tirante*'s deck. In the light of the burning ship, she was spotted by two new Mikura-class frigates, which headed in for the kill. To the first one, Street delivered two bow torpedoes, then, swinging at full speed, fired his last torpedo from a stern tube at the second. Both frigates disintegrated in the ensuing explosions and *Tirante* steamed out of an enemy harbor on surface, even as *Barb* had done, without a scratch.

George Street's courage, initiative, resourcefulness and leadership, combined with excellent judgment and skill, served as an inspiration to submarine personnel. George came back to Guam to receive a hero's welcome and to find himself recommended for the Congressional Medal of Honor. For his ship, we requested the Presidential Citation, and both of these awards were made.

CHAPTER 18

The date for penetrating the Tsushima mine barrier and invading the Sea of Japan drew near. For some months, preparations for this bold and dangerous enterprise had included scheduling a series of comparative tests, at San Diego, of the three types of mine-detection gear, then going into production.

At the same time we planned to demonstrate various secret weapons and hold conferences among the officers and scientists responsible for designing such equipment. Decisions reached were then to be taken direct to Washington for confirmation by the various offices and bureaus concerned, in order to expedite the work. Previous conferences at Mare Island and Hunters Point had been so successful, and had cut through so many layers of red tape, that I hoped like results might be obtained in the case of these anxiously awaited installations and secret weapons.

Two new ultra-short-wave radars, then long overdue, were urgently needed to keep ahead of enemy radar countermeasures and to prevent enemy planes from homing on our submarines. Another important reason now existed for speeding up their production. Admiral Spruance, to take the pressure off light craft acting as pickets off Okinawa, had proposed the substitution of submarines for such jobs. The "little ships" protecting the Fleet, destroyers, DE's and smaller vessels, were catching hell from enemy bombers and *kamikaze* planes and their losses had assumed serious proportions. By employing submarines on the picket line, with radar capable of detecting aircraft at long range, the Combat Air Patrol (CAP) could be alerted to the approaching danger and vectored into position by Fighter Director officers stationed in the submarines. If the enemy planes broke through the CAP, the submarine had merely to dive. The scheme looked mighty good and we wanted to get 24 submarines equipped and trained before Operation Olympic—the invasion of Kyushu—scheduled for November 1st.

After some postponement, the trials and conferences at San Diego were set for April 23–27, so I left John Brown holding down the job at Guam and headed back for the Coast. While at Pearl Harbor on the 19th, I took advantage of the opportunity to see test runs of a secret decoy intended to aid submarines in evading counterattacks by escort vessels. *Skate* and the destroyer escort, *Whitman*, put on the show and, after the submarine acquired the proper technique, she succeeded in eluding the DE in both of the final runs. This was the gadget which I had first seen operating in a fresh water reservoir in August, 1944, and for which we had been praying ever since. Its use in enemy waters might have saved the lives of hundreds of submariners and millions of dollars worth of submarines.

Next morning, I went out with *Skate* and witnessed a very pretty performance of her FM Sonar in a dummy minefield. That afternoon, she fired several of our newest secret torpedoes at an LCI on which I was an observer. The results were not perfect but promised well.

With this brushing up in our latest equipment, our Subpac group took off on the 21st for San Diego. Our representation consisted of Captain Bud Yeomans (Subpac Strategic Plans and New Developments), Captain Bill Irvin (Subpac Communications Officer), Commander George Pierce (skipper of the *Tunny*) and Commander Eddie Fahy (Subtrainpac Electronics Officer). At San Diego, we met representatives of CNO's office, Bureau of Ships, Bureau of Ordnance and the Naval Research Laboratory at San Diego. Rear Admiral Styer (Comsublant) and several of his Staff also joined the party. Minefields in deep and shallow water had been laid outside San Diego and *Flying Fish*, Commander R. D. "Bob" Risser, and *Redfin*, Commander C. K. Miller of Williamsport, Pennsylvania, were in port, equipped with the three types of mine detectors to be tested.

Then followed four of the most interesting days I have ever experienced. We had present all the top-flight talent in the mine-detecting business, plus Commander George Pierce, who had conducted the supreme test by actually running through an enemy minefield and charting the mines. We spent two full days running *Flying Fish* and *Redfin* through dummy minefields, in waters where best sonar conditions were not to be expected, but almost without exception our results were excellent. Patches of kelp frequently interfered and some sort of a wreck was located on bottom off Point

Loma, which gave back the unmistakable bell-like echo of a steel hull.

During one of these trial runs with the FM Sonar, which I happened to be operating at the time, an echo and a blob were obtained at an extreme range on what I believed to be a mine. The experts, however, said the sound was a little too "scratchy"; what I had picked up must be a patch of kelp. We continued the run, passing through this "patch of kelp," and when we surfaced, there was a dummy mine hanging from our port bow plane. The experts had to take a bit of ribbing on that one.

We learned, during these tests, about a sea-water condition which the scientists called a "thermal patch"—an area of warm water surrounded by cold, which would return an echo. This was new to us and I immediately radioed the news back to Guam and, just as a joke, added to my message, "Construct thermal patch targets." Imagine my surprise to find, when I got back there, that Barney Sieglaff and his cohorts had devised thermal patch targets. They fired from the signal tube a "pillenwerfer," which produced a cloud of bubbles much like an Alka Seltzer. Then they circled around it. Good echoes could be obtained on the echo-ranging gear for some minutes, and this became a standard means of testing mine detectors while on patrol.

Each type of mine detector had its proponents but, to me, the FM Sonar was most suitable to our purpose. It was the most unlikely to be overheard by the enemy, because its frequency was considerably above the usual enemy frequency. This would be a very important feature while penetrating enemy mine-fields, or while searching for mines along intended landing beaches. Being overheard at such times might be fatal. Too, I preferred the very recognizable blob and bell-like echo produced in the FM by a mine. The other types of detectors produced only a spark, with no audible echo, when any sort of target was picked up. I discovered there was considerable feeling involved in this matter, a sort of an "old school tie" loyalty which amused me. Our interest was in results—not civilian college rivalry.

Conferences held in Washington following these tests were very satisfactory and, by dint of appearing before a Joint Army-Navy Priority Board, I was able to convince the members that we needed, right then, top priority on 24 ultra-short-wave radars (SV type) for aircraft detection, plus 25 sets of FM Sonar, promised for September delivery. In a few minutes of talk we accomplished what months of letter writing had failed to effect.

May 18 found me back on the *Holland* in Apra Harbor, greatly refreshed by experiences of the trip back to San Diego and Washington. I found matters had progressed well in my absence. Rear Admiral John Brown had been detached and sent to a cruiser division in the Aleutians but Captains Dutch Will and Dick Voge had carried on the job. Sinking reports from the patrol areas were meager, but rescue of aviators was proceeding at the rate of nearly 100 per month. Operation Barney, named after Commander Barney Sieglaff, who planned most of the details, our plan for breaking into the Sea of Japan, had made important advances.

Two happenings during my absence were particularly inspiring. The first was a report from the *Cod*, Commander J. A. "Caddy" Adkins of Washington, D.C., which, during the night of April 26, was patrolling on surface in the shallow waters of the East China Sea. Her position was so close to numerous enemy airfields that diving might be required at any moment when, suddenly, fire was reported in the after torpedo room. A short circuit in one of the electric torpedoes had started a blaze, which not only filled the compartment with suffocating smoke, but might have produced a detonation of the war heads. Lieutenant Kenneth F. Beckman, USNR, of San Francisco, California, Henry Krusenklaus, TM2/c, of Louisville, Kentucky, and John A. Grenner, TM3/c, of Duluth, Minnesota, volunteered to extinguish the fire and made repeated trips into the intense heat, suffocating smoke, and darkness of the torpedo room. Despite the use of rescue breathing apparatus, all were nearly overcome by smoke before they finally succeeded in loading the burning torpedo into a tube and firing it. Their heroic work undoubtedly saved their ship and the lives of their shipmates.

During this bit of fire fighting, Lawrence E. Foley, QM2/c, of Newark, New Jersey, requested permission from the CO to go aft on deck and open the after torpedo room hatch, in order to assist in ventilating the smoke-filled compartment. Foley went down the slippery, wave-swept deck and performed this dangerous task successfully, but while still on deck a huge wave washed him and a shipmate overboard—the latter without a life jacket. For eight hours, the

Cod searched in the darkness for these two men and finally recovered them. During that entire time, Foley had kept his shipmate afloat.

The other incident concerned saving the new submarine *Cabezon* from sinking alongside the dock at Sub Base, Pearl Harbor. By an almost unforseeable series of incidents, pressure failed in her hydraulic system, permitting the torpedo tube outer doors to open in the after torpedo room. At that time two torpedoes were being loaded into the tubes and the opening of the outer doors resulted in a terrific rush of water through the tubes. One 3,000-pound torpedo was hurled back into the compartment, and narrowly missed killing the loading crew. The watertight door into the maneuvering room was open, as were also the two deck hatches. Only four enlisted men, R. H. Peach, Jr., TM1/c, Wm. C. Markland, TM1/c, Brownie W. Szczygiel, TM2/c, and Carl C. Florence, a special technician, were in the after torpedo room. Whether or not *Cabezon* flooded and sank depended entirely upon their speed and headwork.

Never has the courage, intelligence and training of submarine enlisted personnel been more splendidly demonstrated, for those four men, working against time, danger and a terrifying inrush of water, overcame seemingly insurmountable obstacles to get the watertight door and the two deck hatches closed in time to prevent flooding of the entire ship. Their "immediate and intelligent actions in the face of considerable danger to themselves," as their Commanding Officer wrote, "undoubtedly saved lives and prevented possible sinking of the ship." What might have been a major calamity, costing hundreds of thousands of dollars, was, by their courage and skill, limited to a week's work of drying out and repairing or replacing part of the equipment of a single compartment.

Commander George Street, who in *Tirante* had won the Congressional Medal of Honor on her first patrol, was again scouring the East China and Yellow Seas in search of targets. Following his former successful tactics, George was hugging the coast line of Kyushu on the morning of June 11, when he spotted a medium-sized freighter alongside a dock at Na Shima, a small island about seven miles southwest of Nagasaki entrance. A hasty conference with the navigator followed and it was decided the harbor could be entered submerged. The waters were alive with fishermen and small shipping, hence there were evidently no mines, but it appeared certain there were plenty of guns in the shore defenses. Nonetheless, it would be necessary to surface after the attack and make a high-speed getaway, because remaining submerged in shallow water would subject the submarine to a concentration of antisubmarine attacks with minimum chances of getting out alive.

However, *Tirante*'s resolution never wavered; there was the target and in she went after it. Street worked his way cautiously up the harbor, using his SESE (supersonic sounding machine) with care. The target was loading coal and a navy gun crew could be seen lounging around their 4.7-inch piece on the fantail. At 1115, with range of about 1,000 yards, a single torpedo was fired, aimed at the middle of the target and struck forward, tearing out the side of the ship. George had planned to surface immediately, but the freighter's gun's crew was now at station and firing rapidly at the periscope. That would never do, so a second torpedo was fired but did not explode. Probably it hit the soft bottom and buried itself. A third was then fired, set to run at two-foot depth, and that finished the action. The gun was still mounted but its crew had disappeared.

Tirante ran a short distance toward the harbor entrance, searching the sky for planes, and then surfaced and bent on her highest speed. Immediately automatic gunfire was opened on her from the beach and the bluffs, but it was spasmodic and erratic, though numerous splashes were close.

At this crucial point, *Tirante* had to stop all engines in order to rig in the bow planes. Even with a highly dangerous job on his hands, the skipper had taken, at intervals during the entire approach, attack and race for the entrance, color movies through the periscope or from the bridge.

As our plans for invading the Sea of Japan approached finality, the international situation changed with the surrender of Germany. Most people seemed anxious for Russia to come into the war in the East. I was told that she had agreed at Potsdam to declare war on Japan three months after the surrender of Germany. Eventually, I was directed by Cincpac to submit a plan for dividing the Sea of Japan with the Russians. I did not relish the idea. The entire area was not large, we could handle the situation easily without help, and the introduction of foreign submarines into that small space was likely to result in fatal mistakes in identity. If we could not successfully indoctrinate our own surface ships and air forces in identification of U.S. submarines, how could we hope to educate the Russians? All we wanted from our northern Allies was permission for any submarine which might become disabled, to take refuge at Vladivostok.

This change in the international scene placed additional urgency on our Operation Barney. We wanted to finish the job we had started—to sink everything that floated and flew a Japanese flag—without assistance. By this time, nine submarines were equipped with FM Sonar and had been directed to assemble at Guam during the last week in May for the Tsushima job. Training went on continuously and practically every morning saw Barney and me climbing aboard a submarine at 0600, bound for the training area. *Flying Fish*, *Spadefish*, *Bonefish*, *Tunny*, *Skate* and *Bowfin*, each were given a last bit of checking over.

A rapid shift of equipment had to be made from *Seahorse*—then under command of Commander H. H. Greer, Jr., of Upper Darby, Pennsylvania—to *Seadog*, Commander Earl T. Hydeman of Piqua, Ohio. The former had suffered a severe 16-hour depth charging in the East China Sea, which wrecked her periscopes, radio and radar and caused numerous leaks. She was lucky to come back at all. Her inability to make the trip into the Sea of Japan was a serious disappointment to her skipper, an FM Sonar enthusiast. His mine-detection gear was forthwith installed in *Seadog*, where, remarkable to relate, it performed even better than before.

Mine-detection gear on *Skate* and *Tunny* turned temperamental at the last moment—too many "jury rigs" in the "chasis," so the technicians said, and Lt. (jg) Dye and Chief Radar Technician Nigrete worked night and day on repairs, adjustments and tuning up. Barney and I made the last check training runs with these tailenders on May 26 and, next day, all was in readiness for departure of the first echelon. To make doubly sure that the boats would not foul mine anchor cables, clearing wires had been installed forward of bow planes, stern planes and propellers.

As a final preparation, a conference was held with all skippers, execs and communication officers. We ran off an instruction film on the mine-detection gear, prepared by the Research Laboratory at San Diego, and every phase of the operation was discussed in detail. All comment and questions showed careful study of the problem. The determination and deep-down, cool courage of these lads were splendid to see. Operation Barney was ready to "roll 'em over."

Barney Sieglaff wanted to go along, as did Lieutenant Commander Bub Ward and our British Liaison Officer, Lieutenant Commander Barklie Lakin. I had to refuse the first two, but I gave Lakin permission to take passage in *Crevalle*. I, myself, had asked Admiral Nimitz for permission to make the trip in order to qualify, under actual war conditions, in operating the gear in which I had such confidence. This time the Big Boss put me off with a promise that before the war ended he would let me make a patrol—a promise which he was never able to keep.

The "Hellcats," as we designated the group of nine submarines under the command of Commander Earl Hydeman in *Seadog,* was subdivided into three packs. Hydeman's "Hepcats" were *Seadog, Crevalle,* Commander E. H. "Steiny" Steinmetz of Rockville Center, Long Island, and *Spadefish,* Commander W. J. "Bill" Germershausen of Baltimore, Maryland.

Pierce's "Polecats" included his veteran *Tunny, Bonefish,* Commander L. L. "Larry" Edge of Atlanta, Georgia, and *Skate,* Commander R. B. "Ozzie" Lynch of Citronelle, Alabama.

The third group, called Risser's "Bobcats," was led by Commander Bob Risser in *Flying Fish,* with *Bowfin,* Commander A. K. "Alex" Tyree of Danville, Virginia, and *Tinosa,* Commander R. C. "Dick" Latham.

Departure of the Hepcats, first echelon, was scheduled for the afternoon of May 27 and, to give the lads a good send-off, we organized a luncheon party in the *Holland*'s cabin, inviting all the Hellcat skippers, with several Red Cross girls and two or three nurses from Navy Base 18 Hospital to lend a bit of glamor. Miss Kelly, head of the local Red Cross, had won our great appreciation by opening a "White Hat Club" at Camp Dealey exclusively for enlisted men. The Head Nurse, Lieutenant Fielder, at Base 18 Hospital, had also earned our gratitude by permitting six or eight of her off-duty nurses to attend the semioccasional dances at our rest camp. Later, when we were giving a farewell dinner there for Admiral Nimitz, she gave passes to 18 of her attractive young nurses and permitted them to stay until 11 P.M.—an unheard of hour in their curfew regulated lives.

The luncheon party was a success, I thought, and eased the strain and self-consciousness of saying good-bye to these lads leaving on what was probably the most dangerous mission of the war. However, when Earl Hydeman and his Hepcats shoved off, they left plenty of anxiety in my mind and in the minds of my Staff. Our brain-trust back at the Pearl Harbor HQ had prepared a very pessimistic estimate of the situation regarding Operation Barney, but of course they hadn't been in close touch with our mine-detection training and didn't fully realize its potentialities. After the operation was successfully completed, I sent the paper back and asked if they would like to revise it. The other echelons shoved off at 24 hour intervals and then followed 11 anxious days until the hour for opening fire, sunset of June 9, should arrive.

Meanwhile, two changes in Subpac Staff took place. Commodore Merrill Comstock took Rear Admiral John Brown's place as Commander Subpac Training Command and Commodore Cliff Crawford, who had barely settled in a "cushy" job at Philadelphia, had, at my urgent request, come back to sea duty and taken over the duties of Chief of Staff. Cliff was a submariner of many years experience and had also made a war patrol in a British sub. We did not see eye to eye in many things—a very healthy condition—and one which assured that no half-baked decisions would be promulgated.

Meager reports of sinkings for May were coming in. The enemy had few targets to offer but of them, 15 merchant ships, including two tankers, had carried 30,194 tons to the bottom. Five men-of-war, including two frigates, had contributed 4,484 tons to that already crowded repository. Thirteen submarines had shared in these kills.

Raton, commanded by her veteran skipper, Mike Shea, with three freighters downed in the Yellow Sea, sank the greatest number of targets. *Hammerhead*, Commander F. M. Smith of Danville, Kentucky, contributed the greatest tonnage score—6,823 tons—by sinking a tanker and a passenger-cargo ship in the Gulf of Siam.

Bluegill, Commander Eric Barr, on May 29 added a touch of humor as well as keen initiative to my usual morning stack of intercepted dispatches. Barr, one of Admiral Fife's skippers, aided by two Australian Commandoes, reported that he had captured Bluegill Island, "formerly Pratas Reef," and hoisted the American flag with appropriate ceremony. This isolated reef, 150 miles from the China coast, in the upper part of the South China Sea, had served as a meteorological and radio station for the Japanese after our occupation of the Philippines but later was abandoned. Barr's dispatch report requested "invasion" medals for his landing force.

One submarine paid the price of our successes. *Lagarto,* on her second patrol, commanded by the veteran Commander F. D. Latta, was lost, it is believed, in the outer part of the Gulf of Siam, on or about May 3, due to depth charging. *Lagarto* and *Baya* were working together in the Gulf of Siam when the latter contacted a convoy consisting of a tanker, a naval auxiliary and two escort vessels. *Lagarto* was soon also in contact. Early in the morning of May 3, the two submarines met at a rendezvous and agreed that *Lagarto* would attack first at 1400, while Baya was to lie in wait about 10 miles farther along. About midnight, *Baya* made a prolonged but unsuccessful attack and was driven off by radar-equipped escorts. No further contact of any kind was ever made with *Lagarto.*

Japanese reports state that, on May 3, two escort vessels attacked an American submarine with depth charges in 30 fathoms of water. In such shallow water, the advantage is decidedly with the antisubmarine vessel and it seems likely that attack destroyed *Lagarto.*

Once again our long-delayed decoys and secret torpedoes might have saved a submarine and the 86 officers and men of her crew. After almost four years of war, our submarines were still not equipped with prosubmarine weapons which the Germans developed and used against our Atlantic escort craft in 1942-43. If and when we have another war, will our prosubmarine and antisubmarine weapons be ready, or will we again have to learn the hard way?

After what was to us at Guam HQ an anxious and interminable wait, Hydeman's Hellcats opened the Battle of the Sea of Japan at the appointed hour. Fragmentary dispatches reached us of sinkings achieved and the increased volume of enemy radio traffic told a story of panic and confusion in Japan's private sea.

All submarines got safely through the minefields. Two had mine cables scrape along their sides for what must have seemed an eternity before they were finally cleared. I asked one of the skippers, Dick Latham, how a mine wire sounded when it scraped alongside and he replied, "Well, to tell the truth, I don't know. I was asleep in my bunk." Pretty sound nerves a man must have to "cork off" while underrunning a minefield. He had taken the ship through the first lines and then turned her over to the Exec. One submarine's mine detector turned temperamental so she merely ran at a depth where she believed no mines would be encountered and trusted to her clearing wires to fend off anchor cables.

The details of this raid, as related to me by the skippers concerned and as shown in official reports, make a story as fantastic as it is unprecedented. Never in history had a minefield been penetrated en masse by a force of submariners. And probably never in history has the enemy been taken more aback. So astonished were the Japanese by this invasion of their own backyard that Radio Tokyo announced that American submarines had been "smuggled in"—dropped from B-29's, no doubt. Unfortunately for our raiders, the density of shipping was not as great as expected, but, when they withdrew 17 days later, 28 ships and 16 small craft had been stowed in Davy Jones's locker and five ships and three small craft damaged.

As the Hellcats worked their way to their assigned areas, to await the sunset of June 9—the hour set to commence firing—the sight of well-lighted targets, steaming steady courses across supposedly safe waters, was so tempting that some skippers confessed they had a hard time keeping itchy trigger fingers off the firing button.

As befitting the pack leader, Commander Hydeman, in *Seadog,* opened the battle shortly after the appointed deadline by sinking the 1,186-ton *Sagawa Maru* with a single torpedo. The ship sank in 60 seconds—almost as fast as a submarine can dive. In a surface attack before midnight of the same day, *Seadog* added the 2,211-ton *Shoyo Maru* to her bag. Before the date set for rendezvous and withdrawal—June 24—Hydeman made seven torpedo attacks and sank six ships for a total of 7,186 tons. They were not liners, these last remnants of the vanishing Japanese merchant marine, but they were valuable for carrying food and munitions to the homeland.

In one of *Seadog*'s surface attacks, Hydeman wished he had an amphibious submarine. While firing at three medium-sized cargo ships, an enemy plane forced him to dive. Unfortunately, he misjudged the nearness of the beach and hit bottom before he could get his sound gear rigged in. However, the ship was undamaged and backed clear of the shoal water.

Along the northwest coast of Honshu, *Crevalle* sank three cargo ships (6,643 tons), in torpedo attacks, and two smaller craft, in gun attacks. Commander Steinmetz said that, on one occasion, when he fired three torpedoes at a small freighter, the first two destroyed the target so completely that the third fish was "robbed"—passed over the wreckage without being exploded. *Crevalle* received a severe seven-hour depth charging, but came out of it none the worse. In fact, the adventure inspired our redoubtable British Liaison Officer, Lieutenant Commander Lakin, to write a defiant bit of poetry.

Spadefish, the first submarine on which the detection gear had been installed, was assigned an area along the extreme northwest coast of Honshu, extending up to the Hokkaido. There she found plenty of action and, in nine torpedo and three gun attacks, claimed 10 ships sunk. JANAC cuts this down, but Commander Bill Germershausen, her skipper, still had a fine bag for that period of the war, totaling 8,578 tons.

Bill was interested in getting periscope pictures of his victims and complained, "They sank so fast my photographer couldn't get his camera rigged."

He finally sighted a freighter, anchored in the habor at Maoka. Closing in with his camera already rigged, he fired two torpedoes and sank the target.

"The citizens of that town could have got good pictures, too," Bill remarked, generously.

Commander George Pierce's Polecats found mixed good and bad in the Sea of Japan. In their ranks occurred our only tragedy. The *Bonefish*, Commander Larry Edge, and her fine crew, was lost with all hands. *Skate*, with Commander Ozzie Lynch as skipper, found plenty of targets in the vicinity of the Noto Peninsula. While patrolling submerged on the morning of June 10, Lynch sighted an enemy submarine, the I-122, standing his way. The Jap was legging it for port at high speed and making radical zigs. Evidently the word had got out that "the Emperor's bath tub," as the lads dubbed the Sea of Japan, was no longer a private lake. Unfortunately for the target, the last zig brought her across the bow of the *Skate* at a range of 800 yards where two hits from a four-torpedo spread ended her career. *Skate* sighted two other enemy subs during her patrol but was unable to get a shot at either. However, on June 12, Lynch spotted three ships at anchor in a shallow cove where they had probably taken refuge until adequate escorts could be provided. The situation presented no particular problem to Ozzie who submerged and boldly stood in with, at times, no more than two fathoms of water under his keel. He sank *Yozan Maru*, *Kenjo Maru* and *Zuiko Maru* in one, two, three order. Gunfire and depth charges failed to damage the intruder.

Next day *Skate* sank another freighter and picked up three survivors as proof of the kill but his victim must have been under 500 tons, hence is not shown on JANAC's list. Ozzie reported seeing an aged, coal-burning destroyer of about Russo-Japanese War vintage trying desperately to keep up with its convoy. Evidently the enemy was scraping the bottom of the escort craft barrel.

The area assigned *Tunny* was in the vicinity of Shimonoseki Strait where we hoped to intercept the Korea–Inland Sea traffic but bombing and mining had probably caused abandonment of those routes for no targets appeared. Commander Pierce headed northward and combed the coast line, actually entering two ports "trying to beat them out of the bushes," as he expressed it, but without success. He arrived in *Bonefish*'s area in time to hold a conversation by megaphone with that ill-fated vessel before she was lost.

The highlight of *Tunny*'s patrol was a running gunfight with two Japanese destroyers who amused Pierce by dropping "scare" depth charges at a range of 7,000 yards. George wanted to know who was scared, the Japs or *Tunny?*

Commander Bob Risser's Bobcats were given the territory along the Korean side of the Sea of Japan. It proved to be poor hunting grounds for, not only were targets scarce, but the weather was foggy and there were hundreds of fishing craft, which in low visibility constituted a real menace. Nevertheless, Risser's boat, the *Flying Fish*, sank *Taga Maru* and *Meisei Maru* for a total of 4,113 tons. She also damaged two small tugs and, in a gun attack, sank 10 brick-laden barges.

One day while submerged outside Seishin breakwater, Risser observed a small tug approach, towing two barges loaded with large boulders. *Flying Fish* lay doggo waiting for them to pass but when the tug stopped directly above the submarine, her skipper became a little apprehensive and got out from under to have a look-see. On sticking his periscope up, he found the barge crews preparing to unload their cargo which was evidently intended to form part of a new breakwater.

One prisoner brought in by *Flying Fish*, taken from a freighter sunk outside Rashin harbor, was a soldier who had taken part in the invasion of the Philippines.

Commander Alec Tyree's *Bowfin* had the area next to the Russian border and therefore had to be careful to identify her targets. Few ships were sighted but in spite of 75 per cent fog and swarms of fishing junks, Alec succeeded in finding and destroying *Shinyo Maru No. 3* and *Akiura Maru*, for a score of 2,785 tons. He also gunned a 20-ton schooner. The fishermen were most friendly toward the big American submarine and showed no concern when she sank a small freighter in their midst. One fisherman examined just outside Joshin harbor, insisted on donating a fine mess of fish. His reward was a hatful of the coveted American cigarettes.

Tinosa, under Commander Dick Latham, had the southern section of the Korean coast line. Dick also found fishing boats and nets a great hindrance to his operations but his luck in finding targets was good. Four freighters fell victims to his torpedoes, one of them, off historic Tsushima Island, received three hits and sank in a record-breaking 35 seconds. Another freighter estimated at 4,000 tons, was damaged but managed to escape. During a running gun attack on a large "sea truck" off Bokuku Ko in low visibility, the fog suddenly lifted and *Tinosa* found herself close in to the beach, an easy target for coastal guns or planes should any be at hand. However, Latham was determined not to be robbed of his prey and completed the sinking before seeking more sea room.

His score for the patrol was 6,701 tons sunk.

After 17 days in the area, on June 24 all submarines were assembled south of La Perouse Strait. *Bonefish* was missing. She had last been seen by *Tunny*. The day of the 24th was spent in approaching the starting line for the night dash through the strait and at midnight all submarines surfaced, formed two columns, and set course for La Perouse at 16 knots in spite of a pea-soup fog. Ordinarily, fog is a curse to seamen in narrow waters, but in this case, with its dangers removed by radar, its woolly folds were gratefully received to hide their movements.

We believed that La Perouse was mined but our information indicated the mines were laid deep to catch submerged submarines and permit free passage to neutral Russian ships and antisubmarine patrols. Making the exit dash on surface in column would lessen the danger from mines to all except the leading ships, and I expect there were plenty of chills running up and down spines in those two. The leaders reported they never saw more exact columns in their lives. At a crucial point the radar on *Seadog*, which was leading one column, broke down, forcing her to yield her place to *Crevalle*, an honor which the latter probably did not covet.

Just before midnight, radar contact was made with a ship and a few minutes later, in an area of fair visibility, a fully-lighted Russian was seen. Probably alarmed at the sight of darkened, rushing shapes, she turned on a searchlight which might have been bad for us had any patrol boats been near at hand. The submarines increased to full speed and dashed on into the deep waters of the Sea of Okhotsk. At 0250 on June 25, the transit formation was broken up and individual courses set for Pearl. Operation Barney, the greatest of its kind in naval history, was completed.

On getting into the Sea of Okhotsk, Commander Hydeman reported *Bonefish* missing and *Tunny* remained just outside La Perouse for two days, trying to raise her by radio. Our radios on Guam and Oahu joined in the attempt but she was never heard from.

Tunny reported that when she spoke to *Bonefish* on the morning of June 18, Commander Edge asked permission to conduct a submerged daylight patrol in Toyama Wan in the mid-part of western Honshu and, having received it, departed. We had placed no restrictions on the movements of submarines within the Sea of Japan, except to assign certain areas to each one. *Tunny*, pack leader of the Polecats, had come up to *Bonefish*'s area because she found no targets in her own. Edge's request to enter Toyama Bay was merely a matter of form, to let his senior know where he was going, for the area requested lay within his own assigned station.

Toyama Wan is a large bay with an entrance about 40 miles wide. Its length is about 50 miles and the water is about 600 fathoms deep for a considerable distance into the bay. All submarines had been warned not to enter waters of less than 50 fathoms depth on the southwestern half of the

Honshu coast, because the B-29's had been dropping magnetic mines there. I give these details because there has been thoughtless postwar criticism of Commander Edge for taking his ship into "dangerous waters." Toyama Wan was no more dangerous than any other part of the Sea of Japan and *Bonefish*'s operations were no more hazardous than those of the eight other Hellcats.

From Japanese reports we now know that, on June 18, an antisubmarine attack was made by patrol craft near the mouth of Toyama Wan, during which a great many depth charges were dropped. Wood chips and a large pool of oil were brought up. This undoubtedly was the attack which sank the submarine.

Bonefish was lost on her eighth patrol after a distinguished career. JANAC credits her with sinking 12 vessels, including a destroyer and two tankers, for a total of 61,345 tons. Two of her most valuable targets were sunk during the patrol on which she was lost. She was an efficient and well-run ship and her skipper was an expert in electronics. Had he lived to complete his last patrol he would have been shifted to Submarine Training Command for duty in charge of training new submarines in the use of the increasing amount of electrical gear with which they were being equipped.

The loss of *Bonefish* put a severe damper on our feelings of elation at having finally cracked the Sea of Japan, but the fact that she had safely passed through the Tsushima Strait proved we had the equipment which would remove forever the Sea of Japan from the category of private Japanese lakes.

Sinking scores for June were three times those of May, but still not up to mid-war standards. With few exceptions, targets were very, very small. JANAC records that 25 submarines (one British) sank 81,302 tons, distributed among 46 merchantmen, including two tankers, plus 14,442 tons of men-of-war (seven vessels, including one heavy cruiser, one frigate and one submarine). Of this bag, 27 merchant ships (53,642 tons) and one submarine (1,142 tons) were sunk by our FM Sonar-equipped Hellcats in the Sea of Japan.

The exploit of the British boat mentioned was outstanding and involved the last sinking by a submarine of a major Japanese ship in World War II.

H.M.S. *Trenchant*, Commander A. R. Hezlett, RN, on patrol in the Java Sea, intercepted contact reports from *Blueback* and *Chubb* advising that an *Ashigara*-type heavy cruiser had entered the port of Batavia. Commander Hezlett had been ordered to shift his station from the Java Sea to the Malay coast. However, anticipating that the cruiser would return to Singapore, he obtained permission to patrol off Sumatra and selected as his position the north end of Banka Strait. *Trenchant* contacted the British submarine *Stygian* and the latter took station a little north of Banka Strait.

Before daylight of June 8, *Trenchant*, on patrol inside the strait, received a contact report from *Blueback* that a heavy cruiser and destroyer were north bound. Shortly thereafter, the destroyer, one of the *Kamikaze* class, was sighted and *Trenchant* closed in but could pick up no cruiser. Eventually, at a range of 500 yards, the destroyer sighted the submarine and opened fire which forced Hezlett to haul out at best speed. He fired one stern torpedo at the *Kamikaze*, but did not get a hit. The submarine skipper believed this encounter would influence the cruiser to hug the Sumatra coast and he moved over in that direction, until he was only two miles off the beach.

About noon *Trenchant*, through her periscope, sighted the cruiser coming up from the south unescorted and, to Hezlett's amazement, she was steering a steady course. The attack would have been as simple as shooting fish in a rain barrel, had it not been for the fact that the submarine captain believed the *Ashigara* would change course toward his position, in order to leave Frederik Hendrik rocks on her port hand. He, therefore, did not close in, and when she held course and left the rocks on her starboard hand, Trenchant had to use full submerged speed to attain even a mediocre firing position 30 degrees abaft the target's beam, with a torpedo run of 4,700 yards.

British submarines of that class are equipped with two deck tubes forward, in addition to the six built inside the strength hull, and Hezlett fired all eight at the cruiser. The Jap sighted the bubble paths, but not soon enough; unfortunately for the enemy captain, he was forced to run toward the torpedos in an attempt to comb the wakes. With the submarine already abaft his beam, this was the wrong maneuver, but to turn away would have run the cruiser aground. Those must have been agonizing moments on the bridge, while she tried desperately to make a 120 degree turn, with the deadly tracks drawing closer and closer.

Her decks were crowded with khaki-clad figures, probably troops being evacuated from the NEI, watching the race that meant life or death to most of them. Suddenly the first torpedo hit abreast No. 4 turret with a terrific explosion, followed seconds later by two more and then a final two. Five hits out of eight shots at 4,700 yards is very beautiful shooting. The *Ashigara* was enveloped in smoke and flame, but her antiaircraft batteries poured a rain of shells toward the *Trenchant*'s periscopes, both of which were extended while relays of the crew took a peep at the dying enemy. The cruiser's list to starboard increased steadily and she was burning fiercely, while her passengers and crew abandoned ship. Finally, about half an hour after being hit, she slowly capsized and sank in a smother of steam, smoke and foam.

An interested visitor at this time to our submarine activities in Guam was Admiral Sir Bruce Fraser, Royal Navy, Commander in Chief of the British Pacific Fleet. At Camp Dealey he did us the honor of pinning several decorations on officers and enlisted men of the submarines present.

Admiral Fraser had come to Guam with his flagship, *Duke of York*, for conferences with Cincpac and to make investiture of Fleet Admiral Nimitz as a Knight Companion of the Order of the Bath. The impressive presentation ceremony took place on the quarterdeck of the veteran battleship. *Trenchant*'s magnificent feat, climaxing almost two years of cooperation between British and American submarines in the Pacific, fittingly complemented Admiral Fraser's visit.

CHAPTER 19

Conferring with Admiral Halsey's Staff as to the Third Fleet's requirements for the scheduled July strikes and bombardments of the Empire, I found that news of our mine-detecting ability had given them ideas. They wanted submarines to search the waters through which the battleships and cruisers would approach their bombardment positions. With our experience and training, this would be easy, for it would be necessary only to determine the general location of minefields without penetrating. However, the request did catch us short, with all available QLA boats in the Sea of Japan.

However, *Redfin* was at Guam and *Runner II*, Commander Benny Bass, was being fitted with QLA at Pearl.

Runner was rushed to completion and dispatched to two locations on the northeast coast of Honshu, where the Third Fleet planned to wreck industrial targets. We found mines in one or two locations, and the Fleet was so informed. *Redfin*, equipped with OL and MATD (two slightly different types of mine locaters), first was sent up the coast of Hokkaido, where "Uncle Bill" desired to blast two targets, one of them the steel mills at Muroran, and then down to the south coast of Honshu for a repeat performance a few days later.

For the advance of the Third Fleet toward Japan, Admiral Halsey wanted a secret anti-picket-boat sweep such as we put on for Fifth Fleet, plus lifeguard submarines along the coast. These requests presented no special problems and were immediately included in our plans. Seven submarines under Commander B. C. McMahon, of Lakewood, Ohio, in *Piper*, were detailed to make the sweep, at the conclusion of which they assumed lifeguard stations.

No pickets were sighted but a number of downed pilots were rescued. At the end of the Third Fleet's two weeks of harassing the Japanese home islands, we received a dispatch which read:

"Following received from Comtask Force 38 (Vice Admiral McCain) Quote. Once more convey the heartfelt thanks of Task Force 38 to Comsubpac submarines. Unquote. To which I wish to add my appreciation for the excellent services of the Lifeguard League and for the sweeps conducted by *Runner* and *Redfin*. Halsey."

On July 2 I thumbed a ride with Rear Admirals Kauffman and Van Hook, who came through Guam from the Philippines in a special plane, bound for Pearl. I wanted to be there to meet the Hellcats when they arrived. It was indeed a heartwarming sight, on the morning of Independence Day, to see them standing up the channel and mooring at the Submarine Base, and to witness the enthusiasm of the Base personnel, who manned the piers and windows to welcome them. The newspaper men and photographers had already gone out in a destroyer to meet them. One of the pictures they produced, of five boats steaming in line with battle flags flying, is a splendid historical "document." The band was out in full force and, as was customary, my Staff and I boarded each submarine as it came alongside.

All hands were in highest spirits and looked in the pink of condition. They had cracked the Sea of Japan! Our forefathers, who, with their blood, consecrated that first Independence Day, would have been proud of those lads.

Commander Barney Sieglaff was just back from the Coast where he had been pepping up deliveries of more QLA sets. He arranged a critique for Operation Barney two days later, so that all submarines present might hear the Hellcat Commander and other Commanding Officers, tell us how the deed was done. Cincpac HQ, Pearl, arranged a submarine press conference and for the first time during the war, the lid was taken practically off to tell the world just what had happened. I felt, as did everyone, I believe, that the Japanese were so nearly finished they would be unable to profit from any useful information which might be released.

Back at Guam HQ on July 10, I found our veteran Operations Officer, Captain Dick Voge, packing his bags. With the war tottering to its close, it was time a real submarine man began putting together the historical data which had been collected for transmission to future generations of submariners. Hence I had requested Dick be relieved by Commander John Corbus, ex-*Herring*, ex-*Haddo* and ex-*Bowfin*, in order to take up the historical burden. Reams of data and hundreds of patrol reports awaited him in Pearl and no one was better qualified than Dick to bring some order out of chaos. He, who had written most of the submarine operation orders issued in the Pacific, was about to set down in the record the results of his work.

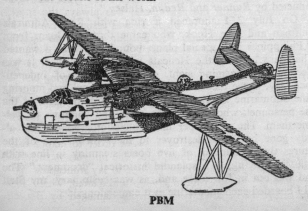

PBM

My long-delayed visit to Admiral Fife's command finally got under way in a PBM from Saipan—shortly before midnight of July 20. Lieutenant Commander Ed Hynes, the Flag Secretary, accompanied me. Cavite and Manila were pitiful to behold. These once beautiful and picturesque Spanish-built cities lay in ruins. Their harbors sprouted forests of masts from sunken ships.

On the north shore of Subic Bay, 60 miles up the coast, I found Rear Admiral Jimmie Fife building a submarine base and rest camp in jungles where, in bygone days, we hunted wild pig and deer. The setting, with quonsets, frame buildings, temporary roads, above-ground piping and mud holes, was pretty raw but, given time, it would develop into a beautiful spot. Two pile-built piers extended into the bay, while two American and two British tenders, with submarines alongside, lay at anchor farther out. Amusements for the personnel, except for movies and a swimming beach, were nonexistent.

Jimmie and I had never anything but minor points to bring into agreement, so let our Staffs battle over numerous questions. Jimmie's Chief of Staff was an old shipmate, Captain Bull Wright, ex-skipper of *Sturgeon*. Both he and Admiral Fife had recently suffered attacks of malaria and atabrin tablets were always ready to hand. I took mine conscientiously but hoped I would not stay long enough to acquire the saffron hue of Fife and his Staff.

Aboard the tender *Anthedon* anchored off the Base, I found Commander Dick Hawes, an old friend of earlier submarine days. Dick had served in subs of every type, had won his commission from the ranks, and was always the spark plug of any organization to which he was assigned. Even this fine, new tender command was not big enough to absorb Dick's energies, so he had salvaged a small Japanese freighter and had it moored alongside. Repair crews worked elbow to elbow on the decks and in machinery spaces preparing her to run rations and materials up from the Fleet Base at Leyte Gulf. Across her stern was painted *Dick Hawes Maru*.

That afternoon I went aboard the British tender *Bonaventure*, Captain Fell—who was also the commander of the submarine flotilla based on her—in order to take a dive in one of the XE midget submarines. The midgets were training for a break into Singapore Harbor to lay mines and limpets under the heavy cruisers *Myoko* and *Takao*, which had taken refuge there after being heavily damaged by *Bergall* and *Darter*. They also intended to cut the Hongkong-Singapore cable off Saigon. The plan for the first venture, was daring in the extreme. Two XE boats were to be rowed by larger submarines to the Singapore entrance, after which the midgets would enter, cutting through nets if necessary, lay their explosives, with a sufficient time delay, under the cruisers and then run for it. The escorts were to await them at a rendezvous. It looked like a suicide job to me but they carried out their plans and lived to tell the tale.

Aboard the other British tender, the *Maidstone*, I found Captain L. M. Shadwell, the Flotilla Commander, and Commander Tony Miers, winner of the Victoria Cross for his submarine exploits and formerly Liaison Officer on my Staff. I met there also Lieutenant Commander Hezlett, a very modest and unassuming lad who, in June, had done such a fine job in sinking the *Ashigara*.

On arrival at Guam Admiral Nimitz sent for me and again warned me to be prepared to divide up the Sea of Japan with Russia as she was coming into the picture on August 15. I had already submitted a plan and asked for procedures and signals necessary to effect mutual recognition and we even had a volunteer—Commander Bill Post—who wanted to be Liaison Officer at Vladivostok. But I still took a poor view of the impending situation. We had skimmed the cream off the Sea of Japan and there would not be much of a job for anyone in those waters except to pick up dunked zoomies, smuggle in commando troops and land secret agents. Already an OSS officer had approached me with a proposition to put agents ashore on the west coast of Korea. Landing and supplying agents would have required no special preparation for we had plenty of boats patrolling those waters.

Haddo, Commander F. C. "Tiny" Lynch, during a patrol in June and July, played a dangerous game of hide and seek with two Japanese frigates and sank one of his playmates by the use of our newest special weapon. "Tiny," whose nickname hardly describes his six-foot-four altitude and Herculean build, was patrolling on July 1 close in to the west coast of Korea in a dense fog. He welcomed the fog for it cloaked his movements in waters that were much too shallow for successful depth charge evasion. He trusted his silent fathometer and the radar to keep his ship off the beach. Shortly after noon, a Japan-bound convoy, headed straight for the submarine, was picked up on the radar screen. There appeared to be five ships in column with an escort on the port flank. *Haddo* therefore opened out to westward and came in to attack from the starboard side.

When in position, *Haddo* opened fire at the largest radar pip and distributed eight torpedoes among the four leading ships. At this critical point a disregarded "fishing boat" developed into a full-sized frigate, and came out of the fog with guns blazing. She and *Haddo* were on opposite courses, converging at high speed, which accounts, probably, for the fact that the Jap's fire was wild. It appeared that the frigate intended to ram and, with the range down to 800 yards, Lynch ordered: "Lookouts below. All ahead flank (highest speed). Left full rudder." When these orders had been executed, the Commanding Officer ordered "Dive!" However, the sharp-eyed Officer of the Deck, Lieutenant J. H. M. Nason, saw the frigate turning away and yelled: "No, don't dive! She's turning!" Quickly the order was given, "Belay the dive. Right full rudder."

This put the two ships on parallel, opposite courses and they passed at less than 500 yards, the frigate "firing a full battle practice," as Frank expressed it, and miraculously missing *Haddo* completely. She swung to follow the submarine which by this time was making a good 20 knots and leaving a smoke screen behind her. The port escort, still unseen in the fog, joined the chase as *Haddo* raced for deeper water.

Meanwhile all eight torpedoes were heard to hit and the high periscope lookout reported mushrooms of smoke and debris flung into the clear above the fog bank. This was all very fine, but the nearest frigate was only 1,300 yards away and pouring steel from every gun that would bear. The situation was far from being well in hand. Sooner or later one of these 4.7's was bound to register.

Frank had only two torpedoes left, both aft, and one of them was a new hush-hush weapon for which we had waited so long. This seemed an excellent opportunity to test its efficacy. A hasty set-up was made and the torpedo sent on its way. Minutes dragged by and nothing happened. The submarine was outrunning her nearest enemy but shells were kicking up waterspouts all around. Frank was just about to give up and seek the scanty protection of the shallow waters when, from back in the fog, came the sound of a heavy explosion, followed almost immediately by four depth charge explosions. It didn't take a soothsayer to guess what had happened. The torpedo had missed the first but hit the second target and, as she sank, the depth charges—all ready to drop on *Haddo*—had exploded, liquidating any survivors.

The nearest escort vessel immediately swung round to go to the assistance of her consort and by the time she discovered that nothing remained to be assisted *Haddo* was out of the fog and 10,000 yards away. As his lone pursuer came out of the fog bank, Lynch "pulled the plug," whereupon the Jap decided he had seen enough and headed back for his convoy. We estimated that all four of Tiny's first targets had sunk, but JANAC credits only two freighters and a frigate—not a bad 15 minutes' work.

Submarines equipped with mine-detection gear bound for the Sea of Japan, continued to arrive and as Barney Sieglaff was back in the U.S. on a QLA boosting mission, I had to pinch-hit for him. *Sennet, Pogy, Pargo* and *Jallao* all were checked out and speeded on their way, each eager to get in before the game was all gone. The newest sets were great improvements over the old ones. We learned to avoid areas where the garbage lighters had been dumped because of the interference created by floating boxes and, when schools of porpoises were encountered, their squealing picked up by the QLA receivers could be heard throughout the boat.

During one of the Third Fleet's raids along the Japanese coast on the night of July 18, *Gabilan*, Commander W. B. "Bill" Parham of Birmingham, Alabama, had a narrow escape from being shot up as *Nautilus* was near Tarawa. She was lifeguarding about 40 miles around to northeastward from Tokyo Bay entrance when Admiral Halsey decided to send a cruiser task force close in to search for enemy shipping.

We immediately radioed *Gabilan* to clear the area and reminded Third Fleet of her location but, according to Admiral Dick Edwards, "There's always some so-and-so who doesn't get the word." Two destroyers of the task force picked the lifeguard submarine up on their radar screens that night and opened fire. Commander Bill Parham says his ship was straddled about 10 times before he could get her down, in a rough head sea, and that it seemed an eternity before the welcome water closed over the hull. *Gabilan* was carrying 15 rescued aviators. Slap-happy incidents of that sort certainly rankled in our souls.

Again on the night of July 14 a lifeguard submarine had a narrow escape from the guns of our rampaging Third Fleet "allies," Toro, Commander J. D. Grant of San Diego, California, was on station close in to the coast of Shikoku but had been drawn off her assigned spot in a fruitless search for zoomies reported downed. At 1800 her air cover departed, leaving her very naked in the path of a friendly task force scheduled to pass through the area. At 1900 Commander Grant opened up with his radio and reported his predicament. Subpac immediately went on the air but in spite of all we could do to inform those concerned, that night the destroyer Colohan picked Toro up at 18,000 yards and headed over to investigate. Colohan tried by voice radio and IFF to establish the identity of her contact but the submarine for some reason, did not have her IFF turned on. Toro did try to communicate with a flashing light but in the existing low-visibility condition her light was not seen.

Finally at 7,400 yards the Colohan opened fire and straddled Toro with the first salvo. Grant, of course, dived on seeing gun flashes and was not hit. The destroyer evidently thought she had sunk a surface vessel for no depth charges were dropped. Toro's recognition signal sent by sonar was not replied to because, running at 28 knots, Colohan could not use her echo-ranging gear. The submarine was lucky to get out of that mess without damage.

The sinking score for July was an emaciated shadow of former ones. According to JANAC, 14 submarines sank 13 merchantmen for a total of 28,452 tons, and nine men-of war, 6,505 tons. Among the former were three tankers, all small, and among the latter were an old destroyer, two frigates and a submarine.

Sennett, Commander C. R. Clark of Plattsburg, New York, was high gun both in numbers and in tonnage. She, in the Sea of Japan, sank a tanker, a passenger-cargo ship and two freighters for a total of 13,105 tons. That area was definitely cooling off and, although we had four or five submarines there, only five ships were sunk. The Yellow Sea, the Gulf of Siam and the Java Sea contributed most of the other sinkings.

Even the Barb, which had been a consistent scorer, could find few targets at her station in the Sea of Okhotsk just outside La Perouse Strait. After sinking a small freighter and a frigate in the first part of July, the supply of enemy ships seemed to have been exhausted. As the submarines patrolled close in to the shore line of Karafuto Island (the north half of which then belonged to Russia) the interest of her personnel was aroused by the trains which ran along the coast, undoubtedly hauling hundreds of tons of enemy goods.—But how could they sink a train?

Before long Commander Gene Fluckey and his cohorts concocted a plan for performing a reasonable facsimile of that difficult sounding job—they would go ashore and blow one up. That would disrupt rail traffic and destroy some rolling stock, and might force the Japs to send freight by sea. A point was selected where the railway line ran close to the beach and *Barb* made a periscopic survey of the terrain. Two rubber boats which could carry eight men, were available and one of the 55-pound TNT demolition charges intended for blowing up the ship in case of dire necessity, would serve to wreck the train and track. Volunteers were called for and so many responded that it became a question of drawing lots. Those lucky enough to win, were offered as high as two hundred dollars for their billets. Everyone wanted the honor of making the first landing in Japan.

Finally an overcast moonless night arrived, *Barb* moved in to about 1,000 yards from the beach and the sabotage party embarked in the rubber boats. Lieutenant Walker— later nicknamed "Choo Choo"—was in charge. For recognition purposes, nightbird calls had been arranged which would have been a credit to the "Last of the Mohicans." Unfortunately the ship's navigational fix was a little bit off and haze covered the landing party's selected landmarks. The result was that they hit the beach practically on some Jap's doorstep. Fortunately no dogs put in an appearance.

After a short reconnaissance, the main party left the boat guards and proceeded cautiously inland, skirting the houses. At this point what had appeared to be grass from the offshore view, turned out to be waist high bulrushes which crunched and crackled with every move. All shapes took on human forms. About 200 yards inland they came to the highway. Another huddled reconnaissance. All clear, so Lieutenant Walker rose to start a dash across the road. "Follow me," he whispered excitedly, and immediately fell headfirst into a drainage ditch!

A hundred yards farther on they arrived at the track, reconnoitered and selected their spots. Digging commenced but the picks and shovels shattered the night with loud ringing sounds, so they were laid aside and excavation continued dog fashion. A flickering light was spotted down the tracks. In proper frontier fashion all ears were pinned to the rails. No sound. Turn to again.

Suddenly, at an estimated range of 75–100 yards, a train loomed up, roaring down upon them. The entire party dived for the nearest cover, trying to hide behind bushes six inches high and two inches wide. The train blared past, with the engineer hanging far out of his cab, looking each of the party over personally. The train safely passed, the project hurried along with no further untoward occurrences. Circuits were checked, the charge was hooked up, the digging disguised and then the night filled with birdcalls. Difficulty was encountered in launching the boats through the surf, with everyone getting soaked. About two-thirds of the way back they sighted the expected train, and thoroughly enjoyed watching the fruits of their labor being explosively plucked.

WHAM! What a beautiful sight! The charge made a much greater explosion than they had imagined, the engine's boiler blew up, wreckage flew 200 feet in the air in a flash of flame and smoke, cars piled up and rolled off the track in a writhing, twisting mass of wreckage. A prisoner taken a few days later said that the Jap newspapers reported the wreck had been caused by an aircraft bomb. Once again the "Silent Service" failed to receive a credit line.

Not content with this invasion of the field normally belonging to the OSS, Barb planned to capture a small island in the Sea of Okhotsk where the Japanese Government maintained a seal rookery. I suspect each man cherished a hope of sending his best girl a sealskin coat. Offers for exchanges of billets this time ran as high as three hundred dollars. The preliminary periscope survey of the new objective, however, developed the fact that it was apparently well garrisoned, had numerous machine-gun emplacements, one 3-inch fieldpiece and several concrete pillboxes. One disillusioned member of the landing force was heard to mutter that he'd sell his billet for a nickel.

Obviously the submarine's eight-man amphibious force was not powerful enough to handle this situation. Barb therefore had to content herself with a bombardment—carried out at 700-yard range—which wrecked warehouses and barracks, knocked a wheel off the fieldpiece and silenced all return fire. As a parting gesture, toward the end of her patrol, she decided to try out an experimental 5-inch rocket launcher which had been mounted on her foredeck. Four attacks were made along the coasts of Hokkaido and Karafuto.

During these varied activities the *Barb* had acquired four prisoners. So contagious was the enthusiasm with which her crew went about their work that one of these prisoners, nicknamed "Kamikaze," begged to go on some of their planned sabotage expeditions. To take him along did not appear advisable but use was made of the valuable information which he gave about the organization and routine of beach patrols.

August 1 found me at sea off Guam in *Torsk*, Commander B. E. Lewellen of Savannah, Missouri, checking the QLA gear before her departure for the Sea of Japan. By that time, we had a very good plot of the enemy minefields in Tsushima Strait but it was still necessary to exercise greatest caution lest they fool us by planting new ones. *Torsk*'s mine-detection gear was excellent and an extreme range of 1,700 yards was obtained. *Piper* followed *Torsk*, with Commander E. L. Beach of Palo Alto, California, a veteran of many patrols, then in his first command. Next came *Stickleback*, with Commander Nauman and his ex-*Salmon* crew, back to avenge the rough handling their old ship had received in October, 1944. They had hurried completion of their new boat in every possible way but unfortunately they arrived too late and were destined to sink no more Japs.

With Okinawa at last secured Cincpac decreed we must give up our old veteran *Holland* to the Service Force for use at a Naval Base there. Sailing date was set for September 15 and that meant fast work to get communications and living quarters shifted to our tiny base on Coconut Island. With so much submarine tradition built around the old ship, it was a wrench to part with her. Generations of submariners had grown up in her and moored their boats alongside. Her prow had plowed the waters of many seas. The Pacific, from Dutch Harbor, Alaska, to Albany, Western Australia, had been her playground.

In her flag quarters had lived famous submariners such as Admiral Hart, Admiral Nimitz and Admiral Edwards. Her machine shops had educated engineers and repair officers no less famous in their own specialties. To turn her over to the nuts, bolts and groceries branch seemed like selling a faithful family horse to the glue factory.

From the Lifeguard League came a stirring dispatch reporting that *Aspro*, Commander J. H. Ashley, Jr., of Clinton, Indiana, had rescued an Army flier in broad daylight deep within Sagami Wan—in fact only eight miles from the famous Daibutsu, the great Buddha, at Kamakura. *Aspro* was lifeguarding south of Tokyo Bay with two B-17's and two fighters as cover. About 1100 Ashley heard over the radio phone that a pilot had parachuted into Sagami Bay. He sent one of the B-17's to investigate and a few minutes later the pilot reported he had dropped a wooden lifeboat to the downed zoomie and was circling him. The position given was about 40 miles distant—20 miles inside the bay. Ashley went full ahead, for it would take a good two hours to reach the spot even if he could get away with it.

Two B-24's (Privateers) relieved the B-17's and the fighters (Mustangs) reported they were running low on fuel and could remain no longer than a couple of hours. Shortly after noon several Jap Zeros attacked the Mustangs as *Aspro* entered Sagami Wan and, in the ensuing dogfights, one of the fighters was shot down, falling about 2,000 yards from the submarine.

There was no sign of the pilot after the crash. The B-24's attacked and drove the Zeros off and the remaining fighter headed back for his base.

By 1 P.M. the lifeboat was in sight and Zeros could be seen strafing it. Ashley called the B-24's and they drove the Japs away. The Privateers then began flying a tight low circle around the submarine. A Jap bomber started a run from the starboard beam but the air cover drove him off. At 1318 the downed flier was reached but at that instant the bomber bored in with both B-24's firing at him. *Aspro* took up the battle with her 20-mm gun and got several hits in the enemy's left wing. Just as the flier was trying to climb aboard, it became apparent the bomber was going to get in his attack, so *Aspro* dived and received two near misses on the way down. Through the periscope the bomber was seen to crash in a cloud of smoke and fire about a mile away.

Aspro surfaced and again was forced down by a bomber as the survivor's boat was desperately trying to get alongside. Two bombs landed close aboard. Things looked pretty grim at this point and the skipper was in some doubt as to whether he should make another try. Risking his ship and crew to save one man did not look like a good gamble and God only knew how many flying fields surrounded the bay. However, as he watched the B-24's "splash" his latest attacker, Ashley decided to try once more. The air cover had certainly done a magnificent job and he couldn't let them down after coming so far. With his radio antenna just above water, the skipper asked the Privateers if it were safe to surface. The answer came back, "I believe so—we just splashed another Jap."

This time, as *Aspro* shot to surface, the Captain and two men popped out of the hatch, got the downed aviator aboard and then directed the Privateers to return to base. They needed no second invitation and instantly started reaching for altitude. Two minutes later radar contact was made on an enemy plane distant six miles, closing. Two seconds after that, *Aspro* pulled the plug.

The rescued pilot proved to be Captain E. H. Mikes, USAAF, in good condition. One bullet had grazed his left arm. His boat and life ring had been badly cut up by strafing but miraculously the Nips had missed the helpless pilot. Ashley's account of the rescue closes with the entry, "Administered medicinal alcohol to survivor." I think the skipper also deserved a dose of "medical red."

Events were marching swiftly and on August 7 Task Force 38 was scheduled to strike Kyushu. Our lifeguards were to take their stations close inshore after dark on the day before. About 6 P.M. August 6, a message was teletyped to my office saying that the strike was canceled. This was nothing unusual but the concluding part of the message directed withdrawal of all ships to positions not less than 100 miles from the coasts of Kyushu.

That puzzled us and after dinner I told Commander Bub Ward, the Staff Duty Officer, to hop in a boat and see if he could find out at Cincpac's office the reason for that last provision and how long it would remain in force.

We were even then training *Catfish*, Commander W. A. Overton of Independence, Kansas, and *Runner*, Commander Benny Bass, for the job of searching the southeast and southwest coasts of Kyushu for minefields. Plans for the big invasion, Operation Olympic, had already been issued to Force Commanders and one of our jobs was to spot all minefields so the sweepers could go to work without delay.

Bub returned after a lengthy stay and reported he could find out nothing—nobody knew anything more than just what the message said. He evidently felt they were holding out on him for he added, "I think it will take at least a Vice Admiral to find out anything about it." I made a note in my little black book to take the matter up with the Big Boss next morning but that was never necessary. About midnight the atomic bomb was dropped on Hiroshima.

There were undoubtedly a few people at Cincpac HQ who knew about the A-bomb, but to the lower echelons, including myself, it was a complete surprise. One of our submarines in the East China Sea, 200 miles from the scene of the explosion, radioed that she had seen the flare and asked with concern about the supposed baleful effects which radio activity might have upon the waters in which she was cruising.

I do not believe that we gave a thought to this event as signaling the end of the war—a significance which has been assigned it in much postwar literature. We thought only of the fact that the destruction of the most important Japanese Army base was a valuable step in isolating Kyushu toward which Olympic was pointed. For months, B-29's had been trying to destroy the tunnel which runs under the Shimonoseki Strait, connecting the islands of Honshu and Kyushu. The next bomb, I assumed, would be aimed at that target.

The second A-bomb wiped out most of Nagasaki, the most important city in Kyushu. It missed the vital part of the target—the harbor area and the shipbuilding yards, but communications with the rest of the Empire were paralyzed. This also we viewed as a part of the Olympic plan and went right ahead with pouring submarines into the Sea of Japan (by this time we had a well-beaten trail through their minefields); sinking remnants of their once mighty merchant fleet in the Sea of Okhotsk, the Yellow Sea; rescuing dunked aviators and searching the waters of Kyushu for mines. Back at Pearl Harbor two submarines were already fitted out and training for duty as radar pickets and fighter directors. A mother back in the states wrote me she had heard the submarine war was all over and wanted her son sent home. I replied that such was not the case; some of our toughest jobs were still to be done but we could send her boy home for a spot of leave.

A preliminary presentation of Operation Coronet (Invasion of the Tokyo plain) scheduled for March 1946, was put on a Cincpac's HQ with participation of Gen. MacArthur's Staff. Certainly there was no thought in our minds at that time the Japanese would surrender their homeland without a last-ditch fight.

At 0600 on August 9 the Staff Duty Officer called me with a dispatch stating that Russia had declared war on Japan. Either the information that Russia would enter the war on August 15 was mistaken or she had seen the handwriting on the wall and wanted to get up to the pie counter before the pie was all gone. Postwar history would indicate the latter.

I immediately called Cincpac Chief of Staff and found him as surprised as I was, for the message had just been handed to him. I asked for recognition codes and found none had been received (they never were received). I had two submarines in areas which had been allocated to the Russians. These we moved to our own side of the line and later pulled another boat out of northern Honshu waters when a Russian submarine made its appearance there, paying no attention to the dividing line supposedly drawn at the Postdam Conference. This Russian skipper evidently declared a private war, for after the armistice, the Japanese complained that two ships were sunk in his area.

A few days later the air was full of messages indicating that the YB's (our private code word for Yellow Bellies) would consider surrender provided the Emperor were not removed. Why we ever acceded to that I will never understand, for certainly in the opinion of everyone I talked to among the fighting forces, he had earned a place right alongside Hitler and Mussolini. I knew the Air Force had orders not to bomb his palace but I thought that was merely to insure saving him for an extraspecial hanging. But once again the bespatted boys in the State Department, who had sanctioned the *Awa Maru* deal, had their way, and at 2304 of August 14 the Big Boss sent the dispatch which, for the Navy in the Pacific, ended the war. The message read:

> Cease offensive operations against Japanese forces. Continue searches and patrols. Maintain defensive and internal security measures at highest level and beware of treachery or last moment attacks by enemy forces or individuals.

When "cease firing" sounded there were in the Pacific 169 Fleet-type submarines, plus 13 S-boats, which were furnishing target services to destroyers and other antisubmarine craft. Twenty-two Fleet submarines were occupied exclusively with lifeguard duties. The remainder were on patrol, under repairs in U.S., or refitting at our various bases. Thus had grown the little band of 51 with which we entered the war.

Gradually reports of the last half month of the war began to trickle in. There were not many, of course, for the Japanese shipping barrel was about empty, but enough to indicate that our lads had been right on the job until the whistle blew. Seven submarines had sunk five merchantmen for a total of 15,433 tons and four men-of-war, 4,060 tons. All but three of these victims were in the Sea of Japan.

Spikefish, Commander R. R. Managhan of Portland, Oregon, in the East China Sea sank the last enemy submarine target of the war. On the night of August 13, she made radar contact and upon closing the range recognized the target as a large Jap sub. However, the American was evidently detected, for the quarry dived. Managhan decided that if he were the Jap, he'd reverse course. *Spikefish* was brought about and slowed to the estimated underwater speed of the enemy. Sure enough, a few minutes after midnight, the target was again picked up on surface.

Meanwhile Managhan radioed Comsubpac and was informed no friendly submarines were in that area. Nevertheless, he decided to wait for daylight and make doubly sure—mistakes do happen. Just before dawn *Spikefish* dived, sighted her target—definitely a Jap—and fired six torpedoes. There was only one survivor. He identified the victim as the I-373.

This brought the Allied score of enemy submarine sinkings in all Pacific and adjoining areas up to a total of 30, divided as follows:

U.S. submarines	23 Japanese
	2 German
Netherland submarines	1 German
British submarines	2 Japanese
	2 German

The two German U-boats credited to British submarines were sunk by *Tally Ho* and *Trenchant* in Malacca Strait. The two Japanese boats credited to the British were sunk by *Taurus* and *Telemachus* in that same Strait, which actually was not within the Pacific Ocean Areas. However, these sinkings occurred within 200 miles of our areas and I have listed them here merely to complete the count for our part of the world since I find no record of other German or Japanese subs sunk by Allied submarines in the Indian Ocean Areas.

Piper, with Commander Ned Beach in command, scouring the Sea of Japan for targets, had an experience in taking prisoners which was typical of many others throughout the war. On August 14, the last day before "Cease Fire," she came upon two survivors of a sunken ship. Several attempts were made to get them aboard but they abandoned their boat and, clinging to a piece of planking, paddled away every time the submarine came alongside. Lieutenant Bowman of Portland, Oregon, and Lieutenant LeClair, of Manchester, New Hampshire, requested and were given permission to bring them aboard. They stripped to their "skivvies" and, each with a knife in his teeth for protection in case of foul play, dived overboard.

The Jap approached by LeClair gave in and allowed himself to be towed alongside. Bowman's quarry, however, had to be subdued with a hammerlock and dragged alongside the bow. There again he put up a fight but found his captor in no mood to tolerate further foolishness. Hardly had these two prisoners been secured below (the magazine, if empty, made an excellent brig) when a life raft was sighted with four men on it. These offered no resistance, grasped a line thrown to them and hauled the raft alongside. Three clambered willingly aboard but the fourth suddenly dived into the water and swam a few feet away. He then turned on his back and dramatically bared his chest, evidently expecting to be shot. LeClair plunged in and after a short tussle, brought his man, gasping and choking, alongside.

We had issued warnings to Subpac against fraternizing with prisoners, pointing out that our fanatical enemies would undoubtedly take advantage of any relaxed vigilance to damage the ship or personnel even at the cost of their own lives. However, the crew invariably made mascots of their prisoners and soon had them working as mess cooks or shining bright work.

Jallao, Commander Icenhower, got the most tonnage for August, with one passenger-cargo ship sunk in the Sea of Japan for 5,795 tons. To *Torsk,* Commander Lewellyn, fell the honor of sinking the most targets—a cargo ship and two frigates, bagged in the Sea of Japan. By her destruction of these two escort vessels on August 14, she earned also the honor of firing the last torpedo from a U.S. ship in World War II.

At that time *Torsk* was carrying some of our newest brand of magnetic exploders and I had hoped we might gain some valuable information as to their performance. However, Lewellyn, knowing the history of our past exploder troubles and realizing that targets were hard to find, was not going to take a chance on some unforeseen malfunctioning, so he set his torpedoes to strike the target's hull instead of running under it—and I can't blame him for his lack of confidence. He got hits and sank his victims, but it was not until after the war, by firing at hulks, that we got the confirmatory information we wanted.

Commander Lewellyn's final coup brought to an end the bitter feud which had raged for almost four years, between submarines and antisubmarine craft, with the score considerably in our favor. Not only had these depth charge carriers and natural enemies of submarines failed adequately to protect their convoys, but they had paid an inordinately heavy price in ships and lives for the 23 American submarines which it is estimated they destroyed. JANAC records that of the Imperial Japanese Navy, 38½ destroyers, 9 old destroyers, 42 frigates and 19 submarine chasers, a total of 108½ antisubmarine vessels, were sunk by United States submarines. The one-half fraction is due to a sinking in which both a submarine and a carrier-based plane participated. The ratio is almost five to one in favor of the submarines, a figure which should give food for thought and some concern to those charged with preparation of our antisubmarine defenses against a possible well-armed, well-trained and daring opponent.

Only one submarine paid the price for our successes in the last month of the war. *Bullhead,* Lieutenant Commander E. R. Holt, Jr., departed Fremantle on July 31 for patrol in the Java Sea, which was to be shared with *Capitaine, Puffer* and the British submarines *Taciturn* and *Thorough.* On August 12 *Capitaine,* the senior ship, ordered *Bullhead* to take position in a scouting line but could obtain no acknowledgment of the message from the latter, nor was anyone ever able to raise her by radio or radar.

Enemy postwar reports record many antisubmarine attacks in the Java Sea area during the first part of August. However, the one considered most likely to account for *Bullhead*'s loss, occurred just north of the island of Bali where a plane claimed two direct hits on a submarine. For 10 minutes thereafter, according to this account, there was a great amount of gushing oil and air bubbles rising to the surface. Since the position given is near the Bali coast it is presumed that the proximity of mountain peaks shortened *Bullhead*'s radar range and prevented her receiving adequate warning of the plane's approach.

JANAC does not credit *Bullhead* with any sinkings but it is known that she did sink several small ships, probably less than 500 tons each, bombarded Pratas Reef and received three downed B-29 flyers from a Chinese junk in the South China Sea.

Bullhead's destruction brought our total losses in submarines up to 52. According to the best evidence (plus some deductions of my own) it appears possible or probable that the causes of our losses were distributed as follows:

Enemy surface ship attacks .... between 17 and 23
Enemy aircraft attacks .... between 11 and 5
(Depending on how six joint attacks are assigned)
Enemy submarines 2
Own surface forces 1
Own aircraft 1
Enemy mines 7
Circular runs of own torpedoes 2
Operational accidents 3
Stranding 4
Unknown 4

At the end of hostilities, the Japanese furnished us with information which claimed the sinking or probable sinking of 468 U.S. submarines. This gross overestimate of our losses does not speak very highly for the work of their assessment committees and certainly flatters our submarine building facilities.

Compared with submarine losses of our enemies, ours were low, for the Germans lost 781, the Japanese 130 and the Italians 85.

Small though our losses were numerically, they amounted to 18 per cent of all submarines that made war patrols and lost with them were 374 officers and 3,131 enlisted men. In a closely knit Force which had, at its peak, not more than 4,000 officers and 46,000 enlisted men (with some 16,000 actually manning the submarines) these losses were severe blows not only to our organization but to our hearts, for we had known or been shipmates with so many of those lads reported "missing presumed lost."

Our records of enemy ships and tonnage sunk, prepared by CO's of submarines and assessment committees of the Submarine Force, show considerable overestimate when compared with JANAC's postwar report. The discrepancy lies chiefly in our estimated tonnage of individual ships destroyed. The number of ships we claimed to have sent to Davy Jones's locker, under the difficult circumstances in which the estimates had to be made, check surprisingly well. Where JANAC does not credit a sinking as claimed by the Submarine Forces, it appears fairly safe to list that ship as having been damaged. There are no official figures in this category. Final sinking scores given below have been compiled from JANAC reports. Estimates of ships damaged are my own based on average patrol reports.

The final submarine score stands:

Naval vessels sunk 214–tonnage 577,626
Merchant vessels sunk .. 1,178–tonnage 5,053,491

One hundred sixteen of the merchant ships sunk were vitally important tankers.

Ships damaged (estimated)
1,200–tonnage (estimated) 5,200,000

According to Japanese figures, about 70,000 personnel of the merchant marine alone were killed or wounded as a result of U.S. submarine attacks. Losses among naval personnel and troops embarked in transports must have been much greater. These losses, inflicted by the Submarine Forces, which, at their peak, were only 1.6 per cent of the United

States Navy, merit careful study of the submarine potential by future Navy and Defense Department planners.

I was devoutly thankful the war was over, the slaughter ended, and humbly grateful that no more would I have to brief outgoing skippers on their missions, while wondering if I were sending them to their deaths. Upon receipt of Cincpac's "Cease firing" order, I sent out one to my own force and for information of all submarines in the Pacific. It read:

> The long-awaited day has come and cease firing has been sounded. As Force Commander I desire to congratulate each and every officer and man of the Submarine Force upon a job superbly well done. My admiration for your daring, skill, initiative, determination and loyalty cannot be adequately expressed. Whether you fought in enemy waters or whether you sweated at bases or in tenders you have all contributed to the end which has this day been achieved. You have deserved the lasting peace which we all hope has been won for future generations. To our brothers in Subs Seventh Fleet, Subs British Pacific Fleet, Subs Royal Netherlands Navy and Sublant hearty thanks for cooperation and admiration for your deeds. May God rest the gallant souls of those missing presumed lost.

CHAPTER 20

With the end of the shooting war came a flood of demobilization duties. Cincpac wanted a submarine tender and spare personnel to take over Japanese submarines at Yokosuka Naval Base. The tender *Proteus* and rescue vessel *Greenlet*, with Captain Lew Parks as Squadron Commander, was rushed off to join Admiral Halsey's Fleet in Empire waters. A similar force was desired for Kure or Sasebo. *Sperry* and *Coucal*, with Captain Stan Moseley as Squadron Commander, were readied for that job. The heavy cruiser *Indianapolis* had been sunk by an enemy submarine on July 30 with heavy casualties, and I was detailed as President of a Court of Inquiry to investigate her loss.*

On top of all this, the Chief of Naval Operations desired recommendations on what submarines and submarine bases should be retained in commission. Comsublant asked for a conference in Washington to handle this last matter, but I could not leave the Pacific at that time. Therefore I asked that Comsub Seventh Fleet, Rear Admiral Fife; and Comsublant, Rear Admiral Styer, come to Guam. This was done and in a three-day session, plans were prepared for demobilization and redeployment, which Comsublant, representing all of us, flew back to Washington. They didn't stand up very well in the postwar politico scramble to "get the boys home before Christmas," nor in the economy wave, but neither did anyone's else.

Requests from reserves for discharge came flocking into our offices until they looked like the fan mail department of a Hollywood star. Everyone wanted to put on his derby hat and go home.

Into this hectic scene, on August 23, came a very gratifying letter which I quote:

HEADQUARTERS TWENTIETH AIR FORCE

Office of the Commanding General

Vice Admiral C. A. Lockwood, Jr.
Commander Submarine Force, Pacific Fleet

My dear Admiral Lockwood:

I wish to take this opportunity to express my personal and official appreciation to you and your command for the splendid Air-Sea Rescue job you did for the XXI Bomber Command and the Twentieth Air Force. From the beginning of operations we were impressed with the interest and enthusiasm you put into your lifeguard work, and the persistent efforts you made to improve the operational procedures and equipment involved. In my opinion your efforts went beyond any routine assumption of an assigned responsibility.

---

* For the full story of this tragedy read *Abandon Ship* by Richard F. Newcomb, another volume in the Bantam War Book Series.

I am told that your submarines picked up 131 of our B-29 aircrewmen from 22 aircraft, and that you manned for us 490 separate lifeguard stations. I feel sure that these rescues will furnish some of the most inspiring history of this war. But even this impressive total of men saved does not tell the whole story. There is no way to evaluate the boost in morale that came to our aircrews from the knowledge that your submarines guarded the routes to and from their targets.

Your staff has always reflected your own personal interest in air-sea rescue, and I wish to convey my appreciation to them. I would particularly like to commend Captain R. G. Voge, Captain W. D. Irvin, Commander N. G. Ward, Commander R. W. Laing, Commander H. Cassidy and Commander J. A. Adkins. These men, from the beginning of our operations from Saipan on 24 November 1944, to our final mission on 14 August 1945, gave unstintingly of their time and energies, and showed the utmost of cooperation in working out common problems.

Gratefully,
N. F. Twining
Lt. General, USA
Commanding

I was sincerely pleased with this bit of cheer, for our lads had worked hard to make our Lifeguard League a success and to rescue downed aviators, not because they belonged to any particular branch of any service but because they belonged to the great Pacific team. As I said before, I did not realize how bad were our relations with the Army and the Army Air Force in the Pacific until after the war, when I got back to Washington and was told about them by the boys in the swivel chairs of the Pentagon and the Navy Department.

Meanwhile Third Fleet was standing guard outside Tokyo Bay, Japanese emissaries flew to Manila to confer with General MacArthur, and operation orders for landing occupation forces in Japan were crowding the air waves. *Segundo*, Commander S. L. "Slick" Johnson of West Lafayette, Indiana, en route to Tokyo Bay, encountered the

Japanese I-14 at sea, flying the black flag which had been specified as the token of surrender, and sent a prize crew aboard. Two others of the huge I-400 class surrendered to destroyers. The islands of Rota, Wake, Marcus and Palau all indicated their desire to surrender. In spite of rumors of a mass *kamikaze-banzai* attack, it looked as though the war really might be over.

One morning at conference Admiral Nimitz announced the plans for the surrender ceremony and invited me to fly to Tokyo Bay in his plane. He considered, so he said, that Submarine Forces rated representation at the surrender because they had played a major part in bringing it about. That, from the Big Boss, was a much appreciated accolade for the services our submarines had rendered to the Navy and to the Nation during 45 months in the front line.

I packed a bag and got permission to order the 12 nearest submarines into Tokyo Bay as representatives of their teammates, living and dead, who had set up this touchdown.

When the long-awaited day arrived for departure for Tokyo, the Guam contingent, having grown to considerable proportions, took off in two seaplanes from Tanapag Harbor, Saipan. Fleet Admiral Nimitz and his Staff led off; with Admiral Kelly Turner, Lieutenant General Roy Geiger, U.S. Marines, Brigadier General Feldman, U.S. Army, myself and a dozen other senior officers following in the second plane, Lieutenant Commander Bob Kaufman, my Flag Lieutenant, went along with me. Everyone was in holiday spirits. We might easily have been bound for an Army-Navy Game—in fact, it was the biggest, most important Army-Navy Game yet played—and for stakes that involved the future of continents.

Those of us who were mere sailors or ground troops, tried to look unconcerned when General Geiger and Admiral Turner—both veteran fliers—took turns at the controls, but when we circled neat but desolate-looking Iwo Jima and Admiral Turner almost scraped the port wing on Mount Surabachi, I voiced a protest.

"Hell," said Kelly, who had commanded the Amphibious Forces at its capture, "why shouldn't I take a piece off it? After all, I've got a half interest in that island!"

As we followed the island chain that led to the Empire, Aoga Shima, Hachijo Shima and O Shima passed under our wings. All were names I had read countless times in patrol reports and all looked peaceful in the sunshine. I was sorry we missed Sofu Gan, Lot's Wife, that pillar of stone which served as a landmark for China-bound submarines throughout the war.

As we neared the Empire, an escort of six Navy fighters hove in sight and took stations above our transport. The day was gorgeous with flecks of cumulus cloud here and there, whitecaps showing on the water below us and majestic-looking Fujiyama blue in the distance. On August 18, 1918, I had climbed to its peak via horseback and foot, while attached to the Embassy at Tokyo. That was near the conclusion of a war when Japan was our ally, but in which her Prime Minister, Baron Goro, and many highly placed Japanese, asserted Japan fought on the wrong side. Well, they had tried fighting on that other side and I hoped they got a bellyful of it.

We passed over a convoy of one escort carrier and three transports guarded by about 10 destroyers and DE's. Admiral Halsey wasn't taking any chances on banzai submarine attacks. A light haze covered the landscape but as we stood up into Tokyo Bay, Japan looked as green and full of rice paddies as ever.—And then the glorious sight of our Fleet, anchored below Yokohama, burst upon us! God! but it looked beautiful!

We sat down off Yokosuka Naval Base and taxied over to the battleship *South Dakota* where Admiral Halsey's flag flew from the mainmast. The *Proteus,* where I would hoist my flag, had not yet arrived, but could be seen standing up the Bay toward her anchorage, so I went aboard the *South Dakota* to pay my respects to Commander Third Fleet. The Admiral received us in his cabin. He looked tired about the eyes but there was nothing wrong with his spirits. He had, mounted on sawhorses, not one, but two, beautifully ornamented saddles which admiring friends back in the States had sent him for that ride he had promised to take on "White Snow" through the streets of Tokyo. Granting immunity to the Emperor had spoiled that jest but I don't believe the fire-eating old seadog ever meant it as a jest—he was in dead earnest.

As the *Proteus* approached, we could see she was followed by two surrendered Jap submarines, the giant I-400 (5,000 tons) and the I-14 (3,000 tons). Each had a huge cylindrical hangar and a catapult. One was designed to carry four planes, the other, two.

I got aboard the big one immediately with Capain Lew Parks and found Commander Barney Sieglaff, whom we had sent with *Proteus* as a spare skipper, Commanding Officer of the prize crew. Except for the Captain and those on watch below, the Japanese crew, 20 officers and 179 men, were lined up on deck, guarded by dungaree-clad tommy gunners.

The Jap skipper was allowed to bring his submarine alongside *Proteus*, with half a dozen of us watching him with eagle eyes for any sign of treachery. It would have been fairly easy to quietly order all engines ahead, full speed, and plow into the tender so I was relieved when her bow came slowly around until we paralleled the tender's side and our lines were shot aboard.

Barney told me the I-400 had been on a supply trip to Truk. Carrying groceries when she should have been working on our Communication lines. The Jap skipper stated he had sunk no American ships—that he hadn't seen any. How he could have run through our "bridge of ships" to Guam and the Philippines without seeing any was beyond me. Our own submarines sometimes ran submerged for hours to keep from alarming our transports and freighters.

I was astonished at the lousy (there is no other word for it) appearance of the enemy crew. Normally a Jap is clean but these were filthy in clothing and person. Barney had been working them pretty hard cleaning out below and had locked up in the hangar some 400 straw-covered flagons of saki. Her lower decks were carpeted with cans of food over which plank walkways had been laid. Empty tins were flung into the nearest corner. The stench of the crew's "benjo" (toilet) was sickening.

The ship was enormous. Built with a double cylindrical cross section, shaped like a figure eight with the middle one-third removed, she had an upper and a lower forward torpedo room with four tubes in each. Her double-decked crew's living compartments were none too large to care for her swarming crew, and her engine room looked like that of an ocean liner.

The principal hope of offensive power of this class (two built and one building) lay in its planes, each of which was capable, so we were told, of carrying a 1,500-pound bomb. The plan was to send these ships with some of the I-14 class, to bomb the Panama Canal locks. Even if they had been able to muster a total of twenty 1,500-pound bombs, the threat to the Canal would not have been serious.

These ships were typical examples of the vacillating, misguided policy of the Japanese submarine arm. They had a dozen different types, some for cargo carrying alone (run by the Army), some for high underwater speed (which never got into the war), and at least four types of midgets and human torpedo suicide craft. They frittered away their building facilities and steel in playing with these side shows, which availed them very little, instead of building long-range, fast, combat submarines of 50–75 days endurance, with which to harass and disrupt our supply lines.

In my opinion, the most valuable type of submarine is one that can strike the enemy life lines and men-of-war areas which cannot be reached by our surface ships or planes. Such a sub will bring back its seasoned crews to make more patrols, not throw away their lives in misguided suicide attacks. It's hard enough to produce skilled, well-trained crews without expending the bravest of them in suicidal missions. I feel that in this war we had the best type of submarine and made the most effective use of it. —And for that last I give full credit to Fleet Admiral Nimitz, for he had a very clear concept of our mission and gave us a free hand in carrying it out.

The next day *Proteus* went inside the breakwater at Yokosuka Naval Station and anchored near the only remaining Japanese battleship, the *Nagato*. Her superstructure was burned out and her mainmast and smokestack were gone. I had seen her at Nagasaki in 1917, just after she was launched. It was difficult to realize she had then been one of the most powerful ships in the world.

The I-401 came in that day with 12 of our submarines, who moored alongside *Proteus*. Both of the 5,000 tonners, when they surrendered, had protested against going into Tokyo Bay. They wanted to go to Aomori in northern Honshu, which was their base and where their families lived. They were "persuaded," however, to head for Tokyo Bay. I-14, which surrendered to Commander Slick Johnson in *Segundo*, had presented a more difficult problem. *Segundo* placed a small prize crew aboard and escorted her toward Tokyo. The personnel of the enemy sub, however, were just barely submissive and the prize officer did not feel that the situation was well in hand. Hence, *Segundo* kept a running

TDC set-up on the I-14 and was prepared to torpedo her at the first sign of trouble. As we later learned, she was carrying the Commander of her division and he was opposed to the surrender. Evidently he sent a dispatch to the Japanese admiral commanding Yokosuka Naval Station, making threats as to what he intended to do. The admiral—one of the old school—with old-fashioned ideas of honor, informed the U.S. naval authorities and a full-sized prize crew from *Proteus* was rushed out to her. Meanwhile the problem solved itself—the Division Commander committed hari-kari, after which happy event, all went well.

Capain Parks and I, with several other submariners, went ashore at Yokosuka to see the Navy Yard and the Submarine Base. I had expected to find a modern and well-equipped Yard since it was one of Japan's best, but what I found was distinctly third class by our standards. The building ways were given over entirely to the construction of midgets and dozens of "Kaitens" were set up on blocks along the quay walls. These latter were about five feet in diameter, 30 feet long and shaped just like a torpedo. Each carried two torpedoes outside the hull along the bilge keels, and each had an enormous war head with which to ram its final target. Needless to say, the pilot would not return from this attack. Some were powered with a small kerosene engine and some were driven by an air turbine, as is a torpedo. Each was equipped with a beautiful little periscope about five feet long. These midgets were designed to be carried on the deck of a large submarine, of which, at that time, the Japanese had practically none in operating condition.

On one of the building ways I picked up a steel-pointed arrow in good condition. I asked both the U.S. Marines and the British Marines, who guarded the Yard, whether this was a part of their equipment, but each laughingly disclaimed ownership. I concluded it must be a new Japanese secret weapon; however, during recent trials by the Allied War Crimes Court of war criminals in Tokyo, it was disclosed that an American airman had been tortured to death by a Japanese officer who used him for an archery target. Perhaps my innocent-looking arrow was not so innocuous a weapon as I had supposed.

There were some 200 Jap torpedoes stored in the Yard and they were definitely not in a "bow and arrow" category. I found representatives of NavTechJap (a U.S. naval technical group) eagerly examining their 24-inch diesel driven fish, which, as I mentioned before, used oxygen and kerosene to produce about 50 knots for 16,000 yards. We could have used a torpedo like that in our own navy.

The Submarine Base we found to be the most one-horse part of the whole Yard. It had only one pier, alongside of which were three HA-class boats with no tubes and large, rectangular cargo hatches. A small gun, about a six pounder, was mounted on deck. These submarines operated under direction of the Army and were used to supply their by-passed island bases.

Another submarine, the I-369, with only two torpedo tubes, also was used for cargo. One ancient RO class completed the force of orthodox submarines. However, moored in various coves, were numerous midgets, some of which had settled to bottom. The shops were of the usual sort, but scantily furnished. This was true in the main Yard also, and we

I-400

found the reason for this scarcity was that a considerable amount of machine tools had been moved into caves dug into the steep hills which backed up the narrow level space around the harbor. These caves had no sheathing overhead, so water dripped on the tools, whose condition can be readily imagined.

The Yard had suffered very little from bombing; a few craters were in evidence and some tattooing by 50-caliber or 20-mm bullets, but in the main, the station suffered from lack of ordinary upkeep. Later, when I inspected Sasebo Navy Yard in western Kyushu, I found much the same situation. There, the center of the town had been burned out but the dilapidated condition of the Navy Yard was due to years of neglect.

It had rained for the last two days but the morning of September 2 (September 1 in the United States) dawned clear as a bell. We were instructed to be aboard *Missouri* by 0815, so we shoved off early from the *Proteus* as we had about 10 miles to go—in a slow motor boat. I left orders to shift my personal flag at 0800 to the I-400 for the period of the surrender ceremony. Perhaps that was gloating a bit over our enemy, but I remembered, and still resented, Admiral Yamamoto's boast that he would dictate terms of peace in the White House. He had long since been gathered to his ancestors, an operation in which American fighter planes played the leading role. Too bad he did not live to see what was about to take place.

We were piped aboard the "Mighty Mo" with due pomp and ceremony, though how the Officer of the Deck could hope to render all honors correctly is beyond me. The gangway ladder looked like a subway entrance during the rush

hour and was continuously crowded with officers of all ranks and nationalities. The boatswain's mate probably wore out a couple of pipes that day. Army, Navy, Marines and Air Forces of all the Allies appeared to be there; British, Russian, Australian, New Zealand, Chinese, French—the old *Missouri* had indeed become a Tower of Babel. Captain Sunshine Murray, who served as my Chief of Staff in the first part of the war, was in command and handled the situation with his usual efficiency, courtesy and aplomb.

One of the first familiar faces I saw was that of Commodore John Collins, RAN, who had been my second in command at Perth. He had been badly wounded in the Philippine campaign but was back to command the Aussie ships participating in the surrender. Rear Admiral Joel Boone, Fleet Medical Officer, was dashing about full of business. He and Commander Harold J. Stassen, ex-Governor of Minnesota, also of Admiral Halsey's Staff, were in charge of POW liberation and had already visited most of the nearby prison camps. Both were bitter about the condition of the Allied prisoners they found there. Our transports were being filled with them as rapidly as possible. I learned to my surprise that Commander Dick O'Kane was alive, though terribly ill and emaciated. We had given Dick up for lost months before. General Wainwright, Commander of Corregidor, was on board, having been flown over from Manchuria. He was pitifully thin and starved looking.

A number of liberated prisoners of war had been brought aboard to witness the ceremony and among them I found L. C. Shaw, MoMM1/c, of the *Grenadier*, who told me the story of her loss. He said that while all hands had been clubbed and starved for no reason at all, the skipper, Commander Fitzgerald, was beaten and tortured for weeks in an attempt to extract from him secret information about our submarines.

Lieutenant Field Harris, Jr., of the Marines, was also on board. He had been captured on Bataan and survived the March of Death. He, in particular, had a hunted look in his eyes, which was not surprising in view of the atrocious treatment he received at Ofuna. As one of his punishments there for some petty offense, he had been triced up before the other prisoners and beaten with clubs until he became unconscious. I met Commander A. L. Maher, who had been a member of the ill-fated *Houston*'s complement. He told me that her Captain, my old friend of early submarine days, Captain Harold Rooks, was killed by a shell as the ship was sinking.

With hundreds of Allied officers and men, I witnessed the surrender. It was a scene that will remain etched in the memory of every man who was there, so long as he may live.

At last the "U.S. flag was flying over Tokyo," as a song writer had promised us some two years before.

After the ceremony, Vice Admiral "Slew" McCain went back to *Proteus* with me, where we had lunch in the Captain's mess with his son, Jack, a veteran submarine skipper, who at the moment had command of the I-14. It was a very cheery meal, for the McCains hadn't seen each other in months, and much good-natured banter as to aviators versus submariners was battered back and forth.

Admiral McCain, who had been detached from duty in command of the Carrier Task Force, shoved off after lunch to catch a plane back to the U.S. He was apparently in good health—though always very nervous and much too thin—and certainly he was in highest spirits at the prospect of getting home now that the job was done. The news, therefore, which came a few days later, of his sudden death at home in Coronado, was a great shock to us all. A daring and skillful leader had gone to his rest.

His was one of many deaths in the first postwar years— Admiral Pete Mitscher, Lieutenant General Roy Geiger, Rear Admiral Dick Voge, among them—of leaders who carried tremendous burdens of responsibility during the war, with apparently no ill effects, only to pay the price of overstrain when the tension relaxed.

After seeing Admiral McCain off, Captain Parks, a reserve lieutenant language officer and I got a jeep and headed for Tokyo. Speed was necessary because my transportation was scheduled to take off for Guam early the next morning. We got no further than Yokohama before we had to turn back but I, for one, had seen enough. The city was leveled to the ground except for a few concrete structures. The roads, due to lack of upkeep, were full of potholes and the people looked ragged and sullen but not undernourished. Remembering how our liberated prisoners of war looked that very morning on the *Missouri*, I could find no sympathy in my heart for these sadistic, misguided, would-be world conquerors.

With the shades of evening closing in, we dashed back to Yokosuka to find a beer party at the Japanese Officers' Club, in full swing. Captain Clark of the *Proteus* and the Flag Lieutenant, Bob Kaufman, had invited all officers off watch and produced numerous cases of beer and huge platters of

sandwiches. An imposing sign was nailed over the front door;
"Submarine Base, Yokosuka, Japan," and we had a mass picture taken under it before darkness shut down. It was a very
quiet and orderly party. I don't believe we fully realized the
war was over. No Fuhrer danced a jig as Hitler had done in
Paris. —What would Tojo have done in San Francisco?

I had no sooner returned to Guam than a stream of our
liberated prisoners of war began to arrive. Those who were in
good health, wild to get home, tarried with us only long
enough to get transportation and their orders. Some, the doc-
tors wanted hospitalized until dysentery, jaundice and malnu-
trition could be taken care of; others we were permitted to put
in Camp Dealey under our submarine doctor's care until they
could orient themselves, get their stomachs used to white
man's food again and put a little flesh on their bones.

Dick O'Kane, when he arrived, didn't want to go
straight home. He probably felt that his condition was too
shocking for his family to see. He was just skin and bones.
His arms and legs looked no bigger than an ordinary man's
wrists, his eyes were a bright yellow from jaundice (the result
of rat-contaminated rice, I was told) and the dysentery from
which he suffered would have killed him in a few more
weeks. Dick's was the worst case I saw but many others were
in pitiable condition.

It made my blood boil to see this human wreckage returning from prison camps of an alleged civilized nation, and
to compare them with the fat, insolent-looking German and
Japanese prisoners I had seen in the United States, in Pearl
Harbor and on Guam.

We organized a regular detail of officers and stenogra-
phers to interview each man and record their stories. I talked
to as many as I could and was shocked to observe the shifty,
hunted look in their eyes and the punch-drunk condition of
many. Some, I feared, would never be quite normal again.
All data collected was sent back to the Office of Naval Intelligence in the hope that it could be used in the trials of war
criminals.

Lieutenant L. Savadkin, who had escaped from the
conning tower of the *Tang*, was among the first to arrive.
When captured he had been taken first to Formosa and later
to the Japanese questioning camp at Ofuna. Its nearness to
Tokyo made it handy for their Gunrabo (Japanese FBI)

agents to work on the prisoners in an effort to break their spirits and make them reveal military or naval secrets. The prisoners were told they were "still fighting the war but without weapons." None were registered as POW's until transferred to some other regularly organized camp such as Omori, which is on an island in Tokyo Bay. Thus the Swiss Embassy, through whom all POW matters were handled, or the Red Cross, knew nothing of them. If any died under the treatment received at Ofuna, the world was none the wiser. Lieutenant Savadkin told me that his skipper, Commander O'Kane, had been treated with special barbarity but had never cracked under it.

Commander Dave Hurt of the *Perch*, and Lieutenant George E. Brown, Jr., Engineer Officer (and only officer survivor of *Sculpin*) showed up in my office on the night of September 6, asking for orders and transportation home. They were terribly thin and white and had that characteristic hunted look. Dave Hurt had been in prison camps for 41 months.

Lieutenant Brown told me the story of *Sculpin*'s loss as I have recorded it in an earlier chapter. He said that while the prisoners from *Sculpin* were at Truk, he was questioned and, with the sanction of a Japanese Rear Admiral, severely beaten for refusing to answer questions which under the Geneva Convention, the enemy had no right to ask. While at Ofuna he was accorded what he described as "the usual treatment; solitary confinement when not being questioned, threatened with death for refusal to answer questions fully and accurately, given reduced rations and frequent beatings." At Omori, treatment was better but discipline was strict and the guards, on their own authority, did not hesitate to administer physical punishment for the slightest offense.

Statements of three other members of the *Sculpin*'s crew taken from the stenographic record are quoted herewith to give the complete picture of what our men suffered at the hands of their barbarous captors:

Paul A. Todd, PHM1/c—"The word had been passed to 'Abandon Ship.' Then someone opened the vents and all men on topside jumped overboard. Some of the men were killed on topside. After we got into the water, the Japs machine gunned us. I swam toward the Japanese destroyer and was picked up along with 41 other members of the crew. One man was thrown overboard because he was said to be severely wounded and the Japs did not want to give him medical attention.

"While at Ofuna, a Lieutenant Commander in the Japanese Navy said that only a miracle could save Japan in this war.

"My impression is that the Japanese Army had confidence in winning the war, but the Naval personnel didn't have.

"On July 10, 1944, all of *Sculpin* prisoners except one officer were transferred to Omori for work. We were registered as prisoners-of-war this date, although we had been captured on November 19, 1943 (8 months before)."

Herbert J. Thomas TM1/c—"Order was given to battle surface. The Jap destroyer, *Yokohama*, was firing on us with 5-inch and machine guns, killing a number of the men on deck. The *Sculpin* returned fire with the 3-inch gun without effect. A total of 42 men were picked up by the enemy, one of them, who was wounded in the arm and chest, was thrown back into the water and left to die. Since the captain of the *Yokohama* was present at the time, it is presumed this was done on his orders. At the same time, Rourke, who was suffering from nausea, caused by swallowing salt water, was about to be thrown overboard in the same manner, but managed to kick himself free, and remain on board."

Edward F. Ricketts, MoMM2/c—"They dove the boat with all hatches open after passing the word to abandon ship. The Captain (referring to Captain Cromwell) never tried to get off. I remember someone saying that Ensign Fiedler, figuring the boat was lost, grabbed a deck of cards and went into the wardroom to play solitaire. He went down with the boat, also. After strafing us in the water for a while and killing several men, the Nips pulled us aboard the destroyer *Yokohama*. One man was wounded in the arm and above the eye. He could have been saved, but the Japs tossed him overboard. Rourke was about to be thrown overboard, also, when he came to and managed to get up forward with us. Pitzer, TM2/c, stayed at his 20-mm gun despite having a shell in the arm. The Japs amputated his arm at the shoulder without anesthetic. Our pharmacist's mate said his arm could have easily been saved. Elliott, F1/c, was shot in the hand, but could move all his fingers, and our pharmacist's mate said it was O.K., but the Japs amputated his hand at the wrist at Truk."

Clifford W. Kuykendall, GM2/c, the only survivor of the *Tullibee,* sunk off Palau on the night of March 26, 1944, had endured particularly atrocious treatment. Lest it lose something in the retelling, I quote his report verbatim, regarding his rescue by and reception aboard the Japanese patrol boat which sighted him floating in the sea about 10 A.M. the morning after *Tullibee* went down. The ship began circling him and then—

"All port machine guns opened fire, the vessel made a complete 360 degree circuit around me, firing all the time. Only damage done to me was flesh wounds in five different places. After making a complete circuit, the vessel came in alongside me and picked me up. First thing after being pulled on deck, an English-speaking officer struck me alongside the head with a large club and knocked me unconscious. After I regained consciousness this English-speaking officer, along with another English-speaking officer, began questioning me. The information that they wanted to know was the captain's name, name of the submarine, where we were operating from, names of the crew, length, dimensions, type of guns and all details covering a submarine. This continued all day but I stuck to international law, only giving them my name, rate and service number. I was treated terrible by these two officers who did all the beating. They beat me with clubs, rawhide thongs, rifle stocks and hit me alongside the head with a pistol barrel. Said they were going to behead me with a saber and made several swings overhead with it but changed their minds and secured the saber."

Lieutenant Kenneth G. Schacht of the *Perch,* had endured 41 months of imprisonment as had his skipper and shipmates. All showed plainly the effects of terrorism. Schacht, who had a talent for sketching, said he kept himself sane by trying to picture the incidents of their daily life. The guards were interested, especially if sketches of themselves appeared, and naturally these had to put them in a good light.

On arrival at Ofuna, he said, all hands were informed they were not yet in any way considered prisoners of war. They were still considered as fighting the war, but without weapons. There was to be no talking among the prisoners and only to the guards in Japanese. Prisoners were beaten, Schacht's report went on, for the slightest infraction of the rules, with wooden clubs which varied in thickness, the smallest being of the same shape and size as a samurai sword.

"Punishments were in two general classes. First, and usually the most severe, were the formal beatings administered when a prisoner refused to answer a question, was suspected of lying, disrespectful to questioner or was guilty of some minor infraction such as sitting on his blankets, whispering to a fellow prisoner or spilling a dish. This last group of minor offenses only brought the severe formal beatings when the prisoners appeared to be relaxing in regards to the regulations. The second class of punishments were administered on the spot, these were for minor offenses such as speaking to the guard in English, not showing proper respect to a guard, taking food from a guard, being late to formation, not counting off properly in Japanese, etc. These infractions were punished by blows on the face with open or closed fist, two or three blows on any part of the body with a stick, physical drills for a long period of time, or being stood at attention for long periods."

Any public punishment seemed to have a sort of chain reaction with the Japanese prison authorities. Beating the culpit or culprits for whom the ceremony was specially arranged, worked them into a frenzy, to the extent that they just pulled anyone who was handy out of the ranks and beat him also.

Lieutenant (jg) J. J. Vandergrift, Jr., also of the *Perch,* said that, while at Ofuna, from time to time examiners from Tokyo would call them singly into a small room for questioning. The questions concerned chiefly communications and sound apparatus. They were searching particularly for someone who could describe the technical end of the sound gear. Beatings were given for refusal to answer, but "I don't know" was generally accepted. In his case, Vandergrift said, his ignorance of all matters finally caused one Jap naval officer to exclaim, "You are a disgrace to your country!" He was never questioned again.

W. F. Jeffries, SC2/c, of the submarine tender *Canopus,* was taken prisoner when Bataan surrendered and survived the March of Death. Some of his observations as to prison life in the Philippines were as follows:

"From Bataan we were taken to Cabanatuan, and then to Manila. We were put into Bilibid Prison. While in the camp at Cabanatuan, four men tried to escape, but were recaptured. They were beaten, and tied in the sun, without water, for 48 hours. We watched their execution, when they were finally shot. They said they were glad to die.

"In the spring of 1945, a Jap hospital corpsman demanded that the camp U.S. doctor give him chocolates from our Red Cross packages. The doctor refused, and the Jap beat him so badly that I was unable to recognize his features."

Lieutenant Commander J. A. Fitzgerald, CO of the ill-fated *Grenadier*, scuttled his ship off Penang, Burma, in the early morning of April 23, 1943, after it had been fatally damaged by aircraft bombs. He probably received more brutal treatment than any other submarine officer. From the time he and his crew arrived at Penang after being picked up by a small merchant ship, their lives were filled with beatings, water cures and standing at attention or in strained positions—hands over heads with knees bent—for hours on end. At the end of the fourth day Fitzgerald received his first food—a small teacup of rice broth and some weak tea.

Meanwhile, in the questioning room persuasive methods such as clubs, pencils between the fingers, the blade of a penknife shoved underneath the fingernails and water cures were used in an effort to make them talk. The water cure given to Fitzgerald consisted in tying him face up on a bench with his head hanging over the end. Then his feet were elevated and water poured from a teakettle into his nostrils. A hand over his mouth forced him to swallow the water and when he was judged to be sufficiently full of water, a club beating would be administered. Usually be became unconscious during this last torture, whereupon they would revive him and try questioning again. When that was unsuccessful, another clubbing followed. The miracle is that he survived and kept his reason.

Grenadier's leading radioman, J. S. Knutson, RM1/c, was questioned by Japanese and German radar experts and, when he wouldn't "give," was starved and hung by his thumbs.

The statement of Robert W. Palmer, CY, after describing the various tortures inflicted, said that Commander

Fitzgerald, in spite of all that had been done to him, would write messages for the crew on the bulkhead every time he went to the toilet, such as "Don't tell 'em anything," "Keep your chins up." At Ofuna, Palmer was questioned by a QK (Quiz Kid) as the Gunrabos were called, a Commander Shinimatzu, who boasted that he graduated from Palo Alto High and Stanford University. When the Pearl Harbor attack was made, he was an attaché in Washington.

Admiration for their skipper was universal among the crew of the *Grenadier*. The statement of William C. Withrow, CTM, said:

"I think as much of Commander Fitzgerald, our skipper, almost as I do of my father. He went through hell for us. They beat him, jumped on his stomach and tortured him by burning splints under his nails. He never talked. They even had him working in the mines for telling the Jap Commander just what he thought of him."

These are only a few of the stories which the 17 officers and 141 enlisted men had to tell of their lives as POW's. The horrors and cruelties to which they were subjected are almost unbelievable, yet I am convinced that not one of these lads told the full story of his sufferings. It was easy to see that—in spite of enemy atrocities which they felt it beneath human dignity to describe—abiding faith in our eventual victory had sustained them through their ordeal.

The aftermath of World War II was not wholly pleasant. Embittered as we were by the treatment of those who had been captured and saddened by the absence of shipmates and friends who had paid the price of our triumph and would never return, it was inevitable that the taste of victory should lose some of its savor. The Submarine Force, in whose esprit de corps and deeds we had the most intense pride, was being dispersed to decommissioning bases; reservist shipmates would soon be returned to civil life; wartime friendships cemented by sharing common dangers and moments of exultation, would be disrupted, perhaps never to be renewed. —A splendid team was breaking up.

However much these thoughts dampened my elation, they could not suppress my feelings of pride and deep satisfaction that, in the acid test of war, submarines and submariners of the United States Navy had proved there is practically nothing they cannot do. They had measured up to their own high standards of performance and certainly no Force Commander ever had a finer, smarter, braver or more loyal Force.

CHAPTER 21

The history of submarine development stretches back through the centuries but it is only within the experience of living men that the submarine has become the sinister, deadly menace in war upon whose control may depend the future command of the Seven Seas.

By careful study and evaluation of the startling advances made in submarine construction, equipment and weapons during the last decade, can we forecast the trend of its development for the next five or 10 years? What will be the most profitable fields of employment for our undersea craft in a possible World War III? What will be the missions assigned to the U-boats of our probable enemies?

Producing the answers to the first and second questions is not too difficult. The trend is unmistakably toward the "true" submarine which can remain submerged indefinitely. As to employment of our own boats, postwar experimentation has developed prototypes which are exploring the various strategic and tactical fields currently considered most profitable.

The answer to the third question is also fairly easily worked out. However, in its train, follows a crop of problems whose solutions are producing headaches and gray hairs in important military, naval and scientific divisions of our National Defense.

Since about 1620, when a Hollander named Van Drebbel took King James the First of England for a ride down the Thames in a leather-skinned submarine propelled by oars, undersea boats have been headaches to countless thousands. Some were headaches chiefly to their inventors and served as tombs for the adventurous souls who attempted to operate them. —The Confederate *Hunley*, for instance, drowned or suffocated three crews before she finally blew up the Federal

Housatanic in Charleston harbor and was herself lost with all
hands. Others were causes of grave worry to governments
whose surface navies were threatened. Fulton, the man whose
genius made steam navigation a success, was paid $75,000 by
the British government for his submarine *Nautilus*, on condition that he would not bring it to the attention of any other
European country. England, then "Mistress of the Seas,"
early recognized the fact that, if this type of vessel were successful, her command of the sea might be endangered.

Development of the submarine was slow because its
success depended upon the progress of three vital, and then
undeveloped, components: the internal combustion engine,
the electric storage battery and the automobile torpedo.
Funds for experimentation could be obtained only from private individuals, because governmental and naval circles were
not interested. However, in spite of indifference and ridicule,
inventors persevered. In 1867, Jules Verne published his
prophetic *Twenty Thousand Leagues Under the Sea*, which
fired the imagination of inventive souls throughout the world.

The histories of the early struggles of our two leading
American submarine inventors—John P. Holland and Simon
Lake—are fascinating and inspiring stories of courage and
perseverance. Handicapped by poverty they nevertheless
worked with dauntless determination for years to perfect their
designs and to create equipment for meeting requirements
then totally unknown to the engineering world. Lack of funds
was no bar to their inventive genius but instead was a spur to
their resourcefulness in devising makeshift, temporary gear.
The devotion and patriotic fervor with which both dedicated
their lives to translating their dreams into successful realities,
have earned for them high places among the great of our nation.

At long last, over the opposition of the conservatives,
submarines began to appear in various European navies and,
in the early 1900's, a Holland boat and a Lake boat were
bought by the U.S. Navy. Models of these same American
types were sold abroad where nations possessing small navies
were taking definite interest in this "weapon of the weaker
power."

Lake smuggled out and sold his *Protector* to Russia during the Russo-Japanese war. The German Krupps by a stroke

of industrial sharp practice, obtained his plans and began construction of Lake-type boats without so much as a "by your leave." England's Vicker's Company bought plans from Holland (Electric Boat Company). France developed her own design of submersibles and Italy's original boats were substantially of the Lake type. The Japanese also bought several Holland-type submarines.

Thus, at the outbreak of World War I, most of the contestants were using submarines whose basic plans were American. This was not the first nor yet the last time that the "Yankee ingenuity" of our inventors produced weapons which eventually were turned against us.

We had not long to wait before the submarine demonstrated its effectiveness in war for, on September 22, 1914, the German U-9 sank the British cruisers *Aboukir, Hogue* and *Cressy* in a single tragic hour. A shocked universe then realized that a new and terrible weapon had been added to the navies of the world. Part of Jules Verne's fantasy had become a deadly reality!

Thus began the first of two world wars in which destruction of life and property at sea surpassed anything the world had ever known.

The problem which the Armed Services and, particularly the Navy, are now facing is the prevention of cataclysmic losses at sea, in the event of World War III, such as the Allies suffered from enemy submarines in the last two wars.

Considered together, the pattern of submarine warfare in both world wars is identical. New undersea weapons, tactics and missions were introduced in World War II but, in the overall picture, we were chiefly concerned with the effectiveness of submarines in destroying the enemy's merchant fleet, thus throttling his war industries and wrecking his national economy. In this struggle enemy men-of-war were targets of secondary importance.

New missions for submarines during World War II sprang up like mushrooms and were so successfully executed that the reputation of these versatile vessels has come to equal that of Rudyard Kipling's Royal Marine, of whom he wrote: "For there isn't a job on the top of the earth the beggar don't know, nor do . . . You can leave 'im at night on a bald man's 'ead to paddle 'is own canoe. . . ."

Some of these uses, such as cargo carrying, had been

discovered in World War I. The German sub, *Deuschland,* built as an undersea freighter, was accorded a rousing welcome in New London and Baltimore on two voyages to the United States in 1916. Her sister ship, *Bremen,* however, had no such luck and kept a rendezvous with Davy Jones. *Deuschland* was eventually diverted to combatant service and was among those surrendered at Harwich in 1918. In the early part of 1942, our own submarines ran many cargoes of food and ammunition into beleaguered Corregidor. From that beginning sprang a thriving trade in supplying Philippine guerrillas as described in a previous chapter, carried on until General MacArthur's troops invaded Leyte.

The Japanese employed submarine blockade runners in a similar manner, trying desperately to supply their by-passed bases.

Troop carrying by submarines was, I believe, for the first time in history, used by the United States Navy in World War II. The idea had long been discussed in submarine circles before the war and actual landings of small sabotage parties were made at the Panama Canal during one of our Fleet exercises. When the opportunity arose early in the war, as related in previous chapters, to create a diversion by landing Marine Raiders or Army Scout troops, submarines were ready to take on the job.

Mine laying by submarines had been carried on extensively in World War I and again in World War II, though in the latter war our own subs used the weapon sparingly because of possible interference with future operations.

The list of other special missions carried out by United States submarines includes:

Evacuation of nationals
Landing coast watchers, agents, commandos
Carrying aviation gasoline
Shore bombardment
Lifeguarding
Acting as beacon ships for landing forces
Photographic reconnaissance, beach and reef reconnaisance
Weather reporting
Anti-picket-boat sweeps
Locating enemy minefields

Sabotage
Radar pickets
Rocket launching

Last but not least in the repertoire of these versatile craft, was the demonstrated ability of the submarine to destroy other submarines. This does not properly belong in the list of special missions since, except in two cases, the enemy submarines so destroyed were operating as surface vessels. In one excepted case a British sub running submerged, picked up on her sound gear the propellar beat of a German submarine, also navigating at periscope depth. The Britisher closed in on the bearing of the sound, sighted the enemy's periscope, fired torpedoes and made one hit. In the other case, an American submarine running on surface, sighted a Japanese periscope, fired one torpedo and destroyed her opponent. Both are elementary examples of what may be expected in future antisubmarine warfare.

The rocket launching listed above as a special mission, was carried out by two submarines only—*Barb* and *Seahorse*—in the closing months of the war. These boats, using experimental 5-inch rocket launchers, bombarded military and industrial targets in northern Japan, from ranges approximating 4,500 yards. These seemingly small incidents I am convinced have cast long and menacing shadows into the future and bring us face to face with a situation which might confront the United States today, or at an enemy's selected moment, if we are so unfortunate as to be forced into another world war.

The idea of using submarines to make surprise bombardments of enemy homeland targets was not new. The Japanese had made such attacks on shore installations on our own west coast, on islands in the Pacific—and even as far south as Sydney, Australia. The Germans, then engaged in buzz-bombing London, intended to launch buzz bombs from submarines against New York and other east coast cities. To accomplish this, they planned that submarines would tow caissons, each containing a V-2 rocket, to positions off the Atlantic coast from which they would fire the rockets from the caissons. Fortunately for us these plans never matured, due, probably, to the terrific pressure brought to bear against German submarines by our air and surface hunter-killer groups. The fact that they lost 241 submarines in 1944 and 153 in 1945 shows how desperate was their situation at sea.

Nevertheless, during this all-time high in their submarine losses, the Germans developed the high underwater-speed snorkel submarine which they designated as Type XXI. The snorkel permitted the submarine to run its diesel engines for propulsion submerged and also to re-charge its storage batteries while submerged. Its greatly increased storage battery capacity enabled it to attain underwater speeds of 16 to 18 knots for about one hour. Many of the slower boats equipped with snorkel made war patrols and furnished us with plenty of trouble but fortunately, none of the high-speed snorkels got into the war.

This is the submarine which we now call a "guppy snorkel." We have converted numbers of our standard submarines to this type and are building others to an improved design. This is the submarine which can cross an ocean without surfacing—as did our *Pickerel*—and its decreased vulnerability to detection from the air or from surface craft is causing our antisubmarine experts grave concern. If discovered, its bursts of high speed, even though limited to a total of about one hour, nearly always insure its escape. This is the submarine which, seized in quantities at Stettin and Danzig at the end of the war, is believed to be the backbone of the Russian undersea fleet. I am convinced that this is the boat which has been sighted off our east coast, off our west coast and off Hawaii.

The Germans also developed the Type XXVI, but never got it into the war. This submarine was likewise snorkel equipped and, for propulsion while completely submerged, it was powered with a hydrogen-peroxide steam-driven turbine capable of developing 25 knots for six hours. The seriousness of this menace can be readily appreciated, for the limitations of our supersonic and sonic listening gear are such that antisubmarine craft cannot run at high speeds and still be able to track a completely submerged submarine. The Russians are known to have seized unassembled parts of 75 of these vessels at the end of World War II.

With those two deadly menaces in their submarine fleet—a fleet which it has been announced, they intended to build up to a strength of 1,000—our position in case of war would be grave indeed. The Reds undoubtedly command the willing or unwilling assistance of many German submarine technicians and scientists and we must assume that these experts will rapidly overcome the ineptitude which the Russians displayed for submarine warfare during World War II.

With an initial force of only 57 submarines at the outbreak of the last war, Germany nearly succeeded in isolating England before we came to her aid, and imperiled not only our supply lines to European Allies but, by inflicting upon us serious losses in tankers, gravely interfered with our flow of oil from Texas, Mexico, Aruba, South America and the Middle East.

What untold havoc could Russia wreak upon us with a starting force of 1,000 modern submarines—or even with her present force, variously reported to be between 250 and 350 boats?

That could be the general situation confronting us at the outbreak of a new world war; a situation in which we could ill afford to move a ship, a gun, a soldier or a ton of freight to the aid of our Allies of the North Atlantic Pact or to start an offensive until we had cleared the seas of the deadly menace of enemy submarines.

Now, let us consider the special situation which might confront us at that same time—a repeat "Pearl Harbor" attack delivered by submarines using atomic weapons—an attack which might lay waste many of our coastal cities and installations, and deal an almost fatal blow to our ability to make war, or even to defend ourselves.

Such an attack would present no great problem to a first-class submarine force—and we must not forget that our most probable enemy is being tutored and guided by submarine experts and scientists from the same nation which has contributed most of the modern improvements to the elementary submarines built by our own American inventors, Holland and Lake.

I have related in foregoing chapters some of the special missions accomplished by our standard World II submarines, many of which necessitated landing secretly on enemy-held coasts. These operations in enemy waters were undertaken by submarines which had to surface each day for a minimum of about six hours to re-charge their storage batteries. When within the bombing range of an alert, radar-equipped enemy, these surfacings often brought on lethal attacks by enemy night fighters or bombers. It was their high losses at such times, that finally forced the Germans to adopt the snorkel.

But, if we could carry out these dangerous operations with the standard type submarine—and the Germans could land secret agents on our supposedly well-guarded coast— how much more simple will it be for modern snorkel-equipped submarines secretly to approach our shores! And I am convinced that numerous Russian submarines have been off our coasts. If their intentions toward us are hostile, what would be more natural than seeking data as to densities, temperature gradients and sonar conditions in waters where they may have to operate? Data of that nature are of great importance in submarine operations. Since it is possible for enemy submarines to arrive undetected off our coasts, nothing more is needed but suitable weapons to set the stage for a sneak attack which could make Pearl Harbor look like a mere Fourth of July celebration.

We have read much of so-called "push button" warfare, of intercontinental bombing by guided missiles fired over the North Pole, but more temperate and better informed writers such as Dr. Vannevar Bush, say that intercontinental guided missiles are a long way in the future. The same eminent authority says that mass bombing is on its way out, that against a radar-equipped opponent armed with jet fighters and anti-aircraft guided missiles and rockets, the cost of such bombing will exceed the damage inflicted and that its chance of getting through to the target will be minute. If Dr. Bush is right, then our enemy will have to depend upon innocent appearing merchant vessels or submarines to deliver his Sunday punch.

Delivery of an underwater missile would not be so simple, but fanatics could solve the problem by running a midget submarine loaded with an A-bomb into the harbor and expending the lives of its two-man crew. For others who believe that every man who goes into action is entitled to a fair chance of survival, there is needed only development of a guided torpedo or midget.

As many of you know, the Germans employed a pattern running torpedo against our convoys. This weapon, whose steering gear was operated through a cam, ran a figure eight, or other pattern, in the midst of a group of ships until some unfortunate was unable to dodge its unpredictable course changes and received a death blow. Navy press releases have stated that we also will use this torpedo, chiefly in antisubmarine work. From this, to a torpedo whose cam-operated steering gear could follow a known channel—say the channel into the Golden Gate—seems only a step. Fitted with special equipment to keep it out of shallow water, it could finish its run, sink to bottom and explode at a predetermined moment.

Scientists tell us that an underwater explosion of the A-bomb is the more deadly since the resulting column of contaminated water, blown by a favorable wind, could render uninhabitable large areas of a city. Thus deep-water ports like San Francisco would be particularly vulnerable to this latter form of attack, while refinery areas and munition factories further inland would be excellent targets for aerial missiles.

Merchant ships we probably can deal with by exclusion or by permitting their entry only into ports whose existences are not of vital importance to our war industries. However, to a nonaggressive democracy, such as we are, dealing with submarines of a potential enemy in the waters off our coasts poses a much graver problem.

Admitting, then, that enemy submarines can put themselves in positions from which sneak attacks could be delivered, how will they accomplish their monstrous purpose? Two methods come to mind immediately—by an aerial missile or by an underwater projectile. Either is feasible. We know that Russia has achieved atomic explosions, we are told that traitors have given her the secret of the hydrogen bomb. Hence, they have, or probably soon will have, the same weapons we possess.

We know that our submarines at Point Mugu and elsewhere have fired and guided a missile which we call the Loon. We must assume that Russia can do likewise. The extreme range of the Loon has not been made public but we have seen press releases to the effect that it is over 100 miles. We have not been informed whether the Loon could carry an atomic war head but it appears probable that it can do so. Thus an enemy possessing such weapons could, with great ease, lob it into ports, oil refining plants and storages, or other important targets. Should the range of the missile exceed the range at which a single submarine can direct its course, other submarines stationed along its path could take

over control and a final one, close inshore, guide it accurately
to its target.

Enemy high underwater-speed snorkel submarines, I am
convinced, we can drive from the seas, eventually, but the initial sneak attack by them can only be warded off by realistic
national preparedness, and national vigilance, plus better intelligence work and keener intelligence evaluation than we
appear to have demonstrated in the Korean affair. Mines,
nets, offshore patrols by our own submarines, with one or two
secret weapons which cannot be discussed here, will help,
provided that early warning of enemy intent is received—but
that intent must be known before our antisubmarine, or any
other forces, can open fire.

Our answer to the deadly threat of the fast snorkel submarine, is the atomic powered submarine whose construction
was authorized by the President of the United States on August 8, 1950. The present cost of a standard Fleet-type submarine is $10,000,000. At a cost of $40,000,000, which will
include the building of the initial atomic pile and the actual
construction of the vessel, in three years the United States—
we hope—will be the first nation to possess the atom submarine, and so lay the foundation for a fleet which will outrun,
outfight and outmaneuver the most advanced snorkel types
that Russia is building behind the curtain, or is likely to
build.

Even in this age of great atomic promise, this estimate
might appear to be optimistic. However, such is not the case.
It is based upon sound factors derived from atomic research
as applied to power plants and naval construction. Earlier estimates gave the period of completion as five to six years,
but, just as in World War II we cut down the building time
of a Fleet-type submarine from two years to seven months,
corresponding technological and engineering advances have
brought the atom submarine much nearer to the day it will
slide down the ways.

When that day arrives we will have a power plant in
which the measureless force that was unleashed to devastate
Hiroshima and Nagasaki will be harnessed for propulsion
purposes and will produce the first true submarine—a vessel
of high speed, unlimited range and operational aiblity. One
which will require no snorkel for air intake and, using the

more effective weapons constantly being perfected, will be the deadliest underwater killer ever conceived.

Formidable as is the fast snorkel submarine on which Russia is reported to be concentrating, it is still tied to fuel and air supply and snorkeling adds to its vulnerability. The snorkel float that it trails along the surface, sucking in air, is as visible as any small boat and kicks up spray. Not only can the float be seen but it can be detected by radar from planes and surface vessels despite its antiradar coating, a protective composition that deflects the beam.

Even more dangerous to this submarine is the noise of the diesel engine, which can be picked up by sonic devices at long ranges. Only when the boat dives and runs silently on its batteries does its chance for survival increase against the detection equipment carried by modern antisubmarine craft. In spite of the snorkel and antiradar coating, the Germans lost 241 boats in a single year, 1944.

We ourselves have not neglected the snorkel, but we regard it as an "ad interim" device. It is a deep source of satisfaction to me as a submarine officer, who has watched our undersea fleet grow from the midget class, that—in true American fashion—we are boldly by-passing the transitional phases in development between the conventional diesel and the atomic engine. The new submarine will outclass the snorkel as radically as the snorkel outclassed the other types.

Nothing can equal the atom boat. Nothing in our present arsenal of antisubmarine weapons can stop it. Its employment will be restricted only by the endurance of the crew, and these men can be rotated frequently. With inexhaustible power derived from atomic energy, its range will be unlimited. It will require no air for its engines and, for the benefit of the crew, need only charge its air banks at three- or four-day intervals. For this purpose, a much smaller and almost undetectable snorkel can be used. Free from the necessity of carrying some 350 tons of diesel oil from a 350-ton electric storage battery, weight saved will compensate for the heavy shielding necessary for the plutonium power plant. Valuable space will be available for greater torpedo storage and for indispensable sonar, radar and radio equipment.

More comfortable accommodations will be provided for the crew, an important psychological consideration under the new conditions of total undersea warfare, where lack of recreation, fresh air and sunshine frays the nerves.

With a plant three or four times the horsepower of our present diesel installation, our engineers believe that the atom boat will run continuously at a speed of 25 to 30 knots submerged. Continuously doesn't mean forever, but, to submariners, the "extended period of time" promised is astronomical in comparison with present performance. This high sustained speed will place these subs on battle stations two or three times quicker than in the past. The U.S.S. *Pickerel*, which made a record-breaking undersea cruise of 5,200 miles from Hongkong to Pearl Harbor in 21 days, would do the same trip in eight to nine days with an atomic plant. By this same great increase in speed, the time required for our submarines to arrive off enemy bases in Europe or Asia, or on patrol station, is correspondingly reduced.

During World War II the normal patrol of a submarine was 60 days but half of that time was spent in unproductive waters, going to and from their patrol areas. To conserve fuel they had to cruise at economic speeds of 12 to 15 knots. With no fuel to be conserved, and machinery designed for high speed, the atom sub will do the work of two or three snorkel submarines, cut nonproductive transit time in half, cover her assigned area more quickly and thoroughly and return rapidly to base for a new load of torpedoes and a fresh crew. She will have no snorkel to reveal her presence to enemy planes and radar and her high submerged speed will let her run away from antisubmarine craft, or sink them, whichever is most expedient. Some undoubtedly will be equipped to launch guided missiles and thus constitute a swift striking force for reprisals or to devastate enemy coastal bases and submarine pens.

This submarine could drive every surface ship from the face of the sea for, with its almost limitless endurance and terrific speed, it will be able to chase them down and destroy them one by one as easily as a greyhound snaps up cottontails. During World War II, fast liners such as the two *Queens* and the *Ile de France*, carried tens of thousands of troops through submarine infested waters protected only by their high speed. Those days are gone.

Against enemy snorkeling submarines, our atom sub will have the advantage of a quiet turbine power plant over the inevitable reciprocating noises of a diesel engine. Operating at depths where sonar conditions are best, snorkeling enemies will be detected at very long ranges, swiftly approached and destroyed with homing torpedoes. Thus she will be the ideal SSK, the submarine which hunts down and kills other submarines. In this employment she will be far more effective than surface antisubmarine vessels whose sonar gear is, of necessity, near the surface and thus handicapped by the less favorable sound conditions existing at shallow depths. It has long been recognized that submarines are among the best antisubmarine vessels. In both world wars British submarines established very creditable records in destruction of enemy subs and, as related in previous chapters, United States submarines in the Pacific sank 23 Japanese and two German undersea boats. Three of the Japanese were bagged by one of our boats in 77 hours. All of these attacks, except one, were made against enemy boats operating on surface. Now, confronted with submarines of possible enemy powers which can operate submerged over long periods, our answer is the atom-powered submarine—a weapon which will prove itself a tower of strength in our national defense.

The conception of the atomic submarine is the greatest stride ever made in naval science since Ericsson's *Monitor,* but the increased security it promises must not be allowed to lull us into national complacency. It is to be expected that Russia is aiming at the same goal. Engineers, technologists and physicists behind the iron curtain also are working feverishly on atom projects, rockets, jets and antisubmarine devices. They now have the A-bomb and Russia and the United States are running a technological race—with our national salvation as the stake.

During the last war the United States never built more than 10 boats a month, but Germany reached a maximum of 30. Russia may well equal or even top the Nazi record. If the Soviet Union decides upon war with the United States, we shall encounter the most formidable submarine fleet ever built, even though we have a technical advantage in the atom boat.

The pity of it is that we didn't start earlier on the project, for the atom-powered submarine, first planned by the Bureau of Ships in the Navy Department in 1946, has not been achieved without a struggle. Three years were required to obtain permission from the Atomic Energy Commission to build the necessary atomic reactors—questions of policy and of funds hampered development. Now, thank God, public interest has been aroused and the acuteness of the antisubmarine problem facing us has forced the issue. We can only hope that there will be no further delays and that funds will be forthcoming for hulls and reactors as fast as the inevitable bugs are ironed out of the first atom powered submarine.

Although the efforts of the Navy Department to strengthen our national defense by production of this well nigh inevitable submarine were retarded for years, the Bureau of Ships, the National Research Council and the Office of Naval Research were not idle. Plans for this newest power plant were developed, and intensive study was initiated in naval, industrial and university laboratories to solve the difficult engineering problems presented by this radical new prime mover.

Thus, even though we are years later in realizing the original conception, the project has a good technical head start. For this, the nation should be grateful to the submariners, engineers and scientists who never lost hope, but stood by their guns.

Scientific cooperation with our armed forces helped us to win the last war. This latest contribution of science, the atomic-powered submarine, to which, as yet, there is no answer in the sea or in the sky, is, in itself, the answer to the prayer in the hearts of loyal, farseeing and God-fearing Americans who hope to guard the fragile peace of today with the weapons of tomorrow.

CHAPTER 22

In concluding these stories of the part played by Submarines in the Pacific during World War II, I cannot lay down my pen without making very sincere and grateful acknowledgment to a number of persons, corporations and services who lent aid, encouragement and strength to our arms. A war is fought not with weapons alone. The patriotism, hopes and prayers of our people at home; the skill, determination and genius of technicians, scientists and workers in our industries and repair yards, are living forces which can fire the souls of fighting men and bring about final victory quite as effectively as the weapons they put in our hands.

Nothing brought more discouragement and discontent to our fighting forces, or was productive of more condemnation from them, than strikes back in the homeland. The war was inevitably prolonged thereby, exposing men in the forward areas to danger of life and limb for just so much more time. This callous disregard for our lives by fellow countrymen, deferred from the draft, drawing fantastic wages—plus overtime—was infuriating and should have been handled, we felt, by exchanging those "Fancy Dans" (a term borrowed from General Bradley) with an equal number of men in the front lines.

Conversely, nothing whetted the fighting spirit of our lads more than cheerful, resolute, enthusiastic letters from home. Efficient mail service to our submarines was most important and we left no stone unturned to provide it.

High upon the list of individuals who helped, I place the Australians. They are a people we should know better. Their country is much like our western states, with climate about the same. They took us into their homes and hearts with openhanded hospitality, at a time when we were badly beaten down and a long way from home. Throughout the war there was one request I learned to expect from skippers of submarines who felt they had earned the right to ask a favor for their crews. This request was to end their next patrol in Fremantle, and have their two weeks' rest period there. The beer is excellent, the beaches are better than many of our own and the girls are good to look upon. Hundreds of international marriages grew out of the "American invasion" of the hospitable shores of Australia.

Of the British and Netherlands submarines, we saw a great deal in Australia and in the Philippines. Their crews were hardy and determined and their submarines, while smaller than ours, and not so well equipped for habitability and comfort, were thoroughly effective. The skippers handled their boats with great skill and need take off their hats to no one, with respect to daring in making their attacks. I became acquainted with the British submarine service in World War I and contacted it again—also Dutch submariners—while on duty in England in 1941. My observation of their capabilities and their performance in the Southwest Pacific, merely confirmed my former high regard for their hardihood and fighting qualities. When there's a tough job to be done, I'm ready at any time to team up with a Britisher or a Dutchman.

The Red Cross was a source of pride to all of us. Their snack bars in Perth (Australian Red Cross) at Camp Dealey and at the Royal Hawaiian, were "manned" by attractive, understanding girls and matrons—most of them unpaid—whose mere presence or helpful advice was a great comfort to many a homesick lad. The generosity with which the Honolulu branch provided warm clothing, sweaters, mittens, for patrols in icy northern waters, as well as its thoughtfulness in sending trees and boxes of Christmas presents to submarines due for patrols during the holiday season, will endear to us always the Red Cross and its workers.

In 1916 President Wilson, in his wise discretion and foresight, assembled a group of top-level scientists for volunteer study and work on the technological phases of war problems. This organization of patriotic citizens became known as the National Defense Research Council and from them sprang branches and special units in all the Armed Services, which attacked problems of every sort with zeal and consumate skill. Many of the devices, procedures and weapons which they produced for submarines are still classified as secret. However, I may tell you that some of the most effective offensive and defensive equipment developed in World War II, is owed to this same devoted band of scientists and to the naval officers who worked with them. I had not previously had the privilege of working with the NDRC or its ancillary units. They speak a totally different language from us sailors, but I know that I am expressing the sentiments for the entire Submarine Service in saying that we developed a very deep respect and admiration for those earnest and zealous men.

At the end of the war Dr. Harnwell, whose UCDWR unit at San Diego produced, among other things, our QLA gear, originated a letter proposing continued liaison between the NDRC and the submariners. To this I was happy to give hearty endorsement and, due largely to the combined efforts of Dr. Tate and Dr. Harnwell, an annual Undersea Warfare Symposium has been held where able presentations and discussions have given constructive aid to naval programs concerning this vitally important subject.

For our submarine designers and builders I have not words to express my admiration and appreciation. Due to conscientious work on the part of the Submarine Officers' Conference at the Navy Department, sympathetic and far-sighted action by the General Board of the Navy and skillful design development on the part of the Bureau of Ships, we were able to start World War II with a standard type of Fleet submarine. This boat, with 10 tubes, 20 to 21 knots surface speed, long cruising radius and endurance, was built for just such work as was required in the Pacific. No major changes were made in it during the war. This elimination of design alterations was instrumental in cutting down building time to seven or eight months, and permitted a degree of standardization never before known in submarines. New ideas and improvements in instruments and weapons under its cognizance, were produced by the Bureau of Ships and by builders with a speed and perfection unknown in peacetime.

To me, one of the most amazing wartime successes was the development of a submarine building yard at Manitowoc, Wisconsin, 1,000 miles from salt water. There, using Electric Boat Company plans, and with no previous experience in this type of construction, 28 boats were produced which were the equals of any turned out elsewhere. They were then run, or floated in a small dry dock, down to New Orleans and given their final preparation for sea.

Manitowoc did more than just build submarines; it established a reputation for cooperation and excellence in living conditions which placed it high on the list of choices among submarine skippers detailed to go home and put a new boat in commission. To Mr. Charles C. West, President of the Manitowoc Shipbuilding Company, belongs much of the credit for this well-deserved popularity.

Portsmouth Navy Yard, Mare Island Navy Yard and the Electric Boat Company all did superb jobs, as they have done for years, in building submarines and in repairing them throughout the war. Many of the ships we sent back to them for repairs had taken the worst punishment—short of total destruction—which the Imperial Japanese Navy could deal out. With hull plating dished in, torpedo tubes knocked out of alignment and frames buckled by depth charging or aerial bombs, many of our battle damaged ships presented king-sized problems to the repair yards. Some that I saw pass through Pearl Harbor, homeward bound, had escaped annihilation at the hands of the enemy only by the combination of a miracle and perfect construction, yet nearly all of them were successfully reconditioned and returned to avenge their rough treatment.

The interest of the Electric Boat Company did not end with the completion of its boats, but extended to doing everything possible for the benefit of the submarine service—a spirit of cooperation based on mutual esteem which had grown up through generations of association.

One particularly generous and thoughtful act, initiated by its President, Mr. L. Y. Spear, was the gift of a beautiful set of stained glass windows to our little Memorial Chapel at the Submarine Base, Pearl Harbor. I tried to convince Mr. Spear, known and revered by all submariners, that one or two windows would be adequate, but he declared that "anything worth doing at all is worth doing well," and insisted on having every window beautified with a Biblical scene.

One of them contained a dedicatory inscription which read:

Sacred to the Memory of Those Who Gave Their Lives in Submarines.
May Their Gallant Souls Rest in Peace.

The most important installation in a submarine is the main power plant—the diesel engines which drive generators to charge the storage batteries, energize all the electric circuits of the ship and provide propulsion with which to take the submarine on its patrols—and bring it home. In the early 1930's when Munich was still just a place where the Germans made good beer, an important development was initiated in Cleveland, Ohio. Sparkplugged by Mr. George W. Codrington, Vice-President of General Motors, American railway engineers, naval engineers from the Bureau of Ships and the Winton Engine Division of GMC, began a collaboration. Working together, they produced the prototype of the modern, high-speed submarine diesel engine. Originally it had been designed to fulfill the requirements of streamlined trains. As modified, it piled up a brilliant record for reliability and ruggedness in our undersea boats. To the men who designed, developed and built that engine, our hats are off. During the development stage, one of the General Motors engineers, Mr. Don Smith, was lost in the sinking of the *Squalus* in May, 1939.

We did have a complaint which I remember, about this Winton General Motors engine. One night we received an urgent dispatch from a submarine skipper off the China coast, who was trying to escape from Japanese escort vessels. He had made an attack on a convoy close inshore and was using every last ounce of horsepower to leg it for water deep enough to dive in. He told us of his dire predicament and closed with the despairing words: "Four Wintons cannot outrun four destroyers." However, I am happy to say, they did hold their own long enough to get him into deeper water and bring his ship safely back to base.

The Fairbanks-Morse Company of Beloit, Wisconsin, also developed during the early 1930's in keen competition with other builders, and in cooperation with the Bureau of Ships, a sturdy two-cycle, opposed piston-type diesel engine which eventually powered about half of our Fleet submarines. In the opinion of many who served with those engines they were absolutely tops. Their reliability was almost incredible and speed records turned in were outstanding.

Tunny, for instance, under pressure of war exigencies, made a 1,200 mile run at full speed, averaging about 19 knots, without any sort of a casualty. To those of us who had grown up in submarines, where power plant breakdowns were a matter of routine, with a resultant deplorable condition of engine room paint work, the spotless, white-painted Fairbanks-Morse engineering spaces looked like paradise.

There were, of course, many other clever and efficient builders of submarine equipment. Among these were the Kollmorgen Optical Company, which built optically beautiful periscopes in unbelievably short time; and the Westinghouse Electric Company which manufactured three types of much-needed electric, wakeless torpedoes. The Farrel-Birmingham Company built silent-running reduction gears which linked our high-speed main motors to slow-speed propellers. Its Vice President, Mr. Austin Kuhns, spent hundreds of hours, surface and submerged, in submarines to make sure these installations properly performed their vital service. The Electric

Storage Battery Company and the Gould Storage Battery Company have, over a long period of years, given very close attention and much research to the problems of submarine battery design, hydrogen elimination and so forth. In the earlier days of submarine history, serious, often fatal, hydrogen explosions were not uncommon. The fact that, during World War II, there was, so far as I know, only one such explosion, proves the success of their labors. To the Bell Telephone Laboratories, the Ford Instrument Company, the Western Electric Company and the Submarine Signal Company, we owe radars, radio phones, radio sets, instruments, sonar, and much other equipment which contributed vitally to the success of our submarine effort.

Almost innumerable other firms and corporations contributed directly or indirectly. There is no intent to overlook their help, but space and my memory do not permit mentioning all.

Last but not least among those who contributed to the moral and spiritual *esprit de corps* of the Submarine Service, is a lady beloved by submariners high and low for her never failing interest and encouragement, her kindness, generosity and hospitality, her tireless efforts in behalf of her "sons"—in short, for her great heart. I refer to Dr. Margaret Chung of San Francisco, "Mom" to all her "Golden Dolphins," their wives, children, sweethearts and widows.

Early in the war, Mom, already fairy godmother to hundreds of aviators, including the original Flying Tigers, and her modest home a refuge for shelterless dependents, decided to add submarine officers to her adopted "family." Thereupon she organized her "Golden Dolphins," each selected for his war record and because "he makes the world a better place to live in," as her citation reads. Every Sunday throughout the war she held open house and served a barbecue dinner to scores of her "sons" and their families or best girls. The steadying influence thus exerted on youngsters just back from patrol to fight the battle of Market Street, cannot be overestimated, nor can we overpraise the unselfishness and generosity with which she gave and still gives of her time, of her substance and of herself.

In spite of having a busy medical practice on her hands, Mom, with her seemingly inexhaustible energy, manages to send a Christmas present to each of her 1,500 sons—and many of their families—to work for adequate pensions for war widows who have young children, and to undertake any worth-while project that affects her sons or her country. I hope that St. Peter has made appropriate commendatory entries in his big book, for, should any submariners get to Heaven, I know they will not enjoy it if Mom Chung isn't there.

To the Reserve Officers and enlisted men, who at the end of the war formed at least three-quarters of our Submarine Forces, we of the Regulars pay our sincere respects. In every submarine, eventually, Reserve Officers far outnumbered Regulars and 11 boats were commanded by Reserves. In peacetime normally two or three tours of duty in submarines were required for an officer to achieve a command billet. The speed with which our Reserves worked up to command and executive officer jobs in World War II, speaks volumes, not only for the efficiency of the Submarine School and the Training Command, but also for the quality of the men from civilian life who poured into the Submarine Service. They came equipped, in many cases, with skills which were new and invaluable to us. They had acquired technical training which fitted them for jobs with highly complicated gear such as radar, radio and sonar. They were eager to learn, to qualify as submarine men, and their zeal and fighting spirit were all they could be desired.

While charges of discrimination against Reserves were being aired in the press and in Congress, I do not recall that a single such allegation was made against submarine administration. We of the Regulars were proud of our Reserve shipmates. We were doubly proud of the fact that when the debacle of demobilization struck us, thousands of them stuck by their ships and transferred to the regular Navy.

Whether Regulars or Reserves, the lads who fought in submarines, who served in tenders or bases, or who composed the relief crews, were a part of a splendid team of fighting men, which I had the honor to command and of which I am tremendously proud. Their resourcefulness, skill and courage won the admiration of all who knew them. No one can deny that they won their spurs in World War II.

They were no supermen, nor were they endowed with any supernatural qualities of heroism. They were merely topnotch American lads, well trained, well treated, well armed and provided with superb ships. May God grant there will be no World War III; but, if there is, whether it be fought with the weapons we know or with weapons at whose type we can only guess, submarines and submariners will be in the thick of the combat, fighting with skill, determination and matchless daring for all of us and for our United States of America.

INDEX

Relive the American Experience in Vietnam

BANTAM VIETNAM WAR BOOKS

Special Offer
Buy a Bantam Book
for only 50¢.

Now you can have Bantam's catalog filled with hundreds of titles plus take advantage of our unique and exciting bonus book offer. A special offer which gives you the opportunity to purchase a Bantam book for only 50¢. Here's how!

By ordering any five books at the regular price per order, you can also choose any other single book listed (up to a $4.95 value) for just 50¢. Some restrictions do apply, but for further details why not send for Bantam's catalog of titles today!

Just send us your name and address and we will send you a catalog!